The
Deviance
Process

The Deviance Process

Erdwin H. Pfuhl, Jr.   Arizona State University

D. Van Nostrand Company
New York   Cincinnati   Toronto   London   Melbourne

D. Van Nostrand Company Regional Offices:
New York   Cincinnati

D. Van Nostrand Company International Offices:
London   Toronto   Melbourne

Library of Congress Catalog Card Number: 79-2137
ISBN: 0-442-26241-8

Published by D. Van Nostrand Company
135 West 50th Street, New York, N.Y. 10020

10 9 8 7 6 5 4 3 2 1

To my wife, Joan, and our children, Chris, Stacey, and Lisa

Preface

This text introduces undergraduate students to the sociology of deviance. The book has grown out of my students' and my own dissatisfaction with much of the traditional sociological material devoted to the study of deviance and deviants.

On the students' part, many have been critical of explanations for rule breaking that do not speak to their own existential condition. As for myself, decades of academic life have convinced me that students are best served when they are equipped with an analytic framework with which to make sense of the daily experiences of their lives. They need a framework that encourages questions and at the same time enables them to acquire answers, even though the answers may not be consistent with current sociological dogma. The goal calls for an analytic system that allows for the appropriate interpretation of new facts as they emerge. Hopefully, the perspective used in this work will be found to meet these criteria, and students will find in the text the core of a framework with which they may make sense of their social world.

Use of this perspective, along with a desire to discuss the *phenomenon of deviance* (rather than merely talking about deviant behavior) call for a processual (as opposed to a topical) arrangement of material. Accordingly, the material is organized in accordance with several stages of the deviance-producing and deviance-maintaining business of society. Types of deviation—obesity, blindness, deafness, drug use, mental illness, homosexuality, and so on—are subordinate, used only to highlight select aspects of the deviance process.

To allow for flexibility, we must avoid the absolutistic impression that there is something about certain conditions and behaviors—some inherent property—that results in their being deviant. By focusing on aspects of the larger deviance-producing process, such as defining and banning certain behaviors and the indeterminate nature of rule enforcement, I am consciously contributing to a morally relativistic view. We do not live in an absolutistic world; in our daily life each of us behaves as a relativist. Ours is a heterogeneous society where progressively fewer things remain sacred and unquestioned, where rules seldom go unchallenged, and where behavioral styles are revised daily.

Focusing on the phenomenon of deviance has another consequence that concerns me, namely, avoidance of the tendency to study deviance in apolitical terms. While standard approaches do not preclude discussion of the politics of deviance, neither are they known to promote it. In the present volume deviance is expressly viewed as an outgrowth of making, enforcing, and administering social policy, that is, the business of politics.

The book is organized to provide an overview of the deviance process. The first chapter, "Studying Deviance," offers a theoretical framework to aid in understanding this process. This framework is followed throughout the remainder of the volume. In Chapter 2, "Breaking Rules," we examine some major biological, psychological, and sociological explanations of rule-breaking behavior, subject them to examination in terms of theory established in Chapter 1, and provide an explanation for breaking rules that conforms to that general framework. Chapter 3, "Counting Deviants," focuses on official statistics, their history, how they are constructed, and their weaknesses. These considerations are used to evaluate the validity of theories that rest on official statistics. Chapter 4, "Banning Behavior," is an excursion into political sociology. Here we seek to examine the ways in which select patterns of behavior come to be defined as deviant. The role of the law and the media are stressed. Deviance also includes the official identification and public labeling of a select number of rule breakers. The social agencies involved in this process of labeling, particularly the courts, are examined. In Chapter 6, "Consequences of Labeling and Stigma," we discuss the theory behind the concern over the consequences of labeling people deviant, and give consideration to the personal and social consequences of being publicly identified as a deviant. Special attention is given to the idea of deviance amplification and its validity. Consistent with our theory, people do not accept labeling passively; rather, both individually and collectively, people seek to manage labels and the stigma imposed on them. How these things are managed is considered in Chapter 7, "Managing Stigma." We conclude with a brief epilogue, focusing on deviance as an enduring, though ever changing aspect of collective life. In each chapter, critical terms are italicized and a working definition provided. A more complete definition of terms is provided as a glossary in the appendix. There is an instructor's manual available which contains instructional information, and multiple-choice, essay, and true-false questions.

I am grateful to many people for their assistance and support throughout this project. To my colleagues and friends David L. Altheide and John M. Johnson I owe a very special and substantial debt for their critical comments, thoughtful suggestions, wise counsel, and encouragement. My thanks, too, to John Bignall for an "insider's" perspective, and to my many other students who were unwilling to take things for granted. I also wish to thank Professors Margaret Zahn, Temple University; Stephen J. Pfohl, Boston College; Charles McCaghy, Bowling Green State University; and Herman Schwendinger, State University of New York College at New Paltz for their support. But most of all I thank my wife, Joan, who managed to endure it all.

E.H.P.

Acknowledgments

Acknowledgment is made to the following publishers and individuals for permission to reprint material:

Saul D. Alinsky. *Rules for Radicals*. Published by Random House, Inc., Copyright © 1972.

Howard S. Becker. *Outsiders: Studies in the Sociology of Deviance*. Published by Macmillan Publishing Co., Inc., 1973.

Claude Brown, *Manchild in the Promised Land*. Published by Macmillan Publishing Co., Inc., Copyright © 1965.

Vincent Bugliosi and Curt Gentry, *Helter Skelter, The True Story of the Manson Murders*. Published by W. W. Norton & Co., Inc., 1974.

Werner J. Cahnman, "The Stigma of Obesity," *The Sociological Quarterly*, Journal of the Midwest Sociological Society, 1968.

Fred Davis, "Deviance Disavowal: The Management of Strained Interaction by the Visibly Handicapped," *Social Problems*. Published by the Society for the Study of Social Problems, Fall 1961.

David Dawley, *A Nation of Lords, The Autobiography of the Vice Lords*. Published by Doubleday Anchor, Copyright © 1973.

Jack D. Douglas and Paul K. Rasmussen with Carol Ann Flanagan, "The Nude Beach," *Sociological Observations*, Vol. 1, p. 199. Published by Sage Publications, Inc., Copyright © 1977. Reprinted by permission.

Stephen L. Fink, James K. Skipper, Jr., Phyllis N. Hallenbeck, "Physical Disability and Problems in Marriage," *Journal of Marriage and the Family*, February 1968. Published by the National Council on Family Relations. Reprinted by permission.

Charles E. Frazier, *Theoretical Approaches to Deviance: An Evaluation*, Published by Charles E. Merrill Publishing Co./Bell and Howell Co., 1976.

Erving Goffman, *Stigma: Notes on the Management of Spoiled Identity*. Published by Prentice-Hall, Inc., Copyright © 1963. Reprinted by permission.

Joseph R. Gusfield, "Moral Passage: the Symbolic Process in Public Designations of Deviance," *Social Problems*. Published by the Society for the Study of Social Problems, Fall 1967.

Ronald A. Hardert, Howard A. Parker, Erdwin H. Pfuhl, and William A. Anderson, *Sociology and Social Issues*. Published by Holt, Rinehart and Winston, 1974.

Jerry Jacobs, Deviance: *Field Studies and Self-Disclosures.* Published by Mayfield Publishing Co. (formerly National Press Books), 1974.

Peter Letkemann, *Crime As Work.* Published by Prentice-Hall, Inc., Copyright © 1973. Reprinted by permission.

Stanford M. Lyman, *The Asian in North America.* Published by ABC-Clio, Inc., Copyright © 1977. Reprinted by permission.

David Matza, *Becoming Deviant.* Published by Prentice-Hall, Inc., Copyright © 1969. Reprinted by permission.

Merle Miller, "What It Means to be a Homosexual," *New York Times Magazine* October 10 and January 17, 1971. Published by the New York Times Company, Copyright © 1971. Reprinted by permission.

C. Wright Mills, *The Sociological Imagination.* Published by Oxford University Press, 1959.

Irving Piliavin and Scott Briar, "Police Encounters with Juveniles," *American Journal of Sociology,* 70:2. Published by The University of Chicago Press, Copyright © 1964.

David J. Pittman and Duff G. Gillespie, "Social Policy as Deviancy Reinforcement: The Case of the Public Intoxication Offender," *Alcoholism.* Published by Harper & Row, Publishers, Inc., Copyright © 1967. Reprinted by permission.

Barbara Ponse, "Secrecy in the Lesbian World," *Urban Life,* Vol. 5, No. 3, October 1976. Published by Sage Publications, Inc. Reprinted by permission.

Richard Quinney, *Crime and Justice in Society.* Published by Little, Brown and Co., 1969.

Robert Ross and Graham L. Staines, "The Politics of Analyzing Social Problems," *Social Problems.* Published by the Society for the Study of Social Problems, Summer 1972.

Joseph Sataloff, *Hearing Loss.* Published by J. B. Lippincott Co., 1966.

William H. Sheldon, *Varieties of Delinquent Youth.* Published by Harper and Brothers, 1949.

James P. Spradely, *You Owe Yourself a Drunk: An Ethnography of Urban Nomads.* Published by Little, Brown and Co., 1970.

Edwin H. Sutherland and Donald R. Cressey, *Criminology.* Published by Harper & Row, Publishers, Inc., 1974.

Frank Tannenbaum, *Crime and Community.* Published by Ginn and Co., 1938.

W. Clinton Terry III and David F. Luckenbill, "Investigating Criminal Homicides: Police Work in Reporting and Solving Murders," W. B. Sanders and H. C. Daudistel, *The Criminal Justice Process*. Published by Praeger Publishers, 1976.

Charles A. Varni, "An Exploratory Study of Spouse-Swapping," *Pacific Sociological Review*, Vol. 15, No. 4, October 1972. Published by Sage Publications, Inc. Reprinted by permission.

Samuel E. Wallace, *Skid Row as a Way of Life*. Published by Bedminster Press, 1965.

Leslie T. Wilkins, *Social Deviance: Social Policy, Action, and Research*. Published by Tavistock/Prentice-Hall, Inc., 1965.

Jacqueline P. Wiseman, *Stations of the Lost: The Treatment of Skid Row Alcoholics*. Published by The University of Chicago Press, Copyright © 1970.

Contents

Ascriptive vs. Achieved Rule Breaking—Power and
Socio-economic Status—Motives—Other Factors

Summary   245

7. Managing Stigma   247

Introduction   248

Individualized Stigma Management   249

The Discreditable   **249**

Secrecy and Information Control—The Role of Others

The Discredited   **254**

Deviance Disavowal—The Disavowal Process—Deviance
Avowal—Stigma Management and Socialization—
Accounts: Excuses and Justifications—Covering

Collective Management of Stigma   262

Origins of Voluntary Associations   **263**

Secret Societies—The Deviant Community

Organizing for Change   **266**
Types of Associations   **269**

Expressive and Instrumental Groups—Conformative
and Alienative Groups

The Deviant as Moral Entrepreneur   273

Forming Entrepreneurial Groups   **274**

A Sense of Dissatisfaction—The Quest for Change

Tactics of Change   **277**

Troubles and Issues—Gaining Legitimacy—Use of the
Media—Reconstructing Reality—Altering Public Policy

The Politicization of Deviance   285

Summary   287

8. Epilogue   290

Glossary   296

Bibliography   305

Author Index   **337**

Subject Index   **343**

Studying
Deviance

Introduction

Everyone, it seems, has at least a superficial interest in rule breakers and their behavior. The popularity of the subject can be noted every night of the week as millions of Americans spend hours watching an incredible variety of fictional and not-so-fictional TV presentations having rule-breaking behavior as the theme. One wonders what we would do for "entertainment" were it not for this element of popular culture. This interest is also reflected in the press and other news media where information about crime and other morally objectionable behavior rates a distinct place equal to news of international events, business and the economy, art, theatre, music, and sports. Clearly, rule breaking is well established in our society as both an attention getter and a money maker. It may be that nothing else is so capable of titillating the masses while at the same time leaving them horrified.

People's interest in deviance takes various other forms and has several bases. For example, students sometimes enroll in courses on deviant behavior because they anticipate a vicarious thrill from examining ethnographic accounts of the exotic lives of "whores, hoods, and homos." Sometimes interest stems from having personally been victimized by rule breakers. Perhaps a person's car has been the target of a gasoline thief or has been crunched by a hit-and-run driver, their home broken into or vandalized, or they or a member of their family assaulted or victimized in some way. Perhaps a person's interest is aroused by the periodic reminders from the Federal Bureau of Investigation, local police departments, and a variety of politicians that crime and deviance are among our nation's major social problems. And what better evidence of their being widespread than that chapter in public life known as Watergate? On the other hand, one's interest may stem from his or her own participation in socially discreditable and proscribed forms of behavior: pot smoking, publicly disavowed sexual behavior, fudging on income tax, petty (grand?) theft, and the like, ad infinitum. After all, it's been said that we are a nation of law breakers and someone must be doing the things authorities claim go on (Wallerstein and Wyle, 1947; Short and Nye, 1958; Murphy, Shirley, and Witmer, 1946; Robin, 1969; Gold, 1966 and 1970).

Whatever the interest and regardless of its basis, deviance is widespread in our society. To be sure, not all forms of rule breaking elicit the same response. Sometimes the action evokes smiles or a chuckle, as when it was announced that a number of call girls in San Francisco accept payment for services by credit card. On other occasions one is struck by the rule breaker's audacity. For example, a would-be bank robber in Florida phoned a savings and loan association to tell an employee to "Put your money in a bag. I'll get there later to rob you." Police were called and staked out the place for several hours, finally deciding it was a hoax. After they left the robber appeared and made off with $3,000 (*New Times Weekly*, 1977:4). Other forms of rule breaking arouse a feeling of impotence, as, for example, when a newspaper carries a story indicating consumers in a western state are being cheated, a penny or two at a time, by a variety of merchants who use improperly adjusted scales, meters, and other devices to measure the products they sell: foodstuffs, gasoline, natural gas for home heating, electricity, and so on. The "take" is estimated to be millions of dollars annually, yet there is little hope for reform ostensibly because of a lack of funds and manpower to police the situation. Some other events leave one stunned, as do reports of the death by suicide and murder of some 900 members of the People's Temple in Guyana, South America. (*Time*, 1978).

These and similar situations, anecdotal in nature and perhaps interesting in their own right, major and minor, funny and deadly serious, immediate and abstract, could be listed indefinitely. However, these anecdotal materials are to the sociology of deviance what the tip is to the iceberg; by themselves they are only a small part of what sociologists mean when they speak of deviance. Sociological interest runs to far greater depth and breadth. It involves the identification of common elements among forms of behavior regarded as deviant, arranging these behaviors in categories, and investigating a host of related personal and social elements. Let's talk about how sociologists study deviance.

Investigating Deviance

In doing their work, sociologists have been guided by a variety of general theoretical models. As one sociologist put it:

> Each sociologist carries in his head one or more "models" of society and man which greatly influence what he looks for, what he sees, and what he does with his observations by way of fitting them along with other facts, into a larger scheme of explanation. In this respect the sociologist is no different from any other scientist. Every scientist holds some general conception of the realm in which he is working, some mental picture of "how it is put together and how it works" (Barber, 1973:2).

Models, then, guide investigations intended to assist us to understand our world. However, at the same time that models promote understanding, they also impose limitations, partly because of the assumptions about man and society on which they rest. Given these assumptions, models simultaneously "illuminate" some aspects of the human condition and "cast a shadow" on others. While a theory may open one avenue of explanation, it precludes use of other possible explanations. The implications of this are far-reaching, extending into areas well beyond the scope of this volume. However, an appreciation of the approach used in this book, in contrast to that of traditional studies of deviance, calls for a brief examination of their respective origins, their assumptions, and how they apply to the study of deviance.

In discussing these matters it is important to note that the theoretical model employed here and that used in traditional studies of deviance rest on different paradigms or models of intellectual thought. That is, differences between these approaches involve such fundamentals as "what should be studied, what questions should be asked, how they should be asked, and what rules should be followed in interpreting the answers obtained" (Ritzer, 1975:7). We shall refer to the traditional intellectual model as the *Paradigm of Fact* and the model used in this book as the *Paradigm of Definition*. Each model consists of several elements, as Table 1-1 indicates. Included is a philosophical base, a notion of how the subject matter should be studied, beliefs about the nature of reality, man and society, and, finally, a perspective on the basis of human behavior. How each paradigm treats each of these matters will be considered. One final point is in order; referring to these models as *factist* and *definitional* is not to suggest that the former deals exclusively with fact and the latter concerns things that are unfactual or nonfactual. Nothing could be more misleading. Indeed, both models deal with "factual" matters, that is, things that are done or that exist. The difference between these models lies in how they approach "facts" and the questions they raise concerning them.

The Factist Paradigm

Philosophical Base and Nature of Reality

The paradigm of fact has its roots in the philosophical idea that things about which man has knowledge have meaning independent of man's consciousness. Accordingly, the world consists of a set of "real" or objective elements. *Objective*, in this case, refers to the idea that such things as truth and natural principles or laws of human behavior exist independent of the mind of the observer and operate whether or not people are aware of them. This tradition also holds

TABLE 1-1

Paradigmatic Distinctions

	Philosophical Base	Nature of Reality	Method of Study	Nature of Man	Nature of Society	Basis of Behavior
PARADIGM OF FACT	Realism Essences held to exist outside the mind Reality is objective	An objective condition Extrinsic	Variable analysis Scientific causation Discover inherent essences of reality	A scientific object A responding organism	Stable Harmonious Consensus	Causes Forces and factors internal and external to people Impersonal Deterministic
PARADIGM OF DEFINITION	Nominalism Reality is essentially mental	A human construction Socially constructed	Systematic observation Social emergent Investigate social basis of reality construction	An active agent An inter-active organism	Changing Internally conflictive Constraint and coercion	Reasons The meanings people create and assign to things in the world Voluntaristic Purposive

that things that are real (tangible) and populate the world have inherent meanings or essences. Given these ideas, the task of investigators (researchers) is to examine things, discover their inherent or essential meaning and any patterns (natural laws) governing their existence, and bring the whole under human control. In brief, philosophical realism suggests the existence of a real world consisting of things that have essences.

Method of Study

Consistent with its philosophical base and view of reality, the fact model regards the scientific method as the proper way to study the human condition. Belief in the scientific method is based on a set of postulates called the *canons of the scientific method*. These postulates are taken for granted; that is, they are assumed to be valid but may only be defended philosophically. These postulates are (1) the world exists, (2) the world is knowable, (3) the world is knowable through our senses, and (4) the elements comprising the world are related in terms of cause and effect (Goode and Hatt, 1952:20). The continuity between these postulates and the assumed nature of reality are apparent.

Further, the proper way of "doing science" calls for a heavy emphasis on *positivism* and *empiricism*. Positivism refers to the historic tendency of Western thinkers to study and reason about human nature and behavior in the same way natural philosophers since the ancient Greeks approached the world of nature (Rossides, 1978:8–9). That is, human nature should be studied using the methods of science. These methods, commonly referred to as empirical, are based on ". . . the conviction that sensory experience should be regarded as the most reliable source of knowledge" (Lastrucci, 1967:30). As this method has evolved it has called for the analysis of *variables* (any phenomenon that can change, be measured directly or indirectly, or be quantified) to determine their objective character. Overall and historically, this orientation rests on the idea that knowledge (such as natural law principles, truths, and so on) has an *absolute foundation* (is independent of and external to the knower, not determined by anything outside itself), and the knowing person is a passive entity so far as "shaping" that knowledge is concerned (Brown, 1978:89). We will return to these considerations in the pages to follow.

Nature of Man and Society

As expressed by Wrong (1961), traditional sociology and the paradigm of fact have adopted an "oversocialized" conception of man. Explicitly or implicitly, this conception holds that man is basically a conforming creature who is guided by a superego or con- science as a result of having internalized social norms. Man is a responding organism, reacting to institutionalized norms, values, and expectations. It is on the basis of this model of man that sociol- ogists have tried to explain how social order is possible. According to the fact model, social order is possible because, among other things, man is a conforming creature.

Linked to this conception of man is the proposition (expressed in what is known as structural functional theory, to be discussed in Chapter 3), that society is characterized by stability, internal har- mony, and value consensus among the bulk of its membership. The link between this conception of society and the oversocialized con- ception of man is seen in the idea that a well-integrated society exists when actors are engaged in compatible roles (such as parent- child, husband-wife) and the roles are being carried out in terms of internalized norms based on agreed-upon social values (Davis, 1975:74ff).

The use of these conceptions of man and society has been partic- ularly stressed in the study of rule-violating behavior. As will be noted shortly, deviant conduct has traditionally been regarded as statistically exceptional, exceptional because people are assumed or- dinarily to be striving for normative conformity. Departure from these norms often has been explained on the basis of some imperfec- tion—either a fault in an essentially integrated and harmonious so- cial system or a fault among persons violating the norms. This leads to the final property of the fact paradigm.

Basis of Behavior

As noted above under Method of Study, the fact paradigm has embraced the notion that the elements comprising the objective world are related in terms of cause and effect. Causes are things that make other things happen. Nothing happens without a cause and every effect ultimately becomes the cause of a future effect. The cause-effect chain is uninterrupted. As employed to account for human behavior, causes take both an internal (psychological) and external (social) form. They are factors to which people are subject and over which they have little or no control. Operating in an im- personal fashion, as, for example, in the case of the often-heralded influence of poverty on crime and the effect of the broken home on delinquency, these elements are regarded as *deterministic*, that is, as elements necessary to the occurrence of the behavior in question (Hoult, 1974:47–48).

In summary, then, the paradigm of fact rests on philosophical realism, according to which the real world is populated by elements having objective meaning and inherent essences. These elements are related to one another in terms of a sequence of cause-and-effect associations. The study of these elements is properly engaged in when guided by the principles of the scientific method. In addition, man, too, may be scientifically studied; man is a scientific object.

Implications for the Study of Deviance

Deviance as Objective Condition

Among the implications of the fact paradigm for the study of deviance is, first, that this orientation suggests that deviance is a real and objective condition existing independent of man's consciousness. This means that deviant acts are inherently and essentially undesirable (immoral), and are disapproved because of their undesirability. An expression of this orientation is found in the once-popular distinction between acts identified as *mala in se*, acts held to be "wrong in themselves," vs. those called *mala prohibita*, wrong because man defines them that way. Examples of the former would include murder and rape, while the latter would include violation of business regulations and licensing codes. This distinction is quite misleading. First, it suggests that some behaviors are prohibited because they are wrong, while others are wrong merely because they are prohibited. However, so far as man is consciously aware, only the latter designation applies. Second, the distinction suggests the existence of *inherently different qualities* of rule-breaking behavior. Careful examination of the behaviors to which these labels are applied reveals they do not differ in *kind* of wrongfulness. An act of one sort is as much a violation of rules (criminal laws or some other) as an act of the other type. At best, these terms refer to acts that differ in perceived degree of seriousness. To the extent that degrees of seriousness are matters of perception (rather than *essences* of the acts) these designations are misleading.

To be sure, no contemporary student of deviant behavior speaks of essences or of deviance as an inherent property of certain acts. For example, no one challenges the view that deviance is relative to time and place. And behavior patterns defined as deviant are always presented as exemplifying a specific and concrete (rather than abstract) instance of deviance (Sherif, 1961:59; Akers, 1973:23–24). Nonetheless, a careful reading of much literature on deviance reveals a sense of some sociologists' unquestioned acceptance of the inherent moral meaning of behavior designated as deviant. Despite paying lip service to moral relativity, relatively few sociologists spend time investigating the basis of the moral meaning of acts that are unlawful. It is in the lack of such effort, together with the ease with which official moral meanings are accepted, that one finds an implicit acceptance of the idea that things have essences—inherent moral meanings.

What is implied in the language of some social scientists is occasionally made explicit in the language of lay people and officials. Thus, in seeking to preclude recruitment of homosexuals into the ranks of police, R. L. Vernon, Deputy Police Chief of Los Angeles is quoted as saying that "Homosexual acts are *inherently* immoral, abnormal, perverted, disgraceful, degenerate, degrading, and criminal . . ." (*The Advocate*, 1975:8. Emphasis added.). Clearly, some people *do* speak and act as if they subscribe to the notion that things have essences.

Focus on Origin of Behavior

By taking the immorality of deviant conduct for granted, few (if any) questions are raised concerning the sociological basis of meaning or the origins of normative prescriptions and proscriptions. Called a "normative" orientation, good and evil are judged in terms of existing social norms. The deviant quality of the act is not regarded as problematic or uncertain. This follows from the first postulate of science; deviance exists as part of the real world.

Taking deviance for granted also encourages scholars to investigate people's behavior to the exclusion of other things. If deviance may be taken for granted, there is no logical reason to investigate other things, such as the social basis of the meaning of behavior. Consistent with the fourth canon of the scientific method, scholars are then free to develop a research method designed to discover some causal nexus (link) of physiological, psychological, or sociological factors (variables) that explain why people violate moral rules. However, as noted earlier, while models are intended to promote understanding of one thing, they may well obscure another ("casting shadows" as well as providing "illumination").

By "casting shadows" is meant that the questions one may ask about a thing are limited by the assumptions and boundaries of the model within which they work. For example, equipped with a medical model of deviance and based on the assumption of societal perfectability (if not perfection), early students of deviance asked questions reflecting (1) their acceptance of existing social rules and values as right and proper (Mills, 1943) and (2) the view that people violate rules for pathological reasons; they are either dependent, defective, or delinquent (Rubington and Weinberg, 1977:22). Limited by these premises, scholars concentrated on investigating and specifying the conditions under which groups or individuals "adjusted improperly" (a euphemism for breaking rules) to social conditions. Tests were conducted to determine if the lower class or the foreign born adjust differently (had higher rates of deviance) than the upper class or the native born, whether young people adjust differently than older people, and whether males adjust differently than females. In short, restricted by a model that equated morality with individual and societal health (and the status quo), discredited behavior could only be viewed as a reflection of individual or group maladaptation, that is, pathology. Later the notion of pathology was applied to social conditions, resulting in the belief that problem situations arose under pathological or abnormal social conditions (Krisberg, 1975:3–4). In either case, however, the fundamental premise is that rule breaking reflects an abnormal (pathological) condition. Popular conceptions of deviance continue to reflect this notion (Simmons, 1969). The difficulty with such conceptions is that they may well restrict understanding.

That a conception or model may restrict understanding, that it "casts shadows" at the same time that it sheds light, may be demonstrated by our general orientation toward crime. As a general phenomenon, crime is most often viewed in moral terms. That is, most forms of criminal behavior are considered to be immoral and those who engage in them are regarded as lacking in moral worth. In turn, their lack of morality is ordinarily taken to mean there is "something wrong" with the offender.

Closing Off Alternative Conceptions

Viewing crime and criminals in that way effectively limits the use of alternative ways to conceive of why people engage in criminal behavior. For example, what can be learned about criminal behavior (at least some forms of it) by examining it as *work*, a matter of gainful employment? Is it possible to understand prostitution (among other things) as an economic endeavor, entered into voluntarily for monetary gain, flexibility of working hours, or other work-related conditions held to be desirable by the prostitute? Would the concept of *moonlighting* (Polsky, 1967:102) add to our knowledge of why some college girls and others engage in prostitution on an irregular basis? Might the same concept shed light on some bank robberies, some burglaries, and some efforts to hustle (Polsky, 1967:102ff; Letkemann, 1973:6ff)? and would the extremely widespread practice of employee theft be better understood as an extension of the historical custom of "perks" or *perquisites*, a gain or profit obtained incidental to employment but separate from wages or salary (Ditton, 1977a and 1977b)?

What of the concept of *leisure?* Might we promote an appreciation of some forms of unlawful behavior by examining them as forms of play or recreation? While a few scholars (Thrasher, 1927; Matza, 1964) have made references to the recreational, play, or thrill-seeking dimensions of crime and delinquency, and despite solid information suggesting a strong play or recreational element in much rule breaking, this facet of the phenomenon of deviance is generally lacking in orthodox theories. That such matters are ignored has continuity, it seems, with the tendency to explain such behavior on the basis of some presumably abnormal condition or defect.

And what of mental illness? What might we learn of this phenomenon if we perceived its various manifestations, not as evidence of a pathologically based disorder, but as *adjustive mechanisms* used by people in order to "manage" situations they regard as irresolvable? Perhaps our understanding of what we now perceive as mental illness would be enhanced if we were to suspend the use of that term, declare it a myth, and seek to investigate such matters as expressions of ". . . personal, social and ethical problems in living" (Szasz, 1961:296).

Finally, much recent criminal and deviant activity may best be understood if viewed as *political action* rather than simply illegal or immoral behavior. Can we really apprehend and understand the activity of the Symbionese Liberation Army, the Weatherunderground, Vietnam war resisters, or advocates of gay liberation, to name a few, when these are cast in moral/legal terms alone? Are these simply groups of immoral, irrational, strange, cowardly, perhaps "crazy" people? Or is light shed and understanding (*not* acceptance) promoted by perceiving their actions as (perhaps ill-advised) behavior engaged in to promote change in public policy or public policy-making processes? Hopefully, these cases make clear that students of society must be sensitive to the limitations of standard concepts and ought not be misled into taking their illuminating potential for granted. It is important to establish whether our conceptual tools, including definitions, reflect accurately the world they are intended to represent or, on the other hand, whether they reflect the moral meanings embraced by persons representing dominant American culture (Spradley, 1970:68).

The limitations imposed by a conceptual model may also be demonstrated in the case of two outstanding social theories of deviance, both of which were intended to "make sense" of the real world. First, *social disorganization* theory (about which we will say more later) models society after an organism. The organism's parts occasionally get out of adjustment because of social change. As a consequence of change, old rules and norms are said to lose their effectiveness as controls on people's behavior. People are then free to behave on the basis of expedience. Deviant behavior is thought to result when people (especially the poor) are not restrained by social control agencies such as the family and other community institutions (themselves the weakened victims of social change). A second theory, *structural functionalism*, employs a similar image of the social system. In this case, however, the factors leading to deviance are "built in" to the social structure. As expressed by Merton (1957), these factors are characteristic (rather than anomalous) features of the social structure. They are things that raise people's hopes and aspirations, while they simultaneously are denied a legitimate opportunity to realize them. According to this theory, some people relieve the frustration by resorting to deviance—crime, gambling, drugs, alcohol, and suicide.

However different in detail, these theories share the assumption of *social perfectability*. For example, even though societal harmony or cultural integrity are temporarily disturbed by social change, or the social structure is arranged so as to systematically disadvantage select groups, neither theory departs from the idea that society can be made more perfect, that it is perfectable, and that the problems are corrigible. Problems are reduced to "technical" or "mechanical" dimensions, and people are assumed to possess the wisdom and humanitarian inclinations necessary to repair the social machine (Erickson, 1964:9). Thus, the theory goes, people in slums and ghettos will engage in less deviance when they are assimilated into the mainstream of society and/or when more legitimate opportunities are made available to them. So, as a matter of social policy, let's keep the kids in school and one day they may grow up to wear Brooks Brothers suits and I. Magnin dresses. Or, by opening up opportunity structures, by making more educational, occupational, and housing opportunities available to depressed and disprivileged minorities, deviant behavior will subside. This idea of social and human perfectability is clearly noted in the New Frontier and Great Society programs of the Kennedy and Johnson presidential administrations, both of which reflected the application of orthodox sociological knowledge to public policy formation.

A word of caution is in order. Increased educational opportunities, jobs, decent diet, good housing, and quality clothing are not suggested as unworthy goals. The point is that *such things have no essential relation to people breaking rules*. It is all too obvious that the abundance or absence of material things does not distinguish between violators and nonviolators. People from all walks of life, all levels of material abundance, and all degrees of social opportunity break society's rules. That we so often forget this seems largely a consequence of the "theory" we employ to make sense of the world. Certainly the data do not compel such an interpretation. To the extent that we persist in using these ideas to make sense of things, alternative and perhaps more plausible interpretations are precluded.

Causality and Determinism

Let's turn to another feature of the fact model and its implications for the study of deviance. By embracing the postulates of the scientific method, the fact model, as we have seen, rests on the premise that elements in the real world (external to man's consciousness) are related to one another in terms of cause and effect and that these cause-effect relationships form an uninterrupted continuum. Thus, every effect is the product of a prior cause and the cause of a posterior effect. A causes B, B causes C, C causes D, and so on ad infinitum. As ordinarily employed, a "cause" is something that makes other things happen. In that sense, causes *determine* other things; that is, they have rather conclusive and authoritative influence. Causes are things to which their effects are subordinate. Following from that, it should be no surprise that in the fact model we encounter the notion that human behavior is rather conclusively and authoritatively influenced by select other factors (Thomlinson, 1965: Chapter II; Hoult, 1974:47–51).

Perhaps to soften the tone of finality surrounding rigid determinism and to acknowledge fact, some social scientists have suggested that the concept of cause does not mean there exists a perfect relationship between causes and their effect; no perfect 1:1 relation exists between the two. Rather, rigid determinism is thus replaced by *probabilism,* the idea that the occurrence of events is *more or less* likely (rather than certain) given the presence of some prior condition. A probabilistic position rests on the belief that "chance" factors are at work in the real world; because of them, the scientist's predictions cannot be perfect, they may only be more or less true. As it is currently expressed, then, determinism takes a modified form (Thomlinson, 1965:31–32).

Despite this modification, the principle of cause continues to pose issues of importance for explaining human behavior. Particularly important is how one reconciles determinism and the exercise of choice. Some social scientists have suggested that determinism does not force people to do things against their will. "We do what we will," they say. Interestingly, however, they continue to insist that "what we will" is determined—". . . choice itself is determined" (Hoult, 1974:48). If that be the case, the ideas of choice and self-control are meaningless; the "exercise of options" is a sham, a deception. If the very thing used to defend the idea that man is free of deterministic influences (choice) is itself determined, then the notion of the "oversocialized man" takes on new meaning. The paradigm of fact would have it that man is bound by the limits of whatever factors are assumed to determine his actions.

If people are subordinated to and bound by these elements, if people are "oversocialized" creatures and have internalized society's norms, how then shall we account for their efforts to break with the established social system, violate its rules, impose lasting changes on societal processes, or embrace countercultural values? The idea that people act voluntaristically, free of deterministic influences, is quite implausible within the limits of the fact model. Given an "over-socialized" conception of man and a model of society characterized by value consensus and internal harmony, it strains credibility to posit an explanation for deviance based on forces arising from within that society.

Summary

The strains and contradictions contained in the fact model have not gone unnoticed. Several students of rule-violating behavior have challenged the fact model and its determinism (Michael and Adler, 1933; Sutherland, 1947:23; Reckless, 1950; Lejins, 1951; Matza, 1964; Quinney, 1970). In its place is the idea that seeking after order between phenomena is not coextensive with seeking after cause-effect relationships. Causal relations are but one logical form of an ordered relationship. Further, critics have suggested that causal statements do not necessarily indicate conditions existing in a state of nature, independent of human consciousness. What we refer to as "cause-effect" relations may be no more than human conceptions of things. Thus, Norwood Hanson has stated that "Causes certainly are connected by effects; but this is because our theories connect them, not because the world is held together by cosmic glue" (Hanson, 1965:64).

Finally, is a model that focuses principally on human behavior and its presumed causes equipped to answer questions about conditions that may be antecedent or subsequent to that behavior? For example, while it is one thing to try to explain *behavior* that is deviant, it is quite another to explain the *deviance* of behavior. Thus, to concentrate on *behavior* that is deviant is to accept and take for granted the existing public moral meanings of behavior. To explain the *deviance* of behavior, however, one investigates the basis for that moral meaning, trying to understand how specific behaviors come to be defined as deviant. For example, how is it that homosexuality came to be defined as an illness (Bullough, 1974), that taking another's property without their permission came to be labeled "theft" and declared a crime (Hall, 1952), and what circumstances preceded the medicalization of hyperkinesis as a behavioral disorder among children (Conrad, 1975)? In short, how do things that once had little or no moral meaning come to be defined as deviant? More basically, how are moral rules developed in any case? Questions of the subsequent sort include the following. What are the consequences of rule making? What does it mean to a person to be defined as a rule breaker? How do people adjust to having that definition applied to them? How do people adjust to having yesterday's morality defined as today's immorality? Once established, how is it that moral rules that are theoretically universal come to be applied to some groups but not others?

Our understanding of deviance is not complete until consideration is given to these and related questions. To address ourselves to these questions, however, calls for an alternative paradigm or model. That alternative is the paradigm of definition. Let's examine this perspective.

The Paradigm of Definition

As noted earlier, paradigms differ in terms of their fundamental conception of the subject matter under study and how it should be investigated. In contrast to the social fact paradigm is the social definition paradigm. Included under this paradigm are elements of several theoretical positions: action theory, symbolic interaction theory, phenomenological sociology, and existential sociology (Ritzer, 1975:91). In the following paragraphs elements of this orientation will be presented.

Philosophical Base

Let us begin by suggesting that musical notes and colors do not exist as tones or light beams floating about in the atmosphere. "A flat," or the name of any other specific musical tone, has no existence outside man's mind. To be sure, audible vibrations of various frequencies occur when a hammer strikes a taut wire; however, to assign to these vibrations a name such as "A flat," "C sharp," "F," is an *act of mind*. Similarly, light waves of differing frequency occur in nature. But designating light waves of a specific frequency as a color, such as red, is an act of mind. By "act of mind" is meant that things like "B flat" and "red" are mental constructs; they are concepts and words that people use to identify classes of things perceived to have elements in common. Most important for our purpose is the fact that *the name does not exist outside the human mind* and should not be confused with the thing it symbolizes. A map is not the terrain to which it refers.

Accordingly, things are whatever people name them. In the case of musical notes and colors, the name "A flat" may just as well have been applied to the vibrations we now call "C sharp" and the word "red" could just as well have been assigned to the light waves we have named "blue." What is important is only that there be agreement among people as to the name used to refer to specific things. For example, regardless of the name, we should agree that the keynote of the normal or natural major scale be referred to in some consistent way. The specific symbol used to refer to that tone, C, is unimportant.

The position stated above regarding musical notes and light waves is referred to as a *nominalistic* position and may be useful in helping people make sense of issues involving morality and immorality—deviance. Rather than assume that acts are moral or immoral in their own right, nominalism frees us from the idea that there are universal essences, that things have inherent meaning, and that meaning exists independent of man's consciousness. Alternatively, we are encouraged to consider whether qualities like moral and immoral, deviant and nondeviant, are human constructions (concepts) imposed on things and reflective of man's attitude toward them. An appreciation of this calls for a brief examination of ontological and epistemological matters as they relate to the nature of reality.

Nature of Reality

We may begin our examination of ontological and epistemological matters with a tale concerning three baseball umpires, each of whom is seeking to describe how he approaches his work. The first umpire says, "I call them as they are!" The second umpire says, "I call them as I see them!" The third umpire says, "They're nothing until I call them!" This parable points to three major Western theories of knowledge. The first umpire apparently regards knowledge as objective and independent of mind, and regards himself as a passive agent (see above, page 4). The second umpire's position represents the Kantian perspective, according to which people mediate knowledge of the real world. Accordingly, the nature of the real world must be approached in terms of the categories of thought through which it is filtered and interpreted. Finally, the third umpire represents a constructionist perspective. Because this is the position to be used in this book, let us expand on these perspectives and link this parable to the issues of ontology and epistemology.

Ontology (the study of being or reality) is concerned with the nature of the world. It asks questions about the nature of reality and the properties and relations of being. It asks "what is the real world like?" The first umpire, representing the paradigm of fact, is prone to reply that the "real" world is validly described as one that operates according to the laws or principles of logical systems "discovered" by man. And, consistent with traditional rationalist thought, the first umpire intimates that human reason is the principal instrument and final authority in the search for truth.

The second umpire is far less assured in responding to the ontological question. This umpire implies that he is a conscious being and that his consciousness must be considered in any evaluation of the validity of his descriptions of the "real" world. This leads to the third umpire and the social definition paradigm.

Unlike the two preceding cases, the third umpire (and the paradigm of definition) suggests there is no such thing as a "real" or objective world consisting of things that have essences. Surely, there are all manner of things in people's environment with which they must deal. However, the way people respond to these things reflects their perception of them rather that the thing's "essence." In short, as the last umpire implies, the real world is whatever we perceive it to be. Beauty and ugliness, morality and immorality, deviance and nondeviance—these represent states of mind, resulting from the assignment of meaning to the things themselves. In accepting this position one is led to conclude that the world to which people respond is a world *without essential meaning*. In response to the ontological question, then, the paradigm of definition leads to the conclusion that the real world has no objective character. As the wag says, there are no dirty words, only dirty minds.

Epistemology raises related questions: "How do we know about the world? How certain is our knowledge of the world?" If man assigns the qualities (ascribes meaning) to the world, it follows that man cannot have knowledge (certain or otherwise) of an external world. Moreover, it is suggested that even if there is an external or objective world of meaning (one existing independent of human consciousness), people are unlikely to apprehend it because of their being "encapsulated" by a world of socially constructed meaning. If man never confronts the hypothesized "real" world, then, he can never have knowledge of its properties. Consequently, man is left with knowledge of things to which *he* has given meaning rather than knowledge of things that supposedly have independent meaning, that is, independent of human consciousness. To apprehend the basis of the meanings people assign to things in their world, then, it is suggested that we must look to people themselves, to their everyday life and their social experience. This is the position to be followed in this book. It is a position that is consistent with existential sociology. It is also a position that has an important bearing on the method of study according to the paradigm of definition.

Method of Study

Is it possible that this same interpretation can be applied to the idea of cause and effect? Earlier it was suggested that the world is held together, not by cosmic forces, but only by our theories of it. Is "cause," then, a concept developed and used by people in an effort to impose order on a world that is without essential order? For example, is it in the objective nature of things that broken homes *cause* delinquency, that the disruption of a family has an authoritative and conclusive effect on the moral behavior of its members? Is it in the nature of things that violence in the media *increases* crime, that social change *produces* a reduction in social control, or that "imbalances" in the social structure *cause* deviant behavior? Or do these linkages reflect the way sociologists and others perceive them to be? If these linkages are human constructions (rather than properties of a "real" world), are there other ways than cause and effect whereby we may order the elements of a socially constructed reality? Let's briefly explore these questions.

Under the influence of the fact model, sociological research has been dominated by *variable analysis* (Blumer, 1956). According to Blumer this has resulted in examining human groups as if they consisted only of variables and their relationships. Thus, as the above questions suggest, there is assumed to be a relationship between deviance (viewed as a dependent variable), on the one hand, and broken homes, violence in the media, and social structural conditions (the independent variables), on the other. The fact paradigm posits a causal relation between these things. This is done by contending that A causes B if (1) they occur together in the way the hypothesis predicts, or (2) A occurs prior to B, or (3) B occurs simultaneously with A. In practical terms this means that phenomena occurring together are likely to be regarded in cause-effect terms. That is, by embracing the concept of cause, one is inclined to perceive causal relationships. Thus, if higher delinquency rates occur in areas with more broken homes, not only are these factors said to be related, but the latter is prone to be viewed as a cause of the former. Alternative interpretations (other than cause-effect) tend to be precluded since, according to the fact model, things that exist in the real world are objectively united that way. Alternative ways of ordering the universe are ignored (Kotarba, 1975).

Continuing with the example of the broken home and delinquency, research studies using large samples of official delinquents have shown that between 30 percent and 60 percent of them have come from broken homes. At best, concordance at that level provides weak support for the "broken homes cause delinquency" hypothesis.

This relationship is even weaker when careful matching of delinquents and nondelinquents has been attempted (Smith, 1955:307). Despite weak data and deficient methods of study (Wilkinson, 1974:734), acceptance of the causal importance of broken homes on delinquency has persisted. Weak relationships led researchers to expand the referent of existing concepts rather than to use different concepts. The concept "broken homes" was expanded to include not only homes broken physically (such as by death or divorce), but psychologically as well, that is, those in which the relationships between parents and children are "disturbed" in some way. Investigation also focused on the relative effects of different types of broken homes (death vs. divorce, mother absent vs. father absent), on the relative influence of broken homes on male vs. female children, and on comparisons of the effect of broken vs. reconstituted homes (Cavan, 1969; Nye, 1958; Perry and Pfuhl, 1963; Toby, 1957). Rarely, however, was consideration given to the idea that the presumed link between these variables is a consequence of (1) the *meaning* of the broken homes (however defined) among police, juvenile court personnel, and other officials and (2) the long-range influence of these meanings on social policy(ies) that produce statistics supportive of the "broken homes cause delinquency" thesis.

For example, to what extent has the relationship between broken homes and delinquency been a result of differential treatment given such youngsters by police and juvenile court? Are victims more prone to report offenses committed by juveniles from broken than unbroken homes? Is the absence of a parent taken as an indication of lax parental control necessitating official intervention? Are children from unbroken homes released with a warning, while their counterparts from broken homes become subject to official processing (Smith, 1955:309)? Questions of this sort are critical in that they call attention to variation in response patterns by officials in terms of their *definition of the situation* rather than in terms of objective differences between adolescents from broken and unbroken homes. The relationship, then, is not causal, but an artifact based on the intervening process of defining (Blumer, 1956:686).

Let's explore this intervening process just a bit. Karen Wilkinson (1974) has suggested that the importance attached to the influence of the broken home on delinquency has varied markedly over the course of this century. Between 1900 and 1932 there was widespread acceptance and support of the idea that broken homes caused children to misbehave. Yet this acceptance rested less on irrefutable empirical evidence (actually, the strength of the evidence was weak) than on the bias of the sociologists of that time. This was a bias composed of an implicit belief in the indispensable role of the family in society and a high evaluation of the family as an institution. Because they defined the family positively whatever seemed to threaten the family or to be a departure from an ideal conception of it was perceived (defined) negatively. Instability in the family or divorce, for example, were among the negatively defined conditions. The link in the belief that broken homes cause delinquency was provided by those persons who, in addition to having strong valuational roots in the family, became involved in the "child saving" movement of the late nineteenth and early twentieth centuries (Platt, 1969). The concern of these reformers for both the family and children led them to define the broken home as one incapable of socializing children properly—a task that demanded the attention of a pair of stable parents. Lacking adequate socialization was felt to lead to maladaptation or delinquency on the part of the child (Rubington and Weinberg, 1977:22).

Between the years 1933 and 1950 emphasis on the role of the broken family as a cause of delinquency declined greatly from the early period. However, that change in emphasis rested not on empirical evidence so much as on (1) sociologists' declining interest in the family as an institution, (2) an increased tolerance and acceptance of urban social conditions among sociologists—including divorce, and so on, (3) changes in the roles of women such that family-related matters became less important and the importance of meanings derived from extrafamilial sources (as from employment) increased, and (4) the increasing methodological sophistication of sociologists and their rejection of the "value judgments" of their predecessors (Wilkinson, 1974:732–733).

In summary, this change in emphasis, which continues into the present, demonstrates that the alleged relationship between variables does not reflect an immutable condition found to exist in "objective" reality. Quite the contrary, the presumed relationship between variables appears to be a consequence of general cultural and ideological factors influencing the meanings assigned to the family by these generations of sociologists. In short, the change in emphasis is a definitional matter.

The essential implication of this observation is that human beings do not respond to *things as they are* (in an objective sense), but to their definition of them. For example, research in delinquency has shown that police often employ offender's speech patterns, grooming, dress, and general demeanor as cues, that is, hints or intimations of the character of offenders. These cues have no objective meaning; they have only the meaning assigned to them by police. Yet on the basis of these things police make inferences about the youth's character and respond accordingly. For example, Piliavin and Briar have noted that police assess the seriousness of delinquent conduct by juveniles on the basis of whether the youths are ". . . *contrite* about their infractions, *respectful* to officers, and *fearful* of the sanctions that might be employed against them" (Piliavin and Briar, 1964:210–211). Such youth are considered salvageable. On the other hand, youth who are unruly, stubborn, nonchalant, or "cool" are defined as "tough guys" or "punks" who deserve severe sanctions. On the basis of the belief that certain groups, especially blacks, are more disposed to the latter traits, police become sensitized to and concentrate their energies on policing such youth. As one police official commented:

> They (Negroes) have no regard for the law or for the police. They just don't seem to give a damn. Few of them are interested in school or getting ahead. The girls start having illegitimate kids before they are sixteen years old and the boys are always "out for kicks." Furthermore, many of these kids try to run you down. They say the damndest things to you and they seem to have absolutely no respect for you as an adult. I admit I am prejudiced now, but frankly I don't think I was when I began police work (Piliavin and Briar, 1964:212).

The role of these symbolically meaningful elements will be further examined when we consider rates of deviance and the process of labeling rule breakers.

Failure to consider the role of defining as an integral part of the perceived relation between variables has produced a sociology in which the very things that should be under investigation (the social basis of meaning) are taken for granted. We have a sociology in which the common-sense meanings of things are replaced by those of the sociologist. As Howard Becker has noted:

> . . . we often turn collective activity—people doing things together—into abstract nouns whose connection to people doing things together is tenuous. We then typically lose interest in the more mundane things people are actually doing. We ignore what we see because it is not abstract, and chase after the invisible "forces" and "conditions" we have learned to think sociology is all about (Becker, 1973:190).

Not the least of the forces and conditions pursued by generations of sociologists are the illusive "causes" whose presumed "effects" so trouble us.

The alternative way of "doing science" (alternative to examining a presumably deterministic world populated by elements having intrinsic and fixed meaning and seeking after abstractions) is to base concepts and principles of human behavior on careful and systematic observation of the social world as it is constructed and experienced in terms of everyday life. This way of doing science, following the paradigm of definition, calls for relinquishing the idea that things have intrinsic and fixed meanings. It calls for examination of the social origins of meaning, how meanings are evolved and applied to things in the environment, the consequences of applying these meanings, and, finally, how meanings change. The remaining chapters of this volume will deal with these issues.

Nature of Man and Basis of Behavior

In addition to providing a substitute for the idea that an external world is populated by inherently meaningful entities related by cause and effect, the paradigm of definition allows man to be perceived as something other than an object. According to this model, man is not to be viewed as an object propelled by causal agents (independent variables) over which he has little or no control. Man is not cast in the image of a billiard ball or a hockey puck. Nor is human behavior to be understood as a matter of stimulus and response. On the contrary, man takes an active part in shaping his destiny; he is an evaluative and judgmental creature, a conscious being who *interacts with* the elements in his world in terms of the meanings he imposes on them.

Further, if we view people as interactive agents, notions about the basis of human behavior must change accordingly. That is, if human behavior (deviant or otherwise) is the action of conscious beings, it becomes explicable in terms of the *choices* people make, in terms of *reasons* rather than causes (Brown, 1977:84). The reasons are to be found in the meanings people create and project to the world around them. Reasons serve to explain the actions of those engaged in both deviant and nondeviant behavior. Both cases involve people behaving in ways meaningful to them. Thus, while the fact model seeks after causes in the form of external forces, the model of definition seeks explanations based on people's existential situation and the actor's values and meanings.

The meaningfulness of the actor's conduct may be apprehended in the *accounts*, the excuses and justifications (Scott and Lyman, 1968) people offer for their acts. An *excuse* is an explanation for behavior that permits the actor to avoid acceptance of full responsibility for it; a *justification*, on the other hand, involves the actor's assumption of responsibility but denies any negative (for example, immoral) element in the behavior. Both these forms allow people to "make sense" of their actions. What is most important about these excuses and justifications is that they form the motive basis of human behavior—the meanings that render our actions sufficient (Weber, 1962:39). If behavior rests on motives, it is unnecessary to resort to deterministic forces in order to explain it. Again, the model employed here rests on an indeterminist position; human conduct is voluntaristic, based on reasons rather than causes.

Nature of Society

Sociologists have long posited the idea that social order rests on moral (value) *consensus* among people. Accordingly, morality is viewed as rather monolithic, consisting of an ". . . organized set of normative values governing behavior which is common to members of a designated society or group" (Merton, 1957:162). Let's ask if that is the most fruitful way to account for social order. Let's ask if it is more consistent with everyday experience to say that people behave in ways *others define as deviant* precisely because of the *absence* of moral consensus. That is, the phenomenon of deviance rests on the absence of agreement as to what is right, proper, moral, and so on, and reflects an ongoing social *conflict* over such matters. These two ways of viewing society and morality—called the consensus and conflict perspectives—deserve brief comment.

As noted earlier, the *consensus perspective* posits the idea that the elements of society are in basic agreement with one another; various age, sex, occupational, racial, ethnic, and other groupings are assumed to share a set of core values and meanings. On that basis there is said to exist some durable relation between these segments and, overall, they form a meaningful whole. Further, the notion of consensus suggests that each part of the social system makes a contribution to the maintenance of the whole. In short, value consensus is said to underlie social structure (Dahrendorf, 1959:161).

The consensus perspective also implies that deviance is a "foreign" element. That is, deviance arises either as a result of unintended conditions that are alien to the ongoing social system (such as a disparity between people's goals and the means to achieve them) or as a consequence of groups embracing values and interests that are contrary to those of "right-minded" citizens—all of whom are assumed to agree on a single moral code. Out of this model come corrective suggestions calling either for social change, that is, social engineering or, more frequently, the rehabilitation of the offender, meaning that the offender's values ought to be brought into harmony with the values of those who are "right-minded." Fundamentally, however, there is assumed to be one reality, a single moral code, to which the bulk of the population subscribes.

An alternative view is called the *conflict perspective*. Point for point this viewpoint is in sharp contrast to the consensus perspective. First, rather than perceiving society in a condition of stability, it is seen to change; social change is omnipresent. This means that the elements comprising the social system have no lasting relationship with one another. Second, rather than being well integrated with one another, as if they were created by some transcendental planner, the elements are in conflict. Workers and employers, consumers and producers or distributors, voters and elected representatives, are all in conflict. There is generational conflict, as well as that based on religious, racial, and sex differences. Third, the factor of change being everywhere and constant means that each element of the social system contributes not to the persistence but to the disintegration of the whole *as it exists at any point in time*. In dialectic fashion, a dynamic system is ever changing, each element contributing to the instability and flux of the whole.

Given this position there is no basis upon which to assume the existence of a transcendent set of values regarding which one may find consensus and *in terms of which people's everyday actions are organized*. To be sure, one may find instances in which there exists widespread public agreement, where consensus appears to prevail. For example, on a *very general level* one will certainly find widespread support for abstract values such as justice, progress, and the like (Williams, 1960). However, it is most problematic that the various age, race, socioeconomic, or sex groups in society agree with one another (or even among themselves) as to precisely what the *specific* referents of these values ought to include.

In the context of everyday life such general and abstract ideas as "fair play," "justice," "decency," and other values take on meaning relative to specific situations. Thus, while most people may subscribe to a general morality on the public level, the private morality that influences our everyday life consists of *situated moral meanings*, interpretations of abstract morals applied to concrete situations (Douglas, 1970:20). For example, doubtless, in terms of public (abstract) morality such things as rape and murder are widely condemned in our society. However, as we will note in Chapter 3, not every "common-sense" behavioral instance that reasonably fits the legal definitions of these things comes to be so defined. Everyday life clearly shows that moral meanings have a contextual base. We will return to this point shortly.

Finally, the values and interests that prevail at any point in time, relative to any specific issue, do so as a result of coercion rather than consensus. For example, regardless of the outcome of present social conflicts over abortion, homosexuality, and marijuana use, the views that "win" will do so at the expense (public condemnation and/or suppression) of their opposite. As we will note in detail, this is a consequence of the perceived mutual exclusiveness of the moral issues with which deviance is inevitably involved. In the final analysis, then, conflict and coercion (rather than cooperation and consensus) are the most valid characterizations of society.

To summarize briefly, this text proposes to analyze the phenomenon of deviance by employing the paradigm of definition. Accordingly, it is necessary that social reality be viewed as a human or social construction rather than an objective condition. Associated with this is the suggestion that we employ the notion of social causation instead of scientific causation, and that man as an active agent replace man as a scientific object. Thereby, man becomes the creator of his own reality as well as one who is influenced by it. This also allows substituting reason for cause as an explanation for social behavior. Finally, it is suggested that society be viewed as an arena of social conflict and change rather than one of consensus and stability.

With these preliminaries in mind, let us now turn to a more concentrated examination of the idea of socially constructed definitions (or social reality) and how socially constructed meanings apply to the study of deviance.

Constructing Social Reality

Social reality refers to the meanings (definitions, conceptions, and typifications) people assign to things in their environment and in terms of which they seek to introduce order to their world. By order is meant the regularization of behavior and human relationships to the point that society is possible. Unlike bees and other forms of social life, wherein behavioral regulation is based on instinct, humans develop this condition through learning. Order exists when people learn to successfully predict one another's behavior and, hence, are able to direct their own actions vis-à-vis others so as to achieve need satisfaction with a minimum of frustration. That is, order occurs when people share meanings of their own and others' behavior as well as of things in their environment. Such order is a product of people interacting with one another in terms of shared meanings.

The construction of meaning is an elemental aspect of our daily lives, so elemental that few people are even aware of being engaged in the process. Nonetheless, as we deal with one another, oftentimes under new and strange conditions, and as we confront existentially unique situations, that is, as we face circumstances calling for some mode of adaptation, we are "writing the script." So, too, are others. Out of these efforts come socially constructed and shared meanings.

A problem with this view is that few of us experience the knowledge underlying social order as a socially constructed element. Rather, most people apprehend reality as a thing to be discovered, not constructed (Holzner, 1972:14). At least that is what everyday, common-sense experience would lead most people to conclude. For example, we are socialized to a set of beliefs, meanings, definitions, values, rules, understandings, and the like, that have the appearance of permanence. This seems to be the case in matters of socializing new family members, providing orientation for entering students in school, recruits to the armed forces, newly recruited club members, "fish" in a prison, or what have you. As a result of socialization and the usual way people are introduced to the social realities of these groups, it is difficult to regard them as social constructions. How is it, then, that what is presented to each new generation as firm, reliable, objective knowledge can be reconciled with the view that reality is socially constructed and has its origin on the private and subjective level? How does the subjective come to be objective? One answer lies in the processes of externalization, objectivation, and internalization (Berger and Luckman, 1967). Let's briefly explore these processes.

Externalization

At the risk of oversimplification, we may begin with the fact that people can and do engage in solitary activity. Much of this activity is *habitual;* that is, it occurs repeatedly and, despite its sometimes complex character, without benefit of conscious reflection. We engage in a variety of daily routines of this sort—brushing teeth, combing hair, dressing, and a variety of other tasks—all of which provide satisfaction. But note, the satisfactory outcome of these actions is not dependent upon the sharing of meanings with others. There is no need to communicate to others "how" I brush my teeth or "why" I put on my clothes the way I do. Certainly the utility of these acts is not enhanced by my doing so. The meanings of these things may remain subjective.

But not all human activity is solitary. People are social animals, engaging in a wide variety of behaviors in concert with others. To move from the level of solitary activity to that of pair relationships (the smallest group and the most limited form of social interaction) calls for coordination if order is to be achieved. That is, whether two people wish to build a log cabin, cook a meal, make love, or whatever, the outcome of their effort will likely be enhanced if they share their respective subjective meanings, preferences, and definitions with each other. For example, does one have a preference for building log cabins with cedar as compared to tamarack logs, for beef steak over pork chops, or for "his thighs outside" as compared to the "woman above, across his thighs" as a coital posture? By "preference" I refer to *how* and *why* people wish to have things done as they do. Given these preferences, sharing them may be expected to promote people's goals, if only for the reason that sharing reduces the likelihood of chaos through misunderstanding. This exchange of meanings, preferences, techniques, and the like may be referred to as *externalization.*

In interaction at the pair level externalization may but need not be elaborate. At a minimum, coordinated and orderly interrelations may be achieved by the language of gesture. That is, bodily movements and facial expressions, demonstrative of acceptance or rejection, approval or disapproval, agreement or disagreement, and so on, may be sufficient for many purposes. For example, male homosexuals unknown to one another and meeting for the first time in *tearooms* (public restrooms where impersonal homosexual encounters occur) effectively convey their interest in sexual relations to one another by means of various forms of "signaling." Included is engaging in pseudomasturbation in view of others, eye contact, beckoning hand and head motions, foot tapping, and note passing (Humphreys, 1970:63–64). In other cases some form of verbalization is required, as when one person seeks to tell another "how" to do something. But whether gestural or verbal, at the level of pair relationships this communication may be informal. What seems certain is that for any prolonged interaction to occur, individual private meanings must be externalized and shared. As a result, one acquires *recipe knowledge*—information about what is and is not considered correct and what must be known to get along when engaged in routine activities (Berger and Luckmann, 1967:42). It is on the basis of this shared knowledge that social order is possible.

Objectivation

However, social groups are not limited to pair relations. As group size increases, so do the variety and complexity of relationships between members. This, in turn, gives rise to a need for more elaborate efforts to achieve order. Ways must be found to introduce new members to standard group definitions and practices— to recipe knowledge. Formulae for coordinated activity for large groups must now be formalized. There are two noteworthy elements involved.

First, names are given to things and activities to which new members must be introduced. By naming something we *reify* it, that is, what was subjective and personal is given objective and social quality. To use an earlier example, while there may be audible vibrations in nature to which we give the name "A flat," "A flat" does not exist in nature. Yet we commonly find people who fail to make this distinction, who give little thought to the distinction between names and things. The name and the thing become indistinguishable. For example, it is possible for one to take another person's property without his or her permission. For one losing property in that way, the event is a substantive matter, possibly of great importance. However, giving the name "theft" to that behavior reifies it. Reification involves ". . . treating a notational device as though it were a substantive term, . . . a construct as though it were observational" (Kaplan, 1964:61). The "name" and the meanings assigned to it become the thing to which we react. The thing is symbolized by the name; the name takes on an existence of its own. Thus, people can be as fearful of and horrified by a word (and the images it connotes) as they can by the substantive matters to which it refers. In many of our large cities people who have never experienced criminal victimization (substantively) nonetheless take great precautions when traveling at night because of "horror stories." And people can become quite sexually stimulated by looking at pictures, reading so-called "dirty" stories, or attending skin-flicks—none of which are more than symbolic representations. What each of these cases entails is creating and imputing meaning to things that are essentially without meaning. It is but a short step to reacting to the event *as if* the assigned meanings were inherent.

Second, information about how things are done in the group may be supplemented with "why" things are done as they are. This calls for the formulation of a rationale or justification that may be appended to the recipe knowledge. Prisons, for example, assemble and print inmate rule books, information on the how and why of inmate conduct during imprisonment. In the armed forces this type of information is called a "code of conduct." In some social groups, for example, a sorority, it may be called "standards." For members of some religious groups it may appear as doctrinal summaries called catechism.

Regardless of the name given this knowledge, externalization of rules (the foundation of which consists of meanings) results in their *objectivation*, "the process by which the externalized products of human activity attain the character of objectivity . . ." (Berger and Luckmann, 1967:60). That is, by naming things and assembling formal statements about "how" and "why" things are done, groups bestow objective quality on things, a quality that is social in origin. Were it not for the fact that order requires some degree of communication and that communication calls for sharing perceptions through verbalization, naming, and so on, these meanings would remain private and subjective, which is where they originate.

Internalization

Each of us apprehends objectivated knowledge during socialization. The *institutions* of society, which are no more than ". . . commonly accepted and established ways of doing things . . ." (Scott, 1972:18) are *presented* to us. But they are presented to us as nonnegotiable conditions. They are not presented as merely *one way* of doing things, but as the *only way* to do things. And in communicating these ways and meanings to people, parents and others in authority reinforce their own acceptance of the objectivated knowledge. In a sense, then, both the socialized and the socializer *internalize* this objectivated knowledge.

By internalizing this knowledge, which is the objectivated product of human activity, it comes to be perceived as having an independent existence. The end product is that a socially constructed reality appears to be ubiquitous and inescapable. Not the least important basis for this is that by internalizing—incorporating—institutionalized knowledge, self and others become fused.

The social order that is created by these means is not limited to integrating interpersonal relations. On a far grander scale, we create meanings that consolidate all institutionalized activity into one coherent whole. These meanings or integrative ideas are referred to as the *symbolic universe*. The symbolic universe consists of ideas that provide a transcendant orderliness to our world. All things come to have a place in "the scheme of things" and a place is provided for everything. We create meanings about how the abstraction "family" harmonizes with an equally abstract notion called "the economy," how the "economy" and "education" complement one another, and how all is unified into a coherent whole referred to as "one nation under God." Birth, our own as well as that of our ancestors and descendants, death, and all in between, is incorporated into one meaningful, ongoing process, and is assigned a place in the cosmos. These integrative ideas, constructed by man, externalized, objectified, and internalized, are referred to as the "symbolic universe" (Berger and Luckmann, 1967:92ff). In everyday terms, they appear as mythologies, cosmologies, theologies, and similar constructions.

By these processes—externalization, objectivation, and internalization—an illusion is created suggesting that reality is external to man, independent of human consciousness, absolute in character, and ontologically certain and orderly. Together, these processes result in the reification of humanly constructed phenomena. What is human appears to be suprahuman (Berger and Luckmann, 1967:89). Man comes to identify with and be influenced by his own creation. What he has created becomes part of him through internalization. Thus, as Berger and Luckmann state: "Society is a human product. Society is an objective reality. Man is a social product" (Berger and Luckmann, 1967:61).

Multiple Realities and Problematic Meanings

Having introduced the paradigm of definition and the notion of the social construction of reality, let us now try to refine these fundamentals. Particularly, it should be noted that socially constructed reality is not all of a kind. As ontologically certain as the world may at first appear to be, life's experiences reveal to all that the certainty we once held concerning the unity and absolute nature of reality is unfounded. Likewise, despite the strength of the *legitimations* (explanations and justifications) underlying institutionalized meanings, our experiences serve to challenge these and weaken our convictions. For example, during early socialization children are introduced to the "right way" of doing things and to the "why" of them. They are taught to go to school, to develop effective study habits, not to hit their little brother or sister, to obey their parents, not to pick their nose in public, and so on. Each of these do's and don'ts, pre- and proscriptions for behavior, is supported by some justification, a legitimation, that seeks to provide either instrumental (utilitarian) or spiritual foundation for the rule. Moreover, these rules are presented in non-negotiable form. Oftentimes this means that the rules are given the status of *moral absolutes*, universal standards applying everywhere and at all times. The consequence is a sense of moral certainty and unity.

The initial sense of certainty and unity may well survive until we move beyond the sheltering effect of home—most often a morally homogeneous environment. As horizons broaden we are exposed to different, sometimes conflicting and mutually exclusive realities. As children move from home to neighborhood, from neighborhood to school, and on to other progressively more heterogeneous social situations, they are introduced to social realities and subuniverses of meaning other than those originally presented to them. They encounter idiosyncratic belief systems reflecting differences in age, sex, religion, social class, occupation, ethnicity. Taught tolerance at home, one soon learns it is an abstraction more often spoken about than practiced. Weaned on the idea of human equality, one is faced with acknowledging that some people are more equal than others. Taught to respect the nation's leaders, one finds them standing before the bar of justice. In these and countless other ways, we are exposed to conditions and contradictions reflecting markedly different meanings, that is, different constructions of reality that challenge the validity and universality of our own. In short, we are exposed to multiple realities.

Our initial sense of stability and unity also founders on the rocks of contextually based meanings. Moral absolutes again begin to appear as something far less certain. We are told that killing violates a divine sense of morality, that it violates the natural order of things and is therefore proscribed in the Ten Commandments. Yet it is all too apparent that the applicability of the code varies with the context. Thus, it is one thing to oppose killing, but not to the extent that it precludes war. Similarly, while "thou shall not kill" is the rule, an accused killer may avoid conviction and public condemnation by successfully pleading self-defense. Using the same rule, many people oppose the death penalty; simultaneously some of the same people advocate more liberal abortion laws. Apparently, though the death penalty and abortion interfere with the life process, that interference has different meaning depending on the context in which it occurs.

Contextual variation in moral meaning is also found in the case of several symptoms of psychiatric disorder. Depending on the context in which they occur and the social position of the person exhibiting them, these symptoms may or may not be taken as evidence in mental illness (Scheff, 1966:34). Daydreaming or engaging in reverie, hallucinating, and talking to "spirits" are such symptoms. None of these have explicit rules against them; nor do we have explicit labels for people who engage in them. Indeed, in our society we have "holy persons" who have been elevated to high status on the basis of their professed ability to experience revelations, have visions, or otherwise bridge the gap between this world and the hereafter. Joseph Smith, founder of the Church of Jesus Christ of Latter Day Saints, and Mary Baker Eddy, founder of Christian Science, are cases in point (Brodie, 1945; Powell, 1940). When these activities are engaged in by such persons a favorable definition is fairly certain; yet if engaged in by one not held to be competent in such matters, or if engaged in under circumstances defined as inappropriate, the same behavior may serve as evidence of mental illness.

The contextual basis of meaning may also be noted in how people respond to events that comprise everyday life. In a study of persons having visible physical (war-related) injuries (White, Wright, and Dembo, 1948), men were asked how they perceived others' curiosity, questions about, or attempts to discuss their injury. One important factor influencing the reaction of the injured men was the situational context of the discussion about the injury. Fundamentally, if questioning or discussion of the injury seems to the injured person to grow out of the context; that is, if it "comes up naturally" as part of a broader conversation, it is more likely to be defined as acceptable. If, however, questioning occurs "out of the blue," or if it is seen by the injured person as an unwarranted intrusion on his privacy, the questioning is regarded as morally offensive. Such instances include "off the wall" queries or questions from total strangers. In short, like many other things people deal with, absolute meanings are abstractions and may well have little use in helping us understand how people behave. More pertinent is the contextually based meanings we assign to things and events. Clearly, these meanings are problematic or uncertain. They are part of the "script writing" it was earlier suggested all people engage in.

Evidence of this may also be noted in our everyday language. For example, politicians frequently send up "trial balloons" to see how their constituency will respond to a legislative proposal or other action. If meanings were clear, unequivocal, and absolute (and, hence, people's behavior highly predictable), no metaphorical balloons would be needed. Likewise, if meanings were unproblematic we wouldn't have to "play it by ear" or "fly by the seat of our pants." We would behave on the basis of more certain understandings. Lest these linguistic forms be understood to reflect the actor's ignorance rather than the problematic nature of meaning, we may point to things regarded as "blessings in disguise." How can a thing simultaneously be a beneficent gift and a malediction unless it be that meanings are situational and, hence, problematic? It would seem that uncertainty and ambiguity of meaning (rather than ignorance) underlie each of these phrases.

To summarize briefly, then, the absence of moral certainty precludes the idea that socially constructed reality is a unitary whole, that it is all of a kind. Social reality is *multiple* rather than singular, and, given multiple realities, it is often *contradictory* rather than consistent. The elements comprising social reality are in *conflict* rather than harmony. Consistent moral definitions of things may be said to exist only in the abstract. As they apply to concrete events, these definitions are highly variable, fluctuating from one setting or context to another. It is out of the conflict between the elements of social reality and variable moral meanings of things that deviance emerges. Indeed, deviance (connoting a definition) is part of social reality. Let's turn now to a consideration of deviance as social reality.

Deviance as Moral Meanings

By extension of the principles already presented, we may regard *deviance* as a concept reflecting the socially constructed moral meanings attached to select behaviors (for example, crime, suicide, and mental illness) and personal attributes such as obesity, physical handicaps, disfigurement. In the first instance, then, *deviance is a social creation.* Deviance is the name (a reification) given to those conditions that run counter to the moral meanings possessed by some groups. Between the thing held to be deviant and the assignment of the label are moral meanings. Deviance, then, is an expression of moral meaning.

But what is meant by the term "moral meanings"? Though subject to extensive philosophical scrutiny, the meaning of the term "moral" remains terribly abstract and seemingly unrelated to our daily affairs. Yet people do have a "commonsense" understanding of things as being moral, respectable, virtuous, and right. The everyday meaning of these terms is known only by their opposite, with which they are linked (Douglas, 1970:3–4). In terms of such opposites we can best know our sense of morality (what is right) by pointing out what we consider wrong. Thus, many people believe abortion is wrong because it is right that pregnancies come to full term; that it is wrong to steal because people have a right to hold and dispose of their own property. Left-handedness is wrong only in relation to right-handedness. In short, goodness is relative to evil, morality relative to immorality. Even Lotsa Luck (see below) seems to have grasped the relativity of meaning.

While for most of us morality may be understood in terms of these dualities, it is still possible to differentiate between moral meanings and meaning in general. As a class, moral meanings are recognizable by the fact that their violation may result in the violator being defined as a socially unacceptable person. That is, moral meanings are distinguishable by the reaction that may result from their violation. (The qualifier "may" is inserted on the grounds that

Copyright © 1973, United Feature Syndicate Inc.

not every violation results in public rejection of the violator. For example, violation of criminal law is *punishable*, but not every known violator is *punished*. Nonetheless, it remains true that violation of moral meanings carries the *threat* of punishment and public stigmatization of the violator).

Defining rule violators as socially unacceptable persons means that such persons may be subject to a public transformation of their character. As Howard Becker states: "When a rule is enforced, the person who is supposed to have broken it may be seen as a special kind of person, one who cannot be trusted to live by the rules agreed upon by the group. He is regarded as an outsider" (Becker, 1963:1). Rule breakers, then, may be defined as qualitatively different from others. Investigation of public conceptions of deviants reveals that people construct and assign stereotypic character traits to different types of deviant actors. Adulterers are perceived to be insecure, lonely, self-interested, passionate, and irresponsible. Homosexuals are perceived to be effeminate, lacking self-control, secretive, sensual, and sensitive (Simmons, 1969:29). Each category of deviant has a somewhat unique set of assigned characterological traits.

As these examples show, the expressions of the violator's unacceptability, of his or her being an outsider, take variable form. One may be declared criminal, mentally ill, a heretic. The attachment of these labels, however, is not simply a consequence of the person's behavior (alleged or otherwise). Labels reflect the moral sense of the labelers. As we noted, deviance is an expression of moral meaning.

Defining Deviance

We began this chapter with several examples of rule-violating behavior. Very commonly, deviance is defined in such terms—that is, *deviance* and *deviant* are terms used generically to refer to conditions (primarily behavior) and people that depart from a norm or a rule (Hoult, 1969:105). Having dwelled at length on the paradigm of definition, it should now be clear that such definitions are insufficient to convey the full range and complexity of the *phenomenon of deviance*. This is particularly apparent when we note that deviance and deviants are outgrowths of the social construction of reality—of the processes of creating and applying moral meaning.

Viewed from this perspective, how shall we define deviance and deviants? Basically, *deviance* refers to behavior and conditions that people so define. The basis of this labeling rests on the labeler's interests (which are felt to be jeopardized by these acts) together with their power and legitimacy. *Deviant* is a label attached to persons or groups defined as violators of moral rules; it reflects the discreditable character attributed to them. *Deviant*, then, is a status assumed by people identified as rule breakers.

Such definitions are deceptively simple. An understanding and appreciation of the phenomenon of deviance calls for a grasp of more than definitions taken out of context. In the final analysis, this phenomenon is best apprehended as a complex social process, a process we will explore in depth in the chapters to follow. In Chapter 2 we will consider how and why people engage in behavior known to be deviant and that puts them in a position to be declared an "outsider." In exploring this matter we will consider explanations based on the fact model as well as the model of definition. In Chapter 3 we will explore the distribution of rule-violating behavior in society. Our "knowledge" of how deviance is distributed is influenced by the problematics or uncertainties associated with defining people and their behavior as deviant. Of particular importance are official rates of deviance and how they are constructed. In Chapter 4 we will examine the process of *banning*, how moral meaning comes to be assigned to behavior. Understanding that process calls for an investigation of the sociological basis of law. Chapter 5 will explore the work of rule-enforcing groups, official agencies having the authority to assign the formal label "deviant" to actors. In conjunction with this, we will examine how people seek to negotiate, moderate, or otherwise resist being labeled. Try though they may, not everyone is able to resist being labeled. In Chapter 6, then, we give extended consideration to the social and social psychological consequences of being labeled—of being stigmatized. Viewing people as interactive agents, however, suggests they may not simply accept and resign themselves to a degraded social status or "wear their chains with honor." Rather, many people seek to manage their stigma. The variety of forms this effort may take on an individual and a collective level is treated in Chapter 7.

Though these aspects of the phenomenon of deviance do not exhaust the matter, they do suggest that it is far too complex to be defined in simple terms. It is perhaps valid to say that this entire volume is devoted to defining deviance—perceived as an ongoing social process that is seemingly without end.

Summary

The present chapter has been concerned with providing a theoretical foundation for the study of deviance. This involved the presentation of alternative paradigms and the assumptions on which they rest. Traditionally, sociological studies of deviance have focused attention largely on questions of etiology, seeking to discover and explain the basis of behavior. This has led sociologists to seek "truth" about an objectively real world. This effort has been accompanied by a "correctional" attitude toward rule-breaking behavior. Sociologists have been guided in this effort by the paradigm of fact.

A contrasting approach, to be used in this volume, is the definition paradigm. In contrast with the fact model, this orientation rests on nominalism. Its major thrust is to help man understand the process by which he introduces order to his world, a process called the social construction of reality. By this means people create and assign meanings to things, reify these meanings, and then apprehend them as if they were objectively real. Included among these socially constructed and reified meanings are the moral meanings that underlie deviance. Deviance, then, is a product of the complex, ongoing effort whereby man seeks to create social order; deviance is part of that social order. Using this approach, behaviors are deviant not because of some moral essence but as a result of human activity.

In contrast with the fact paradigm, then, the definition model seeks no information about the inherent meanings of an objectively real world. Indeed, this approach questions whether such a world exists. And, even if one does exist, it is of no consequence since the meanings to which man responds are those of his own making.

With this general orientation in hand we may proceed to examine deviance in an interactional framework, that is, understanding deviance calls for investigating how rule breakers and others interact to shape the direction and outcome of the deviance-producing process. For example, how people define and respond to things serves to diminish or enlarge (at least perceptually) the issue at hand. As regards behavior defined as deviant, these responses may serve to aggravate or mitigate the situation, with the outcome being either more or less costly to society. Interactionally, then, who defines behavior as deviant? How do they do this? How do individuals labeled deviant respond to that definition? And with what consequences? By these questions, which will be considered at length, it is clear that the definitions paradigm calls for more than an investigation of the deviant actor—no matter how extensive that investigation may be.

With these considerations in mind, let us begin to examine the process of deviance in detail.

Breaking
Rules

38

Introduction

Having established the guidelines for analysis, we now commence our investigation of the deviance process with an examination of people's involvement in rule breaking behavior. Traditional explanations of rule breaking behavior have taken two quite distinct orientations. One of these, with which this chapter will be concerned, seeks to explain individual conduct. This segment of theory focuses on the question of how individuals come to display the behavior in question. The second orientation (dealt with in Chapter 3) is the epidemiological; it seeks to explain how phenomena (in this case rule breaking behavior) comes to be distributed among the various groups comprising society. As such, this segment concerns rates of behavior. This distinction between segments of theory will become clear as we proceed.

In developing the perspective to be used in this book we noted that people are evaluative and judgmental creatures, conscious beings who interact with the elements of their world in terms of socially created and assigned meanings. Consistent with that model it was suggested that human behavior, including rule breaking, be perceived as a result of conscious choices and reasons rather than the result of forces over which people have little or no control.

However that may be, it is well to recognize the scientific and lay popularity of a rather different model of man and behavior, one suggesting that a number of elements—some environmental, some personal—exert a rather determinative influence on human action and that, however things may appear, human beings are "responding organisms" rather than interactive agents. To have an appreciation for the view presented here, then, calls for a brief examination of some historic and contemporary biological, psychological and sociological explanations of individual behavior, with particular attention being given to how the assumptions of these theories "fit" those of the paradigm of definition. Following a critique of traditional theories we will turn to an alternative explanation of "doing deviance."

Explaining Deviant Conduct

Trying to explain why people behave in objectionable ways probably predates man's first effort to make and enforce rules. Certainly it is difficult to conceive of rule making in the absence of some prior offensive behavior. In any event, systematic investigation of why people break rules has interested Western man for hundreds of years. A large part of that interest has been shaped and guided by the premise that rule-breaking behavior is an outgrowth of some aspect of the person. As historically popular expressions of this premise reveal, the deviant has long been viewed as an "abnormal" person. Early biologists, psychologists, and social philosophers operated from this general idea. The representatives of these fields offered different explanations, but they shared a tendency to employ a medical model reflecting the idea of abnormality. Accordingly, deviant actors were perceived as either lacking or possessing something that distinguished them from so-called normals (Vold, 1958:43ff). The goal of representatives of these fields of study was to isolate the factor or factors that differentiated offenders from other people and that could, simultaneously, explain the offender's antisocial conduct.

The early effort to explain deviant conduct reflects the *dualistic fallacy*. This fallacy assumes the existence of a distinct difference between deviants and nondeviants; occupants of these categories are assumed to be *essentially* different, representing mutually exclusive segments of the population (Reid, 1976:97–98). Though recognized now by contemporary scholars as unacceptable, the "knowledge" derived by these investigators continues to circulate and influence many people's thoughts on the subject. For that reason we will briefly examine a sample of the more outstanding examples of such theories.

The Biological Perspective

Physiognomy and Phrenology

Among those who early assumed a biological stance were the physiognomists and phrenologists. *Physiognomy*, the art of determining a person's temperament and character from the external configuration of the face, never reached great heights. Yet it attempted to systematize beliefs that some people think survive to the present— beliefs expressed in folk terms such as "evil eye," "strong chin," "weak mouth," and the like.

Phrenology, the study of the shape of the skull as an indicator of mental faculties, was both the immediate successor of physiognomy and a more sophisticated perspective. This orientation consisted of three propositions and several corollaries. The propositions were (1) that the shape of the skull conformed to the shape of the brain within, (2) the mind consisted of faculties or functions, and (3) the development of these faculties was revealed in the shape of the skull (Fink, 1938:2ff). Further, the brain was held to be the organ of the mind and the mind was a series of psychological characters or faculties. Each of these faculties was located in a given area of the brain.

Several of these faculties were assumed to be related to rule-breaking behavior. Called "lower propensities," these faculties included amativeness (related to sex crime and rape), acquisitiveness (bearing on property crimes), combativeness (related to assault and murder), and secretiveness (associated with treason and fraud) (Vold, 1958:47; Fink, 1938:5). It was believed that if a person had a well-developed propensity for any of these faculties and lacked the development of its corresponding control (also located in the brain and developed through education), he or she would engage in that behavior. The overall development of one's faculties and controls was thought to be discernible by feeling the conformation of the skull. That is, by locating the depressions and bumps on the skull—assumed to correspond to the under- or over-development of the various faculties and their controls—behavior tendencies could be detected and controlled.

In general, according to this perspective, deviance is defined as behavior engaged in by those having well-developed lower propensities and who lacked appropriate controls. On the other hand, reflecting the dualistic fallacy, nondeviants (normals) were those whose propensities were held in check by exercise of will and educational training (Fink, 1938:6ff).

The popularity of this view was cut short, among other reasons, because it ran counter to the then-popular notion of free will. The central idea survived, however, as the search for the basis of deviant behavior spread from the head to the balance of the anatomy. Such was the direction of *criminal anthropology.*

Criminal Anthropology

Led by Cesare Lombroso, an Italian physician, criminal anthropology originated with the idea that deviants and nondeviants were *phylogenetically* different; that is, they had different evolutionary histories and hereditary bases. Crime was thought to be rooted in heredity. Accordingly, systematic rule violators were believed to be *atavists* or throwbacks to an earlier period in the evolution of the species. This idea is reminiscent of the then-popular work of Charles Darwin. Followers of this view set out to measure a variety of human physical traits in an effort to identify the *stigmata* (indices of a discreditable condition) of these atavists. Head size, amount of body hair, lip shape and size, dentition, and ears were among the things measured. Measurements were made of convicted criminals and these were compared with measurements of non criminals (erroneously defined by the absence of a criminal record). These comparisons yielded too few differences to adequately support the view that crime was based on heredity. Nonetheless, on the basis of measures used as an index of physiological inferiority, the view prevailed that criminal behavior reflected an inferior heredity (Vold, 1958:50–52). In short, a so-called inferior biology was used to explain discreditable behavior. Deviants came to be categorized on the basis of their presumed stigmata; systematic deviance was behavior engaged in by atavistic people.

Hereditarians and Eugenicists

In time this general argument of constitutional (biological) inferiority came to be highly refined. Supplemented by increasingly sophisticated research efforts, the first third of this century witnessed the playing out of the nature (heredity) vs. nurture argument, with biology pitted against psychology. One who was involved in this argument was Charles Goring, an English researcher. Goring tried to make statistical tests for the independent effect of heredity and of environment in order to determine which was the more influential factor; he concluded it was heredity (Vold, 1958: 52–55, 92–96). Another figure involved in the nature vs. nurture debate was Johannes Lange. In the 1920's Lange compared the criminal records of identical twins, fraternal twins, and siblings to determine whether behavior of monozygotic (one-egg) twins was more concordant (alike) than that of dyzygotic (two-egg) twins and siblings. He concluded that some people were destined by heredity to engage in crime (Vold, 1958:96–98).

Also in the 1920's investigations were made of the relation between endocrine glandular activity and deviant behavior. Though the results were questionable, they were heralded as the foundation of a "new criminology," with at least certain types of crime being regarded as the product of glandular malfunction (Vold, 1958:102–104; Barnes and Teeters, 1951:148–150).

Almost simultaneously, Earnest Hooton, a Harvard University anthropologist, carrying on the theme pursued by Lombroso and Goring, sought to ". . . study the physical characteristics of criminals for the purpose of discovering whether or not these are related to antisocial conduct" (Hooton, 1939:5). His assumption was that just as chimpanzee behavior is an expression of that animal's morphology, physiology, and psychology, so, too, is this the case for humans. Since deviant and nondeviant behavior were held to be qualitatively different orders of behavior, those engaging in them should reveal appropriate biological differences. Professor Hooton gathered evidence in support of the contention that criminals and deviants are low-grade organisms. To Hooton, crime, war, totalitarian oppression, and other socially questionable behavior stemmed from human deterioration. All such issues revolved about human biology; his proposed solution was eugenics (Hooton, 1939:396ff). An effort to establish a psychobiological basis for delinquent behavior was also attempted by William H. Sheldon (1949). Building on the earlier work of Emil Kraeplin and Ernst Kretschmer, specialists in constitutional psychiatry, Sheldon attempted to establish a typology of human physique and to relate human temperament or characteristic mood to these various types of physique. This typology and their related patterns of temperament may be summarized as follows (Vold, 1958:71):

Physique	*Temperament*
1. *Endomorphic:* relatively great development of digestive viscera; tendency to put on fat; soft roundness through various regions of the body; short tapering limbs; small bones, soft, smooth, velvety skin.	**1.** *Viscerotonic:* general relaxation of body; a comfortable person; loves soft luxury; a "softie" but still essentially an extrovert.
2. *Mesomorphic:* relative predominance of muscles, bone, and the motor-organs of the body; large trunk; heavy chest; large wrists and hands; if "lean" a hard rectangularity of outline; if "not lean" they fill out heavily.	**2.** *Somotonic:* active, dynamic person; walks, talks, gestures assertively; behaves aggressively.
3. *Ectomorphic:* relative predominance of skin and its appendages which include the nervous system; lean, fragile, delicate body; small, delicate bones; droopy shoulders; small face, sharp nose, fine hair; relatively little body mass and relatively great surface area.	**3.** *Cerebrotonic:* an introvert; full of functional complaints, allergies, skin troubles, chronic fatigue, insomnia; sensitive to noise and distractions; shrinks from crowds.

Related to these types are three psychiatric classifications: the manic depressive (which overlaps the endomorph and mesomorph), the paranoid (overlapping the mesomorph and the ectomorph), and the hebephrenic (which overlaps the ectomorph and the endomorph) (Sheldon, 1949:59). To these complexes of body, temperament, and personality Sheldon seeks to relate a variety of "delinquencies" based on (1) mental insufficiency, (2) medical insufficiency, (3) first-order psychopathy, (4) second-order psychopathy, and (5) primary criminality. Though his data do not support his contentions, Sheldon concludes that delinquents are different from nondelinquents, that delinquents are inferior, and that their inferiority is inherited. For Sheldon, as for Hooton, the final solution lay in eugenics (Sheldon, 1949:872).

The XYY Controversy

A more recent chapter in the effort to account for deviance in terms of a person's biological condition involves the investigation of chromosomal imbalance, that is, the XYY chromosome pattern. According to this theory, a normal X or Y sperm, uniting with a normal X ovum, results in either an XY (normal male) or an XX (normal female). However, on occasion (theoretically, less than once in 1,000 live births) a YY sperm unites with an X ovum resulting in an XYY male. This XYY aberration, the extra Y chromosome, is said to produce a person with an increased tendency toward aggressiveness. The extra Y chromosome is not regarded as sufficient to account for violent or criminal behavior, but in combination with environmental pressure, an XYY male is felt to be more vulnerable to criminogenic stimuli than the XY (normal) male (Montagu, 1968; Fox, 1971).

Some celebrated offenders have been thought to provide support for this explanation of violent behavior. Thus, Richard Speck, convicted murderer of eight Chicago nurses, was once believed to have an extra Y chromosome. Speck's attorney reported, however, that his client's chromosome structure was normal. Despite the application of these beliefs to sensational cases such as Speck's, more recent and considered evaluation of chromosomal research has led to the conslusion that ". . . definite causal links between the XYY complement and deviant, criminal or violent behavior cannot be established" (U.S. Department of Health, Education, and Welfare, 1970:33). Despite the evidence, some students of deviance have suggested that male homosexuality may be attributable to chromosomal abnormalities (Storr, 1964:81).

Summary

The foregoing represents a mere fraction of the studies seeking to establish a biophysiological difference between known rule breakers and so-called normals or nondeviants. Clearly reflecting the dualistic fallacy, this effort attempts to (1) differentiate rule breakers from nonrule breakers and (2) on the basis of the differentia account for their respective behavior patterns. Despite great expenditure of resources, in several ways these efforts have failed to meet the requirements of scientific proof embraced by their authors. First, *control populations* (supposedly nondeviant groups) with which deviant groups could be compared were either too small or too unrepresentative of the "nondeviant" population to allow for a valid comparison. Second, the *statistically significant differences* (differences in excess of what would result from chance) were too few to support the weight of the argument. Third, there are no objective (independent of the researcher's consciousness), agreed-upon criteria of biological inferiority, just as there are no generally accepted criteria for normality or good health. Finally, the abundance of *negative cases* (those that contradict a predicted relationship) strongly suggests the weakness of the argument (Sutherland and Cressey, 1974:125–126; Vold, 1958:107–108; Reid, 1976:98; Becker, 1963:8).

In summary, despite the devotion of great quantities of time and energy in researching and defending this general hypothesis, we may conclude that an answer to the question "Why do they do it?" seems not to lie in the creation of categories such as "normals" and "abnormals" based on insubstantial biological differences between known rule breakers and others.

The Psychological Perspective

What was sought in vain on the physiological and anatomical levels has also been pursued on the psychological level. There, rule breaking (especially crime) has been held to be a consequence of a person's psychological character.

Mental Defectiveness

Investigations of this proposition have included examination of the relationship of crime and mental defectiveness. In the extreme, it was once contended that most offenders were mentally defective (feeble-minded). Based on his study of the Kallikak family (a pseudonym), and his work at the New Jersey School for Feeble-minded Children, H. H. Goddard (1922:72–73) noted:

> It is sufficient to state that every investigation of the mentality of criminals, misdemeanants, delinquents and other anti-social groups has proven beyond the possibility of contradiction that nearly all persons in these classes and in some cases all are of low mentality . . . a large percentage of the groups are of such low mentality as to properly be denominated feeble-minded . . . In view of these facts it is no longer to be denied that the greatest single cause of delinquency and crime is low grade mentality . . .

Goddard's views were quite popular during the early portion of this century. Presently, however, based on results of more recent research and psychological tests, the view that inferior intelligence is a prime cause of rule-violating behavior has been rejected (Vold, 1958:Chapter 5). Even modest claims of the relation of feeble-mindedness to antisocial behavior have been rejected (Sutherland and Cressey, 1974:152ff).

Mental Illness

In addition to mental defectiveness, investigators have tried to establish a causal link between deviance and mental and emotional illness. The idea that some or all offenders are afflicted by such conditions, that is, that they are cognitively or volitionally incapacitated, has a lengthy history. In English common law children under age seven, as well as persons recognized as mentally incompetent, were considered incapable of committing felonies because of their mental state. This does not mean they did not commit acts disturbing to others, only that because of their mental condition these persons were not held legally responsible for their deeds.

Presently, mental illness, whether temporary or prolonged, is widely accepted as a defense against prosecution for crime. Mental illness loosely translates into the legal term *insanity*, referring to a state of mind in which the offender is alleged not to have known right from wrong or that what he or she was doing had wrongful consequences (Vold, 1958:111). Thus, according to the McNaghten Rule of legal insanity, a person is legally insane if he or she can be shown to have suffered an intellectual impairment. A second rule of insanity, the Pinel Rule, posits that one may experience an emotional state rendering him or her incapable of resisting an impulse to behave in a way he or she knows is wrong (for example, commit murder). According to this rule, called the irresistible impulse rule, insanity is an emotional rather than an intellectual condition (Hartung, 1965:190ff). A third rule of insanity, the Durham Rule, involves the demonstration that the defendant committed the alleged offense as a consequence of a mental disease or defect. Psychiatric testimony supporting that belief may result in an acquittal based on insanity (Kittrie, 1971:43; *Durham* v. *United States*, 1954).

What is most important for our purpose, however, is not so much the legal aspect of these presumed states of mind as the medical and psychological realities that allegedly lie behind them. Despite widespread popular acceptance of "craziness" or mental illness as a characteristic of deviants and an explanation for their behavior (Simmons, 1969:13–16), studies reveal that no more than 1 to 5 percent of prison inmates experience *psychosis*, that is severe personality disturbance (Sutherland and Cressey, 1974:155). Psychosis, whatever its referent, is hardly synonymous with crime and deviance.

In addition to psychosis is the condition called *psychopathy*, defined as a condition of emotional abnormality. Persons in this state, sometimes called psychopaths, psychopathic personalities, or constitutional psychopathic inferiors, have been held to be involved in a variety of socially unacceptable behaviors including drug addiction, alcoholism, and various forms of aberrant sexual behavior. Despite such claims, others scholars maintain that these psychiatric categories (labels) are simply catchalls for persons that are otherwise psychologically unclassifiable and that the vagueness of the terms render them useless for research and scientific purposes. These terms, some believe, should be discarded along with other outmoded classifications (Sutherland and Cressey, 1974:159ff).

Despite the problems associated with terms such as psychopaths, etc., some authorities continue to investigate personality in general, and social-emotional development in particular, in an effort to distinguish between deviant and nondeviant actors, and to understand and account for forms of rule-violating behavior. For example, according to some authorities, difficulty in one's social-emotional development often underlies alcoholism (Lisansky, 1968:266). Other investigators maintain that while there is no such thing as an *alcoholic personality*, a personality configuration with which alcoholism is most likely to be associated, there are several personality characteristics that underlie alcoholism (Cantanzaro, 1967:38ff).

Three other patterns of behavior that have been linked to personality are homosexuality, prostitution, and crime. Regarding male homosexuality, a wide variety of test methods have been used to discover a cluster of personality traits relatively unique to homosexuals and that may be causally linked to their sexual preferences. Despite this effort, little supportive evidence has been found (West, 1967:48–53). In a classic study of the personality structure of overt male homosexuals, three psychiatric clinicians were asked to distinguish between the projective test response patterns of thirty homosexuals and thirty heterosexuals. The homosexual-heterosexual pairs were matched by age, I.Q., and level of education. In an attempt to classify the response patterns by the sexual preference of the unidentified respondent, ". . . neither judge was able to do better than chance. In seven pairs both judges were incorrect, that is, identifying the homosexual as heterosexual, and vice versa; in twelve pairs the identifications were correct; and in the remaining eleven they disagreed" (Hooker, 1958:23). On the basis of such evidence it is questionable to maintain that homosexuality is a *clinical condition*, that it is attributable to a personality structure distinct from that of heterosexuals. Nonetheless, constructs such as narcissism, unconscious castration anxieties, unconscious incestuous attraction to women, and incapacitating fear of the opposite sex and of heterosexuality continue to be created and given causal significance in an effort to explain homosexuality (Bieber, 1962:303).

Second, we may note that women's involvement in prostitution has been linked to a variety of personality characteristics. Included are masochism, infantile mentality, inability to establish mature interpersonal relationships, regression, anxiousness, having a confused self-image, excessive dependence on others, sex role confusion, aggressiveness, and a lack of internal controls (Bryan, 1967). As in the cases of alcoholism and homosexuality, claims regarding the link between these factors and a person's involvement in prostitution remain largely hypothetical.

Finally, we may note the extended effort put forth to distinguish between offenders and nonoffenders in terms of a complex of personality traits other than mental defectiveness and mental disorders. In pursuit of this elusive complex, "studies have been made of instincts, emotions, moods, temperaments, moral judgments, ethical discriminations, as well as specific tendencies such as aggressiveness, caution, conformity, consciousness, deception, self-assurance, social resistance, suggestibility, and many others" (Sutherland and Cressey, 1974:161).

The most recent effort of this sort is the work of Samuel Yochelson and Stanton E. Samenow (1976). Based on interviews with 240 male offenders, their families and friends, Yochelson and Samenow contend that offenders are not ill and that "insanity" as a legal defense is a charade and a subterfuge calculated to reduce the offender's penalty (Yochelson and Samenow, 1976:227–235). Rather than being ill, it is contended that offenders are distinguishable by fifty-two "errors in thinking" concerning such things as fear, anger, pride, power, sentimentality, religion, perfectionism, sexuality, and lying—among others. By "errors in thinking," Yochelson and Samenow refer to thought processes which, though not found *only* among offenders, are held to be *more characteristic of offenders* than nonoffenders. Thus, the "criminal personality" represents a position on what these researchers define as a continuum of "responsibility-irresponsibility" (Yochelson and Samenow, 1976:252–253). Rather than consisting of a complex of personality traits (characteristic of earlier works), the criminal personality as conceived of by Yochelson and Samenow represents a relatively unique pattern of thought-ways. Unfortunately, however, no evidence is provided to support the claim that these faulty thoughtways do differentiate between offenders and non offenders.

Summary

In summary, as we noted with regard to the biological perspective, claims that rule violators are psychologically different (abnormal) tend to lack support. At the very least, the extravagant claims by spokesman for such a position well exceed the evidence. Many of the claims made concerning the psychological abnormality or uniqueness of known deviants rest on evidence gathered from an extremely limited number of cases and generalized to the entire deviant population. In addition, these relatively few cases often consisted of those who had not adjusted to their involvement in rule-violating behavior. Included among these "nonadjusted" persons were those who, because of their difficulties, sought relief by submitting to psychiatric treatment (for example, homosexuals). Finally, these research groups included those who had been identified and processed as deviant. Publicly unidentified rule breakers and those who are comfortable in their variant behavior are systematically excluded from these studies. Thus we are faced with a classic case of generalizing to an entire class of people on the basis of information gathered from an extremely limited, atypical, and biased number of cases. This has led to opinion parading under the color of fact and to an abundance of contradictions and confusion (West, 1967:188; Hartung, 1965: Chapters 6 and 7). Oftentimes, too, the reasoning, as in the case of psychoanalytic and psychiatric explanations of deviance, takes a tautological or circular form. Thus:

Q: Why did he do it:
A: Because he is (psychiatrically) ill.
Q: How do you know he is ill?
A: Because he did it.

The existence of a presumed causal factor is therefore based on its hypothesized effect. Yet empirical research reported by a number of scholars indicates that no particular personality trait is sufficiently linked to criminal or deviant behavior to support the claim of causality (Schuessler and Cressey, 1958; Lowrey, 1944; Waldo and Dinitz, 1967). As in the case of biological explanations, psychological answers to the question "Why do they do it?" remain unconvincing.

The Sociological Perspective

The question "Why do they do it?" has also been asked by sociologists. The distinction between the biological and psychological approaches, on the one hand, and the traditional sociological approach based on the fact model, on the other, rests on the conceptual tools employed in these respective fields. Whereas the biological and psychological perspectives perceive deviance as an emergent of people's biological and psychological character, the sociologist has tended to focus on the cultural influences commonly experienced by people held to be deviant. Thus, rather than being concerned with deviance as behavior engaged in by certain "kinds of people" (definable in biological or psychological terms), the sociologist has traditionally viewed deviance as behavior engaged in by persons having a common sociocultural background or similar social experiences. This leads sociologists to focus on variables such as the properties of groups or collectivities (social classes, for example) and things that collectivities commonly experience (Cohen, 1966: Chapters 4 and 5). As we will see, attention is focused on the *structural* aspects of society as well as on the social *processes* that are felt to influence human conduct. In examining leading sociological explanations of rule-violating behavior it will be noted that some theories emphasize social psychological processes while other theories stress societal conditions. Ultimately, sociological explanations of behavior combine these dimensions to provide what is felt to be the most comprehensive statement on the issue. Let's examine some historically significant sociological approaches to rule-violating behavior.

Multiple Factor Approach

Early sociological students of deviance tended to use the *multiple factor approach* (Hirschi and Selvin, 1967:178–181; Cohen, 1970). This approach has several identifying characteristics. First, it is unencumbered by theory or the need to set forth a statement of the relationship between variables. Rather, the multiple-factor approach generally relies on the establishment of a statistical relationship between the presumed cause and its supposed effect. Thus, a correlation between A and B, together with the assertion that A is the cause of B, is generally sufficient. This leads to the second characteristic of the multiple-factor approach, namely, that it tends to avoid analytic entanglements. Precisely how A produces B, that is, the mechanics of the relationship, is rarely dealt with. Rather than delve into the component parts of the thing under investigation and examine their relation to one another and to the whole (engage in analysis), the multiple-factor argument rests on an assumption. It is assumed that supposed causal factors possess *intrinsic pathogenic qualities* (Cohen, 1970:124). This means that select factors are assumed to have the capacity, singly or in combination with one another, to produce the rule-violating behavior. But precisely how the behavior is produced is not dealt with.

Third, this approach rests on the idea that "evil causes evil"

(Cohen, 1970:124). This means that the factors or variables felt to have pathogenic qualities are themselves lacking desirability. One early expression of this idea is Cyril Burt's comparison of delinquents and nondelinquents in which he concluded that delinquents generally suffer four or five physical, psychological, or sociological *handicaps.* That a factor is a handicap, an evil, is regarded as self-evident and is taken for granted (Burt, 1925). More contemporary thinking of this sort lists the following factors as the "handicaps" of juvenile delinquents: homes broken by divorce, separation, or desertion, parental rejection of the child, homes in which the parents are themselves engaged in immoral behavior, defective social training, low socioeconomic status of the family (including "bad" housing), a lack of recreational opportunity, a lack of effective guidance and training of youth for effective citizenship, high unemployment of youth not in school, and the law-violating traditions and customs of low-income peoples and those residing in deteriorated areas of cities (Elliott and Merrill, 1961:79ff). This list hardly exhausts the number of factors (such as exposure to crime and violence in the mass media) considered to have pathogenic properties.

A final characteristic of the multiple-factor approach is the tendency to accept statistical evidence as an adequate indicator of causality. However, while things may occur together in some regular way, thereby giving rise to a high correlation, that fact is not sufficient to posit a *causal relation,* one in which one condition *makes* another happen. Statistical relationships do not necessarily translate into causal relationships. For example, a positive statistical relationship (one in which an increase in the presumed cause is associated with an increase in its alleged effect) between broken homes and delinquent behavior does not tell us how many reverse cases may be observed. That is, what correlation may be established between unbroken homes and delinquency? How much delinquency occurs among youth from unbroken homes? In research comparing the social adjustment of boys and girls in broken, unbroken, and reconstituted homes, no significant differences in adjustment were found. That is, measures of "adjustment" (amount and variety of delinquency, school performance, and neurotic tendencies) indicated that boys and girls in different home situations are not appreciably different from one another (Perry and Pfuhl, 1963). Such evidence is consistent with the contention of contemporary scholars that the multiple-factor approach lacks scientific and substantive adequacy.

Differential Association Theory

A more contemporary and sophisticated sociological explanation of individual conduct, one departing from the foregoing approach in several ways, is the theory of differential association. Formulated by the late Edwin H. Sutherland, this theory maintains that while some people engage in rule-violating behavior and others behave in law-abiding ways, the social psychological process leading to these qualitatively different behaviors is the same. That is, deviant and nondeviant behavior are learned in precisely the same way. Sutherland's theory consists of the following nine propositions (Sutherland and Cressey, 1974:75–76):

1. Criminal behavior is learned.
2. Criminal behavior is learned in interaction with other persons in a process of communication.
3. The principal part of the learning of criminal behavior occurs within intimate personal groups.
4. When criminal behavior is learned, the learning includes (a) techniques of committing the crime, which are sometimes very complicated, sometimes very simple; (b) the specific direction of motives, drives, rationalizations, and attitudes.
5. The specific direction of motives and drives is learned from definitions of the legal codes as favorable or unfavorable.
6. A person becomes delinquent because of an excess of definitions favorable to violation of law over definitions unfavorable to violation of law.
7. Differential associations may vary in frequency, duration, priority, and intensity.
8. The process of learning criminal behavior by association with criminal and anticriminal patterns involves all of the mechanisms that are involved in any other learning.
9. While criminal behavior is an expression of general needs and values, it is not explained by those general needs and values, since noncriminal behavior is an expression of the same needs and values.

As these propositions indicate, the origins of *both* deviant and nondeviant behavior rest on the same social psychological process. Any complex pattern of behavior is said to be learned in the same general way. In slightly different terms, Sutherland contends that in complex societies such as ours, all people are exposed to *patterns of verbalization* (meanings, rationalizations, definitions of things, attitudes) that are both law-violating *and* law-abiding. *Both of these patterns* of verbalization are part of the general culture to which all are exposed. Depending on the frequency, duration, priority, and intensity of a person's association with these patterns (Note: "association" refers specifically to exposure to patterns of verbalization, *not* necessarily to affiliation with persons who are criminals), a person may become involved in either criminal or noncriminal behavior. Thus, Sutherland tells us, the definitions necessary to engage in deviant behavior already exist and are shared by others. By affiliating with groups "possessing" them, one becomes similarly socialized. Thereby one is "converted" to behavior that is normative for others. For example, to be a member in good standing of a motorcycle gang calls for a person to behave in ways consistent with the meanings and interests of other gang members. Values, interests, and attitudes are shared in largely similar ways by individual members. Similarly, a person learns to be Roman Catholic (or a member of any other religious faith) by associating with the meanings, definitions, and so on, that are the property of the Roman Catholic church. A woman learns to behave as a call girl by serving a specific apprenticeship period during which she is exposed to the "cultural stuff" of prostitution (Bryan, 1967). By careful socialization of the blind, such people learn to behave as sighted people would have them behave (Scott, 1969).

Viewed in terms of Sutherland's theory, each of these examples involves actors associating differentially (in terms of frequency, duration, priority, or intensity) with one set of meanings rather than another. Whether the meanings support behavior held to be deviant or nondeviant, the social psychological process involved is the same. Sutherland maintains that this process is necessary (but not sufficient) to account for an individual's involvement in rule-violating behavior (Sutherland, 1956b:30–31).

Despite several attempts to test Sutherland's theory, no fully successful effort has yet been made (Short, 1958 and 1960; Glaser, 1956). In part, this is due to the enormity and difficulty of measuring the differential association one has with criminal and anticriminal patterns. Despite these problems, the Sutherland thesis is one of the most popular sociological explanations of individual conduct. Differential association or some variant of its basic premises, such as differential identification, differential reference, and differential learning, has become a major sociological explanation of deviant behavior in general and criminal behavior in particular (Glaser, 1958 and 1962).

A Critique

Despite its wide and enduring popularity, the theory of differential association poses at least two major difficulties relevant to our understanding of deviant behavior. The first problem becomes apparent when the theory is examined in terms of two of the fundamental assumptions of the definition paradigm: (1) that behavior is a result of reasons, choices, and judgments rather than being determined by causes and (2) people are not simple, reactive organisms, but interact with elements in the environment. People are not helpless and hapless victims of forces that propel them through life like pinballs. Let us examine Sutherland's theory in terms of these assumptions.

Clearly, Sutherland's notion is that man, to a great extent, is a prisoner of his environment (Matza, 1969:107; Davis, 1975:137). According to Sutherland, people find themselves in an environment consisting, in part, of established meanings and definitions. Without any effort on their part, that is, in a passive manner, without making any decisions or exercising choices, without being able to opt for or against dominant meanings in that environment, people become victims of those meanings and definitions. Man ". . . is like the tree or the fox without the capacity for choice and sometimes like the insular primitive without alternatives from which to choose; he could not create meaning, shift it, or shift himself away from it" (Matza, 1969:107). Given sufficient exposure to meanings and definitions conducive to rule-violating behavior, one automatically "contracts" the deviation. Cast in this way, people are rendered passive entities; people are regarded as subjects. Their behavior is *determined* by the meanings to which they are exposed.

Contrary to that, as the notion of multiple reality suggests, people exist in environments containing a wide variety of meanings and definitions. In a "cafeteria-like" manner people make choices as to which meanings and definitions and, consequently, action patterns, are appropriate for them at any given time and place. On the basis of judgments and choices people move from one alternative to another. As noted earlier, people do not simply *react to* these meanings. Rather, they *interact with* them and, in doing so, contribute to the creation of new meanings and definitions. The Sutherland theory does not allow for these considerations.

The second major difficulty with the Sutherland theory stems from its contention that learning the meanings and definitions conducive to rule violating behavior is a necessary *precondition* of that behavior. This is clearly noted in Sutherland's sixth proposition that one *becomes* delinquent because of what one has learned.

However logical that may appear, this proposition conflicts with observations of everyday life where it may be seen that untold numbers of people break innumerable rules without benefit of having learned the things (motives, drives, rationalizations, and attitudes) Sutherland's theory claims are necessary to the behavior. For example, rather than being privy to sophisticated intelligence concerning its use, novice pot smokers are generally seen as ignorant (Becker, 1973:41ff). Learning to smoke marijuana, to recognize its mood-altering properties, and to identify and define those properties as pleasurable—all these are acquired (if at all) *incidental to using* marijuana and to having contact with experienced users. That is, *learning results from doing* rather than doing resulting from learning.

That doing precedes learning is also noted in the case of professional thieves, many of whom begin their careers with a remarkably low level of knowledge and expertise. This means that inexperienced (ignorant) thieves must often work with other ignorant thieves learning by trial and error. As Letkemann (1973:135–136) noted, learning to be a thief is a matter of "experiment and experience." Indeed, Sutherland, too, seems to have recognized this in his study *The Professional Thief* (1937), in which he notes that one does not become a professional thief unless and until he acquires proficiency in that business. How does one acquire proficiency; how does one learn the things necessary to being recognized by others as a professional thief? The genesis of the professional thief commences with the selection of a promising novice for instruction by more accomplished (professional) thieves. During a probationary period

> . . . the neophyte is assimilating the general standards of morality, propriety, etiquette and rights which characterize the profession, and he is acquiring "larceny sense." He is learning the general methods of disposing of stolen goods and of fixing cases. He is building up a personal acquaintance with other thieves, and with lawyers, policemen, court officials, and fixers. . . . As a result of this tutelage during the probationary period, he acquires the techniques of theft and consensus with the thieves (Sutherland, 1937:213–214).

As this passage makes clear, one learns to be a sophisticated thief as a result of doing thieving. In turn, being recognized by one's peers as a professional thief, that is, acquiring the prestige of a particular position, depends on one's proficiency in that business. However, that one may engage in theft without achieving such a level of sophistication is all too clear. In any case, one learns as a result of doing.

A further case demonstrating that rule-breaking behavior is not determined by prior learning in the manner prescribed by Sutherland is found in Diana Gray's study of teenage prostitutes (1973). The teenage girls Gray studied had little or no knowledge of the skills, techniques, and so on, of prostitution prior to their entry into that business. Prior to their first act of prostitution these girls received no training in such matters. Indeed, skill and training was not required. The most that was available to these girls was "informal information" incidentally acquired as part of their "recipe knowledge." This knowledge, however, was incredibly meager. As one girl stated:

> We got the idea in our heads that we were going to try it [do prostitution]. We went down on Pike [Street], downtown, and we were walking down there. I didn't say anything. I didn't know how the girls called out to ask for a date. We both went down there and we didn't say anything . . . then another girl explained that I would have to call out to them and speak to them [potential customers.]. I did like she told me and caught my first trick (Gray, 1973:412–413).

In short, the occupational tools of the prostitute were unknown to these girls. How to initiate a contact with a "john," how to examine a john for venereal disease, what forms of personal hygiene need be engaged in, how to practice contraception and prevent pregnancy, how to collect money and what to charge, how to watch for and recognize police, how to perform specific sex acts, and so on, are among the basic skills, techniques, and meanings to be learned by women engaged in prostitution. Girls learned these things while on the job, by trial and error (Gray, 1973:413). James Bryan (1967) makes the same point concerning call girls. The apprenticeship period served by these women is one of *practice*. During this time they are observed by their pimps or other trainer while they serve customers. Their behavior is evaluated and criticized. Beyond behavior, these women are introduced to the "philosophical" aspects of prostitution, that is, the rationalizations, justifications, and defenses—the value structure—that support prostitution. In both these cases, then, learning is a consequence of participation in rule-breaking conduct rather than the reverse.

In summary, given the unacceptable characteristics of the multiple-factor approach and the fact that the Sutherland thesis runs counter to fundamental assumptions of the paradigm of definition as well as demonstrable aspects of everyday life, we are faced with the task of providing an alternative account for individuals' involvement in rule-violating behavior. Let us now turn to such an alternative.

An Alternative View

As indicated, limiting an explanation of individual conduct to prior learning is to embrace the notion of passive conversion. More important is the need to consider the basis of people's action when they are viewed as objects, that is, agents capable of reflexive thought and who act on the basis of choice (though not always well-informed choice) and reasons. Let us seek to account for behavior while viewing man as one who *interacts with* elements in the environment rather than simply *reacting to* them.

Biography and Affinity

The specific basis of one's initial involvement in any pattern of behavior, deviant or otherwise, must, of course, remain obscure, a manifestation of one's unique and continually developing biography. However, it is on the basis of their biographies that people acquire a greater or lesser affinity for particular patterns of behavior. Two terms, *biography* and *affinity*, call for explication.

Nothing mysterious is meant by the notion of biography. In literal terms, it refers to the events that make up one's life. One's biography may consist of the experiences that comprise growing up in a ghetto or on a farm, being accepted or ostracized by one's peers, growing up male or female, being black, Indian, oriental, or white, being poor, comfortable, or wealthy, being considered attractive or unattractive, and so on. Each of these conditions or circumstances is linked with an incredible variety of complex social experiences to which all people are subject. These experiences are a consequence of one's being situated in a complex social structure. We are situated in terms of race, religion, socioeconomic status, sex, and age, among others. Being situated in these "places" means that people who are similarly located will experience events in a *roughly* similar way, while those located in different "places" within the social structure will have correspondingly different experiences. That is, they will have different biographies.

It is important to recognize that biography, as used here, has no final form. *A person has no definitive biography. Biography is constantly in the making; it is constantly being redefined and reinterpreted in each new situation.* Today's experiences make tomorrow's biography different from yesterday's. Acknowledging this, one may only conclude that the influence of biography is problematic, to be understood situationally.

Affinity may also be interpreted quite literally. The experiences that comprise one's biography leave one more or less attracted to (having an affinity for) particular other behaviors. That is, experience provides a foundation for subsequent behavior. Experience is the context within which one acquires and constructs meanings and definitions of things. Future behavior will be influenced (albeit imperfectly) by these meanings. Affinity, then, as a general condition, consists of the meanings consistent with being favorably disposed toward any particular course of action.

Being Willing

To say that affinity leaves one favorably disposed to engage in a particular pattern of behavior means that people are *open* or *willing* to engage in such actions; they are *free to enter into such activity.* Willing, in this sense, is *not to be equated with determinism.* Nor is willingness to be confused with the notion of *free will.* "Free will, as the phrase itself implies, takes will out of context . . . Will is the conscious foreshadowing of specific intention capable of being acted on or not. It is a sense of option that must be rendered in context" (Matza, 1969:116). That context consists of the everyday conditions faced by us all, including the opportunity to do deviance.

Willingness or openness must be understood as consisting of a set of meanings applied by the actor to a particular course of action at a specific time and place. As noted, biography leaves people with an affinity (a greater or lesser attraction) for specific behaviors. However, affinity is only a *general* condition. Whether or not one is willing and open to any *specific act* at a *particular time* is problematic, subject to the influence of a variety of related meanings. For example, many readers of this volume are likely quite open to using marijuana (a general condition), yet decline the opportunity to get high just prior to going to class to take a major exam. The meaning (definition) of the exam, together with their sense of the consequence of using marijuana at that specific time, the meaning of the classroom as a particular place, and perhaps several other things, combine to form the context in which smoking pot seems inappropriate. Likewise, many married people are open to swinging (extramarital sexual relationships); however, it strains credibility to suggest they actually engage in such relations at each and every opportunity. Nor do people engage in cheating, exceed the speed limit, or break other rules at every opportunity—despite their being willing to do so under *some* circumstances. To repeat, then, an affinity may be regarded only as a general condition; it is not to be seen as a determinant of all future actions.

One's willingness to engage in rule-violating behavior needs also to be understood in terms of the actor's self-conception. In addition to influencing the meanings one has of elements in the environment, biography also leaves us with a definition of self, that is, a *self-concept.* Just as our definition of things shapes our responses to them, so, too, does the meaning we have of self influence our willingness to engage in this or that behavior. Given the combined factors of (1) opportunity to engage in proscribed behavior, (2) a set of meanings supportive of engaging in the behavior (affinity), and (3) a particular conception of self, one is faced with an option; a decision or choice must be made. The choice, however, is *not preordained*. Rather, the meanings one has of self permit *self-ordination* (Matza, 1969:112). That is, how a person responds to the opportunity reflects his or her definition of the behavior (part of affinity) and whether participation is consistent with self-concept. This is not something to which self is subjected. Is self the type of person who would engage, even experiment, in the behavior in question? Does the conception of self as a participant leave one disgusted, mildly intrigued, pleasurably excited, or strongly attracted? How one defines the situation vis-à-vis self strongly influences one's willingness. As the following cartoon suggests, in the final analysis to "do deviance" is a matter of self-ordination.

In summary, as an alternative explanation of doing deviance it is suggested that people are more or less attracted to particular patterns of behavior; that attraction is based on the meaning, definition, and understanding (sometimes quite deficient) one has of the behavior. These meanings and knowledge are derived through experience, a product of biography. Included, too, is self-concept, the definition one has of self. When faced with the option of doing or not doing any particular form of deviance, people are willing or unwilling to varying degrees; they are open or closed to the situation. Thus, on the basis of a complex variety of fortuitous and situational factors that comprise one's biography, a person arrives at the "threshold of deviant conduct." But let's cast these abstract notions in the context of everyday experience.

Willingness and Everyday Life

That experience may promote an affinity for a life style others regard as deviant has been noted by Wallace (1965) in his study of recruits to skid row. The biography of the majority of men coming to skid row left them with no "fixed place" in society. Working as lumberjacks, migrant farm workers, or serving in the military required them to be absent from home for long periods of time. As a result they were not practiced in living with members of their family— parents, spouse, or children. Commitment to family and its associated values are given low priority by these men. Frequently enough, these men are not accepted back into their families. In short, biography leads some men to define home as an irrelevant and/or unpleasant place (Wallace, 1965:166).

Supplementing this experience are the job-related contacts and

"I didn't take a wrong turn anywhere. Ever since I was a little kid, I've always wanted to be a pimp."

associations some men have with skid row men. Interacting intimately with skid rowers over prolonged periods exposes these men to that subculture; they become aware that an alternative life style exists.

It is at this point . . . that an unsatisfactory home situation becomes relevant in explaining a man's move to skid row. If before he left home he was at constant odds with his family, he may be less inclined than ever to "put up with it"—now that he knows another way of life complete with a few friends is open to him. Problems at home plus the weakening of family ties brought about by his absence reinforce his sense of isolation, push him further adrift, and help sever the few remaining roots he has in the respectable society. The skid row way of life—a life without care, worry, and responsibility, a life with friends, drink, and plenty of time in which to enjoy them—begins to look better and better (Wallace, 1965:167).

In short, it is the unique character of their biography that leads these men to have an affinity for skid row living and to be willing to exchange one life style for another.

Unique experiences associated with occupation (that is, elements of their biography) also serve to explain lesbianism among striptease dancers. "Specifically, conditions supportive of homosexual behavior in the stripping occupation can be classified as follows: (1) isolation from affective social relationships, (2) unsatisfactory relationships with males, and (3) an opportunity structure allowing a wide range of sexual behavior" (McCaghy and Skipper, 1969:266). Absence of affective ties may be a consequence of marital problems and/or the job-related difficulties strippers have of establishing relationships of trust with others. Working at odd hours and touring from city to city leads to loneliness. Further, the males with whom strippers have the most frequent contact comprise their audience, unattached men they frequently characterize as "degenerate" because of their tendency to engage in exhibitionism and masturbation during the stripper's performance. Add to this the warm reception strippers are likely to receive from those who frequent gay bars where they may go for relaxation and the presence of lesbians among the strippers. En toto, this complex of biographical factors may be expected to promote the actor's willingness to engage in homosexual relations.

Consider, too, the following lines from the autobiography of a female heroin user regarding her introduction to "smack."

I learned [about] smack from a boyfriend . . . I met the guy on a farm in Oregon . . . Because of a fortuitous combination of circumstances I ended up back here in school, the guy followed, did about a year [in jail], and got out, with the intention of turning middle-class. He and I and a buddy of his . . . used to go around together a couple of nights a week, usually not doing much except getting loaded—smoking marijuana or maybe dropping reds or rainbows—none of which I much liked except that it was a rather different social activity.

Then the buddy got a girlfriend who was a hype from way back . . . I never knew anyone who took so much dope. All she cared about was getting loaded and that's all she ever did. My boyfriend and I often dropped by their pad . . . One night they had just bought some smack and offered us some. My boyfriend demurred but I said "Hell, yes, I want some," just because that's about the only thing I'd never done. Everyone was rather surprised at *my willingness* . . . (Anonymous, 1974:60–61. Emphasis added.).

In this case, as in so many others, the opportunity to use heroin was a chance affair. However, the company this girl kept, her previous experiences, and the circumstances under which she had the opportunity to try heroin and other drugs—all elements of her biography—may be considered to have continuity with the use of drugs. *But none of these factors may be regarded as decisive or compelling.* In the final analysis, her use of heroin was volitional. It was a matter of choice. She was willing.

The role of choice and willingness may also be noted in the case of a black youth nicknamed Goat, a member of the Van Dykes, a Chicago fighting gang. When Goat was twelve years old his family moved from California to an area of Chicago where access to school playgrounds, public parks, movie houses, street corners, and so on, was controlled by gangs. Two weeks after his arrival, while on the way to the store, he was confronted by ten members of the Braves (another gang) who beat him up and took his money. Goat had to make a decision. He knew only that he needed protection in order to live in the neighborhood.

So I asked a cat how do I become a member of the Van Dykes . . . and he say you gotta fight one of the baddest cats in the club and even if you lose, long as you give a good thumpin', you can become a member.

I went home and thought about it. Do I fight this dude and become a member or do I just don't fight him and become a rebel? Then I thought that rebels can't go to the show, can't go to the beach, can't go to house parties, can't have no girlfriends and walk the street. I went back and said "OK, Jack, I'll thump one of the tough cats." (Dawley, 1973:23).

Finally, we may examine the biography and decision-making process leading some young blacks to enter pimping as a way of making a living. In studying the biographies of pimps, Christina and Richard Milner (1972) found the early life of many of these men involved their being exposed to the ubiquitousness of sex, to hustling as a way of life, and led them to define formal education as largely unrewarding and irrelevant to their existence (Milner, 1972: 137–138). Yet in no case are these factors compelling. Rather, they are situational elements that influenced the perception (definition) these men had of pimping and other alternative ways of making a living. Simple observation led them to conclude that despite its hazards, pimping pays more handsomely than "chump jobs" such as being a delivery boy as a youth or, later in life, occupying some "straight" job. Some men become willing in high school when they encounter a girl who will trick for them, or perhaps because they have an uncle who is a pimp.

> Others get turned out after they have been married and had children, been in the Service, and tried working to support their wives. They are disillusioned with what society offers them because . . . they have tried living "straight" as adults and found the experience not only wanting but emasculating (Milner, 1972:142).

Willingness and the Support of Others

In addition to the above, a person's initial willingness to participate in deviance may be promoted by the support and encouragement he or she receives from others, particularly those he or she trusts. Of particular importance are friends. In his study of drug use, Erich Goode (1972:40) identifies three ways friends may influence a person to engage in deviance (in this case, smoking marijuana). First, friends may serve as examples, thereby making the behavior seem acceptable. If friends are doing it, perhaps it can't be so bad. "Doing it" is "in." (And logically, to refrain is to be "square.") Second, friends are often a source of justification for the behavior. They provide a rationale—a reason, a foundation—for the behavior. Third, with particular relevance to behaviors that depend on the use of "facilitating substances" (such as smoking pot), friends may make such substances available. In these ways, the contribution of friends toward one's doing deviance is crucial and, in some cases, quite indispensable.

On occasion the support provided by others well exceeds the above, helping people to manage their reluctance and overcome negative attitudes they may have toward the behavior itself. Such encouragement reinforces affinity and supplements a lagging willingness. For example, Martin Weinberg (1978:306) notes the importance of interpersonal relations in helping people overcome their reluctance to participate in nudism and nudist camp activities. One of Weinberg's female interviewees, commenting about her ambivalence over participating in nudism, remarked as follows:

> [Whether or not I would go to a nudist camp would] depend on who asked me. If a friend, I probably would have gone. . . . If an acquaintance, I wouldn't have been interested. . . . If it was someone you like or had confidence in, you'd go along with it. If you didn't think they were morally upright you probably wouldn't have anything to do with it (1978:307).

Weinberg further notes that over three-fourths (78 percent) of his female interviewees became interested in and were introduced to nudism through their husbands, parents, or in-laws. Only 20 percent became interested through impersonal sources such as magazines or motion pictures (1978:306).[1]

A similar condition is reported by Charles Varni. In studying spouse swapping, Varni found that, initially, women typically perceived mate swapping with revulsion. This reaction was followed by the husband's efforts to alter his wife's definition of mate swapping. This involved a "convincing" or "coercing" process which, at least, brought the wife to the point of experimenting in this behavior (Varni, 1972:511–512).

The support and encouragement of friends and acquaintances is also apparent in the introduction of people to the nude beach scene. Referring to "nude beach seductions," or ways people are encouraged to take off their clothes in public when they are reluctant, Douglas et al. (1977:74) indicate these "seduction" attempts frequently involve the subtle pressure put on a girl ("nude beach virgins") by their boyfriends, as well as friendly persuasion of boys by girls. To be sure, the effect of these efforts is variable, but, again, it frequently results in bringing the novice to the point of experimentation.

In addition, the support provided by others enables some predeviants to perceive rule breakers as "people like themselves," people who are not different in any appreciable way. As Weinberg's subjects note, it is important to people that their involvement in question-

---

1. Interestingly, the men in Weinberg's sample were less influenced to try nudism by other persons (33 percent), while 50 percent had their initial interest aroused by media. This is consistent with what is known about males being more responsive than females to such stimuli and with the general biographical experiences of males in our society, particularly their greater exposure to media that might be defined as pornographic. Again, then, these data support the alternative perspective presented here.

able behavior be compatible with a moral self-image. Support of trusted others allows people to overcome the reluctance that may arise when trying to combine a moral conception of self, on the one hand, with participation in morally questionable behavior, on the other. If the behavior is engaged in by "people like themselves," that is, by moral people, perhaps the behavior isn't so bad after all. This same support also permits us to overcome obstructions to participation that rest on stereotyped definitions of "people like that." Again, Weinberg reports that prenudist attitudes of nudists consisted of such stereotypes. One respondent commented, "I thought . . . [nudism] was a cult—a nut-eating, berry-chewing bunch of vegetarians, doing calisthenics all day, a gymno-physical society. I thought they were carrying health to an extreme, being egomaniacs about their body" (Weinberg, 1978:306). Another informant remarked, "I'm afraid I had the prevailing notion that [nudist camps] were undignified, untidy places populated (a) by the very poor, and (b) by languishing bleached blondes, and (c) by greasy, leering bachelors" (Weinberg, 1978:306). To the extent they exist, such attitudes need to be somewhat dissipated or resolved in order that one be willing to engage in deviant conduct.

Willingness and Commitment

In general, willingness is influenced by one's *behavioral commitment* to conformity as a line of action (Johnson, 1973:397; Becker, 1960). Willingness is balanced against the actor's anticipation of the possible consequences of engaging in punishable behavior. A decision to engage in conduct that has some probability of punishment calls for consideration of the material and social consequences—punishments—should one be discovered. Included here is the consequence of discovery for such varied concerns as the preservation of self-image, maintaining relationships with valued others, and the ability to maintain one's present statuses or achieve desired statuses in the future (Briar and Piliavin, 1965:39). In short, each of us possesses innumerable interests to which we attach varying degrees of importance. Behavior consistent with one interest is often considered in terms of the consequences it may have for one's other interests. A person with a high commitment to law-abiding behavior is therefore less likely to engage in deviance than a person lacking such commitment. Thus, commitment entails an appreciation of the factors that encourage one to continue to pursue a line or course of action—in this case, conformity—as opposed to the consequences one may anticipate as a result of discontinuing that action line (engaging in deviance).

As an example of the constraining aspect of commitments, especially the anticipated "costs" of discontinuing a conforming line of action, some sexually inactive co-eds have indicated that their decision to be inactive rests on their parent's expectation that they would avoid such involvement. The co-ed's sense of commitment to their parents, that is, a wish to avoid hurting them by violating their trust and to avoid the costs of damaging a valued relationship, is a major element in these girls' thinking. A similar set of constraints based on commitments was found by Rossman (1976:180) in his study of homosexual pederasts. Among the constraining factors cited by pederasts who choose to refrain from actual sexual encounters are (1) a concern for the feelings of and a desire not to hurt family and friends and (2) a reluctance to do things the discovery of which would destroy one's life, especially (but not only) in a professional sense.

Neutralizing Constraints

In addition to these various commitments, people are restrained by internalized beliefs and ethical systems as well as their acceptance of the norms of the legitimate institutional system. However, neither these restraints nor the possibility of being singled out for punishment serve as permanent or insurmountable barriers to engaging in banned behavior. Indeed, everyday experience as well as systematic research demonstrate the ease with which people may, *at the same time*, preserve their commitment to the values of the legitimate institutional system and violate them behaviorally.

Serving to resolve this apparent contradiction between "saying and doing" are several *techniques of neutralization* (Sykes and Matza, 1957), devices that simultaneously allow for the preservation of one's conception of self as a "moral" person while engaging in proscribed behavior. One may subscribe to a moral code, then, while simultaneously violating its prescriptions. Using these techniques of neutralization *prior to engaging* in deviant behavior makes possible the deflection of self-disapproval that results from internalized proscriptive norms. These are devices that release us from the moral bind of our value commitments. There are five of these techniques. We will consider each briefly.

One technique of neutralization is called *denial of responsibility*. When asked why she engaged in systematic theft, a teenage girl replied that she had no other choice; jobs just weren't available, she had to have clothes, wanted to have some fun, and her unemployed parents didn't have the money to provide these things. The only alternative, she felt, was to steal. That assertion contains the basic element of denial of responsibility, that is, the actor professes to have no control over his or her actions, that he or she is driven by external forces to act or professes to be a "billiard ball." This assertion is contained in the popular notion that poverty is a "cause" of such behavior. Other forces are sometimes enlisted to account for rule breaking such as poor home conditions, alcoholic parents, bad companions, and the like. Given the operation of these elements, elements felt to be beyond the actor's ability to resist, one views oneself as essentially blameless, "more acted upon than acting" (Sykes and Matza, 1957:667).

A second technique of neutralization, *denial of injury*, rests on a morality of consequences. That is, the claim is made that whether or not one's actions may be properly referred to as deviant or immoral depends on the injury or harm resulting from those acts. (This is distinguished from a morality of intentions, wherein culpability rests on one's purpose, knowledge, recklessness, and negligence (Packer, 1968:105; Pfuhl, 1978). Thus, guilt rests on whether one knowingly engages in proscribed behavior. Cases reflective of a "denial of injury" exist in abundance. For some people fist fights are normative though they are legally definable as assault. They are a means of resolving interpersonal problems. Embracing the latter perspective precludes the former—including the sometimes harmful consequences resulting from assault. In similar fashion, auto theft is defined as "borrowing" and vandalism is defined as "mischief" or a "prank" (Sykes and Matza, 1957:667). Obviously, "fist-fighting," "borrowing," "mischief," and "pranks" refer to behaviors that involve no serious injury to person or harm to property.

A third technique is *denial of the victim*. For example, a former shoplifter reported that he had engaged in shoplifting from a major national retail chain store because of the store's policy toward its customers. Given the person's perception of that policy, he defined his thefts as what the company deserved. The company "had it coming." Similarly, "straights" often justify beating up homosexuals with the claim that homosexuals deserve to be assaulted. In both these cases responsibility for the rule-violating behavior is accepted and injury admitted. Indeed, acknowledgment of these elements is necessary to a denial of the victim. However, as these examples indicate, the victim is converted into a legitimate target and the actor becomes a "moral avenger." The rule violator becomes a modern-day Robin Hood dealing out deserved rewards to "evildoers."

In researching the role behavior of "unwed fathers" (Pfuhl, 1978), a man was encountered who, unknowingly, had steadily dated a co-ed engaged to marry someone else. Upon discovering this, the man was infuriated and set out to "punish" the woman by getting her pregnant. Consistent with the essence of "denial of the victim," the man became the offended "avenger" and the woman the "transgressor." He states:

> I found out about the two of them and played the dumb routine. At the time I thought she was a virgin . . . She was pretty religiously hung up . . . She was anti-abortion, anti-sex, and she was kind of a tease—letting you go just so far and then clamming up and saying she had a headache and wanted to go home. And at first I thought she was just hanging on, but then I found out about this other guy. So then I just began trying a little harder . . . so I could get to her. She misled me to think that I was the only one for her . . . it wasn't just that she didn't tell me about this. That was what offended me so much. I didn't like being used this way. She was Miss Socialite, and I was supposed to escort her around, pay her way here and there, and all the time she was tight with this other guy (Taped interview).

Asked how he felt when he learned she was pregnant, he replied:

> I was happy about the predicament she was in and that if everyone found out it would put the damper on the angelic front she was putting up. I wouldn't have been happy had the circumstances been different. I had finally gotten to this girl after she had made a monkey out of me (Taped interview).

A fourth pattern of neutralization, *condemnation of condemners*, centers on those who disapprove, reject, or condemn the deviant on the basis of his actions. In this case the deviant rejects such persons— he "rejects his rejectors" (Sykes and Matza, 1957:668). For example, prison inmates are often heard to make morally condemning remarks regarding police, prosecutors, and judges. To have been rejected and condemned by such "morally reprehensible" people is defined as an honor by some convicts. More, the alleged immorality of one's condemners is taken to be far greater than anything done or likely to be done by the actor. Thus, attention is focused on the condemners rather than the deviant, and the behavior of the condemners is seen as more reprehensible. The utility of this technique lies in its function of redirecting the negative sanctions and condemnation from the deviant to rule enforcers.

The final technique of neutralization, *appeal to higher loyalties*, is commonly encountered as a form of *role conflict*, that is, people are faced with competing demands as a consequence of inconsistency in roles. In the vernacular, people claim to be "caught between a rock and a hard place," disentanglement from which necessarily entails violation of one set of demands or expectations. The expectations, expressed as rules, that are violated are defined as being of lesser importance.

The popularity of this technique is readily apparent. Perhaps the best-known example is the conflict between peer-group and family expectations. More newsworthy, however, was the West Point cheating scandal of 1976. Here the role of cadet and the role of citizen having constitutional rights were in conflict. Many of the cadets involved in the scandal acknowledged the existence of the honor code requirement to report all cases of cheating. Yet many found themselves bound by another set of norms and beliefs. They viewed the code as an anomaly and called for the same constitutional rights granted civilians as well as the elimination of a (military) court system that they viewed as violating the provisions of the 14th Amendment of the U.S. Constitution (*Time*, 1976). As a final example, we may point to people's appeal to "secular necessities" to justify violation of religious codes of conduct. In a study of "religious deviants," Dunford and Kunz (1973) report that Mormon people in violation of that church's rule against Sunday shopping neutralized the rule by citing such things as their need to purchase medicine for a sick family member, or the need to obtain food for unexpected guests—such needs taking precedence over the moral norm. In this way an appeal to a higher loyalty aids in resolving a conflict in roles.

Contracultural Values

Our comments on the actor's need to neutralize value commitments rest on the assumption that the actor's commitment is to values rooted in the legitimate institutional system. Experience demonstrates that such an assumption is not always warranted and may not be taken for granted. That is, not all people who violate public rules do so in spite of their subscribing to these same rules. Given the pluralistic value system in a heterogenous society, it is quite plausible to consider the idea that many rule violations reflect the actor's rejection of the conventional and advocacy of a contrary perspective. Two considerations deserve mention.

First, as many of the events of the 1960's and early 1970's reveal—particularly those centering about the military draft, the Vietnam war, and civil rights—some rule-violating behavior is based on a revolutionary ethos such as embraced by William and Emily Harris, members of the Symbionese Liberation Army (*Newsweek*, 1976). These instances of disobediance to public rules ". . . have as their objective the destruction of the society's system of power, changes of policy by means of violence, or the forceful removal of those exercising power in the system" (Sykes, 1972:413).

Clearly, in such cases commitment is to values contrary to those of the dominant institutional order. These alternative values have been referred to as *contracultural* or *countervalues* (Yinger, 1965:231). Viewed in the context of multiple realities, *contracultural* and *countervalues* are terms applied to values perceived to threaten interests of dominant groups. In that sense, *contracultural* is not essentially different from *deviant*.

Another example of deviance based on contracultural values is *civil disobedience*, carefully chosen and limited behavior known to be illegal and openly engaged in for the express purpose of promoting limited social change (Bay, 1967:166). Embracing this principle and the practical goals upon which it rests means one is unlikely to be constrained by rules that derive their legitimacy from the very system one wishes to change. For example, in April, 1968, Philip Berrigan, a former Jesuit priest, and three other persons (the so-called Baltimore Four) went on trial for interfering with the military draft as an act against the war in Vietnam (Berrigan, 1971). For Berrigan and his associates that act was simultaneously an expression of their profound Christian beliefs and a rejection of the values and interests that sustained and justified America's presence in Vietnam. Breaking the rules, then, was based on a commitment to effect a change in public policy. In this case, moral release from the so-called legitimate order may be regarded as the opposite side of the coin of value commitment.

A second condition in which it is unnecessary to specifically secure moral release from public rules are those situations involving behavior people define as *amoral*, behavior about which people feel no sense of right or wrong. Largely as a matter of social change and reflecting the diversity of moral meanings in a heterogeneous society, behaviors once held to have negative moral meaning undergo a change in definition (Sykes, 1972:415). Behavior once publicly regarded as immoral and taboo comes to be widely engaged in and rules once zealously enforced tend to be ignored. A case in point is divorce, once regarded as a shameful event but currently accepted (though in some quarters with alarm) with few if any moral connotations (Sirjamaki, 1959:164). For a substantial segment of the population adultery and the use of some psychotropic drugs, such as marijuana, fall into this same category.

A Cautionary Note

At this point a cautionary word on willingness and commitment is in order. First, these elements are not to be regarded as the basis of an exclusive condition. That is, deviance and nondeviance are not mutually exclusive. People are not committed *either* to deviant *or* to nondeviant values and behaviors. As we have noted, few persons, including the most dedicated delinquent, engage in rule-violating behavior at each and every opportunity. "Severely disturbed" mental patients conform to most rules most of the time. And even among the most dedicated professional offenders, violation of law is occasional. Rather than being unique, this same observation may be made of anyone. Realistically, then, commitment to legitimate values is a modality, a condition characteristic of most people most of the time. Second, for most people, release from moral constraint is situation specific, short lived, and must be renewed from time to time. This episodic release, as the term implies, is an event that stands out or apart from other customary conditions. Thus, there is no contention here that willingness with respect to one form of deviance is generalized to other forms. Rather, people are released from moral constraint in a specific, episodic, and recurrent manner. After all, many who sin on Saturday night attend church on Sunday and appear for work on Monday.

Summarizing to this point, being willing, in the sense used here, means no more or less than that one is available for participation in a deviant act. Being willing means only that one stands at the vestibule of deviance. Whether one enters the "main chamber" is yet highly problematic, dependent upon a number of conditions. Among those conditions are one's commitments, the influence of others, the degree of one's freedom from moral constraints, and the degree to which the actor embraces countercultural values. However, when all is said and done, one's involvement in deviant conduct continues to be a matter over which the actor has control. That is, people who stand at this juncture make decisions as to whether they should remain on the periphery, become more involved, or withdraw completely. Let's turn to these decisions.

Turning On—Turning Off

Having once engaged in deviance, whether or not one persists is a matter for the actor to decide. The outcome of this decision-making effort rests on whether or not one's experience with deviance results in being *turned on* or *turned off* (Matza, 1969:117ff). One meaning of the term "turned on" is that one is aware of a thing as a consequence of experience (Partridge, 1970:1484). In this sense, being "turned on" is not synonymous with "being hooked" or with having an indelible commitment to the behavior. Simply, experience renders one at least minimally knowledgeable. On the basis of that knowledge one decides that the behavior either is or is not appropriate for him or her. Viewed in the context in which it is experienced, the actor may define the episode as having or lacking utility for him or her. It is through experience that one comes to associate with others who are engaged in the same behavior and through them becomes more knowledgeable, skilled, or sophisticated in the behavior. On such bases, the actor is able to make reasoned choices and decisions.

One consequence of experience is that people may have second thoughts about their actions, leading to a decision to refrain from further involvement. It may lead to people being "turned off." As an example, the initial experience some people have with psychotropic drugs almost precludes anything but future abstinence. Consider the following results of snorting heroin for the first time. After the initial "rush,"

> My guts felt like they were going to come out. Everything was bursting out all at once, and there was nothing I could do. It was my stomach and my brain. My stomach was pulling my brain down into it, and my brain was going to pull my guts out and into my head . . . And then it seemed like everything in me all of a sudden just came out, and I vomited . . . I was dying, I was dying . . . I threw up, and I threw up. It seemed like I threw up a million times. I felt that if I threw up one more time, my stomach was just going to break all open; and still I threw up. I prayed and I prayed and I prayed. After a while I was too sick to care . . . I was sick about two days after that. I didn't even want a reefer. I didn't want anything, anything, that was like a high. I started drinking some of Dad's liquor after that, but I was scared of those dry highs. Anyway, that was the big letdown with horse . . . The horse had turned out to be a real drag (Brown, 1966:111–112).

In other cases of deviant conduct people are overcome with problems of conscience and remorse. For them persistence is psychologically untenable in view of traumatic results. But whether physical, psychological, social, or a combination of these, experience may lead the actor to be "turned off," to become unwilling. That is, what was viewed a highly enticing novelty, a moderately tolerable possibility, or perhaps as a long shot, is now rejected. Unlike the decision to experiment, which was made in the abstract, rejection rests on experience. While the decision to reject may not have indelible results, experience "refreshes" or renews the actor's commitment to a prior reality (Matza, 1969:112). For example, Douglas et al. relate the case of Kay, a young, pretty Kansas schoolteacher whose introduction to the nude beach was with an experienced friend, Diana. At the time of the initial suggestion that they go to the beach Kay ". . . thought it sounded great and decided to go nude publicly for the first time in her adult life" (1977:77). Upon arrival at the beach Diana immediately stripped and encouraged Kay to join her. Despite every gentle encouragement from her friend and other acquaintances, Kay ended the day fully clothed, crying "I can't."

Obviously, however, not all such experiences leave actors in a state of distress. Often satisfaction obtained from the initial experience promotes a decision to persist. For example, Octavio Rodriguez reports the following concerning his encounter with heroin (1974:84):

> I adapted to it very well, probably because I was having a hard time trying to establish relationships with people—I couldn't get to know people very well . . . but I discovered that if you were a junkie in my neighborhood people really didn't expect too much from you. That was an easy way out: if I became a heroin addict, I wouldn't have to try to meet people and people would leave me alone . . . Well, anyway, heroin sort of satisfied my feelings of frustration, and I really became quite involved in it—as a user mostly.

On the basis of positive or utilitarian experiences, then, people may get "turned on" in a second and related sense, that is, they may be "converted" to the behavior. From experience they know (at least to a limited degree) the positive and negative features of the deviation. It is no longer an abstraction. It is now part of their biography. Through experience the actor is able to revise or supplement former meanings attached to the behavior. Nudism, for example, once taboo, comes to be invested with "good purposes" such as healthy bodies and minds cleansed of distorted sex curiosities (Weinberg, 1978:342ff). A similar "conversion" was noted by Varni (1972) in his study of mate swapping. Though they characteristically approached spouse swapping with anxiety, apprehension, and misgivings, many wives reported

> The main effect of the first swinging experience was to greatly reduce the level of anxiety . . . and thus provide a climate in which the experience could be evaluated in a more "objective" light. If anything, the experience was anticlimactic in relation to the woman's expectations. The typical response was that it was not such a big deal after all. Many women made guardedly positive remarks such as "Well, it wasn't as bad as I thought it would be," or *"I might try it again"* (Varni, 1972:512).

Varni also reports that if the initial swinging experience is not traumatic, it is likely that a couple will try it again. On the basis of the
knowledge provided by the first experience and its function of reducing anxiety and apprehension (that is, on the basis of limited experience) people report the second experience to be usually more
enjoyable. Such a reaction, of course, rests on the condition that no
unmanageable or threatening conditions arise to alter the definition
of the experience. "This second experience, if it proves to be nonthreatening—and especially if it is enjoyable—is usually the clincher
in that it validates the non-uniqueness of the first experience"
(Varni, 1972:513). On that basis (and subsequent nontroubling experiences) the actor is proceeding toward acquiring a new set of moral
meanings—a "new" social reality.

Experiences of this sort are legion; they are the stuff of everyday
life. On the basis of just such experiences we validate and reinforce,
or question, revise, and reject, our conceptions of things in our environment. In the context of deviance, it is these experiences that en-
able people to make decisions regarding the appropriateness of their
behavior in light of self-attitudes and their position in society. It is
out of this experience that the once "willing but reticent," now
"turned on" actor, builds a revised social reality. This is a learning
experience in which the actor "gives up" one social reality and
"takes on" another (Varni, 1972:510).

Throughout this learning process, however, the actor is in a position of control and authority (Matza, 1969:123). To have control and
authority in the sense used here precludes explanations of conduct
based on "pressures" by others or "capitulating" to external or immutable forces. The actor perceives himself as an object—as a person
doing the act. It is the actor who perceives himself as a sometime
rule violator in the context of his various social positions. It is the
actor who contemplates himself as a possible candidate for social
rejection. It is the actor who mediates and resolves any conflict between his rule-violating behavior and other commitments. In short,
the actor perceives himself in a *relational sense*. On the basis of such
perceptions and their assigned meanings, the actor "makes up his
mind" (Matza, 1969:122) in a literal sense. It is the actor's decision
to pursue (or not) his deviance. Deviation is self-ordained.

The Question of Motives

It has been indicated that rule-violating behavior is volitional
and is based on reasons. Initimately associated with those reasons
are *motives* or motivation, the ". . . complex of meaning which ap-

pears to the individual involved . . . to be sufficient reason for his conduct" (Weber, 1962:39). In short, the decision to pursue a deviant course of action rests on the behavior's motivation. Stated differently, deviant conduct is intentional; our concern now, and finally, is with various foundations of that intent.

One basis for rule-breaking behavior is people's desire to break with the established order (Quinney, 1965:122). This is the case with several forms of delinquent and criminal behavior as well as mass protest. One classic expression of this pattern of motivation is the over 250 slave revolts and conspiracies engaged in by blacks during the time of American slavery (Aptheker, 1943:162). To black slaves, these uprisings were cases of "carrying the fight to the enemy" and were based on the hope of obtaining personal freedom as well as destroying that "peculiar institution" (Franklin, 1956:208). Black antipathy to the established order did not, of course, cease in 1865. As W. Haywood Burns (1963) makes clear, the "voices of Negro protest" have never been stilled in our society and have been particularly strident since the end of World War II.

Another group in our society that has engaged in mass protest is women. The history of women in America bears great similarity to both the condition and the protest efforts of blacks (Kirkpatrick, 1955:158–160; Hardert et al., 1977:Chapter 8). The history of the feminist movement reveals innumerable cases demonstrating the degree to which women's protest has been considered deviant, particularly by those occupying positions of authority in the established order. So much does the activity of some contemporary feminist groups violate institutionalized expectations (the established order) that the topic of "militant women" has recently come to be included in some topically oriented works on deviance (Bell, 1971). Other examples of domestic protest seen as deviance include student protests of the 1960's and 70's, the activity of the politically radical left, and the gay liberation movement.

Not all forms of protest regarded as deviant are of the mass type. Again, turning to the history of slavery in America we find numerous examples demonstrating that most black protest against the established order, a reaction against subordination, took an individual and private form. Included among these efforts were

> . . . loafing on the job, feigning illness in the fields and on the auction block, and engaging in . . . sabotage. The slave was so hard on the farming tools that special ones were developed for him. He drove the animals with a cruelty that suggested revenge, and . . . was . . . ruthless in his destruction of the crops . . . He burned forests, barns, and homes

. . . [Finally] self-mutilation and suicide were popular forms of resistance to slavery (Franklin, 1956:206).

As viewed by the slave owner, self-mutilation and suicide constituted destruction of property. Equally individualized are such contemporary forms of protest as shoplifting, destruction of telephone equipment, and, at least on one occasion, an airplane hijacking (*New York Times*, 1970) engaged in by persons seeking to redress what they regard as grievances stemming from having to deal with impersonal, unresponsive, and unregenerate bureaucratic systems.

Another pattern of protest against elements of the established order is civil disobedience. As noted in our consideration of countercultural values, civil disobedience is engaged in for the express purpose of promoting social change. On a grander scale, revolutionary activity has the same essential purpose.

Delinquent behavior, too, is sometimes engaged in as an expression of hostility toward and rejection of persons and agencies representing what some young people regard as onerous. Eloquently symbolic of this hostility and contempt is the incident, related by Albert Cohen (1955:23), of the student who defecates on the teacher's desk.

A second motivational base for rule-violating behavior involves immediate, tangible, and utilitarian goals. Theft sometimes reflects this motivational base. For example, a student who engaged in systematic theft while employed as a route salesman for a wholesale bakery put the matter this way. Too frequently and for a variety of reasons, the difference between the cost of the merchandise consigned to him and what he was required to pay the bakery for it left him "short."

> Being a novice, . . . I came up short all too often. The amounts were usually small, but they added up. A dollar or two a day devastated my budget. Even more inconvenient was an occasional major (to me) shortage—$5-$10. I would have to settle all the shortages on the weekly payday. When I would go home with the remains of my check and tell my wife how much I had left, she gave me the practical advice "Either stop coming up short or get another job." She wasn't recommending stealing. She was recommending that I change jobs. I checked the job market and found no practical alternatives. There was no real wrestling with conscience. It was more the feeling of agony, of being substantially short again with my stomach knotting up and muttering a vow, "Shit, this is going to happen to me again." There were no trips to the Garden of Gethsemane in making the decision to

steal; they came later. There was just an awareness of what to do and then doing it (Unpublished paper).

Just as immediate, practical matters influenced this person to decide to steal to supplement his income, so, too, do they influence women in their decision to obtain an abortion. In a study of the motivations of women receiving abortions (Steinhoff, Smith, and Diamond, 1971:3) it was found that 36 percent (116 cases) wanted an abortion because they were not married. Other reasons cited were inability to afford having a child at the time, the belief that a child would interfere with educational goals, that occupational or other activity would be disturbed, or that the woman was too young to have a baby. The reasons cited clearly reflect the personal situation in which these women found themselves. The bulk of the women claiming to be "too young" were, in fact, under twenty years of age. Of those who claimed they already had too many children, 50 percent already had given birth to four or more children. Over half of those citing educational goals as the reason had some college training and, apparently, were desirous of advancing their education.

Henslin's (1971:116–118) study of criminal abortion also reveals the importance of situational (practical) factors in bringing women to the decision to undergo an abortion. Regardless of marital status, Henslin's subjects regarded their pregnancy as a dilemma that could be solved by abortion. In the case of the unmarried woman, the man did not want to (or would not) marry her; the married woman's marriage would be unduly strained (usually financially) by the birth; and the divorced woman anticipated that giving birth would create unsoluble problems with her former husband regarding custody of their children (compare with Manning, 1971a). To the extent that it is regarded as deviant, then, the motives for abortion among these women rest on personalized, situationally based circumstances.

A third pattern of motivation to be considered is the recreational and the general idea that rule-violating behavior is fun. There appears to be a tendency to regard a variety of deviant and delinquent acts as sport or play (Sykes, 1972:411). The idea of deviance as fun has long been recognized. Thrasher noted that "going robbing" was a common recreational diversion among gang boys (Thrasher, 1963:269). Tannenbaum, too, early recognized the play element in rule-violating behavior. He noted that

> In the beginning the definition of the situation by the young delinquent may be in the form of play, adventure, excitement, interest, mischief, fun. Breaking windows, annoying people, running around porches, climbing over roofs, steal-

ing from pushcarts, playing truant—all are items of play, adventure, excitement (Tannenbaum, 1938:17)

And who would deny that a great deal of so-called "sex delinquency" is pleasurable?

More contemporary expressions of recreational deviance include the construction and operation of complex gadgetry in order to "beat" the phone company out of the cost of long-distance phone calls, interfering with national poll samples, rerouting mail, and tampering with radio and television broadcasts (Toffler, 1970: 289–290). Toffler suggests that these diversionary forms of deviance are likely to increase in the future with the development of *"anti-social leisure cults"*—". . . organized groups of people who will disrupt the workings of society not for material gain, but for the sheer sport of 'beating the system' " (Toffler, 1970:289). As social definitions of leisure change, suggests Toffler, the inclusion of socially disruptive forms of behavior under the heading of "fun" is a distinct possibility.

Other expressions of doing deviance for "fun" include the use of mood-altering substances. Erich Goode (1972:172) suggests that at least the "honeymoon phase" of heroin use is based on a desire for its highly touted euphoria and pleasure. In the case of marijuana, intermittent and moderate users, probably the largest proportion of users, use marijuana as a "social relaxant" to facilitate social interaction, just as others use alcohol (Geller and Boas, 1969:65). Particularly important in this respect is the widely held belief that marijuana use enhances the enjoyment and appreciation of shared activities such as music, art, films, and food (National Commission on Marihuana, 1972:37). Thus, marijuana smoking has become the focal point of much social and recreational activity.

Deviance as Situated Transactions

As a final aspect of our consideration of the motivational basis of deviant behavior, let us consider the emergence of these acts in interactional terms. For example, some rule-breaking behavior, such as criminal homicide, assault, and rape, may be viewed as the culmination of *situated transactions*, that is, ". . . a chain of interactions between two or more individuals that lasts the time they find themselves in one another's physical presence" (Luckenbill, 1977:177). These transactions are carried out in a wide variety of settings (bars, automobiles, parties, people's homes, dances) and between persons representing an array of relationships (spouses, friends, co-workers, acquaintances, and strangers). What is critical, however, is the dynamics of these situated activities.

On the basis of an examination of the dynamics of criminal homicide, Luckenbill contends that such acts are frequently the result of an intense period of interaction between persons, one of whom eventually assumes the role of victim and the other assumes the role of offender, the ultimate determination of these positions being entirely problematic. Each of the parties is a contributor to the final outcome of the event.

Quite often these events are "character contests" that commence when (1) one party says or does something to another that (2) is perceived to be a disparagement, insult, or other affront to the other's self-image. This is followed by (3) a retaliatory move by the offended party consisting either of a verbal or physical challenge, or a direct physical retaliation resulting in the death of the original offender. If the third step is limited to a challenge by the offended person, the initial offender is now in a position that marks the fourth stage of this situated transaction: he or she must now ". . . either stand up to the challenge and demonstrate strength of character, or apologize, discontinue the inappropriate conduct, or flee the situation" (Luckenbill, 1977:182). Any response other than the first of these, a demonstration of character, constitutes a loss of face, that is, an abandonment of the self-image that the person has claimed for himself or herself in that situation.

To avoid a loss of face, a demonstration of weakness, many parties at this point enter into a "working agreement" that the situation is one wherein violence is a suitable means of resolving the situation. At this point the probability of violence occurring is enhanced, a circumstance that constitutes the fourth stage of homicide as a situated transaction.

In establishing this working agreement, it becomes incontrovertible that both parties are active contributors to homicide as a situated transaction. Viewed in this way, who ultimately becomes victim and who offender is quite problematic. Becoming a victim or an offender is more a consequence of situationally based conditions than of a set of properties by which these actors may be distinguished in advance and their respective behaviors accounted for. The action of each party to the drama is shaped by the action of the other and by the desire to save face, demonstrate character, and develop or preserve a reputation. In short, the regularities and development of homicide result from an interaction rather than being the consequence of an aggressive offender imposing his or her will on a passive victim (Luckenbill, 1977:185–186). Homicide is a joint enterprise, situationally based, problematic, and reflects people's existential condition.

Continued demonstration of the practical and/or situational

bases of people's decisions to engage in banned behavior would be no more than pedantry. Escape—either from boredom, a "bad" home situation, or poverty—is one possible motivating factor. Expressing hostility and contempt, striving for political change, seeking recreation, seeking to make a living or episodically trying to "keep one's head above water," and, finally, trying to preserve a threatened self-image, are all motivating elements. Not the least important consequence of recognizing these varied grounds for behavior is that they permit an understanding of deviance in nonmoral terms. To regard deviant acts from these alternative perspectives opens doors to analysis and understanding that the more traditional dualistic perspectives are unlikely to reveal. Acknowledgment of these considerations throws light into corners where, largely, only darkness has prevailed (Polsky, 1967:101; Letkemann, 1973:Chapter 1). Finally, perhaps it is sufficient to conclude by reiterating the contention that an understanding of why people behave as they do is best understood in terms of reasons rather than causes and that, as such, human behavior is unpredictable, uncertain. In the final analysis these reasons are best known to the actor. To consider the actor's sense of reality and the situational basis of behavior is consistent with the model employed in this volume.

A Final Word, or, Are There No Exceptions?

To avoid being doctrinaire and to exercise careful judgment, let's once more consider the plausibility of the idea that rule breaking is volitional and a result of individual choices. Thus far we have considered two rather different sociological explanations for such action. The first, in the form of Sutherland's differential association theory, rests on the notion of affiliation (Matza, 1969:Chapter 6). According to Sutherland, one rather passively becomes involved in behaviors that are practiced by others. The novice learns these behaviors simply because of excessive association with their supportive meanings. The second, and alternative, explanation offered here, while not rejecting the interactional element in human behavior, proposes that our actions generally rest on a more active, deliberate, and conscious series of choices, and are situationally rooted. Thus, while behaviors may be established and practiced by others, the actor's involvement is a consequence of decision making rather than resulting simply from association with supportive meanings. The question to be considered is whether such an explanation may be regarded as the only plausible account?

The perspective proposed here suggests that a person's biography provides a foundation for subsequent behavior; through biography one acquires meanings that render one willing or unwilling to experiment with deviance. These meanings are fundamental to the decision-making process. Beyond the point of initial experimentation, actors make other decisions, not the least of which involve self-reflection. At each interval or stage, the events that occur rest on the actor's intellectual and social-psychological maturation—at least to a degree that would permit the actor to make informed choices and decisions.

However reasonable these contentions may be when considering the behavior of persons who have at least reached early adolescence, they seem inappropriate when considering children's involvement in rule-breaking behavior. A case in point is "tiny-doping" (Adler and Adler, 1976), the use of marijuana by children between the ages of zero and eight years and who have been introduced to marijuana smoking by their parents.

Given their age, lack of adult capabilities, and the absence of a developed sense of self, the "tiny-doper" represents a case in which it is somewhat inappropriate to contend that all actors become involved in deviance on the basis of more or less informed choices. Some tiny-dopers are introduced to marijuana smoking (at least to marijuana smoke) while still diapered toddlers as a consequence of being taken to gatherings where their parents and other adults smoke pot. Clearly, this involvement reflects neither decision making nor self-reflection on the part of the child. Prior to one and a half years of age, children are passive subjects; they simply breathe air that is sometimes filled with marijuana smoke. The drug's effects are apparent, however, as this exposure tends to have a calming effect on the child. Between the ages of one and a half and three years, youngsters become more aware of their surroundings and are free to watch adult behavior, imitate these behaviors, and "play" with (sometimes trying imitatively to smoke) marijuana and the paraphernalia. However ineffective their efforts to smoke at this age, that is, to inhale the smoke, retain it, and so on, the breathing of marijuana smoke-filled air continues, sometimes augmented by a mom or dad exhaling a lung full of pot smoke directly into the mouth of the eager youngster.

Around age three or four inhalation is often achieved, as is a more sophisticated appreciation of the use to which roach clips and other paraphernalia are put. By age four or five children acquire at least a vague social sense regarding pot smoking. Rapidly becoming more sophisticated, youngsters of age seven or eight differentiate users from nonusers (who is and isn't cool) and who should and should not know about their pot smoking. In short, by age seven children have learned the rudiments of legal and moral public meanings applied to marijuana smoking as well as the private meanings shared by their immediate family and parents' friends. Moreover, as a direct result of the various strategems employed by the parents, children learn to distinguish between situations when these different meanings are operative. Overall, however, from a state of total innocence to one of active and knowledgeable participation, the tiny-doper's involvement rests on intergenerational transmission in which children are passive agents.

In summary, from their earliest years these children are exposed to (associate with) meanings supportive of marijuana use. Pot smoking is normative in their families. It is learned in a process of interaction within intimate personal groups. It is a pattern of behavior engaged in by significant others such as parents. By parental "instruction" children are directly or indirectly introduced to the legal and moral meanings of pot smoking. Taken together, these elements lead to the conclusion that tiny-doping rests on normal socialization. Tiny-doping thus displays the essential properties of the process of differential association set forth by Sutherland. In critical respects it reflects an earlier and more "primitive" expression of conversion via affiliation and indoctrination.

A second instance in which the applicability of a traditional learning model or an existential model may be questionable is that of homosexuality. Thus, the question frequently asked is "why are some people homosexual and others heterosexual?" In the view of some contemporary students of sexuality, the idea that a person's *primary sexual identity* is learned is an illusion created and perpetuated by Sigmund Freud and many others (including social scientists) following in his footsteps (Whitam, 1975). By primary sexual identity is meant the gut-level feelings about the objects of sexual attraction—be they male, female, or both—that people have in the privacy of their sexual fantasies. This primary identity is *not* to be equated with sex roles, sex norms, or sex-related behavior. Restricting our concern, then, to fundamental sexual inclination, there is increasing cross-cultural evidence suggesting that sexual preference—homosexual or heterosexual—originates in early childhood and substantially predates the actor's knowledge about sex. Data also suggest that a homosexual orientation is not an outgrowth of "disturbed" parent-child relations, is not determined by aspects of the social structure (such as family configurations or social class), is ahistorical, and transcends culture. In short, homosexuality, it is suggested, ". . . is not learned, but rather emerges in much the same way that a heterosexual orientation emerges" (Whitam, 1975:5). As such, homosexuality should not be perceived as a role, either achieved or ascribed. Roles are cultural elements, while homosexuality is an orientation that likely gives rise to a particular sex role (Whitam, 1977a:2; 1977b). Finally, Whitam suggests, homosexuality as an orientation should not be confused with the concept of role since children who experience this orientation are neither socialized to it in the traditional sense, nor do they choose it on some rational basis (1977a).

Clearly, then, there are alternatives to the explanation of "doing deviance" proffered herein. These cases, however, rather than nullifying our alternative explanation, provide a supplement to it. That supplement is welcomed rather than resisted since it serves to reinforce the fundamental dictum that nothing so complex and varied as the broad spectrum of human behavior may be accounted for by a single explanation. Nor is it unreasonable to contend that assumptions that apply to the bulk of the population may not be applicable to all. Thus, rather than subordinate facts to theory, theory must be shaped by facts. Only then may our accounts be regarded as valid and faithful representations of the world as seen and experienced by the actor (Matza, 1969:25).

Summary

In this chapter an effort has been made to consider a wide range of historical explanations for people's involvement in deviant conduct. We have considered early biological, psychological and psychiatric, and sociological explanations. For methodological and substantive reasons, each of these were found to be deficient. A more contemporary sociological explanation for deviant conduct, Sutherland's theory of differential association, was also considered. Though extremely popular, Sutherland's thesis was set aside as not meeting the assumptions embraced in this volume. An alternative explanation of deviant conduct, one meeting the assumptions of the paradigm of definition, was proffered. On the basis of available evidence it is concluded that involvement in much deviance is a consequence of a variety of elements comprising one's biography, elements that are fluid, contingent, and situational (Schur, 1973:136; Matza, 1964; Lemert, 1967:40). Finally, consideration was given to Sutherland's thesis on the basis of the "tiny-doper," a case reflecting indoctrination of rather passive subjects to marijuana smoking, and to homosexuality, which, it has been suggested, is an "emergent" that predates learning.

Having sought to explain individual conduct, consideration must also be given to those explanations that focus on the epidemiology of rule-violating behavior, that is, on the statistical distribution of deviant behavior in time and space. It is to this second aspect of explaining rule breaking that we now turn.

Counting
Deviants

Introduction

In the preceding chapter consideration was given the question of why people engage in rule-breaking. The focus of attention was on the individual *qua* individual. However, seeking to explain how individuals come to engage in deviant acts is only one of the sociologist's concern for "doing deviance." A second concern, with which this chapter will deal, is with explaining *rates* of these behaviors among different segments of the population. This is sometimes referred to as the *epidemiological* issue and focuses on the distribution of deviant conduct in society, the expression of this distribution in statistical terms, and variations in these rates relative to other social conditions. In this chapter our attention will be directed to these and related matters as well as to the theories based on the use of official rates of deviance. Before turning to these considerations, however, two questions deserve attention: (1) precisely what is meant by the term *rates* and (2) why study rates when our concern is with individual behavior?

The Meaning of Rates

The term *rates* refers to a type of ratio, a way of relating the size of one number to that of another. Official rates of deviance, such as official police or Federal Bureau of Investigation statistics on crime, or a city or county health department rate on sucide, are numerical expressions of how the known frequency of the behavior (one number) relates to units of population (expressed by a second number). For example, the F.B.I. Uniform Crime Reports (1976:15) estimates there were 56,730 forcible rapes committed in this country in 1976. Taken out of context, that is, without giving simultaneous consideration to the size of the population among whom these rapes occurred, that number is relatively meaningless. Converting that number to a rate or ratio, however, provides a more meaningful statement of the extensiveness of the phenomenon. Thus, given the total U.S. population for that year, the estimated rate of rape was 26.4 per 100,000 persons; here we have the size of one number in contrast with the size of another. By establishing rates of deviance for known segments of the population, for example, women or men, blacks,. whites, or Indians, juveniles or adults, metropolitan areas, rural places, or other cities, it is felt that changes in the volume and character of criminal behavior may be determined relative to these different segments of the population. Further, as we will see later, changes in rates of deviance are also studied in terms of changes in rates of conditions to which deviance is thought to be related. For example, changes in crime rates may be correlated with changes in employment rates. As we examine theories of deviance employing these official statistics, we will have occasion to refer to the uses made of these data as "building blocks" for the construction and "testing" of theories.

Studying Rates

Turning to the second question, three reasons exist for considering rates of deviance and theories based on them. The first reason for examining official statistics on deviance rests on their use as a means of objectifying the phenomenon of deviance. As we saw in Chapter 1, deviance involves the application of subjective meanings to events. Thereafter those meanings are reified and given objective character. A prime means for making the transition from subjective meaning to objective condition is by the use of statistics dealing with arrests, suicides, child and spouse battering, and other offensive behavior. By amassing statistics alluding to "deviation as an objective condition," we bypass the idea that deviance (*not* rule breaking) has a subjective origin. In bypassing this critical notion the impression is created that deviation (a series of events having inherent moral meaning) is an objective phenomenon. Seldom, if ever, do officials, researchers, or the general public examine statistics with the idea in mind that they reflect the assignment of meaning to events. Rather, the data are taken as a valid index of "what's out there." An understanding of deviance as a social construction, then, necessitates an appreciation of these figures and how they are amassed.

A second reason for examining rates is that these statistics are *official;* that is, they are produced and disseminated by public (ranging from the municipal to federal levels) and publically approved agencies charged with the responsibility of dealing with deviants. The production and dissemination of these data by control agencies is consistent with the legal definitions that prevail in our society. As we will see in Chapter 4, many forms of deviance have been defined in law. Thus, the official declaration of a form of behavior as deviant is an act of the state. As a consequence,

> . . . *most forms of deviance today cannot be said to exist until they are legally (officially) defined in concrete cases.* That is, crime, suicide, and so on, exist only when the legal procedures have "certified" them . . . Basically, then, most forms of deviance today are constructed by official action and by law (Douglas, 1971a:68).

Recognition of this is critical since, quite clearly, not all behavior that might reasonably fit the official criteria of deviance comes to the attention of officials and not all behavior that fit the criteria and come to their attention is defined as deviant. Whether any given act is classed as deviant is problematic and subject to the influence of a variety of conditions. When considering explanations of deviance based on these official data, then, it is essential that one be aware of the manner in which rates are constructed. As we will note shortly, the meaning of these statistics cannot be taken for granted.

The "legal" basis of these data relates to the third reason for considering official statistics, namely, the use made of them by sociologists seeking to explain deviant conduct. Several generations of sociologists have built and/or relied upon theories of deviance utilizing these official sources. For example, in 1897 Emile Durkheim published his classic study of suicide having used suicide statistics from France and other European countries as his basic resource (Durkheim, 1951). Since that time students of suicide have consistently relied upon official data (Schmid, 1928; Cavan, 1928; Powell, 1958; Gibbs and Martin, 1964; Maris, 1969). Students of crime have similarly relied on officially created statistics. In 1833 Andre-Michel Guerry published his essay on French "moral statistics," a work regarded as the first "scientific criminology" (Vold, 1958:167). By 1929, in the United States, standardized (uniform) offense categories of criminal law violations were established and employed by the Federal Bureau of Investigation in reporting national crime data (Barnes and Teeters, 1951:52). The establishment of these standardized categories allowed for comparison of crime rates between cities and states at various points in time, as well as the establishment of "trends in crime." Most important, however, and despite criticism based on their biases and other deficiencies, sociologists came to accept these data for the purpose of establishing and testing theory (Douglas, 1971a:67–68). Let's turn now to an examination of some of these theories.

Rate-Based Theories of Deviance

The Ecological School

One of the earliest systematic efforts to work with and explain rates of deviance was that of the cartographic or ecological "school" of crime. (As used here, "ecology" refers to *human ecology*, the study of the spatial and temporal distribution of man and his institutions). This "school" consisted of a group of nineteenth-century European thinkers interested in how crime and other socially morbid conditions varied with changing geographic and social conditions (Radzinowicz, 1966:Chapter 2). In pursuit of these interests, members of this school stressed epidemiology and took medicine as a model to emulate. That is, just as the known volume of disease in general, as well as specific diseases, waxes and wanes, so, too, does the known volume of crime in general and specific offenses. From the outset, human ecologists investigated the relationship of crime to a variety of demographic (age, sex, and race composition of the population) and other (professional, educational and socioeconomic) characteristics of populations. In several cases climatic and seasonal changes were also studied to discern patterned changes between them and rates of criminality. On the basis of these data, known as "moral statistics," impetus was given to the idea that behavior is socially determined (Radzinowcz, 1966:42–43).

Though with fewer political implications than contained in some earlier studies, twentieth-century human ecologists and criminologists tend to support several of the general findings of their nineteenth-century counterparts (Winslow, 1973:Chapter 5). When studied by means of official crime statistics, patterns of crime within and between cities display discernible spatial and temporal consistencies. For example, except for areas within a city that undergo drastic change in land use and/or population composition, areas having high crime rates in one period are likely to have high crime rates in another time (Winslow, 1973:127). Extending over a period of at least forty years, ecological studies of Chicago crime rates revealed a constant decline in those rates as one moves from urban areas where poverty is concentrated to suburban areas populated by persons in a relatively affluent state. Correlations between crime rates and other socially morbid conditions continued to reveal high and significant associations between crime, on the one hand, and rates of truancy, infant mortality, tuberculosis, mental disorder, housing, and low education and income levels, on the other (Winslow, 1973:127–130).

Other studies, focusing on the age, sex, nativity, and ethnic and racial composition of populations, have revealed higher official rates of crime and delinquency among youth and young adults than among older persons, higher rates for men as compared to women, higher rates for native born than foreign born, and higher rates for blacks than for whites (Sutherland and Cressey, 1974:149).

Finally, contemporary application of ecological methods in studying crime rates has contributed to the elaboration of the concept of the *culture area*, that is, a physical area defined in terms of cultural homogeneity, particularly focusing on variation in crime rate from area to area. On the basis of these studies relatively consistent patterns of crime rate distribution have been reported. Thus, the southeastern United States has been found to reveal a higher rate of homicide than other areas of the nation. Urban areas are found to have consistently higher rates of crime than rural places. Finally, in terms of a variety of factors, variation in rates have also been established for culture areas (such as ghettos, ethnic enclaves, and the like) within large cities (Sutherland, 1974:Chapter 9).

On the basis of investigations such as these, reflecting acceptance of the etiological ideas discussed under the heading of the multiple-factor approach (see above, page 49), popular views of deviance have been substantially influenced. For example, ecologically oriented studies were taken as scientific support for the idea that crime and other forms of deviance were associated with poverty, though it was never quite clear whether the poor were simply more prone to crime than the more affluent or whether poor people who incidentally engaged in deviance "drifted" to high crime and deviance areas (Winslow, 1973:139). Similarly, the consistently higher official rate of such behavior among blacks has, in the hands of racists, been used as an argument against desegregation in this country. Simply stated, the traditionally higher rate of crime among blacks has been used as "evidence" of hereditary black inferiority—a clear justification for segregation of the races (Garrett, n.d.:22–23). In truth, however, the establishment of these associations between rule-violating behavior and other indices of human misery served less to contribute directly to theory construction than they did to the general idea that behavioral patterns among groups of people—races, sexes, age groups, and socioeconomic levels—reflected the conditions of life under which people lived. In the hands of select scholars, however, particularly those known collectively as the Chicago school, these data melded into what has come to be known as the social disorganization perspective. We will examine that perspective at some length.

Social Disorganization

Social disorganization theory dominated American sociology between 1925 and the post-World War II period (Hinkle and Hinkle, 1954:Chapter 2; Rubington and Weinberg, 1977:Chapter 3). According to this perspective, culture is an organism whose parts are ideally in harmony or integration with one another. (Of particular importance as "parts" of culture are institutions, customs, expectations, values and their associated rules—elements that serve as restraints on human behavior.) However, the cultural organism is not static. Rather, it is subject to change, thereby precluding the ideal of harmony and producing some degree of disharmony.

Regarding this disharmony, it is proposed that culture consists of material (technological elements, means of production and transportation, for example) and nonmaterial (rules, values, beliefs, elements. The material elements are believed to change more rapidly, causing the nonmaterial to lag behind and play "catch-up." This is because material culture is more responsive than nonmaterial culture to changes brought about by scientific and technological innovations. This disparity in the rate of change in these two spheres has been called "cultural lag" (Hinkle and Hinkle, 1954:39). When cultural lag occurs society is said to be disorganized. Note, however, that disorganization does not mean a benign transformation of culture over time; it refers to a conflict between old and new cultural elements— a conflict that is believed to have behavioral consequences.

By "consequences" is meant that social disorganization produces a condition in which people find it meaningless to follow old rules to achieve desired goals. For example, the rule that young people should stay in school and earn high grades in order to get a secure, good-paying job (the goal) is believed to make little or no sense either to youth who are members of depressed segments of society or to a broader spectrum of youth during times of economic recession. This same sort of meaninglessness applies to the situation faced by countless retired people who, after a lifetime of labor (playing by the rules) and relative restraint in an effort to enjoy their "golden years," find themselves victims of pervasive economic difficulties. For youth and the aged, as well as others, social change has resulted in norms becoming irrelevant. Thus, the harmony between effort and reward has declined.

This lack of integration and conflict between the parts of culture—disorganization—is held to be the common experience of groups displaying high rates of deviance and is thought to explain variations in rates of rule-violating behavior. Theory predicts that fluctuations in deviance rates will be associated with fluctuations in indices of social disorganization.

For the social disorganization theorist, evidence of the impact of disorganization lies in the failure of established customs, rules, and expectations to guide behavior. Immigrant groups, the unemployed, ethnic minorities, and others experiencing this type of change are held to be victims of social disorganization. Such a view seems logical enough given the usually heavy concentration of such groups in the central city areas where one finds, as did the ecologists, relatively high rates of traditional forms of deviance: delinquency, crime, sucide, gambling, drug addiction, and prostitution.

According to social disorganization theory, the presence of these behaviors among a people is not a simple or automatic result of cultural change. Change results in the breakdown of social control. That is, change brings about a decline in importance of customs, norms, rules, and expectations. In turn, families, neighborhoods, and communities (places where these social control mechanisms have their most immediate impact) are no longer in a position to exert a favorable (nondeviant) influence on the life of their members. As David Matza has stated, "Social disorganization . . . [theory amounts] . . . to the liquidation of ordinary controls; among the poor especially, . . . the breakdown of communal organization released deviant impulses. Vice and crime . . . magnetically attracted the unrestrained" (Matza, 1969:95).

The case of social disorganization reveals characteristics of the traditional sociological perspective. The impact of social forces, specifically the impact of cultural change on collective or group life and individual conduct, is clearly of major importance. Specific examples of the application of this theoretical orientation are abundant in sociological literature. Included are Shaw and McKay's study of delinquency (Shaw and McKay, 1942), Ruth Cavan's work on suicide (Cavan, 1928), Thrasher's study of juvenile gangs (Thrasher, 1927), and Faris and Dunham's investigation of mental illness (Faris and Dunham, 1939), among others. The popularity of these investigations promoted the idea that deviance, defined generally as a lack of conformity to social norms, has its origin in sociocultural conditions rather than personal atttributes. The distinction between social disorganization theory and the earlier multiple-factor and ecological approach lies in the more sophisticated conceptual and theoretical nature of social disorganization theory.

Social Structure and Anomie

While social disorganization theorists were explaining rates of deviance in terms of the *process* of social change, other sociologists were concerned with how the *structure* of society relates to rates of deviant behavior. One of the best-known exponents of a structurally oriented explanation of rates of rule-violating behavior is Robert K. Merton (Merton, 1957:Chapters 4 and 5).

Using the concept of *anomie* (a social condition lacking norms for the governance of individual and group behavior), Merton contends that high rates of problematic behavior should be associated with a relative absence of normative restraints on behavior, while low rates of deviance should be associated with an abundance of restraints. The question, then, is what is there about the structure of society that leads to an absence (or abundance) of normative controls.

Merton theorized that the answer lay in the relationship between the dominant *goals* of our society and the *means* provided (as part of the structure or organization of society) to achieve them. These goals, including but not limited to pecuniary success, are associated with legitimate means for attaining them. It is Merton's view that while these goals are embraced by groups experiencing widely different circumstances (rich and poor, Catholics, Protestants, and Jews, minorities and others), not all groups have equal access to socially acceptable ways of attaining them. For example, reflecting the idea of value consensus, Merton maintains that despite differences in race, sex, age, or religion, most people in our society have internalized and strive for a place of dignity and have accepted work as a principal means to its attainment. However, substantial segments of society have been denied access to dignified work. Racism, sexism, the generally low regard accorded the aged as employees, and discrimination against some religious groups constitute evidence of this condition. Using Merton's terms, discrimination against these groups is part of the structure of society; that is, rewards are granted and withheld on the basis of people's race, age, and sex, among other things. Society is structured so as to prevent select segments of the population from having equal access to the legitimate goals. This structurally based disparity between goals and the means to attain them, existing in a context of equalitarianism, that is, a condition of *anomie,* is seen as leading to a variety of behavioral responses.

Despite continued frustration of one's goals, probably the most frequent behavioral response is to persist in normatively prescribed behavior; that is, people try and try again. Merton refers to such behavior as *conformity,* defined as continued adherence to socially approved behavior and continued belief in the moral legitimacy of normatively prescribed behavior. A second response is called *ritualism* and involves continued acceptance of the means (conforming behavior) along with reduced emphasis on (or renunciation of) the goals. This response has little relation to deviant behavior. Basically, one adjusts by reducing frustration through lowered or redirected aspirations. Third, Merton speaks of *retreatism,* a response involving simultaneous rejection of both means and goals. In this case the legitimacy of both elements is challenged and one exhibits a kind of defeatism or quietism. A principal characteristic of this mode of adjustment is its individual rather than collective nature. Fourth is *rebellion.* This mode of adaptation is marked by the actor's rejection of socially legitimate goals and the means to achieve them and simultaneous embracing of an alternative set of goals and means. Moreover, the rebellious deviant publicly dissents from and challenges the legitimacy of public policy, and seeks to change that policy, sometimes for purposes that transcend individual gain, while subscribing to and being sustained by a "higher" morality, such as a revolutionary ideology (Merton and Nisbet, 1971:830ff). Finally, Merton speaks of *innovation.* In this case the actor continues to accept the legitimacy of the goal—wealth, power, status—but, finding legitimate means unsatisfactory, turns to illegitimate (deviant) means to obtain them. Thus, for example, Merton would explain the relatively higher official crime rate among the poor (as compared to wealthier groups) by the pressure the social structure exerts on that segment of society.

Implicit in this model is the view that ". . . deviant behavior refers to conduct that departs significantly from the norms set for people in their social statuses" (Merton and Nisbet, 1971:824). In this respect, the anomie model bears considerable similarity to the social disorganization perspective; both perceive deviation as resulting from imperfections in the social system. However, while social disorganization focuses on social processes, the anomie model addresses the structure of society. As such, there exist marked differences in their respective consideration of antecedent conditions. In the case of social disorganization theory, deviance allegedly emerges as a result of a temporary disruption of a potentially harmonious cultural system. In the case of *anomie* theory, meaninglessness is an integral element of the social system. Deviance, then, is a response to endemic conditions.

In summary, we have focused on the core elements of several prominent approaches to the study of deviance. While not exhaustive of these efforts, the approaches discussed do provide a fair representation of the major explanatory systems. Though differing in specifics, these theoretical perspectives have a number of common elements, largely a result of their shared view that deviance is satisfactorily understood simply as rule-violating behavior, that the moral meaning of so-called deviant behavior may be taken for granted, and the etiological (causal) explanations of such behavior are sufficient. Accordingly, each approach *explicitly* addresses the question of what leads people to engage in deviance and *implicitly* suggests ways society can rid itself of such people and/or behavior.

However legitimate these concerns may be (and their legitimacy is not at issue), the sufficiency and adequacy of these explanations ought not be taken for granted. Let us turn, then, to a critical examination of some features of these theories.

A Critique

The foregoing theories, like those constructed to account for individual conduct, have attracted great following in this country and elsewhere. Between 1918 and 1954 the concept of social disorganization dominated American sociological thought (Rubington and Weinberg, 1977:150; Hinkle and Hinkle, 1954:Chapters 2 and 3). Since its inception Merton's theory of anomie has been equally influential. In his discussion and critique of that theory, Clinard (1964) included a forty-page inventory of empirical and theoretical works based on anomie. But even this list was incomplete. Despite such extended attention and influence, when viewed in terms of the characteristics of the paradigm of definition, these theories contain several shortcomings.

Moral Objectivity

First, contrary to the view that reality (including moral meanings) is a social construction, these theories rest on the assumption that the moral quality and meaning of behavior is objective and nonproblematic. Characteristically, officially declared meanings and definitions of acts as deviant are taken for granted. In addition to taking meanings for granted, these theories tend to reflect a morality consistent with established public morality in our society. This tendency has two interrelated implications. One, by reflecting the dominant or public morality, these theories assume the existence of moral consensus (Davis, 1975:68) and, by definition, preclude giving consideration to the existence of multiple realities (to say nothing of their legitimacy). Second, the "brand" of morality reflected in these theories stems more from the homogeneity of thought among "professional pathologists" than from the nature of our society. In a survey of the work of thirty-two leading early American social scientists, men who had a lasting influence on the nature and direction of sociology for several generations, C. Wright Mills (1943) noted that the overwhelming bulk of these men were either born on farms or in small towns, that they tended to participate (though independent of one another) in similar types of "reform" groups and societies that were identified with the business and professional classes, that they tended to be academics, and that they tended to marry persons who were similarly situated. On these grounds, then, the "moral consensus" assumed to exist and reflected in these mainstream sociological works was that of small-town, white, Anglo-Saxon, Protestant America. Thus equipped, it becomes relatively simple for *seemingly objective* (that is, value-free) observers to assume the moral superiority of behavior displayed by persons of their membership and reference group, while assigning a different moral meaning to the behavior of others. To be sure, over the years, the value preferences of sociologists have undergone considerable change. Nonetheless, the impression remains that deviants are still judged in terms of the standards of "conventional society," whatever those standards might be (Davis, 1975:38,44).

As an example of the consequence of this position, we may point to the ease with which some students of society identify "lower class culture" as a "deliquency generating milieu" (Miller, 1958). Underlying this position is the assumption of the nonproblematic moral meaning of behavior and that reality is an extrinsic, objective condition. This tendency is noticeable in both the social disorganization and anomie theories.

Social Stability and Harmony

Second, in addition to the assumption of moral consensus, these theories (especially anomie theory) conceive of society as being *essentially* stable and harmonious. Derived from the broader functionalist perspective, anomie theory stresses the universality of cultural goals. Thus, in anomie theory emphasis is placed on "cultural wholeness" (Davis, 1975:101). This cultural unity (or sharedness) of goals is accompanied by structural division or disunity. As we noted, persons located at different positions in the social structure experience different opportunities to achieve satisfaction of the culturally universal needs. Thus, anomie theory combines cultural unity (goals) and structural diversity (means) into one model. However, while structural problems exist, implicit in this orientation is the idea that with some adjustment, such as extending legitimate opportunities to groups that lack them, structural problems may be reduced and the true unity of society achieved. By equalizing opportunities in this way, anomie or normlessness, the condition to which people adjust in deviant ways, may be eliminated.

As exhibited by social disorganization theorists, this issue takes a somewhat different form. In social disorganization theory change is an inevitable and constant element in society working to frustrate social harmony. However, cultural unity and harmony (equilibrium) may be achieved in this scheme as groups become accommodated to changed circumstances (and, hence, embrace the attributes of conventional society). A second way of achieving unity involves bringing those parts of the social system that are out of adjustment into harmony with the balance. Direct intervention and guidance of technological change is hypothesized to provide such adjustment (Rubington and Weinberg, 1977:63). Indeed, the theme of amelioration or improvement of social ills runs throughout the history of American sociology. In either case, then, the presumption of societal harmony is part of the social disorganization perspective.

This orientation is inconsistent with the social definition paradigm, according to which society is ever-changing and the scene of constant conflict. However, these conditions are not the result of variable rates of change between material and nonmaterial culture. Rather, change is a consequence of the conflict within society; in turn, conflict is a consequence of the existence of mutually exclusive interests and the unequal distribution of power. Change and conflict, then, are endemic to any society in which heterogeneous values and interests exist and in which interest groups seek to have their interests translated into rules. Conflict becomes the locomotive power of change.

The Matter of Determinism

The epidemiological theories considered here run counter to the social definition model in still another way. To varying degrees, epidemiological theories employ a deterministic model of causation. Accordingly, much deviant behavior becomes an expected consequence of certain environmental conditions. Behavior is explainable in terms of these "causes." That is, the ecological and the social disorganization approaches appear to embrace a form of environmental determinism. Perhaps the most accurate characterization of this determinism is to refer to "free-will environmentalism." According to Sprout and Sprout (1965:71),

> Those who speak in [the idiom of free-will determinism] populate their universe with "influences," derived in the main from the non-human environment, sometimes called simply "geography" or "nature." But they avoid verbs that might cast doubt on volition. In this watered-down derivative of environmental determinism, man is assumed to have a free will. Nature gives him instructions, but he is capable of choosing, however unwisely, to disregard them.

In terms of the approaches we have considered, the "influences" of greatest importance are cultural, for example, the influence of a cultural area, and the influence of the strain produced by social and cultural change. These elements serve as external constraints on people's behavior.

> . . . the external constraints are influences on social action and yet men somehow assert an ambiguous free will (e.g., to become criminal or not). Free will is the added factor which may propel people into natural areas of criminal residence [an area wherein the traditions and customs of the population are largely criminal]. There is no sense of men struggling against social arrangements as such; no sense of a social structure riven by inequalities and contradictions, and no sense of men acting to change the range of options (Taylor, Walton, and Young, 1973:114).

Though somewhat more sophisticated than the earlier ecological and social disorganization approaches, anomie theory, too, casts human behavior into a deterministic mold. Human behavior (either legitimate or nonlegitimate) is an expression of the kinds of opportunities fate appears to have made available. To be sure, problems of anomie give rise to efforts to evolve solutions (modes of adaptation); in that sense anomie perceives humans as responsive organisms. However, regardless of how they may be subdivided, the adaptations are either legitimate or nonlegitimate and are determined by the character of the social organization in which people find themselves (Cloward and Ohlin, 1960:Chapter 7). At best, the adaptations posited by Merton (1957:Chapters 4 and 5) and by Cloward and Ohlin fail to reflect the diversity of human behavior and mankind's seemingly endless capacity for creative innovation (Taylor, Walton, and Young, 1973:134).

In taking a deterministic position, epidemiological theories run counter to the idea that man is an interactive organism. Earlier it was suggested that human behavior is not simply a response—individual or collective—to external stimuli. People are not well described as either billiard balls or hockey pucks. Behavioral choices reflect one's biography, self-identity, commitments to others and to statuses, as well as situational circumstances. Viewed in terms of this complex of elements, to which little consideration is given in these epidemiological theories, deterministic approaches appear to fall short of providing an adequate account of human behavior. We will return to these considerations in Chapter 5.

The Validity of Social Statistics

A final element to be considered in appraising these theories is their reliance on official statistics. For the social disorganizationists, this took the form of "mapping rates and distributions of suicide, venereal disease, alcoholism, mental illness, crime, vice, and other indicators of social disorganization . . . [and] contributed to the formulation of a general sociological rule: deviant types are concentrated among the poor, foreign-born, black or other minority populations" (Davis, 1975:60). Among theorists of the social structure-anomie orientation, official statistics became a major, if not the sole source of data for determining the distribution of etiological factors in deviance. Thus, segments of the population experiencing high rates of deviance and crime were predicted to be those segments likely experiencing limited opportunity and vice versa. The best-known theoretical expression of the supposed link between official rates of deviance (especially delinquency) and limited opportunity is that of Richard Cloward and Lloyd Ohlin (1960).

It is Cloward and Ohlin's basic thesis that delinquency, specifically gang delinquency, is a collective adaptation to failure to achieve success goals when that failure is rationalized as being due to institutional defects, such as racism, rather than individual deficiencies (Cloward and Ohlin, 1960:125).

The merits of this perspective rest very substantially on the acceptance of official statistics as valid indices of the distribution of deviant and criminal behavior in society. In turn, the acceptance of official data rests on the assumption that they are based on objective criteria and that their meaning is certain (nonproblematic). Given this line of reasoning, it is obvious that these theories must stand or fall on the strength (or weakness) of official statistics as objective measures of deviant conduct. Let's turn, then, to an examination of these statistics, how they are constructed, and what factors contribute to their variation.

Official Statistics as Social Constructions

Official statistics on crime and other forms of deviant conduct have long been accepted by authorities, scholars, and lay people as acceptably valid measures of "moral phenomena." That acceptance rests, in part, on the abiding belief in the Western world that enumeration is the "cornerstone of knowledge." In Chapter 1 we discussed epistemology, the basis or method by which one claims to know things (see page 17). In the Western world it has been a common-sense assumption (an epistemological assumption) that ". . . one knows something only when it is counted (Douglas, 1967:163)." Thus, in a half (but only half) facetious way, scholars have been heard to say "If you can't count it, it's not worth knowing."

Counting things certainly has advantages. Perhaps the greatest of these is that numerical information is readily systematized; that is, it may be arranged in terms of some supposed interrelationship, and may then be proffered as rational knowledge. Operations of that sort derive a great deal of their respectability and acceptability from the faith the Western world has always attributed to the methods of the physical sciences. Aided by this respectability from its very beginning, the rational knowledge accumulated by the nineteenth-century "moral statisticians" (such as Lambert-Adolphe-Jacques Quetelet and Andre-Michel Guerry) became the basis for establishing and administering social policies designed to curb immoral behavior (Douglas, 1971b:52). In the hands of moral statisticians (persons dedicated to the statistical analysis of moral phenomena) data of this sort was used to "prove" the existence of "dangerous classes"—segments of society believed to contribute most to crime and social disorder and commonly referred to as parasites, criminals, nomads, barbarians, strangers, and savages. Such "proof" as moral statisticians provided, of course, was consistent with popular opinion of that day, particularly the upper-class view that a well-ordered society existed only when people, especially the lower classes, were engaged in honest and steady work (Radzinowicz, 1966:38–39). By generalizing to the data of the moral statistician the objectivity and rationality assigned to the data of the physical sciences, the "proof" or validity of the *objective* existence of the "dangerous classes" became unquestionable. At least the claims were not questioned. ". . . What could be more certain than ideas and findings based on the ultimate criteria of scientific methods and knowledge? . . . Who could deny the truth of a finding or an explanation obviously based on the forms of science?" (Douglas, 1971b:53) Thereby, knowledge was advanced by the "magick of number."

Given an aura of respectability derived from science, the validity and moral implications of official statistical data was (and to a very great extent still is) taken for granted. Not the least of those taking them for granted are sociologists. However, in taking the meaning of these official statistics for granted and by assuming they refer to objective conditions, sociologists, public officials, and lay people have failed to acknowledge that ". . . from their very beginnings official statistics were policy oriented and determined primarily by the political goals of the officials" (Douglas, 1971a:49). Records on immorality kept by church officials in the seventeenth and eighteenth centuries were used to demonstrate the efficiency of officials responsible for operating houses of confinement. In addition, these data could be used as a rational basis for making judgments regarding allocation of monies and other resources to control immorality. What seems true of seventeenth- and eighteenth-century church officials is true of police and other officials in twentieth century United States. For example, in our society *clearance rates* (the proportion of crimes known to the police which they have solved and for which an offender has been arrested) have long been used by police departments to promote an image of police efficiency. Some authorities regard the clearance rate as the most important index of police performance (Skolnick, 1966:167). Similarly, official crime statistics are used by police for purposes of self-justification, organizational survival, and improvement of community relations (Manning, 1971b:175). By raising or lowering statistics police departments seek to validate their claims for additional budget allocations or, on the other hand, to demonstrate the efficiency with which they do their job. As one officer reported,

Pretty regularly people call in saying they think their car is stolen. We check the report out and after a little checking we locate the car in some great big shopping mall parking lot where the owner left it. They just forgot where they parked and called us. They are real embarrassed. But it don't matter. We just list the thing as another stolen auto we recovered. It makes us look pretty good.

Rather clearly, then, clearance rates, as well as the crime rates, may be (and are) inflated or otherwise "adjusted" figures (Sutherland and Cressey, 1974:26).

The danger and consequences of assuming the "adjusted" figures are valid and objective measures of crime may well be obvious. Yet the matter of bias in official statistics deserves extended examination.

The Problem of Bias

The term *bias*, when applied to social science research data, refers to a condition of that data such that conclusions drawn from it are systematically distorted (Cohen, 1954:80). According to some observers, these errors of bias creep into social science data as a result of ". . . carelessness, incompetence, or poor judgement" (Thomlinson, 1965:70). In the case of official data, however, far from being inadvertent, bias often appears to be a matter of design or, at the very least, a reflection of the very operation and organization of social control agencies.

To understand how official statistics become warped, one must recognize that there is no necessary or consistent relationship between the *actual volume of offender behavior* and statistical indices of that behavior. That is, statistical rates may vary (increase or decrease) without any corresponding change in the actual volume of the behavior to which they refer. That is because *statistical rates reflect official action; they are social constructions.* They are created by official agencies (police departments, psychiatric hospitals, public health facilities, coroner's offices, drug rehabilitation centers) which have the task of managing one or another form of deviance. These agencies, and only these, have the legal authority to decide when a specific behavioral act shall be designated as a case of deviance. It is these agencies that give the *official* moral meaning to behavior coming to their attention. As we have noted (see page 85), given the role of the state in defining deviance, it is readily apparent that official action is critical in shaping the statistical record.

However, official agencies do not exist in a vacuum. To appreciate the complexity of biasing official statistics, the operation of official agencies must be viewed in context. Several factors deserve consideration.

Underreporting

Before officials may act to construct a statistical record, information must come to their attention. Bearing very heavily on the ultimate validity of the statistical record is the fact that not all behavior that might reasonably fit the official criteria of deviance is brought to the attention of official agencies. A survey of criminal victims in three Washington, D.C., police precincts reported that

> . . . for certain specific offenses against individuals the number of offenses reported to the survey per thousand residents 18 years of age or over ranged, depending on the offense, from 3 to 10 times *more* than the number contained in police statistics (President's Commission on Law Enforcement, 1967:21).

Victim survey data for the entire nation revealed an amount of crime against persons almost twice that shown in the F.B.I. Uniform Crime Reports (based on police department data), and a volume of crime against property was revealed that more than doubled the Uniform Crime Report figures (President's Commission on Law Enforcement, 1967:21). In another victim survey 2,077 incidents were discovered that reasonably fit legal definitions of crime. Of those 2,077 cases, 1,059 (51 percent) had not been reported to police and, hence, were not part of the official crime statistics (Ennis, 1967:49).

Data reported by Ennis have been supplemented by more extensive and recent information. National crime surveys in many U.S. cities reveal that in the area of personal crime (including crime against person and property) the percent of victimizations reported to police ranges from a low of 25 percent (Houston, Texas) to a high of 42 percent (Washington, D.C.). Household offenses (burglary, household larceny, and auto theft) reports range between 36 percent (Houston) and 50 percent (Boston and Washington, D.C.). Crimes against commercial establishments (burglary and robbery) are reported most often, ranging from 72 percent in Houston and New Orleans to 85 percent in Cincinnati (U.S. Department of Justice, 1975).

Overall, it is estimated that perhaps half of the crimes that occur become part of the official record. This does not mean that only 50 percent of the murders, robberies, or burglaries, and so on, come to the attention of the police. Indeed, the extent to which behavior of any sort is reported to police is highly variable. Murder and auto theft are, perhaps, the most fully reported offenses. For example, 93 percent of all completed auto thefts are reported to police in Buffalo and New Orleans. On the other hand, only 11 percent of household larcenies under $50 get reported to police in Houston (U.S. Department of Justice, 1975). Equally low in reporting rate is consumer fraud; since its effect is widespread and because it occurs sub rosa, it is a low-visibility offense and is seldom reported (Ennis, 1967:42).

Why officials lack more complete information is believed to be largely attributable to underreporting of incidents by victims and others. The reasons why crime victims underreport are numerous, as Table 3-1 indicates. It is worth noting that in over one-third of these cases (reasons 2 and 4) the incidents were not regarded as police matters, while an additional 55 percent (reasons 5, 6, and 9) of the victims did not feel police would take effective action.

Beyond the "garden variety" crimes dealt with in victim surveys are the far more frequent "crimes without victims," referring to ". . . the willing exchange, among adults, of strongly demanded but legally proscribed goods or services" (Schur, 1965:169). Homosexuality, drug addiction, gambling, sale of pornographic materials, prostitution, and other forms of socially proscribed sexual behavior are included under this heading. Given the fact that these goods and

TABLE 3-1

Reasons for Not Notifying Police Among Those Not Reporting Incident

Reasons for Not Notifying Police	Mentioned at All	Most Important
1. Did not want to take time	13%	6%
2. Did not want to harm offender	12	7
3. Afraid of reprisal	5	2
4. Was private, not criminal, affair		2
5. Police couldn't do anything about matter	58	36
6. Police wouldn't want to be bothered	28	8
7. Didn't know how or if they should notify police	6	1
8. Too confused or upset to notify police	6	2
9. Not sure if real offenders would be caught	31	12
10. Fear of insurance cancellation	1	0
Total		100%
N	(1,017)	(906)

SOURCE: P. H. Ennis, *Criminal Victimization in the United States: A Report of a National Survey*, Washington, D.C.: U.S. Government Printing Office, 1967, p. 44.

services are sought by people and that there are no victims in the usual sense of that term, one would expect few complaints. That expectation is confirmed. How much of this behavior occurs that would reasonably fit legal definitions is unknown. It is not implausible to assume, however, that the amount coming to the attention of authorities is no more than the tip of the iceberg (Rossman, 1976:11–13).

In addition to the standard crimes without victims there are a wide variety of low-visibility offenses that relatively rarely are mentioned in the press and only occasionally dealt with by authorities. These behaviors range from diverse forms of white-collar crime at one extreme to male prostitution, incest, sexual fetishisms, sadomasochism, pederasty, and the like, at the other. No accurate figures on the extent of such behavior exist. Since these behaviors receive so little public (official) attention, one may surmise that a relatively modest increase in *known* cases would represent a sizable *proportional* increase in official rates. What is most important to note is that an increase in *known cases* does not necessarily reflect an increase in the actual frequency of these behaviors. All that may be involved in a change in perception.

The problem of undercounting is by no means limited to criminal behavior. Additional examples may be noted in the cases of mental illness and child battering. In the instance of mental disorder, little or no confidence may be attached to official rates of mental illness being accurate reflections of the actual incidence of these conditions among a population. Psychiatric *nosology* (a branch of medical science dealing with the classification of disease) has led to the belief that qualitatively different categories of mental and personality disorders do exist in fact and that persons either do or do not display the unique symptoms from which the existence of these "diseases" may be inferred (Taber et al., 1969:351). That is, there are those who contend that personality disorders, schizophrenia, and neuroses are on the same existential level as malaria, tuberculosis, or a kidney disorder (Movahedi, 1975:313).

Despite these nosological pretensions, many psychiatrists recognize that

. . . the epidemiology of the mental illnesses is at a quite primitive level, particularly in regard to its most important problems—schizophrenia, depression, and the various neuroses. Depression and schizophrenia are better studied than the neuroses, probably largely because they are more reliably diagnosable, though *they leave much to be desired in this area. Diagnosis of neuroses is far from reliable, that is, reproducible by equally qualified diagnosticians* (Lemkau and Crocetti, 1967:228. Emphasis added.).

The diagnostic difficulties alluded to are attributed by some observers to a lack of sufficient contact between patient and physician prior to diagnosis, a lack of psychiatrists trained in research methodology which would sensitize them to the importance of classificatory criteria, and a general disinterest among psychiatrists in problems of classifying illness (Clausen, 1976:113). Given these conditions, it is not surprising that psychiatrists display sometimes grossly different diagnostic practices. In turn, these varying practices lead to the contention that most large differences in hospital admission diagnoses are the result of diagnostic practices rather than a result of real differences in the volume of behavioral disorders (Schwab and Schwab, 1973:69).

The problem with mental health rates does not rest solely on the diagnostic idiosyncracies of the medical profession, however. In addition, it has long been recognized that ". . . treatment rates [of mental illness] vary with the availability of facilities and with public attitudes toward their use . . . [Therefore] treated rates do not tell us much about . . . the occurrence and distribution of true rates of disorder" (Dohrenwend, 1975:366). Forty years ago Faris and Dunham (1939:162) recognized this condition when they noted that mental hospital admission rates among higher-income groups may be artificially low because of a tendency among such people to have family members treated at home or otherwise avoid their inclusion in official statistics. The result was a bias, an overestimate of the incidence of mental illness among the lower class relative to the upper classes.

The concern registered by Faris and Dunham rests on the fundamental issue of how official rates of these disorders are influenced by when people seek help with emotional and mental problems, when and under what circumstances people come to define the bizarre or threatening behavior of others as mental illness, and when and under what circumstances people are defined as mentally ill. Since such qualities and actions do not inhere in either the person or their behavior, but rest only on the meanings attributed to persons and their behavior by others operating in varying situational contexts, any assessment of the accuracy of rates of mental disorder must reckon with the highly subjective basis of these meanings.

In the final analysis it appears that rates of crime and rates of mental illness have broadly similar characteristics stemming from roughly equivalent circumstances. As in the case of crime, a substantial but unknown and unknowable proportion of the behavioral episodes that fit standard categories never get reported to those with the authority to assign the designation "mental illness." Further, not all reported cases are defined by psychiatrists in terms of standard psychiatric classifications. On such grounds it is perhaps no over-statement to suggest that, like crime rates, the validity of statistics on mental illness may not be taken for granted.

As a final example of underreporting, let us turn to *child abuse,* defined as the deliberate inflicting of painful injuries and indignities upon children by parents. Prior to the early 1960's, few cases of child abuse were reported or recorded in this country and even fewer cases were defined as deviant (Pfohl, 1977:311). At that time, how-ever, the number of cases of child abuse that were observed and recorded began to rise, not only in the United States but in other na-tions as well (Fontana, 1973:27). Rather than a function of an in-crease in the true incidence of child abuse, this change in statistics stemmed from reporting differences generated by the child-abuse reporting movement (Pfohl, 1977:319). That is, current and rising statistics on child abuse do not reflect any known increase in paren-tal abuse of children. Rather, the current statistical rate increase reflects an increasing responsiveness by observers to an already exist-ing, age-old phenomenon. This responsiveness is a manifestation of a change in meaning regarding the limits of parental authority in im-posing physical or corporal punishment on their children. This change, finally, is the outgrowth of an effort by a number of inter-ested groups: the medical profession, especially pediatric radiol-ogists, social welfare organizations such as the Children's Division of the American Humane Association, governmental agencies, and the media.

Despite the relatively precipitous rise in rates of child abuse over the past several years, official data on child abuse are still ex-tremely limited in validity. As Fontana (1973:34) notes,

> The means to accurately pinpoint the incidence of abuse are not yet at our disposal. (A national registry might be a help though not the complete answer.) It is difficult to estimate the number of children being physically abused or neglected in the course of a year. We do not even know how many cases of child maltreatment are *reported* across the nation; we do not know how many reported cases refer to neglect, how many to abandonment, how many to sexual abuse. We do not know how many cases go *unreported,* although we cannot help suspecting that what we see is only the tip of the ice-berg.

It is apparent, then, that official statistics covering a variety of phenomena rarely, if ever, provide a valid picture of the actual volume of rule breaking in society. Invariably these data constitute an underrepresentation of the true incidence. Variation in rates, rather than reflecting a change in the actual incidence of these behaviors, more often are a consequence of a change in the awareness (sensitivity) of persons reporting these phenomena and in the organizational apparatus established to compile and maintain such records. In no sense may the validity of these statistics be taken for granted.

Defining Deviance

Another major reason why official records of deviance are biased involves a number of factors influencing authorities' definition of that behavior. Not all behavior coming to the attention of rule enforcers and that reasonably satisfy official criteria of deviance are so defined. The classification of any instance of behavior is problematic. For example, though a "common-sense" case of rape may occur, police may label it "unfounded"; that is, the case has no factual basis. That does not mean the victim was not subjected to forced sexual intercourse; rather, it is a technical-legal term bearing on the prosecutability of the case. Thus, most "unfounded" rape complaints result from at least one of the following "flaws" (LeGrand, 1973:928):

1. Evidence that the victim was intoxicated;
2. Delay in reporting by the victim;
3. Lack of physical condition supporting the allegation;
4. Refusal [of victim] to submit to a medical examination;
5. The previous relationship of the victim and the offender; and
6. The use of a weapon with accompanying battery

Such factors represent conditions that substantially reduce the probability of obtaining a conviction against the alleged assailant. On that basis no "official" recognition is given the case; not the least result is a bias in rape data.

Similar biasing of official data results from the variability of police assigning criminal definition to people's actions. Research among youth (Piliavin and Briar, 1964) reveals that in managing police-citizen encounters that may lead to arrest, police respond not simply to the "objective" and legal criteria related to the suspect's actions. Rather, the decision to arrest often rests on the officer's inferences about the suspect's character. These inferences, in turn, stem from the police officer's definition of cues that are unrelated to the alleged offense but that emerge during the course of the police-citizen encounter. Included among these cues are the suspect's age, group affiliation, race, dress, general grooming, and, most important, the youth's general demeanor. An older youth known to be a member of an outlaw gang, a black youth, a youth wearing a black jacket and soiled blue jeans, or one who behaves toward the police in a way defined as "disrespectful" is more likely to be defined as a case calling for arrest and formalization. On the other hand, youth who display cues likely to be defined as consistent with one who is law-abiding tend to have their cases defined and responded to in a different manner. This tendency is reflected in the following cartoon. The consequences for biasing official data need no elaboration.

Funky Winkerbean by Tom Batiuk. Copyright © Field Enterprises, Inc., 1978. Courtesy Field Newspaper Syndicate.

Another factor influencing official definitions is the private conceptions and typifications possessed by rule enforcers. As noted in Chapter 1, how people react to things in their world depends on how they are defined. This applies to rule enforcers as well as others. For example, research has shown that the moral beliefs and stereotypic definitions a police officer has about offenders, whether a police officer is politically liberal, conservative, or reactionary, and how an officer categorizes various groups are things likely to influence his definitions of and reactions to people's behavior. A study of police recruits reports that young officers are likely to categorize people in depersonalized terms. It is reported that police recruits see people as ". . . either law-abiding or not. Radical students were spoiled. Liberal politicians were subversive. Blacks were criminally inclined. Intentions had no place in law enforcement, especially if the [offender] belonged to a major out-group" (Harris, 1973:127). Categorizing of that sort is felt to promote intolerance on the part of police toward some groups while serving to provide a kind of immunity for others. Differential enforcement results. In turn, differential enforcement (a kind of official action) helps produce biased data.

   Examples of how categorization and stereotypy relate to differential rule enforcement and distorted statistics is contained in

Chambliss and Nagasawa's (1969) study comparing self-reported and official arrest rates of white, black, and Japanese-American youth in Seattle, Washington. In this study—to be discussed more fully in Chapter 4—police rather consistently overemphasized the involvement of black youth in delinquency and underestimated the involvement of Japanese-American youth. These erroneous estimates were based on prevailing stereotypes of the involvement of these youth in unlawful behavior, stereotypes leading to the idea that blacks are more inclined to criminality and Japanese-Americans are less so.

Similar biases were noted among department store detectives contacted in Cameron's study of shoplifters. While only 6.5 percent of the arrested shoplifters were black, they accounted for 24 percent of all prosecutions. Further, while only 10.9 percent of nonblacks were charged with larceny, charges were brought against 58 percent of the blacks. Finally, though only 8.85 percent of the apprehended white women were charged with larceny, 42 percent of the black women shoplifters were formally charged. Cameron concludes that "decisions as to which people will be released with an admonition and which people will be formally charged with larceny are made . . . by members of the store protection staffs . . . *decisions reflect the biases and prejudices of these staffs*" (Cameron, 1964:136. Emphasis added.).

Suicide is another instance in which official data are likely subject to systematic bias. For example, given the relatively stronger condemnation of suicide among Roman Catholics than among people of other religions, one would expect a greater effort by Catholics than others to hide the occurrence of suicide (Douglas, 1967:207). For this and perhaps other reasons one may expect that among various subgroups there will be a variable rate of attempted concealment of suicide. Douglas, for example, has hypothesized that ". . . the rate of attempted concealment will vary directly with the degree of negative moral judgement associated with the act of suicide and with the degree of negative sanctions *believed* to be imposed for violations of moral judgements (Douglas, 1967:208)." Douglas further suggests that concealment will likely vary in terms of the degree to which the suicide victim is involved in supportive social relations and according to the social status of the deceased (Douglas, 1967:209).

Biasing statistics on suicide is also promoted by the *post hoc* or "after the fact" definition of suicides. For example, suicide has been defined as self-imposed extinction by methods the deceased knows will result in death. Thus, *knowledge* possessed by the deceased and the *role played by the deceased in their own death* are two critical elements influencing the decision to legally and officially declare a death as suicide. The mere identification of these elements and their indeterminateness suggests how equivocal will be the assigning of official meaning to suspected suicides. At one extreme is the clear case of the person who has long talked of suicide, and who, after leaving an explicit note indicating his or her suicidal intentions, proceeds to take an excessive dose of sleeping pills. At the other extreme is the person whose body is found floating in San Francisco Bay. Did he or she jump, or fall, or get pushed into the water? From a bridge or boat? In the absence of notes or other hard evidence to answer these questions, the labeling of unattended deaths as suicide (or murder or an accident) must rest on circumstantial evidence. The open-ended nature of such evidence and the ambiguous meanings attached to it, are an invitation for the introduction of bias (Douglas, 1967:185–190).

The way in which actual suicides may be misclassified has been investigated by David Phillips (1974 and 1977). Based on Goethe's novel *The Sorrows of the Young Werther,* in which the hero commits suicide, Phillips has coined the term *"the Werther effect,"* referring to the rise in *actual* suicides immediately following publicized suicide stories in the media. Alledgedly, such publicity leads to an increase in suicides as a consequence of suggestibility and imitation (1974:341). Using the *New York Times* and the *New York Daily News* as media sources, Phillips found that suicides do rise well above the expected level in the period immediately following the time a suicide story appears in the press. On the average, each suicide story results in an excess of 58.1 suicides above the expected number (1974:343). In more recent research, more pertinent to our concern for biased statistics, Phillips has shown that many deaths heretofore officially classified as motor vehicle fatalities (and, hence, accidents) are most likely disguised suicides (1977). Using an index of front-page publicity given to California suicide stories, Phillips correlated suicide publicity with fluctuations in motor vehicle fatalities. It was predicted that ". . . publicized suicide stories help stimulate a brief increase in motor vehicle fatalities" (1977:1465). Moreover, Phillips predicted that the correlation between the rise in "motor vehicle fatalities" and suicide publicity would increase as the number of newspapers circulating the story increased. Both predictions were sustained by research data. Phillips concludes that ". . . some of these imitative suicides are disguised and recorded as motor vehicle accidents" (1977:1465). Though the magnitude of this misclassification remains to be determined, it seems clear that official suicide rates are anything but valid. The biases we have examined, stemming from definitional matters, tend to (1) promote differential rule enforcement and/or (2) contribute to the construction of biased statistics.

Finally, whether or not a specific instance of behavior is defined as deviance and included in official statistics is a consequence of how officials classify ambiguous events. As we noted in Chapter 1, the moral meaning of behavior is often quite ambiguous; under such conditions the assignment of appropriate meaning calls for an exercise in constructing reality. This is well demonstrated in the difficulty police personnel sometimes have in attaching an appropriate label to events coming to their attention. Let's consider a few examples of the role of ambiguity in police work where death is involved.

On the basis of careful observation of police investigative methods, Terry and Luckenbill (1976) conclude that homicide detectives tend to divide cases into one of two classes: *walk-throughs,* those in which there is little or no ambiguity as to the legal classification to which a case should be assigned, and *whodunits,* cases in which the nature of the events that transpired are problematic (crime, or accident, or suicide,) and, hence, subject to variable interpretation and labeling. Characteristic of the walk-through type is the case in which a person responsible for the death of another calls the police, informs them of what has happened, and then awaits their arrival and his or her arrest. In such a case the identity of the victim and the offender, the nature of their relationship, and some plausible explanation of the act and what prompted it are all rather readily available. In sharp contrast is the whodunit investigation wherein the identity of the deceased, the identity of the assailant (if, indeed, there is sufficient evidence to justify referring to the deceased as a victim), the events leading to the death, and other possibly relevant information is lacking. In such a case the nature of the event (and how it should be classified and treated) becomes a matter of social construction. For example,

> Detectives entered the scene of an apparent suicide. They found a "suicide note" written in the victim's own hand; her relatives and a close friend related that she had been very depressed the previous few weeks over her family affairs; the room was locked from the inside; she was found slumped on her bed with a pump-action shotgun wedged between her legs. The victim was dead, the top of her head splattered against the ceiling.
>
> Closer examination of the scene gave investigators cause to consider the possibility that there had been another person

who either assisted in the suicide or killed the victim. Of primary importance in this regard was the observation that the breach of the pump-action shotgun was open and the shell casing in the wastebasket on the other side of the room.

By testing the victim's shotgun as the victim would have had to use it in order to have shot herself—that is, with the gun stock on the ground and light pressure applied to the slide—it was discovered that a shell would indeed eject from the chamber. That the casing landed in the wastebasket was held to be pure happenstance. Consequently, the case's designation changed from "possible suicide" to "suicide" (Terry and Luckenbill, 1976:85).

In this case the initial classification was "possible suicide"—a term clearly indicative of ambiguity or uncertainty that could only be resolved by careful investigation. The essential point, however, is that meanings and the classification of cases are far from certain and may, in an unknown number of incidents, result in misclassification. Related to this is the fact that detectives, no less than other officials, are,

. . . not neutral observers of unambiguous events. They are active agents. Their activities determine whether a set of events will be placed within the criminal-homicide column or seen as instances of suicide or natural death . . . To assume, therefore, that statistical data accurately represent the universe of criminal homicides overlooks both the ambiguous and perplexed, albeit reasonable, nature of investigations and the probable inaccuracy in the reports of homicides. In the light of these difficulties, the thought must at least be entertained that official documents reflect only those homicides that are readily visible and capable of being investigated. Thus, murders committed by urban ghetto dwellers of the lower socio-economic and racially disadvantaged classes are heavily overrepresented in the official statistics (Terry and Luckenbill, 1976:92–93).

Visibility

Also contributing to the construction of biased official statistics is the fact that by reason of life circumstances some segments of the population are more subject to observation than others and, hence, their involvement in rule-breaking incidents is more readily observed and recorded. This is particularly the case for persons on welfare, ADC mothers, and others whose lives, as part of the price of obtaining public assistance, are subject to sometimes microscopic scrutiny. This provides increased opportunity for authorities to become aware of behavior definable as rule violating. For example, regarding the relationship of poverty to the discovery of victims of statutory rape, Skolnick and Woodworth report that

. . . the largest single source of [statutory rape] reports is from the family support division (40%). At the time of the study ADC aid could be given to a mother only if her real property was worth less than $5,000 and her personal property less than $600. One social worker reported that most applicants possessed no real property; those who had originally owned such property had exhausted its value prior to applying for aid. Thus, statutory rape is punished mainly among the poor who become visible by applying for maternity aid from welfare authorities (Skolnick and Woodworth, 1967:109).

The influence of life conditions on the "visibility" of rule-breaking behavior is further demonstrated by the increasing reliance of people on insurance to cover property losses. Because claims against insurance companies for property lost through theft must be validated by the insured filing a report of the theft with police, the official data on theft is increased. Such increase, however, may not be assumed to reflect a simple increase in offender behavior. A statistical increase does not necessarily mean a "real" increase.

The distortions due to differential perception and law enforcement have never been more noticeable than as a consequence of the research based on the technique of "reported behavior" (Short and Nye, 1957). Developed in the mid-1950's, a substantial amount of research using this technique has revealed systematic evidence indicating that official statistics, especially those on delinquency, provide a distorted picture of the actual pattern and distribution of offender behavior (Short and Nye, 1958: Dentler and Monroe, 1961; Clark and Wenninger, 1962; Akers, 1964; Gold, 1966 and 1970; Williams and Gold, 1972). Using an anonymously administered questionnaire designed to measure the range and frequency of involvement in delinquent behavior, Short and Nye compared responses of high-school students in three western and three midwestern communities with responses from a western training school group (adjudicated delinquents). From this comparison they concluded delinquency is distributed far more evenly in the general population than official statistical data would suggest. These conclusions have been further confirmed by Ronald Akers in a retest of the original Short-Nye investigation. Akers reported ". . . no significant differences in delinquent behavior by socio-economic status, and analysis revealed no correlation between the two variables" (Akers, 1964:38). Finally, on the basis of an extensive interview study among over 500 randomly selected Flint, Michigan, teenagers, Martin Gold concluded that official data are selective and incomplete and therefore indicate a ratio of five lower-class youngsters to one higher-status youth. It is suggested that if the most highly delinquent youth were dealt with in a complete and unselective manner the ratio of lower- to higher-status youth would be closer to 1.5:1, a clear indication of a more even distribution of rule-violating behavior than is ordinarily acknowledged (Gold, 1966:44).

More recently Williams and Gold (1972) studied the differences between self-reported and official delinquency among a national sample of 847 boys and girls, age thirteen through sixteen. In conducting this research Williams and Gold examined boys' and girls' admitted (self-reported) delinquencies as well as whether or not they were caught by police, if caught whether or not a record was made of their offense, and, if the youth had an official or quasi-official record, whether or not they had been declared delinquent by the court. On the basis of this extensive investigation, Williams and Gold conclude that actual delinquency is not at all accurately reflected in official records (1972:226). Indeed, official records tend to amplify (that is, overstate) and present a distorted picture of the actual delinquency engaged in by these youth. These authors state: ". . . both delinquent behavior and official delinquency are important phenomena deserving attention, but they are not by any means the same thing. Measures of one . . . are far from isomorphic with measures of the other" (Williams and Gold, 1972:227). This study, then, confirms the general conclusion reported by Gold (1966) on the basis of the study of a single city.

As we have noted, one area of distortion in official data on rule-violating behavior involves the underrepresentation of violations of upper-status persons. This distortion does not result simply from police and other officials focusing attention on lower social status groups. Equally involved is an active tendency to underplay violations of higher-status persons. Ordinarily, police and others simply withhold negative judgment of influential persons or groups in deference to the moral meanings associated with those people. On the basis of positive qualities assigned to residents of "better" neighborhoods, police tend not to perceive them as potential or actual violators. Rule violations committed by these people, then, have a low level of *social-psychological visibility*, that is, authorities are not prepared to officially define these behaviors as intentional violations. It is more likely that these behaviors will be defined as "exceptions" and dealt with as informally as possible (Westley, 1970:97–98).

A most graphic instance demonstrating this and the subordination of police to the power-wielding capacity of upper-status groups, is the case, stumbled on by a cub newspaper reporter, of the *premeditated shooting* of a member of one of Long Island, New York's wealthiest families by his wife. All newspaper coverage of the event was immediately supressed and within hours of the murder the physical evidence was removed never to be seen again. Witnesses to events associated with the death were never permitted to be heard in public. At an inquest held five days after the death it was officially established that the wife was awakened when she thought she heard burglars, went to investigate, and, because she was groggy with sleep, accidentally shot her husband. The death was officially declared an accident (Chambliss, 1975:259–261). Rather clearly, the elements of murder are not always defined that way.

The definitions authorities assign to behavior is also influenced by the necessity, particularly of police, to rely on citizen complaints to initiate the rule-enforcing process. Basically, police may pursue law enforcement in either of two ways. They may perform in a *proactive* manner, that is, discover rule-violating behavior on the basis of extensive patrol and search operations, or they may operate on a *reactive* basis by relying on citizen complaints to initiate the law-enforcement process (Reiss and Bordua, 1967:25). To the extent that police are organized to operate on a reactive basis, the construction of official statistical records will in some measure reflect the moral meanings, prejudices, and stereotypes of the complainant. For example, the greater awareness people have of being victimized by burglary or auto theft (as contrasted with being victimized by means of consumer fraud) suggests people will be more prone to report blue-collar types of crime. Obviously, then, regardless of the actual frequency of blue-collar vs. white-collar offenses, selective reporting will result in the inflation of statistics on one type and deflated statistics on the other.

Further, the general citizen, like police recruits and store detectives, is prone to possess stereotypes of various categories of deviant actors (Simmons, 1969). As with other segments of the population, complainants respond in terms of these stereotypes and are prepared to perceive (define) and report offenders who fit their stereotypes. As we have noted, the popular social construction of crime and deviance in this country suggests that offenders are more likely to be male than female, black than white, and lower class than upper or middle class. Given this construction, one would expect complaints to be more frequently lodged against lower-class black males than more affluent white females. This expectation is supported by the data collected in Cameron's (1964) study of the disposition of shoplifters and by a study of how corporations respond to employee thieves (Robin, 1967). For example, *holding the dollar value of the theft constant,* comparison of publicly exposed and prosecuted employee thieves revealed that significantly more men (60 percent) were prosecuted than women (47 percent) and significantly more lower-status employees (cleaners, servicemen, and stock workers) were prosecuted than were higher-status workers (executives, salespersons, and white-collar workers), Of the former group, 73 percent were exposed and prosecuted, compared with 50 percent of the latter. Robin concludes, "thus, it has been possible to offer empirical evidence that the offenders with whom the enforcers can more easily identify are treated more sympathetically—and what better way to express such identification and empathy . . . than by not exposing him publicly" (Robin, 1967:129). Such selectivity, a seemingly fundamental characteristic of all rule enforcing, has an ultimate effect on official statistics, rendering them unreliable as measures of the actual volume of offender behavior.

Data Bias and Organizational Interests

Our discussion thus far clearly notes that how behavior is defined and rules are enforced is highly problematic, and suggests that full enforcement of law is nonexistent. It is nonexistent, first, because it is physically impossible in an open society where the legitimate activities of police and other rule enforcers are restricted by procedural law. But full enforcement is nonexistent for a second reason; namely, because proscriptive rules are enforced in ways that maximize organizational rewards and minimize organizational strain (Chambliss, 1969:86; Chambliss and Seidman, 1971:100-101). That is, people are arrested, tried, sentenced, hospitalized, declared mentally ill, have their deaths declared suicides, and so on, in inverse ratio to the trouble such official actions and declarations may bring to the respective agency.

Maximizing rewards and minimizing trouble is a principle element in many bureaucratic organizations. To appreciate the relevance of the principle to official statistics it is necessary to note that rule enforcers operate in a context of value pluralism. There is no single set of values and moral meanings to which the entire population subscribes. Social reality is multiple. To be sure, there are some behavior patterns regarding which there exists overwhelming public moral consensus, but even in the case of murder there are times when the apparent meaning is withheld. Further, though most people subscribe to the ideal of "law and order," the practical meaning of that term for one group is not shared by all. We should also note that a substantial variety of behaviors, particularly "crimes without victims," are subject to very different meanings and serve as the basis for significant social conflict. Examples of this conflict include the current controversy over abortion, decriminalization of possession of marijuana for personal use, and the definition of pornography. Each of these is an expression of value pluralism.

Pluralism influences law enforcement in that no matter how they perform their assigned tasks, rule enforcers will likely be damned by some and praised by others. In a pluralistic society rule enforcers will inevitably interfere with some group's interests. Enforcing rules that contravene a group's interests will promote opposition and antagonism. In order to maximize rewards and minimize strain, then, rule enforcers may be expected to exercise discretion in performing their duties. In the case of police, laws will be enforced when doing so is either independent of strains or when enforcement is likely to bring positive recognition. However, when enforcement is likely to promote strains, discretionary *nonenforcement* will occur. Discretionary nonenforcement is sometimes the most rewarding course of action.

The existence of value pluralism and an abiding interest in organizational rewards and strains raises the question of how rule enforcers know whether enforcement or nonenforcement is the most judicious course in any given situation. Certainly, they do not know these things in any definitive sense, but there are factors that aid in the determination. One of these is that power in our society is differentially distributed. The police, for example, must deal with persons occupying lower-, middle-, as well as upper-class socio economic positions. These people differ not only in values and interests, but have differing degrees of power—degrees of ability to impose strain on police should their interests be threatened by public policy. Full enforcement directed against powerful segments of the community is likely to produce criticism, and, perhaps, influence the resources of the rule-enforcing body.

Allocation of resources is another element influencing the enforcer's decisions on how and when to exercise discretion. Like many service organizations, rule-enforcing bodies seldom, if ever, produce their own resources (Chambliss and Seidman, 1971:266). They are dependent on others—legislative assemblies, city councils, executive bodies—for operating funds, personnel allocations, salary and benefit increases, among other things. Astute rule enforcers do not operate in ignorance or disregard of their dependent position and do not "bite the hand that feeds them." Among other things, that means they will select and respond to their clientele with care; that is, they will respond to persons and groups on the basis of their potential for making trouble for the organization. Disregard for the practical implications of the distribution of power and their dependent status may have politically disadvantageous consequences for the offending organization.

Let's relate these matters to official statistics. For the reasons cited, rule-enforcing bodies exercise discretion. That is, practical considerations influence organizational action and bring about a substitution of informal goals for the formal goals on which the organization is based (Etzioni, 1964:10–11; Chambliss and Seidman, 1971:266). Previously we noted that official statistics were records of official actions. That is, how many people are arrested, convicted, or imprisoned reflects actions engaged in by officials. How many official suicides there were in your home county last year reflects the action of your county coroner. Because these actions are to some extent discretionary, the statistics they generate are biased in particular directions. Discretion is not exercised randomly; it is systematic and has a discernible direction. Groups with power are systematically dealt with in ways different from those who lack power and the ability to make problems for the organization. An awareness that official data are influenced by organizational discretion, a concern for minimizing trouble, and that agency actions are sometimes influenced by stereotypes and other factors, should serve as a basis for interpreting such data with caution.

As we have seen, arrest statistics indicate an overinvolvement of poor, blacks, and youth in crime; however, the apparent meaning of these data ought not be taken for granted. Let's reverse the situation and ask if the relatively low rate of arrest and conviction of white-collar offenders may be taken at face value; do the data mean that men of business are really men of virtue? In his study of white-collar crime, Edwin Sutherland (1956a) investigated 980 adverse decisions against corporations. These decisions were based on cases of fraudulent advertising, violation of labor laws, violation of antitrust laws, embezzlement, and violation of trust by corporate officials. *Each case involved violation of criminal law.* However, only 159 (16.2 percent) of these decisions were made by criminal courts. Decisions for 786 of these criminal law violations were handled by civil courts or by commissions. It seems quite apparent that examination of conviction statistics (a record of criminal court actions) would yield invalid information concerning the unlawful activity of corporate groups and their representatives. Teasing out the meaning of these and other official statistics necessitates careful examination of the rates and the rate-producing process.

That the meaning of statistics on crimes known to the police and arrest statistics may not be taken for granted is also indicated by the fact that these data are sometimes purposefully and consciously manipulated by police in order to promote organizational interests. For example, rather than reflecting genuine increases and decreases in unlawful behavior, it is contended by Rosett and Cressey (1976) that these data have been juggled to satisfy federal regulations regarding the distribution of financial grants. Rosett and Cressey comment:

> The artificial nature of these statistics became evident when the federal government modified its law enforcement grant policy, which had been to give financial aid to cities with high crime rates. The new policy gave large grants in proportion to the reduction of the crime rate in target cities. A city no longer would receive extra money because its crime rate was high, but if the rate went down, it would be granted more money for police equipment and services. This amounted to thinly concealed bribery of police departments to make "the crime problem" go away statistically, and impressive results were obtained (Rosett and Cressey, 1976:177).

It is again clear that the apparent meaning of offical data may not be taken for granted. In a substantial proportion of cases they may be found to be self-serving (Weis and Milakovich, 1974:33). That statistics are used by organizations for self-serving purposes is not, of course, limited to police. Use of official data for that purpose extends to the highest levels of national government, including the White House and executive agencies such as the Bureau of Narcotics and Dangerous Drugs (B.N.D.D.). Thus, in 1971 then President Richard Nixon sought emergency powers (including no-knock warrants, pretrial detention, wiretaps, and unorthodox strike forces) to deal with what was hailed in the media as an "uncontrollable heroin epidemic" which "will surely in time destroy us (Epstein, 1977:51–52)." Rather than the consequences of increased numbers and activity among heroin traffickers, this "epidemic" was a social construction, the work of B.N.D.D. statisticians and White House strategists, manufactured in an effort to create sufficient concern and fear to win public support for the White House's "war on crime." Information supplied to the media in support of the claim that the nation was in the throes of an epidemic purported to show that ". . . the number of addict-users [in the nation] had increased from 68,000 in 1969 to 315,000 in 1970 to 559,000 in 1971" (Epstein, 1977:52). These data— representing an eightfold increase in the number of addicts in the short span of two to three years—were produced simply by applying a "new formula" to old (1969) figures. Of course such prodigious increases may also produce a sort of backlash, which in this case was soon feared. Thus, it soon became apparent that this "increase" in addicts occurred *under the Nixon administration*—hardly consistent with that administration's goal. Thereafter all statements emanating from the B.N.D.D. had to be cleared by White House staffers (Epstein, 1977:52).

Summary

This chapter has focused on theories designed to explain rates of deviance. Following consideration of a sample of such theories, a critical examination was offered of the data on which they rest. Several elements were considered in terms of their influence on the rate-producing process and the rates themselves. Of particular concern is whether these data may be accepted as valid; that is, do they measure what they purport to measure? Can their apparent meaning be taken for granted?

The answer to both these questions is an unequivocal "no." The research and analysis presented clearly demonstrates these data contain a systematic bias. The implications of this conclusion, however, are not limited simply to such questions as whether it is true or false that middle- and upper-income groups engage in unlawful and deviant behavior, or whether whites and blacks engage in objectively similar or different patterns of behavior, or whether police and other agencies manipulate arrest data for organizational benefits. Rather, the crucial question is whether materials of the sort presented in this chapter reveal sufficient information to challenge the validity of theories based on data abstracted from these records. For example, are the data presented here sufficient to challenge the deeply rooted belief, legitimized and reinforced by anomie theory, that delinquency, crime, and deviance are functions of lower-class living and a response to frustrations of ambition, meaninglessness, and anomie? The analysis presented seems to do just that. Moreover, how adequate can be the explanatory power of theories based on data that are demonstrably biased? The answer is all too obvious. As a consequence of our analysis it is concluded that juvenile court records, police arrest statistics, records of correctional institutions, mental hospitals, coroner's offices, and other official agencies are highly suspect when employed in defense of epidemiological theory—when used to explain alleged objective differences in the distribution of deviance in society. Official data may be adequate for research on the operation of agencies that compile them since they are, in the first place, indices of agency operations. In that sense they may be used to study *official* delinquency, *official* crime, *official* deviance. However, as an index of *delinquency, crime,* and *deviance* in the general population they are inadequate.

Nonetheless, it is on the basis of such distorted data that a number of highly popular social psychological and sociological theories of deviance (for example, Cohen, 1955; Cloward and Ohlin, 1960) have been built. By embracing and perpetuating these theories sociologists have not contributed to a faithful rendering of the phenomena of deviance. Inferences about deviance drawn from questionable data must themselves be questionable. To construct elaborate theories on such bases and tender them as "scientific evidence" is, at least, to distort the purpose of the sociological enterprise (Davis, 1975:121). Others would contend that sociologists have, albeit unintentionally, prostituted themselves. That is, they have abandoned their intellectual responsibility and have allowed themselves and the product of their labor to become part of the established social control machinery. As we have shown, such theories, since the time of the early moral statisticians, have granted an undeserved legitimacy to social control policies designed, not to curb rule-violating behavior (defined in objective terms), but to facilitate the aims and interests of those groups in positions of power to influence control agents. Such was never the intended purpose of sociology.

4
Banning
Behavior

Introduction

In the preceding chapters extensive consideration was given to matters of perspective. Briefly stated, our purpose has been largely that of trying to "get a handle" on the phenomenon of deviance, to "clear away" some taken-for-granted assumptions and interpretations based on them, and to establish a foundation for the analysis to follow. In the present and subsequent chapters we turn to the heart of the deviance process, to the assignment of moral meaning, to resisting its assignment, to its consequences and how they are managed, and to how those meanings may be changed.

We may begin our analysis by noting that the deviance process has three phases whereby ". . . a group, community, or society (1) interpret behavior as deviant, (2) define persons who so behave as . . . deviant, and (3) accord them the treatment considered appropriate to such deviants" (Kitsuse, 1962:248). Kitsuse's comments are consistent with the position established in Chapter 1, namely, that deviance is a social construction involving the assignment of moral meaning to things and people and acting on those assigned meanings. If deviance is a consequence of an observer's interpretation of things, rather than an inherent part of them, how are these interpretations arrived at? How do private and subjective meanings become public and objective rules of behavior? Stated differently, how, in the course of everyday affairs, do we attach moral meaning to things? How do things perceived as amoral or moral get defined as immoral? The present chapter is concerned with these questions. Together they focus on one aspect of the deviance process, one called *banning*, imbuing the activity with guilt, and proscribing it as bad, evil, wrong, or immoral (Matza, 1969:146). Banning refers to the first of Kitsuse's three phases of deviance.

The Deviance-Making Enterprise

The process of constructing and applying moral meanings may be understood as a *moral enterprise* (Becker, 1973:162). The term enterprise means that creating moral meanings is an undertaking of major proportions, calling for considerable management and initiative. It does not occur without conscious human intervention. The business of making deviance is an enterprise in two senses. First, it is an enterprise consisting of rule making (without which there could be no deviant behavior), and second, it entails the business of rule enforcing, the application of rules to some specific group of people. These two activities are the work of two subtypes of moral entrepreneur: *rule creators and rule enforcers*.[1] For the present we will focus on the work of the rule creator.

Many individuals play the role of rule creator. At the time of writing these lines Anita Bryant is well embarked on a crusade against homosexuality and other forms of behavior she regards as sexually deviant. However, the term *rule creator* is most appropriately applied to groups of people joined together by a shared concern. (Indeed, Anita Bryant is a symbol, a representative of a far larger collectivity of concerned persons.) Rule creators are *interest groups*, that is, groups organized on the basis of shared and distinctive interests among the members. When seeking to convert these interests into public law the interest group may be identified as a *pressure group* (Hoult, 1969:169, 247).

In terms of creating deviance, the existence of these groups in heterogeneous societies like ours is extremely important; their existence assures a constant supply of deviance and deviants. As indicated previously, in societies like ours there exist all manner of idiosyncratic belief systems. Social reality is multiple. These belief systems are the stuff of varying and often conflicting social realities; out of this conflict (ultimately) comes deviance. Howard Becker comments:

> Social rules are the creation of specific social groups. Modern societies are not simply organizations in which everyone agrees on what the rules are and how they are to be applied in specific situations. They are, instead, highly differentiated along social class lines. These groups need not and, in fact, often do not share the same rules. The problems they face in dealing with their environment, the history and traditions they carry with them, all lead to the evolution of different sets of rules. Insofar as the rules of various groups conflict and contradict one another, there will be disagreement about the kind of behavior that is proper in any given situation (Becker, 1963:15).

Rule-creating groups, then, are a product of moral heterogeneity. The belief that one group's interests are mutually exclusive of those of another, together with the almost unlimited variety of interest groups in heterogeneous societies, makes it inevitable that the goals and purposes of some will purposely or accidentally encroach

---

1. The distinction between rule creators and rule enforcers is analytic. In the actual process of deviance the same individuals and groups that are instrumental in the creation of rules may be equally active in their enforcement. For example, police departments may suggest legislation to municipal and state authorities as well as enforce the ensuing laws.

upon the interests of others. But even when no direct encroachment occurs, a heterogeneous and highly impersonal society like ours is characterized by the perception of threats, fears, distrust, and suspicion of one group's behavior by another (Lofland, 1969:13). That such emotions play a prominent role in initiating the work of the moral entrepreneur is noted in Sutherland's work on the diffusion of sex psychopath laws (Sutherland, 1950a). These laws are established because of the fear aroused by the occurrence of sex crimes in a community. Sometimes subject to substantial amplification by the news media, the perceived danger and fear resulting from these events may be sufficient to give rise to corrective efforts—efforts to seek relief. In seeking that relief interest groups may be transformed into rule-creating assemblages. In broad terms, then, the work of the rule creator begins with dissatisfaction over some facet of the status quo.

Awareness

The work of the rule creator takes time. To create something is to invest it with new form, or to bring something to pass. In manufacturing this entails the production of finished consumer goods out of raw materials. Not only does the creator (manufacturer) bring something to pass, but it comes to pass in a new form. In much the same way, those who create rules invest things with new form and bring them to pass. In a very literal sense, moral entrepreneurs are *creators of new moralities*. But new moralities are created slowly.

The process of creating rules commences with *awareness*, defined as the time when ". . . some person or group sees a set of objective conditions as problematic, posing a danger or containing the seeds of some future difficulties" (Becker, 1966:12). This occurs substantially in advance of the time rules are created and is a precondition of that later development. As used in this definition, "seeing" means "defining." That is, a person or group attaches particular meaning to an objective state of affairs. They define it. When this occurs, the process of rule creating commences.[2]

Ostensibly, the goal of rule creators is to forestall anticipated problems or to correct conditions they experience as a problem. On relatively limited scale, these perceptions and rule-creating efforts occur when, in support of their respective interests, parents set down rules for their children, teachers set behavior standards for students in the classroom, and employers regulate the general business deportment of their employees. In each case the rule maker seeks to

2. Awareness and the assigning of problematic meaning to objective conditions does not inevitably lead to the creation of new moral rules. However, as a precondition of rule making, it may be said to be necessary without being sufficient.

prevent or correct conditions they think interfere with their interests. Though they use the same principle, the rule creators we will deal with operate on a far grander scale. They seek to translate private interests into public law and, at least in theory, have the rules apply to all persons. Deviance making is therefore an aspect of making public policy. Making deviance is an act of politics.

Given their dissatisfaction, moral entrepreneurs work for the promotion of a change in social policy. This may consist of either a call for progressive or for conservative changes. They may advocate "returning" to an earlier social condition or they may seek a progressive form of change. The dissatisfaction may be due, for example, to an increase of traffic in one's neighborhood resulting from the "wildcatting," that is, establishment, of a nude beach along the California coast. It may arise when parents see their neighborhood being invaded by adult movie houses and adult bookshops. Possibly one's dissatisfaction is based on the existing definition of rape as a sex crime rather than a crime of violence. Or it may take the form of a person who objects to the presence of "dirty books" on the shelves of the high school and town libraries. In fact, dissatisfaction arising over these and myriad other situations, commonly regarded as actual or potentially evil, immoral, or threatening conditions, underlies the work of the moral entrepreneur.

Practical Examples

The rule creator defines these conditions and those who engage in them as inimical to his or her values and/or interests. Thus, public nudity is seen to threaten the moral superiority and challenge the legitimacy of the religiously based idea that displays of the body connote sexual immodesty (Weinberg, 1957). Tramps and hippies are often seen as a threat to the security of so-called "respectable identities" and the values on which they rest (Spradley, 1970:120–121). These are matters involving conflicting life styles. The presence of "adult" theaters and bookshops in one's neighborhood is felt to invite into the neighborhood persons who threaten the sanctity of home and hearth and who pose a moral threat to naïve children. Treating rape as a sex crime rather than a crime of violence is perceived to be symbolic of the psychological, social, and political oppression of women in our society (Connell and Wilson, 1974). Heightened by press coverage, the fear associated with the commission of sex offenses leads to the belief that "women and children are in great danger in American society because serious sex crimes are very prevalent and are increasing more rapidly than any other types of crime" (Sutherland, 1950b:543). Homosexuality is regarded as incompatible with a heterosexual family and sexual bargaining system (Davis, 1971:354). And Anita Bryant sees homosexuality and other forms of unorthodox sexual behavior as threatening the entire nation, claiming that she ". . . came out of the closet to warn that if we continue to get away from God's standards, we as a nation are doomed" (*Arizona Republic*, 1978). Other behaviors, prostitution, for example, are opposed because they are defined as reprehensible in essence—they are vices (Davis, 1966:347).

In each of these examples, the problem situation consists of conflicting if not mutually exclusive values and interests. Something of great value is perceived to be threatened. On these grounds *anything* could be regarded as deviant. Like beauty, deviance is in the eye of the beholder. What is and is not regarded as loathsome, threatening, fearsome, and so on, depends on the perspective of the definer. What distinguishes menacing from nonmenacing conditions, then, is not the objective property of such things (or acts); it is the moral definition assigned to them. In the final analysis, these definitions may be as much (or more) a reflection of the definer's condition as they are of the behavior in question.

Resolving Distress: Instrumental and Symbolic Goals

Rule creators are moved by the lack of available means to solve their problem. That lack is noted by the very term "creator." Rules do not exist, or existing rules are inadequate to curb the condition they find threatening. Even though formal rules may exist, there may be no agencies—police, welfare, medical, and the like—to whom the distressed group may turn for relief. These two conditions, a sense of distress and a lack of ready means for its resolution, underlie the efforts of the moral entrepreneur. They serve as the stimulus to create new rules, alter existing rules, or in some other way set things right.

In seeking to resolve distress, moral entrepreneurs may work toward *instrumental* or *symbolic* goals (Gusfield, 1967). By instrumental is meant the direct influence of law on the actions of people. The essential element of the instrumental function of law is enforcement since, without it, such laws have little effect. As seen in the preceding paragraphs, resolution of the moral entrepreneur's concerns call for control of the behavior of people seen as a threat. Seeking relief by way of the instrumental function of law does not mean that moral entrepreneurs always seek new rules or laws. Equally important is the defense of existing rules that are under attack by threatening forces. For example, fearful of and morally opposed to the consequences of proposed changes in law, defenders of existing relatively restrictive abortion laws in this country have banded together to resist liberalization of abortion policy and defend existing law. A group opposing nude bathing in public places is also likely to be in support of existing codes. In these cases the goal of the moral entrepreneur calls for the direct use of law to serve his or her interests. On occasion, however, these same interests may best be served by working to prevent enforcement of law. For example, farmers who rely on illegal Mexican aliens ("wetbacks") as a source of cheap labor will sometimes seek to block enforcement of immigration laws, especially during harvest time when the presence of large numbers of such workers is consistent with the farmer's interests. After harvest, however, they may assume a different stance and call for more enforcement, perhaps to get rid of a group that has now become a liability (Bustamente, 1972). Instrumental use of law, then, reflects the rule creators' perceptions of their needs and interests.

At other times moral entrepreneurs have recourse to the law for its symbolic effect. This is closely linked to the fact that making deviance is part of the larger process of making public policy (politics). Seen in a conflict perspective, the symbolic function of law lies in its ability to legitimate some groups and interests at the expense of others (Gusfield, 1967:178). Moreover, even though honored only in the breach, passage or defense of legal norms (or others) reflects the distribution of power in a community. Therefore, to allow previously discredited behavior to be engaged in with impunity may be taken to mean that the power of one interest group has been succeeded by another. A concern over this issue is noted by Gusfield in his comments on efforts to legalize gambling in Boston. He notes:

> The threat to the middle class in the increased political power of Cornerville is not that the Cornerville resident will gamble more; he already does gamble with great frequency. The threat is that the law will come to accept the morality of gambling and treat it as a legitimate business. If this happens, Boston is no longer a city dominated by middle-class Yankees but becomes one dominated by lower class immigrants . . . The maintenance of a norm which defines gambling as deviant behavior thus symbolizes the maintenance of Yankee social and political superiority. Its disappearance as a public commitment would symbolize the loss of that superiority (Gusfield, 1967:181–182).

Concern for the legitimating (hence, symbolic) function of the law has also been noted with respect to the Catholic Church's position regarding homosexuality. As Simpson notes, "In addition to its clear position that homosexuality is patently inadmissable, the Catholic Church has another reason to oppress homosexuals: in order to maintain its status as a 'moral leader.' It must fight any change in attitude toward the church-state laws on homosexuality . . . or it will lose its 'moral' credibility" (Simpson, 1976:60–61).

A similar attitude exists among some attorneys and legislators for whom the absence of a law against something is equal to an official endorsement of the thing (Blaustein and Ferguson, 1957:110–111). This is known as the *declaratory argument*, according to which the repeal of a prohibitory law is seen as a public declaration that the conduct at issue is no longer considered morally wrong. That repeal of law has this effect has been challenged by the findings of a number of research studies (Walker and Argyle, 1964; Berkowitz and Walker, 1967). Nonetheless, the opinion persists in some quarters that repeal of or failure to enforce laws against marijuana, prostitution, abortion, gambling, pornographic literature, and other things is taken as an official endorsement of these things. Such contentions fail to reckon with the highly important symbolic function of law.

On occasion, it seems, the effort to create rules and expand the scope of deviance stems not from moral concerns of an instrumental or symbolic sort, but from threatening conditions faced by formal organizations. Such a case involves the Narcotics Division of the Internal Revenue Bureau in the years immediately following passage of the Harrison [narcotics] Act in 1914. Severely restricted in its field of operations, the Narcotics Division strove for growth and expansion, normal tendencies among most bureaucratic organizations. It was hampered in this by an apathetic public and an unresponsive Congress. To bring about change

> . . . the Division launched a two-pronged campaign: (1) a barrage of reports and newspaper articles which generated a substantial outcry against narcotics use, and (2) a series of Division-sponsored test cases in the courts which resulted in a reinterpretation of the Harrison Act and substantially broadened powers for the Narcotics Division. Thus the Division attained its goals by altering a weakly held public value regarding narcotics use from neutrality or slight opposition to strong opposition, and by persuading the courts that it should have increased powers (Dickson, 1968:149).

Though subject to variable interpretation (Galliher and Walker, 1977), Becker (1963) and Reasons (1974) maintain a similar campaign was waged by the Bureau of Narcotics in the 1930's in an effort to win passage of the Marijuana Tax Act in 1937. This is alleged to have again been an attempt by the bureau to rescue itself from the organizational perils of a decreasing budget and power by means of heightening public awareness of the "dangers" of marijuana use. What is most important is that these cases reflect the sometimes problematic intention of rule creators.

Holy Crusades

These comments do not preclude the idea that moral entrepreneurs are often moved by a sincere and unwavering belief that their expressed views and interests are correct and that they oppose things that are absolutely evil—evil at all times and places. As noted, belief in the objectivity of moral meanings is an important element in the social construction of reality. Some moral entrepreneurs are so convinced of the objective rightness of their position that their efforts take on elements of a *holy crusade*. That is, the rightness of their "cause" is no longer defended (if it ever was) on rational, empirical, or this-worldly bases, but is supported by scriptural and other references to supernatural entities. One is reminded of John Brown of antislavery fame who felt he had a divine mission to take vengeance against proslavery forces and effect the freedom of all enslaved blacks. Carry Nation, noted prohibitionist, was also a holy crusader. Fancying herself a messiah, standing six feet tall and weighing about 175 pounds, dressed in black and white clothing of a somewhat religious nature, and often assisted by hymn-singing women, ". . . she would march into a saloon and proceed to sing, pray, hurl biblical-sounding vituperations at the 'rummies' present, and smash bar fixtures and stock with a hatchet" (*Encyclopaedia Brittanica*, 1974:207; also see Taylor, 1966). Similarly, Anthony Comstock, noted for his lifelong fight against pornographic and salacious art and literature, is felt to have been "possessed of a curious, vague, sense of sin . . ." and a "determination to exorcise sin from the whole of the . . . environment" (*Dictionary of American Biography*, 1930:330). So pronounced was Comstock's dedication that it led to coining of the terms "comstockery," referring to the zealous purging of society of so-called obscene materials, and "comstock" for those who are so engaged. On the latter, Robert Haney comments:

> The comstocks are not merely people with intellectual theories who might be convinced by more persuasive theories; nor are they pragmatists who will be guided by the balance of power among pressure groups. Many of them are so emotionally involved in the condemnation of what they find objectionable that they find rational arguments irrelevant. They *must* suppress what is offensive in order to stabilize their own tremulous values and consciences. Panic rules

them and they cannot be calmed by discussions of legal rights, literary integrity, or artistic merit (1960:176–77).

A more contemporary example of a moral crusade is Anita Byrant's campaign against equal rights laws for homosexuals. Likening herself to Carry Nation, Bryant sees America at a moral crossroads, one path leading to a Sodom and Gomorrah, the other to a life of biblically defined moral virtue. She and her crusade are in the vanguard of those taking the latter course (*Playboy*, 1978).

Whether religiously inspired or not, the moral reform sought by many rule creators is often prompted by humanitarian impulses. An example is found in the American temperance movement. As Gusfield tells us, during the nineteenth century this movement

> . . . was part of a general effort toward the improvement of the worth of the human being through improved morality as well as economic conditions. The mixture of the religious, the equalitarian, and the humanitarian was an outstanding facet of the moral reformism of many movements (Gusfield, 1955:222–223).

The plight of the poor and women, of farmers and workers, of slaves and prison inmates, among others, concerned these reformers. Inspired by their humanitarian concerns and reinforced by notions of *noblesse oblige* and stewardship, members of the predominantly middle- and upper-class Women's Christian Temperance Union marched forth to solve the drinking problem of less fortunate folk— the lower class (Gusfield, 1955:225–226).

A Cautionary Note

A word of caution is in order. In our earlier discussion of the nature of social reality it was noted that there is no external reality, no objective meanings, to which people respond. There are only shared, socially constructed meanings. Applying that observation to banning, we are reminded that the "reality" of the threat underlying banning is as much a social product as any other aspect of reality. The threat need not be validated in objective terms; there need be no "spilling of blood" for one to fear for one's personal safety. In short, the threat may be a thing of the mind. But it may be a thing of the mind in a special sense.

A *perceived* threat can be as important for moral entrepreneurs as one that is objectively validated. Indeed, "objective facts" have no necessary bearing on the matter. Objectively similar behaviors may be defined and responded to in totally different ways. In one study

(Chambliss and Nagasawa, 1969) comparing official and unofficial delinquency statistics for white, black, and Japanese youth, it was found that self-reported (unofficial) rates for these groups were higher and more similar to one another than were the official arrest rates. The discrepancy between these rates is explained by the tendency of police to respond *not* to the behaviors per se, but to their own bias and the meanings they assign to the behavior. For example, though the actual delinquent behavior of the Japanese youth was very similar in frequency and seriousness to that of black youth, the official arrest rates for these two groups was 2 percent and 36 percent respectively. These rates reflect police acceptance of (1) the idea that Japanese youth are seldom if ever involved in illegal acts and (2) the popular notion that blacks are more prone to unlawful behavior than other racial groups.

In a more recent study, Chambliss (1973) informs us of a similar situation in which an upper-middle-class white gang and a lower-class white gang, attending the same high school and engaging in the same type and frequency of delinquent behavior, were subject to quite opposite responses from police and citizen groups. Despite being involved in a greater number of delinquent acts, the Saints (upper middle class) avoided being stopped by police. Indeed, the ". . . townspeople never perceived the Saints' high level of delinquency. The Saints were good boys who just went in for an occasional prank" (Chambliss, 1973:27). On the other hand, and despite their equally episodic involvement in delinquent forms of behavior, the Roughnecks (lower class) were subject to a very different definition; ". . . everyone agreed that the not-so-well-dressed, not-so-well-mannered, not-so-rich boys were heading for trouble" (Chambliss, 1973:27).

The differential perceptions people had of the Saints and the Roughnecks was not based on objective differences in the gangs' behavior. Rather, differences in perception stem from and reflect the bias of the police and citizens. That is, the "visibility" of the Roughnecks and the relative "obscurity" of the Saints reflects the definitions people had of these boys. Indeed, citizens and police were prepared to "see" the delinquency of one group and the innocent pranks of the other.

To the degree that perceptions influence (bias) the response of moral entrepreneurs they may be regarded as *self-fulfilling prophecies* (Chambliss and Nagasawa, 1969:76). That is, a prophecy (a definition) may be reacted to in ways that bring about its validation (Merton, 1957). In the studies reported, delinquency, when engaged in by Japanese youth or the Saints, was perceived as a prank or some other transitory, nonthreatening form of behavior. When engaged in by black or lower-class youth like the Roughnecks the probability of it being defined as persistent delinquency rose. The consequent differences in official response are reflected in arrest statistics—official data that provide "validation" of the accuracy of the original prophecy (definition). In short, the meanings of behavior are problematic. Nonetheless, as W. I. Thomas suggested long ago, once people define situations as real, they are real in their consequences.

In summary, moral entrepreneurs or rule creators are those who seek to alter the content of rules, establish new rules, or influence the enforcement of existing rules. They are initially moved by real or anticipated threats that others pose to their interests, goals, and values. The purity of their motives ranges from that of the self-seeking bootlegger who, fearing a decline in business, sanctimoniously opposes repeal of prohibition, to the genuine self-sacrifice of an Anthony Comstock, a John Brown, or a Carry Nation.

Moral Conversion

In and of themselves, the perceptions, fears, and interests of the moral entrepreneurial group are never sufficient to bring about the desired change. The "awareness" that originates with the crusader must be disseminated to and accepted by a significantly broader segment of the community. Achieving this may require the rule creator to (1) overcome the effect of contrary realities (remember, reality is multiple) and/or (2) convert persons who are neutral on the issue into supporting partisans. This means that to achieve the desired goal the moral entrepreneur may have to alter a variety of perceptual and cognitive structures. To begin with, it is likely that most people have little or no interest in the crusader's views, one way or other, and are barely cognizant of the troubling condition. Among those who are aware of the troubling condition there may be a variety of views. Some may regard the matter as a passing event; these people may be said to have *optimized* the condition. Other groups may have *neutralized* it; that is, they have accommodated to it and no longer define it as deviant. Others may have *normalized* the matter to the point that it is perceived as "normal though unusual." In contrast to these cognitive structures, the would-be rule creator *pessimizes* the situation in that the evil vested in the matter is so great that it may not be tolerated (Rubington and Weinberg, 1973:31). In short, the moral entrepreneur must work to bring individual and collective perceptions into line with his own.

Should rule creators succeed to any significant degree, they may look forward to change in public policy consistent with their interests. Awareness, then, must be extended to others to bring about individual and collective "moral conversion." Though the scope of this effort may vary, it is necessary in order to create the desired moral environment. Another term for this is *legitimacy*, the achievement of a public, legal, and authorized status. In itself, achieving legitimacy is part of the process of constructing reality—of changing the official or public moral meanings of things and altering the applicable rules.

Legitimacy is a critical need. To be effective in any ultimate sense, rule makers must appeal to people's sense of propriety. When rules are approved by members of one's reference group they are likely to be obeyed and those who violate them will likely be sanctioned. This means that people tend to follow rules and rule makers they think have a right to rule, that is, have legitimacy. This tendency has been referred to as the *rule of law.*

> The phrase [rule of law] is useful to describe the willingness of a people to accept and order their behavior according to the rules and procedures which are prescribed by political and social institutions . . . and enforced, when necessary, either by those bodies or by other institutions such as governors, police, and courts. The "rule of law" expresses the idea that people recognize the legitimacy of the law as a means of ordering and controlling the behavior of *all* people in a society, the governors and the governed, the rich and the poor, the contented and the discontented (National Commission on Violence, 1970:8–9).

Achieving this legitimacy is part of the enterprise of deviance. To have rules promulgated that will have legitimacy assigned them seems first to require the transformation of *personal troubles* into *public issues.* C. Wright Mills distinguishes between troubles and issues as follows:

> *Troubles* occur within the character of the individual and within the range of his immediate relations with others; they have to do with his self and with those limited areas of social life of which he is directly and personally aware. . . . A trouble is a private matter; values cherished by an individual are felt by him to be threatened. . . . *Issues* have to do with matters that transcend these local environments of the individual and the range of his inner life. They have to do with the . . . institutions of an historical society as a whole, with the ways various milieus overlap and interpenetrate to form the larger structure of social and historical life. An issue is a public matter: some value cherished by publics is felt to be threatened (Mills, 1959:8–9).

For Mills, the critical element is whether the situation has personal or institutional roots. What is important for our purposes is the enlargement of the private trouble to the point that it comes to be defined as a public issue. Enlargement consists principally of moral entrepreneurs seeking to raise levels of consciousness and win adherents to their perspective, a tactic well institutionalized among advocates of women's liberation. This process consists of converting occurrences into public events. Essentially private matters are rendered "experience" for great numbers of people (Molotch and Lester, 1974:103). This transformation is achieved by the dissemination of meanings and their acceptance by an audience. As a subaspect of banning, dissemination of meanings and broadening of social awareness deserves extended comment.

To disseminate these meanings calls for the moral entrepreneur's views to be at a high degree of visibility. Public visibility and the opportunity to broadcast one's views is extremely critical; one's claim to legitimacy hangs in the balance. Prior to the advent of modern mass communication techniques, particularly the electronic media, dissemination of a perspective to a nation of millions was a monumental task. Such was the case in nineteenth-century China when moral entrepreneurs sought to eliminate the centuries-old custom of binding the feet of young Chinese girls. The goal was to convert an erotic custom long held in esteem to one regarded with disdain and to have rules established banning the practice. One means used to circulate the desired meanings and challenge the customary definitions was poetry and song. These were designed to appeal to the emotions. One popular poem, written by a natural-footed poetess was as follows:

> Three-inch bowed shoes were non-existent in ages before,
> And Great Kuanyin has two bare feet for one to adore.
> I don't know when this custom began;
> It must have been started by a despicable man (Levy, 1966:68).

In addition, essays and tracts, widely circulated and addressed to the masses, extolled the virtues of the unbound foot. Adding to the impact of these efforts was the influence of posters, placards, slogans, and critical catchwords. These things were distributed by the million. Being easily recalled and repeatable, they became highly popular. Some examples:

> One pair of bound feet, but two cisterns of tears.

or,

Once feet are bound so small,
Such effort to do any work at all!

and

Once feet to a sharp point are bound,
The woman's cries to Heaven resound (Levy, 1966:86).

To be sure, the impact of such effort was centered largely in urban places and their immediate rural surroundings, places easily reached by existing means of communication. Yet out of these efforts came the eventual emancipation of the female Chinese foot.

Role of the Media

Like his nineteenth-century counterpart, today's moral crusader also faces the task of bringing his message before large audiences. Though aided by the tools of the mass communications industry, contemporary entrepreneurs are confronted by problems unique to the present. Despite these, use of the media provides a degree of visibility not otherwise available. Daily newspaper circulation in the United States is estimated at over 60 million and Sunday newspaper circulation exceeds 50 million (*World Almanac and Book of Facts*, 1977:428). It is estimated that over 20 million Americans read weekly news magazines (Haselden, 1968:57). Television sets in use in 1970 exceeded 60 million (U.S. Bureau of the Census, 1972:254). Overall, Americans are estimated to average thirty-five hours of exposure per week to media of all sorts (Heselden, 1968:59). It is in terms of such facts that the word "visibility" must be understood.

The initial problem, of course, is whether or not the media will deign to consider or carry the matter. In this sense it is essential to recall that the establishment of a public definition of a thing as a problem involves the interaction of various interest groups. Not the least influential of these groups is the media industry itself and those persons and groups with whom media officials identify. In light of this, access to the media often requires negotiation between media and other interest groups and the moral entrepreneur.

Under the influence of their own interests and those of the groups with whom they identify, media officials authoritatively protect access to these many organs. They promote one social reality often at the expense of others. Therefore, though all parties to a conflict may regard their position as the most valid, it is a virtual certainty that not all views will have equal access to the media. Some may have no access at all.

Research clearly demonstrates that information carried by the media is neither randomly selected nor all-inclusive. A study of sound-on-film stories carried by one major West Coast television station revealed that military, county, and city officials (public information representatives) were involved in 34.5 percent of the stories; other public officials were involved in 29 percent of the stories; spokesmen for private interests were involved in 16.5 percent; public relations workers accounted for 12.5 percent; and independent citizens were involved in only 7.5 percent of the stories (Althiede, 1974:294).

In short, access to the media seems assured for some groups, while others are systematically and purposely excluded. Information supportive of some group's interests may be excluded because it is perceived to be incompatible with the interests of media officials and other significant interest groups. Further, for practical reasons associated with the management of the news business, information vital to the goals and interests of crusaders is seen in opposite terms by newsworkers (Althiede, 1976:112ff). Exclusion, of course, does not mean groups are without recourse. "News" is as important to the newsworkers as it is to the newsmaker (crusader). That fact, together with a variety of tactics, makes it possible for moral entrepreneurs to strategize to gain access to the media.

Managing the Media

Access to the media and visibility, though necessary, is not sufficient to bring about legitimacy. For example, depending upon how the media present the issue, the legitimacy of the entrepreneur's claim may be enhanced or diminished. Of particular importance is the sequence in which the pros and cons of an issue are presented, the amount of coverage given an issue, and the orientations of those reporting the "facts." By altering these elements, the constructed image of an issue may be varied and the desired definition (meaning) effected. Through variations in visual and auditory stimuli it is possible to increase or decrease the likelihood that a potential audience will perceive a situation as consistent with or inimical to recognized standards or principles. For example,

Among . . . ways in which the media influence legitimacy is the pointed inclusion or exclusion of certain ostensibly critical pieces of factual information. Thus, if a news article reports that a study has shown deafening noise levels in a residential area near an airport, a reporter, or an editor, may make a point of interviewing a resident who does not mind the noise. Or if the community group has asked an expert to represent them at a hearing, a delegitimizing point may be made merely by giving the information that the expert does not live in the affected area. Legitimacy may be created, in a similar manner, by following up a press conference, e.g., about rising unemployment, with man-on-the-street interviews at the lines in front of a state unemployment compensation office (Ross and Staines, 1972:22).

Additional ways to influence legitimacy include the use of emotionally loaded words or, in the case of television, emotionally loaded visual images, and selectively linking or dissociating a cause and existing positive social values.

Douglas, Rasmussen, and Flanagan demonstrate these points when they note the effort of a group of nude bathers to resist the attempt by beach-front property owners to have their behavior declared unlawful (to delegitimize it). This effort was substantially aided by the nature of television news coverage. "The nude bathers got a great press, especially great TV coverage, partly because they carefully controlled what was presented, . . . and partly because almost all of the newsmen and women who covered the beach were favorable to its existence before and after coverage (Douglas, Rasmussen, and Flanagan, 1977:199). These researchers also note that the politically astute moral entrepreneur (which is the role the nude bathers were playing) will make use of any prior information concerning the ideological predispositions of media personnel:

> Most of the feature news coverage of the nude beach can be
> seen in the major filming and airing done by one of the net-
> work affiliates. The . . . reporter in charge of this pro-
> gramming had done a small program on Cliff Beach earlier,
> so it was known by the beach organizers that he was basi-
> cally sympathetic or, at least, libertarian about the whole
> thing. They [the nude bathing advocates] had decided at one
> of their meetings that they should try to get some more fa-
> vorable coverage on the beach and that the reporter was the
> man to approach. They got hold of him and arranged to let
> him have an exclusive on their side of the story if he'd do it
> (Douglas, Rasmussen and Flanagan, 1977:200).

Manipulating the media to further enhance their legitimacy, some members of the nude bathing group collected trash that lay strewn about the beach and arranged it neatly in sacks. When the sacks were filmed by the TV cameramen, the general scene of cleanliness provided an image connoting the nude bathers' ecological awareness and sensitivity to "nature." Though nude bathing is hardly an ecological issue, the two interests at least may be shown to be compatible. Potential opposition from ecology groups is thereby neutralized.

Skillful manipulation of camerapersons also avoided display of possibly damaging materials: display of nude males with erections, the sexual parts of voluptuous females, or any of the casual or heavy sex (heterosexual or homosexual) that occasionally occurs on the beaches. On the other hand, film of ". . . a lovely young nude mother with long, flowing blonde hair, bending over her toddler in the shallow water, with the sun a little behind her to produce a sparkling halo effect on film . . . and . . . no pubis shot to get it banned by the censor (Douglas, Rasmussen, and Flanagan, 1977:201)" greatly enhanced the image desired by nude bathers; no direct link was made between nude bathing and orgiastic sex, and nudity and motherhood were shown to be quite compatible.

In much the same way, binding of the Chinese girl's feet was linked to select values. Of significance was the effort to define footbinding as contrary to laws of nature as well as a symbol of the oppression and punishment undeservedly heaped upon women. Footbinding was proclaimed to be an evil crippler of women, a condition that intensified the misery of the poor, raised the infanticide rate, made women dependent and reduced their effectiveness as mothers and homemakers, and reduced their intellectual activities (Levy, 1966:77–78). Emancipation of the female foot was also defined as an obstruction to China's entry into the mainstream of world commerce and the modern age. As this economic goal increased in favor, footbinding, symbolic of cultural stagnation, lost favor (Levy, 1966:76–77). Finally, the unbound female foot came to be associated with the liberation of Chinese women in general. In the case of both nude bathing and footbinding, then, the association of the moral entrepreneur's position or goal with other major values—ecology, motherhood, infanticide, poverty, economic growth, national prestige—of both a positive and negative sort proved critical in the effort to win support of others or to preclude effective opposition.

In addition to aligning their own cause with positive values, moral entrepreneurs try to associate the opposition with negative values. In this way the moral entrepreneur tries to denigrate opponents; success assures at least a relative increase in one's own moral legitimacy. To follow our account of nude bathers and beach-front property owners, the latter were cast in the position of wanting to control public beaches for their private interests. Among people living in increasingly densely populated urban areas, such an image can have a negative effect, as it did in this case. So, too, did the image of property owners as reactionaries seeking to repress the enthusiasm and freedom of youth. Skillful use of these themes, together with upstaging the property owners by airing the nude bathers' views earlier and more extensively, so damaged the position of the property owners that they abandoned their effort to present their position through the media, chosing instead to work privately through local governmental functionaries and the courts (Douglas, Rasmussen, and Flanagan, 1977:204-205).

A Cautionary Note

Because it is easy to overstate the impact of the mass media on their audience a word of caution is in order. It is rarely the case that the media convert "puritans" into "hedonists," or that members of an audience are transformed in any substantial ideological way. Nor is it maintained that the media by themselves are able to construct social reality. Nonetheless, the way information is presented, particularly the manipulation of the variables mentioned earlier, may readily give credibility to one set of meanings at the expense of alternatives. As Shaw (1969:126) notes, in a heterogeneous society, *public* expression of morality on any issue reflects a range of attitudes and these attitudes have a modality. By careful engineering, media officials may present an issue so as to place it within or beyond the limits of that modality. While presenting "facts" they simultaneously eschew or espouse perspectives, ideologies, and behaviors. Further, the simple act of withholding contrary perspectives or information may add to (or detract from) the legitimacy or credibility of publicized meanings. The importance of this effort is seen in that "Not only is a symbolic environment created within the society, but personal actions take their referent from that environment. Indeed, the construction of a conceptual reality is also the creation of a social reality of actions and events" (Quinney, 1975:262). Taken together, these matters are all part of what makes deviance an "enterprise."

Obtaining Respectability: Alliances, Testimonials, and Endorsements

To promote their legitimacy rule creators may use other means than manipulating the media. Of great importance to moral entrepreneurs is their public image. For example, an image of humanitarianism is preferred to one of self-seeking. To enlarge on their acceptability they may seek prestige and respectability from others who may be enlisted in their cause. Obtaining this respectability serves to (1) enhance the moral stature of the proposed goal of the crusader and (2) further reduces any question of the legitimacy of the crusading group itself. En toto, such conditions promote the goal of moral conversion.

Alliances

One method of achieving this respectability involves "borrowing" it from existing moral leaders, for example, the charismatic type. To this end moral entrepreneurs may seek to establish alliances or otherwise affiliate with significant persons or groups in the community. This sometimes results in great promotional benefits. Perhaps the most common expression of this is the use of notables' names on the letterhead stationery of special interest groups.

Alliances may also be formed between existing groups. Such a case is the Religious Coalition for Abortion Rights (RCAR), representing twenty-three Protestant and Jewish religious groups, established in January, 1976, in response to the antiabortion rights campaign announced in late 1975 by the National Conference of Catholic Bishops. Members of the RCAR hold the view that the abortion controversy is being fueled by religious beliefs, whereas the right of abortion is a matter of privacy and personal freedom guaranteed by the U.S. Constitution. Operating as a unit, these twenty-three groups, with support from substantial numbers of their respective memeberships, seek a level of legitimacy and respectability, and a degree of influence on lawmaking bodies unavailable to them as single entities, but that collectively may be sufficient to counter the influence and authoritative position of the National Conference of Catholic Bishops (*Unitarian Universalist World*, 1976:1–2).

The antifootbinding crusade in nineteenth-century China was substantially aided by the authority and respectability of Christian missionaries who sternly discouraged the practice among their followers, even to the point of accepting only persons with unbound feet as members of the church (Levy, 1966:75). In still another instance, Edwin Sutherland (1950a:142ff) has informed us of the association between psychiatrists and groups seeking enactment of sex psychopath laws. Given their publicly acknowledged expertise and usually unquestioned authority on the "mental pathology" underlying sex crimes, the instrumental role of psychiatrists in that movement is hardly surprising. However, Sutherland notes, too, that passage of these laws is consistent with and promotes the professional interests of psychiatrists. Each of these cases reminds us that creating deviance (like constructing reality in general) is an interactional process, the behavior of the principals being influenced to a large extent by their self-interest.

Testimonials and Endorsements

Moral entrepreneurs may also seek to enhance their image and that of their "cause" by the use of testimonials and endorsements. In Arizona, for example, where copper mining and smelting is a leading and influential industry, recent conflict centered about the ecological consequences of these activities. An innovation in the battle involved the mine association hiring a well-known and highly popular professional athlete to do spot TV ads supporting mining, the industry's contribution to the state (taxes plus primary and secondary payrolls), and its costly effort to curb all ecologically questionable practices. The athlete's lack of expertise in mining and ecology was compensated for by his popularity and his posing in the ads as a concerned citizen who was "just trying to get the facts," a position with which many confused but concerned citizens could readily identify. In this way the mine association's goals were pursued and perhaps promoted by, first, the status-conferring function of the media, second, by having their activities linked to the economic vitality of the entire state, and finally, by the support of esteemed "opinion shapers" in the local area.

In some instances moral entrepreneurs have less need of outside endorsement. This is particularly so when the crusader has an already-existing public image providing credibility and legitimacy and that may be used to heighten the visibility of the crusade. Such appears to have been the case when Anita Bryant launched her campaign against a Dade County, Florida, ordinance forbidding discrimination against homosexuals in jobs and housing. Miss Bryant's public image, a consequence of her long-term role as a TV salesperson for Florida orange juice and enhanced by her status as a "born again Christian," undoubtedly gave added impetus to her effort, not the least consequence of which was her ability to attract the attention of national media, amplify a local issue, and place it in a more global perspective (Hacker, 1977; *National Observer*, 1977).

Legitimacy and prestige (to say nothing of visibility) may be further enhanced by endorsement of a crusade by public officials. As self-proclaimed defenders of their constituent's views, officials may be expected to be aware of the limits of public morality. Endorsement of a position by officials, then, may be taken as *prima facie* evidence of its legitimacy. Causes based on contrary views are thereby denied some legitimacy and the goal of moral conversion is promoted. Efforts by administrators of philanthropic goals to have their programs endorsed by public officials are neither wasted nor accidental.

In addition, official endorsement may be expected to promote dissemination via the media and, simultaneously, to limit the opposition's access to the media. According to William Wilde's analysis of news organizations, "News is what officials say and do. The more sensational the more newsworthy. Even . . . outrageous charges go unanalyzed. Unsubstantiated statements go unquestioned. They are given the status of news as the media prints them without further comment or analysis" (Wilde, 1969:186). Furthermore, preempting the opposition is achieved by public officials controlling and engineering the flow of information to the media and by making their comments appear to be official pronouncements. Thereby they overwhelm and delegitimize alternative perspectives.

Examples of this are wide-ranging. In 1971

> President Nixon's bitter anti-busing statement was circulated to millions . . . by newspapers, radio and television. But it went almost unnoticed that the very next day the school superintendent of Harrisburg, Pa. (Dr. D. H. Porter), refuted the Nixon position point by point, in an account of the actual experience of that city.
>
> This was a classic demonstration of the extent to which the American press—print and electronic—merely react to the statements of important officials rather than trying to make an independent judgment on the facts. Mr. Nixon's distortions were trumpeted in headlines, because he is President; the facts put forward by Dr. David H. Porter were ignored, because he was not "newsworthy" enough (Wicker, 1971).

In 1976 then secretary of State Henry A. Kissinger seems also to have used his superior official position in an effort to defuse and reduce the impact of the information being revealed by the investigation of the House Select Committee on Intelligence into covert aspects of American foreign policy. Among the obstacles placed in the path of the Committee by Kissinger was "leaking" to the press embarrassing stories about the Committee (Latham, 1976:70). By embarrassing the Committee and its Chairman, Congressman Otis Pike, the Committee's work became at least as suspect as the very activities it was investigating.

It should be noted that these efforts are often aided by the tactic of *advocacy journalism* on the part of the media. By this tactic the traditional roles of "critical questioner" and "investigative journalist" are exchanged for that of "advocate." With advocacy journalism comes the tendency for media to boost "good causes" without a comparable tendency to attack "bad causes" (Ross and Staines, 1972:24). By definition, it seems, by this tactic whatever is presented by the media is "good."

Finally, acquiring the support of respected and prestigious figures may enhance the image of the moral entrenpreneur's goals by reason of *transfer of authority* (Lowry and Rankin, 1969:254). As a result of this process, ideas achieve increased legitimacy by their author being associated with admired or respected others, such as esteemed professionals, public figures, and the like. Social psychological experiments reveal that attitude change (which is what banning may require) is likely to increase if the communicator of a new idea is identified as a member of a prestigious group; as a consequence, the entire group is likely looked upon as being in support of the idea (Secord and Backman, 1964:128). Studies also reveal that negatively labeled proposals have less chance of acceptance than those with liked or prestigious labels attached, even when the substance of the proposal is the same (Newcomb, 1950:235–239).

Myth Making

To this point we have noted that banning involves (1) bringing the views of the moral crusader to the attention of the community, (2) having them endorsed and legitimized by public officials and others in positions of authority and respectability, and (3) avoiding the detractive effort of the opposition. Acceptance of the moralist's view, however, does not depend solely on the appeal of abstract statements and claims. As noted in discussing the media, it is necessary for these views to be made part of the public morality already shared by those to whom the appeal is made. At the very least, there must be some agreement between the social reality being promoted by the moralist and that of the audience. The crusader's position must appear to be compatible with others' thoughts and feelings. The values, interests, and fears of the moral entrepreneur, as well as the "new morality" to be created, must be woven into the fabric of the reality already possessed by his or her listeners. To achieve this unification, moral entrepreneurs may employ myth.

The term *myth* is used to refer to the constructed stories that serve to explain the problematic events in question and that seek to cast these events in counterinstitutional terms. Sometimes these stories are *etiologic;* that is, they seek to deal with the supposed causes of the troubling phenomenon. Too, the "evildoer" is often portrayed in counterinstitutional terms, as one opposed to symbols and values embraced by the community, as one who seeks to undermine the vitality of fundamental moral precepts. Two examples of such myths are those of *white slavery* and the *dope fiend.*

White Slavery

In speaking of the history of public agitation against prostitution, Charles Reasons notes that the myth of white slavery emerged out of the flood of popular antiprostitution literature circulated around the turn of the century. According to the myth of white slavery, "prostitution was . . . a consequence of a class of merchants of flesh who obtained innocent, unsophisticated girls of foreign extraction, often underage, by false pretense, drugs and coercion" (Reasons, 1970:5). In this myth behaviors and persons are explicitly cast in opposition to premarital chastity, the purity of womanhood, and the sanctity of home and hearth. Viewed from the perspective of public morality dominant during the late 1890's and early 1900's, one who sytematically violated these values, especially for profit, could expect only the most severe condemnation. This myth, generated and spread by countless muckrakers and other moralists who published antiprostitution books and tracts, played an important part of incorporating the aims of reformers into public policy, of linking the "new" and the existing moralities. This was a vital element in a vigorous campaign to eliminate prostitution.

The "Dope Fiend" Mythology

Myth has also been employed in the effort to establish prohibitions against addictive drugs. In this situation, termed the "dope fiend" mythology by Alfred Lindesmith (1940), the alleged deviant is cast in the model of a totally discreditable person whose behavior is without redeeming virtue. Consistent with the stereotype that addicts are criminals independent of narcotic drug law violations, the myth provides materials (anecdotes, stories, and so on) supportive of a variety of labels used to refer to addicts: dope-crazed killer, dope fiend rapist, moral degenerate, thief, and liar are a few such terms. The myth also alleges that addicts have a "positive mania" to convert others to drug addiction. The myth also points to the insidiousness of drugs: the use of drugs, even of a mild sort, is said to result in an inevitable progression to the use of stronger drugs and that over time there is a need to gradually enlarge the dose. Finally, drug use is hailed as a certain path to moral degeneracy, debauchery, and the like. This supposedly irreversible process has been referred to as "the path to demoralization and despair (Horton and Leslie, 1965:565)."

Many of these same values, supplemented by visual imagery, appear in motion pictures of the 1930's and 1940's such as "Tell Your

Children" (also known as "Reefer Madness"), "Marihuana," and "Assassin of Youth." In the first of these, Bill and his sweetheart Mary, a "model young couple" symbolizing the innocence of high school youth, fall victim to the blandishments of two unscrupulous drug peddlers and the evil effects of marihuana. Under the spell of the drug, the unsuspecting Bill becomes a moral weakling and allows himself to be seduced by the evil addict, Blanche. Mary and her younger brother Jimmy are also caught up in the debauchery; Mary is accidentally shot and killed. As befits peddlers of the insidious weed, one is killed and the other is adjudged insane. Their female accomplice, Blanche, commits suicide, while the once innocent Bill survives, but his life is wrecked. Thus it is demonstrated in graphic terms that in various ways marihuana destroys the life of all who have contact with it; debauchery, crime, murder, and suicide await the unsuspecting (Look, 1938). Today these films are advertised and perceived by the general public as camp art. Interestingly, however, the same message was regarded as objective truth by an earlier generation. Such are the dynamics of social reality.

The values stressed in these films find expression elsewhere, though perhaps not in so dramatic a fashion. For example, Stuart L. Hills has noted the Federal Bureau of Narcotics' reliance on several American values in its effort to secure passage of the Marijuana Tax Act of 1937.

> In its publicity campaign, the bureau could appeal to a number of traditional societal values . . . it could emphasize humanitarian values as well as those stressing the importance of self control, by portraying the bureau's efforts as preventing persons from becoming "enslaved" to drugs and protecting them from their own weakness. It could further appeal to the values of the "Protestant ethic," which disdains "ecstasy" and pleasure when deliberately sought as ends in themselves rather than as by-products of achievement and work (Hills, 1971:70).

Using the term "ideology," Sutherland found similar materials in popular literature being used to support formulation and passage of sex psychopath laws. Contained in the ideology were several ideas: (1) women and children were in grave and immediate danger at the hands of "crazed psychopaths," (2) such offenses were committed most often by "degenerates" and "sex psychopaths" who (3) are unable to control themselves because of their mental condition, (4) this mental state renders them identifiable as potential offenders, (5) nonetheless, these offenders should be punished and never be free to inflict harm on others, (6) at least not until they are fully cured, and

(7) the care and treatment of these people should be the concern of psychiatrists, the professionals best equipped to deal with them (Sutherland, 1950b:543–544). Unfortunately, Sutherland stated, each of these ideas was factually false or questionable.

Myths vs. Truth

Sutherland's contention concerning the falsity of these ideas raises a critical issue concerning ideology and myth. The content of these myths is often attacked on the basis of the claim that they have limited validity or that they distort reality (viewed as an objective condition). For example, there likely are cases wherein unsuspecting girls have been drawn into prostitution by deception, and cases of persons having been involved in systematic law violations prior to becoming addicted to drugs. That is, there are cases that conform to the elements of these myths. But so, too, can we find cases reflecting a quite different set of conditions. Some women are recruited to prostitution on wholly rational (for example, economic) grounds (Fairfield, 1959). Such is the case of a university co-ed who entered prostitution quite voluntarily. For her, the income earned by prostitution far exceeded what she could earn otherwise and made the difference between a student life free of financial worries and one of an economically marginal sort (Williams, 1974:1). Turning to the "dope fiend" mythology, qualified observers note that a substantial number of practicing physicians are drug addicts (Hessler, 1974:146–147). In 1967 the Federal Bureau of Narcotics estimated the incidence of addiction among U.S. physicians at about 1 for every 867 doctors but only 1:3,228 for the general population (*American Druggist*, 1968). Others have placed the rate of physician addiction as high as 2.5 percent (Hessler, 1974:147). Despite this, it is maintained, most addicted physicians fulfill their professional and community obligations without difficulty. Indeed, in that regard, some researchers have reported addict physicians to be more successful than the average nonaddict physician (Winick, 1964:264; Hessler, 1974:150).

Resolution of what appear to be contradictions between myth and fact is often of concern to those who seek an objective "truth." However, from the perspective of the social definition model, these efforts to resolve "contradictions" are irrelevant in that they obscure the point that myths and the specific charges they contain are dimensions of meaning. What is regarded as "invalid" and a "distortion of reality" by one group is likely to be an expression of another group's sense of reality. What is needed is not a substitution of one construction of reality for another, that of the social scientist, for example, replacing that of the crusader. Rather, as David Matza (1969) states, it is incumbent on students of society to take an "apprecia-tional" stance. This means one must be sensitive to the experience and values of those involved in the situation, the moral crusader as well as others. This calls for a faithful rendering of the phenomenon. To "appreciate" in this sense does not require the social scientist to agree or disagree with the views of crusaders or others. His goal is to understand, ". . . to comprehend and to illuminate the subject's view and to interpret the world *as it appears to him*" (Matza. 1969:25). Again, the Thomas theorum applies (see page 131).

An appreciational perspective helps us to see that notions of "va-lidity" and "distortion" have little to do with the utility of these myths. In this regard it is important to recall that the deviance pro-cess involves defining behavior and actors as discreditable. The aim is to incriminate, to discredit, to control, and to stigmatize, perhaps for symbolic reasons or perhaps to legitimize "treatment" of the alleged deviant. At the banning stage of the process, efforts to fac-tually validate the characterizations of the deviant actor and his or her behavior seem unneccessary. If any justification for incrimina-tion is needed it is provided by the *meaning of the actor's behavior.* Taking the immorality of the behavior for granted leads to perceiv-ing the actor as a discreditable person. As we shall note later, to engage in deviance means one is devious; that is, one's behavior serves as the justification for assigning characterological traits (Matza, 1969:157). The assigned characterizations serve to justify ex-isting (read: appropriate) treatment. In other words, these myths serve to justify (1) the proposed moral environment. (2) the distribu-tion of authority, (3) the proposed disposition of the deviant, and (4) the moral superiority of the nondeviant (crusader). In this regard, myths serve the same symbolic purpose served by rules in general.

One final example of this is found in the media wherein images are arranged and presented so as to "fit" an acceptable world view and a prior existing set of meanings (social reality). Berelson and Salter (1946) long ago noted the consistent distinction in character-ization of heroes and villians portrayed in fiction. Heroes were con-sistently white, Anglo-Saxon, Protestant types, while villians, fools, and other denigrative roles were played by minority group persons and foreigners. Such imagery fits well into an existing world view in which virtue is held to be the exclusive property of the politically dominant group, while all other groups are defined as subordinate. Such imagery neatly divides the world into "good guys" and "bad guys." Further, such images and myths are constructed so as to sup-port the claim that "what is is right," or to otherwise support the claim of the moral entrepreneur. To the degree that the validity of these myths and images is taken for granted and acted upon, our public life is shaped by them. Myths *may* therefore be self-validating. They serve to legitimate the institutional activities called for by the moral entrepreneur.

In concluding these remarks about myths and myth making, it should be noted that these images and meanings are not born full-blown. Rather, they are the consequence of the accumulation of countless individual utterances, definitions, and meanings, each of which is originally private and subjective. Rather than being a consciously sought goal, the myth is constructed of highly specific meanings reflecting the perceptions and interpretations of people who are strategically located (such as having access to the media) so as to influence "official" reality.[3] This accumulation results in a kind of "semantic amalgamation" whereby utterances that bear reasonable similarity are lumped together. By stages, each of which entails progressively higher levels of abstraction, people create subuniverses of meaning (Berger and Luckmann, 1967:85ff). As elements within these subuniverses of meaning, myths take on the autonomous character of the larger bodies of meaning. As a result of increasing abstraction and autonomy, the "knowledge" involved—that whoring is never voluntary, that being addicted to drugs precludes playing legitimate roles simultaneously, or that the Mafia survives on the basis of a code of silence called "omerta" (Bell, 1965:138–141; Anderson 1968:369ff)—becomes separated from the social conditions out of which it develops. This knowledge takes on a "life of its own" and very often is regarded as an accurate, valid reflection of "what's out there." It is reified, becoming objective and independent of individual consciousness. As noted earlier, the meaning and definitions we attach to things (part of the myths) move from a subjective to an objective status. Myth making is an expression of this tendency.

Power

A crucial element in the banning process is power. As noted earlier, deviance is intimately bound to politics. It involves making and enforcing public policy. In an attempt to influence the content of public policy, moral entrepreneurs seek to translate their values and interests into rules (laws) that may be applied to the population at

3. As a case in point, it is now conceded that the events comprising Watergate were not unique in American political life. What led to the *public event* known as Watergate, including the meanings assigned to its components, was the work of the media. Thus, in the hands of several media personalities, conceptually discrete events were linked and given the name "Watergate." As Altheide has noted, ". . . Nixon fell from power because the news perspective transformed the series of events known as Watergate into a whole, which was then used as evidence of corruption and immorality" (Altheide, 1976:159).

large. However, to have one's definition of reality declared to be "official" is not achieved without regard to power, particularly the power to influence the legal (rule-making) process. An appreciation of this aspect of banning calls for an examination of the role of power and of the state in the rule-making enterprise.[4]

Attempts to control others' behavior are widespread in any society. Most of this effort is confined to informal techniques of control: gossip, ridicule, ostracism, and various corporal punishments. These techniques have proven highly effective under specific circumstances such as those of a small, homogenous community, neighborhood, or family setting where primary-group relationships prevail. But in a highly impersonal urban society where members' contacts are limited in time and lack depth, and where pluralism prevails, the informal and individualized application of labels and other control techniques is hardly effective in curbing offensive behavior. For that reason, to be effective, contemporary moral crusaders must ultimately have recourse to the state, where the "signification of deviance become a specialized and protected function . . . The main substance of that state function is the authorized ordaining of activities and persons as deviant and thus making them suitable objects of surveillance and control" (Matza, 1969:145). Access to this state apparatus may be achieved either by direct exercise of power by the moral entrepreneur or on the basis of one's ability to influence those who do have power—influence them to act in accord with the crusader's goals.

Power, Law, and Deviance

The final transformation of values and interests into rules, and their enforcement and administration, is the responsibility of public officials, including police, prosecuting attorneys, court judges, legislators, as well as various standing and ad hoc administrative agencies, such as the Federal Communications Commission, the Securities Exchange Commission, the Federal Aeronautics Administration. Each group has the responsibility of regulating some specialized activity and, as deemed necessary, may engage in the deviance-making enterprise. In ordinary terms, it is these functionaries who ultimately decide what behaviors are officially labeled deviant and which are not. They decide how zealously rules will be enforced and to which groups the rules will apply. Variation in these activities —in the formulation, enforcement, and administration of law—

4.   We must distinguish between power and authority, the latter being a publicly acknowledged *right* to assert control over others. Authority is what distinguishes the passage of prohibition laws by a legislative assembly from the tavern-busting behavior of a Carry Nation.

have led to law being defined as ". . . an instrument for furthering the interests of certain groups within society" (Shaskolsky, 1973:295).

Contrary to the idea that law is a human expression of some divine command or that law serves the purposes of an abstraction like "justice," law is an expression of the values and interests of groups able to influence the actions of the legal role players mentioned. In a politically dynamic, pluralistic society such as ours, the class, ethnic, occupational, cultural, or other interest group that wins the day in the political marketplace is the one with the greater power. In short, banning behavior is a result of the interaction between legal functionaries and representatives of interests, with power being the critical variable.

Working with these same factors, Richard Quinney (1969) has formulated an interest theory of law consisting of four propositions. First, Quinney defines law as the ". . . creation and interpretation of specialized rules in a politically organized society [the state]" (Quinney, 1969:26). By this definition, law is a "way of doing something," it is a kind of action (Quinney, 1970:36–37). Law is not simply a means of social control. Nor is it limited to an abstract body of rules contained in statute books. Rather, *law is a process.* It is an integral part of society in that it arises out of as well as influences society. It arises out of the dynamic character of society in which interest groups compete and conflict with one another for public and official favor. Likewise, law influences these interacts; it is a factor that groups must consider when dealing with one another. Law provides at least the rough boundaries of legitimate group interaction. Most important,

> . . . law is one of the methods in which *public policy* is formulated and administered for governing the lives and activities of the inhabitants of the state. As an act of politics, law does not represent the norms and values of all persons in the society. Legal decisions, rather, incorporate the interests of only some persons. Whenever a law is created or interpreted, the values of some are necessarily assured and the values of others are either ignored or negated (Quinney, 1969:27).

The making and interpreting of laws are acts of politics. This is the politicality of law.

Second, Quinney, notes that "politically organized society is based on an interest structure" (Quinney, 1969:27). By this he means that the state (a politically organized society) is influenced by the interests of certain constituent groups, specifically, those who are equipped to command. This leads to his third proposition: "the interest structure of politically organized society is characterized by unequal distribution of power and by conflict" (Quinney, 1969:28). This means that not all segments of society are equally well situated or equipped to command—to have their interests incorporated into public policy. They do not all have equal amounts of or access to power. Since interest groups have differing amounts of power and conflict with one another, power and conflict become critical factors in the politics of deviance. It is out of the interplay of such differentially situated and equipped groups that public policy emerges. Quinney's fourth proposition is that "law is formulated and administered within the interest structure of a politically organized society" (Quinney, 1969:29). This proposition follows from the fact that it is the groups with the greatest power that are able to influence policy makers. We thus come full circle: law is a way of doing something— it is a way of controlling segments of the society who threaten dominant interest groups. In answer to the question "which groups have the ability to create deviance?" one is inclined to answer "those with the clout!"

The idea that law is a means of control deserves further explication. As used here, "control" refers not only to direct control of some groups by others, as, for example, by exerting coercive force upon people and the exercise of violence. In addition, "law as control" also refers to the legitimizing capacity of the law. As Turk (1976:281) notes, "those definitions of the real, the true, and the worthy given legal expression or approval are thereby given the support of what is not only one of the most prestigious cultural structures, but also that structure most directly supported by the apparatus of political control." In short, by having power, groups are better able to employ the dignity of law to legitimize their interests at the expense of others.

Defining Power

Given these considerations and the model of society within which we are working, how may we define power? Following Dennis H. Wrong, power may be defined as ". . . the production of intended effects by some men on other men" (1968:676). Closely related to force, prestige, influence, and similar concepts, power is a general term referring to a variety of means whereby people seek to control the behavior of others. Consistent with our dynamic model of society, the distribution among groups of the ability to control others is variable and ever-changing. That is, power does not rest exclusively in the hands of some and not at all in others. *Power is bilateral.* Certainly, power relations are "asymmetrical" (Wrong, 1968:673). That is, at any instant in time groups and individuals may be classified as power holders or power subjects. However, in the course of social interaction, superordinate and subordinate positions are far from permanent. Today's "giver" is tomorrow's "taker." Further, as Wrong indicates, people who wield power in some situated activities (*scopes*) are quite subordinate in others. For example, labor unions control hiring while employers control the place and time of work. In short, the model employed here in one of *intercursive power.* "Intercursive power exists where the power of each party in a relationship is countervailed by that of the other, with procedures for bargaining or joint decision making governing their relations when matters affecting the goals and interests of both are involved" (Wrong, 1968:674). Placed in the perspective of "deviance as politics," then, power becomes a vital element in a struggle (conflict) between interest groups. It is a struggle that involves simultaneous movements to impose restraints, on the one hand, and to limit, resist, or escape control, on the other.

These remarks concerning power provoke additional questions. What is the basis of the moral crusaders' power? How do they wield power? What tactics do they employ? Let's turn to these questions.

Bases of Power

Becker (1963:149) notes that rule-creating groups derive power from (1) the legitimacy of their moral position and (2) from the generally superior socioeconomic position of their membership. As to the first of these, a certain degree of power stems from the fact that the moral entrepreneur pursues ends that many people are reluctant to oppose publicly. To do so, it is feared, would result in their being publicly discredited as immoral. As every politician knows, it pays to stand foursquare for "motherhood and apple pie." The reverse of this principle is that public figures, especially officials, do not ordinarily take a stand in support of morally questionable behaviors—even when they are convinced of the "victimless" nature of these behaviors and the pointlessness of legal proscription. And, if asked, the chances are great that public figures will lend at least minimal support to movements to eradicate publicly discreditable behaviors. (It is a virtual certainty that discredited behavior would be opposed.) As a case in point, the author is reminded of a city council member's effort to bring about more vigorous enforcement of anti prostitution ordinances in her city. Publicly this council member received little support (largely because the buildings housing the brothels were owned by wealthy and influential persons in the town). Privately, she was criticized for stirring up an issue that had lain dormant for years and about which the public seemed unconcerned. Frustrated beyond endurance the woman finally resorted to confronting her foot-dragging colleagues on the street and elsewhere announcing she was establishing a committee for legalizing prostitution and intended to nominate them for membership. Needless to say, among the city council members private criticism diminished and public support for the original proposal increased apace.

Similarly, members of a southwestern city police department's "smut detail" publicly called on all state legislators to spend one full day viewing pornographic movies and magazines. Said one officer, "Without the legislators having first-hand knowledge of the type of filth being peddled in our communities, it is difficult to convince many of them of the need for stronger laws and penalties in this area" (Schwartz, 1976:1). For their part, members of the legislature declined the invitation. Nonetheless, this was an astute move by police. What legislator who rose to the bait could then fail to support such restrictive legislation? Having been exposed to pornography in this way, no legislator could then resist supporting proscriptive legislation. In short, exposure to pornographic material under these publicized circumstances would be tantamount to winning that legislator's support.

The point is that the goals of moral crusaders are often consistent with a version of public morality to which all "right-minded" people are expected to subscribe. This is a consequence of the legitimacy of that version of morality. Privately, the same people who support that public morality may behave in a markedly different way, as, for example, when a safe cracker was contacted by a minister offering to provide the combination to his church's safe (which contained a sizable portion of the proceeds of a successful fund-raising effort) if the safe cracker would agree to split the loot with him. Thus, while public and private morality may sometimes differ radically, the position of the moral entrepreneur is often (if not always) publicly unassailable. This forestalls public opposition and promotes public support.

The second source of power Becker mentions is the superior socioeconomic position occupied by many crusaders and their followers. As noted earlier, a number of humanitarian reform movements were conducted by middle- and upper-class persons ostensibly for the benefit of the poorer classes. Their humanitarian quality and the fact that upper-class persons were recruited to lend their name to the crusade (how could they refuse?) results in a kind of "halo effect." The use of testimonials, mentioned earlier, is a case in point. Testimonial support is often necessary to offset the inherent limitations of having one's moral position supported only by obscure or unknown persons. In circular fashion then, unassailability of the crusader's perspective promotes its support by significant public figures, while support by significant public figures contributes to its unassailability.

Wielding Power

Given the factors on which power rests, moral entrepreneurial groups may pursue their goals in a variety of ways. Operating as *pressure groups* these entities have been found to use any means that will maximize goal achievement and minimize the costs (Turner, 1958). One means of achieving the desired goal is to establish a formal group and work to expand membership in order to increase the group's political strength. As group membership increases so, too, does the probability of engaging members in direct political activity: letter writing, soliciting funds (with which to engage in costly advertising or launch an expensive media blitz), applying direct pressure on public figures, seeking to influence the media, phone campaigns, and so on. It goes without saying that the core leadership of interest groups finds it easier to enlist members in these activities if the leadership's legitimacy and integrity have been secured by means discussed earlier.

Another tactic used by interest groups is to establish *coalitions*, formal or informal, covert or overt cooperative relations with other groups for limited periods of time and for the pursuit of limited goals. To the degree that they do not compromise the discrete interests of either group (Carmichael and Hamilton, 1967:58ff), these affiliations may be mutually and functionally advantageous. Thus, legislation proposed by one group may be seen to have advantages for another group, leading to the support of the proposal by the latter body.

Examples of the establishment of coalitions among interest groups seeking change in the "moral climate" are abundant. Among black civil rights groups coalitions have been established between militants and moderates, as well as between representatives of religious, labor, and libertarian groups (Bennett, 1965:162). In the early 1970's it appeared there would emerge a strong coalition between the gay liberation movement, Third World freedom groups, women's liberation groups, and black liberation groups (Humphreys, 1972:161).

Unlike the above examples, some coalitions are covert and their activities illegal. Such is the case regarding the alleged coalition between the Roman Catholic Church and the New York State Right to Life Committee (NYSRTL), groups well known for their shared opposition to abortion law liberalization. In this case the Roman Catholic Church, like all tax-exempt, tax-deductible organizations, is forbidden by the U.S. Internal Revenue Code from engaging in any political campaign on behalf of any candidate for public office. The same code also places restrictions on the political activity of the NYSRTL, itself a tax-exempt body. Contrary to these restrictions, it is alleged, the ". . . NYSRTL, with fundraising assistance from the church, has directly intervened in scores of New York political races, both local and statewide" (Norton and Stokes, 1977:12). Not the least of the charges against the church involves its alleged collection and contribution of $155,000 toward the election of James Buckley to the U.S. Senate.

The contribution an organization may make to a moral crusade may not always involve direct support; indeed, it may sometimes be quite indirect—perhaps a consequence of the groups' respective philosophical and ideological positions. A case in point occurred when the Roman Catholic bishop of the diocese of San Diego, California, issued an order denying elected lay church offices and sacraments to any member of the National Organization for Women or of any proabortion group (*Arizona Republic*, 1975). By this order, the church not only denigrates one group and perspective but places the stamp of approval on its opposite. In still other cases, coalitions are agreed to by support groups simply for the supposed utility of affiliating with a publicly unassailable proposal. Thus, police agencies have commonly enlisted in the "cause" of child abuse by affiliating with child-saving organizations (Hazlett, 1976).

In addition, interest groups are known to focus attention directly on legislators in an effort to promote their own and frustrate others' attempts to shape public policy. Highly trained professional lobbyists, equipped with secretarial services, research personnel, and press agents are readily available in every capital city in the nation for testifying before legislative committees or representing their client's interests whenever possible. Not the least influential aspect of the lobbyist's effort is to impress on legislators their client's ability to reward or punish the legislator and so help or hinder his or her career (Turner, 1958:66). For example, one of the best-known lobbies in the nation is the National Rifle Association. Operating with a budget of $10 million annually and a membership of about one million, the NRA is able to successfully blunt any effort to pass gun control legislation calling for licensing and registration of guns or their owners. On the list of NRA victims is the influential National Council on Crime and Delinquency and the late Senator Thomas Dodd, who was defeated for reelection in 1970 in part because of NRA opposition (Halverson, 1975:18).

In another example, it is alleged that a U.S. Senate resolution calling for a full-scale public investigation of the disappearance of James R. Hoffa in 1975 was effectively stalled because of "high-pressure lobbying" by officials of the Teamsters union. "The day after the resolution was introduced on Nov. 18 [1975] Mr. [Frank E.] Fitzsimmons [Teamster president] sent telegrams to every member of the Senate urging 'opposition to this resolution because the present law contains ample means for protecting working people' " (Frutig, 1975:50). Members of Congress, as well as Justice and Labor Department officials were also contacted in similar manner to get them to stop "harassing the union."

In addition to the legislature, lobbyists also seek to influence the executive and judicial branches of government. As to the former, this pressure is directed not only at governors and the President, but, as the above case indicates, includes the heads of agencies and cabinet officers who regulate and rule on the basis of executive authority. Thus, for example, proecology groups and representatives of extractive industries (Sierra Club, Friends of the Earth, the mining and forestry industries) pursued their respective interests when they sought to influence the President in his choice of a successor to Secretary of the Interior Rogers C. B. Morton. And in 1941 famed black leader A. Philip Randolph, on the basis of his threat of a March on Washington by 10,000 disgruntled unemployed black workers, was instrumental in bringing about President Franklin Roosevelt's issuance of Executive Order No. 8802, establishing the wartime Fair Employment Committee, a forerunner to the Fair Employment Practices Committee (Bennett, 1965: Chapter III).

Concerning the judiciary, efforts to exert pressure and influence decisions tend to be less blatant than in the case of the legislative and executive branches. Yet no astute moral entrepreneur would ignore the fact that policy formulation involves all branches and levels of government. In the case of courts, then, the cause of the moral entrepreneur often calls for initiating litigation. The importance of this effort and the judiciary is reflected in the fact that several national organizations maintain permanent legal staffs whose function includes becoming directly involved in *test cases,* court cases in which the decision is likely to influence or control the decision of future cases resting on similar points of law (Vose, 1958:20ff). The National Association for the Advancement of Colored People, the American Liberty League, the National Consumers League, and the American Civil Liberties Union are just a few of the groups involved in such efforts.

Beyond the use of these socially approved methods, powerful interest groups in our society have always sought to compromise the integrity of the courts. Thus, as Charles R. Ashman (1973) has noted, some of our judges are the "finest that money can buy." To the extent that deviance involves moral and legal issues frequently resolved in the courts, it should be no surprise that judges are targets for those wishing to control the outcome of both criminal and civil cases at both the trial court and appellate court levels. For example, in 1971, U.S. Court of Appeals Justice (and former governor of Illinois) Otto Kerner was indicted by a federal grand jury for ". . . accepting bribes—purchasing race track stock at virtually giveaway prices [buying at 40 cents and selling ten months later at $2 per share—a 500 percent increase] in exchange for seeing that certain race track owners received favorable treatment in the assignment of racing dates" (Ashman, 1973:203). In a somewhat more complex case, Chief Justice Roy J. Solfisburg, Jr., and Justice Ray I. Klingbiel, both of the Illinois Supreme Court, resigned their positions because of the pressure of investigations into some questionable behavior on their part. In this case it was alleged that these justices were "paid off" for having approved dismissal of an indictment (on a technicality) against Theodore Isaacs, an organizer of the Civic Center Bank and Trust Company of Chicago. Mr. Isaacs was charged with collusion and conspiracy in the handling of state contracts. For their approval of the motion for dismissal of the indictment, it is alleged, Justices Solfisburg and Klingbiel were, respectively, offered stock in the Civic Center Bank at below market price and were given "gift" certificates of stock in the Civic Center Bank. These transactions occurred after oral arguments were heard but before Isaacs' indictment was dismissed. The case was terminated upon the resignation (with full pension) of these justices (Ashman, 1973:195ff).

The tactics mentioned are undoubtedly available to large numbers of organizations in this country and have become a standard feature of the American political scene. In utilizing these tactics, those who share the dominent symbols of wealth, property, status, and the like have an obvious advantage (Gable, 1958). But what of groups for whom these indices of power are unavailable and who may embrace a different sense of reality? Given a bilateral and intercursive power model, what can be said of the power-wielding tactics of the "have-nots?"

By permission of Johnny Hart and Field Enterprises, Inc.

One of the most noted orchestraters and solidifiers of latent influence among less privileged groups in this country was Saul Alinsky. What Alinsky lacked in polish he made up for in effectiveness; where others sought for style and sophistication, Alinsky focused on the pragmatic. As such, he once listed thirteen principles that organizations, even tiny ones, could use in formulating operational tactics to influence private and public policy makers. In listing these principles, Alinsky notes that money and people have traditionally been the sources of power. Lacking the former, he maintained the poor had to use their numbers—flesh and blood—to achieve their goals. His suggestions reflect this point.

1. Power is not only what you have but what the enemy thinks you have.
2. Never go outside the experience of your people.
3. Wherever possible go outside the experience of the enemy.
4. Make the enemy live up to their own book of rules.
5. Ridicule is man's most potent weapon.
6. A good tactic is one that your people enjoy.
7. A tactic that drags on too long becomes a drag.
8. Keep the pressure on.
9. The threat is usually more terrifying than the thing itself.
10. The major premise for tactics is the development of operations that will maintain a constant pressure upon the opposition.
11. If you push a negative hard and deep enough it will break through into its counterside.
12. The price of a successful attack is a constructive alternative.
13. Pick the target, freeze it, personalize it, and polarize it (Alinsky, 1972:127–130).

This is not the place to discuss the efficacy of Alinsky's principles. Suffice to say that their use helped make it possible for the black minority of Rochester, New York, to secure concessions from Eastman Kodak of that city and for the Woodlawn Organization of Chicago to force the Chicago City Hall to honor promises to support programs beneficial to its ghetto residents, that is, to establish rules and programs to serve black interests (Alinsky, 1972:140–144).

In summary, then, a wide variety of tactics and principles are employed by interest groups wielding power. No one knows precisely how effective these tactics and principles are since few researchers have directly addressed the question of how much influence pressure groups actually exert on rule-making bodies. One might guess, however, that the continued use of these tactics is the best possible evidence of their effectiveness. On that basis we conclude that power is indeed bilateral and intercursive.

Summary

In this chapter attention has focused on the process of banning, whereby behavior is officially defined as evil, bad, immoral, wrong, and is proscribed. This process is part of the larger deviance-constructing enterprise and involves the work of those moral entrepreneurs called rule creators, referring to groups of persons having common interests and organized to have their interests translated into public policy. Another variety of moral entrepreneur is one who defends the existing network of rules rather than seeking to create new rules. Overall, the interests pursued by these groups and persons may be narrow or broad, humanitarian or self-serving, and may have sacred or secular inspiration. The action of the moral entrepreneur may be a response to real or anticipated threats to the group's interests. In either event, the effort to ban reflects the intention to impose meaning on conditions in the world.

The banning process has been examined in terms of its several elements. Among these is "awareness," defined as the perception by "some person or group of an objective set of conditions as problematic." A second element is moral conversion, during which an effort is made to convert what is a personal trouble into a public issue. This transformation entails the dissemination of meanings and their being defined by others as plausible and legitimate. Meanings that are initially private and subjective are transformed into public and objective beliefs. Achieving this transformation calls for making the entrepreneur's meanings visible. To achieve widespread visibility in our society almost necessitates use of the mass media. Access to this media, however, is far from universal and the visibility it affords must be engineered by a variety of techniques.

Moral conversion and legitimacy are influenced by other factors as well. Included is the prestige and respectability that may be acquired when the moral entrepreneur selectively identifies with publicly important persons or groups. Testimonials and endorsements, to say nothing of organizational alliances, are seen to promote the cause of the moral crusader.

Out of these efforts there may emerge an image or set of meanings regarding the problematic event. Called myths, these meanings seek to harmonize the claims of the moral crusader with the legitimate dominant values of the community. Simultaneously, the troubling behavior is displayed as running counter to dominant norms, values, and interests.

In modern society, the conversion of any given set of beliefs into public law—thereby to control people against their will—calls for the exercise of power. Because the impersonal and pluralistic nature of our society prevents effective use of informal social control techniques, the moral entrepreneur must rely on the state, whose function it is to designate activities and persons as deviant. Access to state functionaries varies, as do the principles and tactics used by moral entrepreneurs to influence the actions of these state functionaries. The successful outcome of such effort is that public policy is shaped by interest groups. The law is shown to be a means whereby the interests of some groups may be secured at the expense of others. In the final analysis, the public meanings of allegedly deviant behaviors may be seen to be those shared by select segments of society. Moral meaning, then, is negotiable and problematic, part of our socially constructed reality. It is expressed in the public rules intended to guide our lives. Expressing values and interests as rules is the "creation," the "new morality," of which we spoke at the beginning of this chapter.

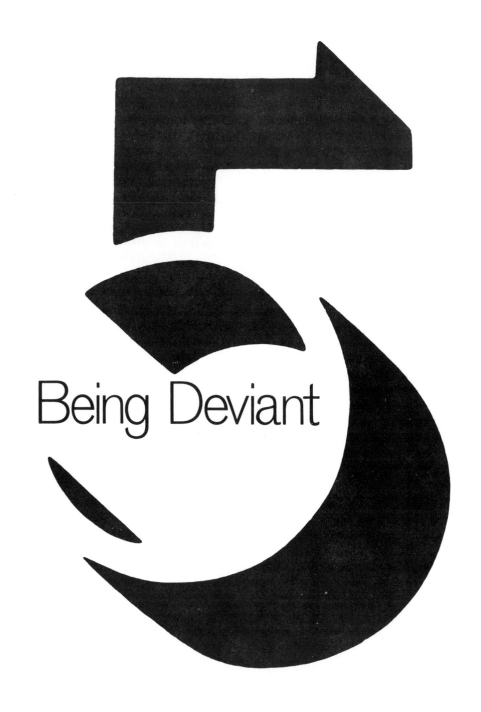

Being Deviant

Introduction

In Chapter 4 we noted that the deviance process consists of three phases. The preceding chapter, dealing with banning, addressed the first of those phases. In this chapter we turn to the second—to the process of defining people who break rules as deviant. In making this shift, two considerations need to be highlighted briefly.

First, we will be considering elements of the process whereby an otherwise "innocent" actor assumes the status of deviant. Examination of the facts of everyday life reveals the need to distinguish between those who break rules and those who get tagged as deviant. By no means are they the same; indeed, the bulk of those who break rules (either formal or informal) are never confronted or charged with violations. Essentially, then, we will be concerned with a relatively small segment of the rule-breaking population. Nonetheless, this is an important segment, as those who occupy the status of deviant will likely attest. The importance of understanding this phase of the deviance process, then, is not a matter of numbers; rather, it lies in the changes in the quality of people's lives that may result from being labeled. The importance of this process will become more clear as our analysis proceeds.

Second, in making the transition from people who "do deviance" (Chapter 2) to people who occupy the status of deviant, it is well to distinguish between "simultaneous" and "sequential" approaches to studying deviance. Becker suggests that students of deviance have most often employed a simultaneous model, one that assumes that all the factors producing deviance, that is, its causes, are operative at one time. This type of orientation involves "variable analysis" such as we discussed earlier. Sequential models, on the other hand, rest on the idea that ". . . all causes do not operate at the same time, . . . that patterns of behavior develop in orderly sequence" (Becker, 1973:23).

The orientation of the present work is patterned on the notions of sequence and process, maintaining that the phenomenon of deviance is not exhausted with the development of individual behavior. Indeed, in the opinion of some observers, the most lasting consequences of rule-breaking behavior follow after such acts become known to others, especially those in positions of authority who have the capacity to apply the label of "deviant" to the actor (Lemert, 1951:75–79; Becker, 1973:31–36). These observers have stressed the importance of *career deviance*, the process of being publicly identified as a deviant and, on that basis (1) being excluded from participating in nondeviant activities and (2) coming to regard oneself as a deviant. To perceive deviance in this way, to consider it as a process influencing one's social position and self-regarding attitudes, calls for an examination of an interactive process between individuals and groups. A major outcome of this interactive process is that *some* rule breakers assume the status of deviant. Moreover, in focusing on the informal and formal aspects of one's induction into that status, attention is given to the alteration in one's existential self from that of a moral person to one who is regarded as *essentially* deviant, that is, immoral. *One's being is deviant.* In focusing on being deviant, we will give attention to the relationship between deviant actors, on the one hand, and social control agencies, on the other (Lemert, 1967:44–46).

Deviance as a Status

What is meant by referring to deviance as a status? *Status* is a social position assigned to and occupied by people on the basis of their being officially recognized in this case as (1) rule breakers or (2) displaying traits defined as objectionable. That is, one may assume this position by achievement or ascription.

Deviance as Achieved Status

Being deviant by achievement means that people may occupy this position by reason of the official definition of their behavior— behavior that is banned. That is, it rests on the public meaning of the actor's accomplishment. Falling into this category is a wide variety of deviations, including any of the following: (1) those who engage in acts destructive of another's property or injurious to their person (such as murder and assault), (2) people who demand and/or consume unlawful goods and services and those who provide them (users of illicit drugs, prostitutes and customers of prostitutes, drug pushers and pimps, to name a few), (3) those whose behavior (streaking and nudity, for example) offends another's sense of propriety, and (4) people whose beliefs challenge legitimated ideologies—as a sect may challenge the beliefs of an orthodox religious group (Glaser, 1971: Chapter 1). In each case some overt action (or suspicion thereof), some accomplishment, underlies one's assignment to a deviant status. In the case of achieved status, then, one's deviance is a matter of doing.

Deviance as Ascribed Status

Deviance by ascription, on the other hand, refers to the assignment of status on the basis of some quality the person is assumed to possess. Like deviant behavior, these personal qualities are seen as departures from expectations and evoke stigmatizing sanctions on the part of others. These qualities include any number of overt conditions: left-handedness in a society where right-handedness is preeminent and its opposite the subject of centuries-old prejudices (Hertz, 1960; *Time*, 1974:85); being short in a nation stressing height (Sagarin, 1969:196ff); being obese in a society where weight watching has become a religious exercise; being an amputee, spastic, or otherwise physically handicapped in a society stressing athletic and physical prowess; or being blind in a society dominated by sighted people. These and other conditions may arouse feelings of fear, loathing, and a sense that the "deviant" is in some way inferior to normals—inferior physically, psychologically, emotionally, or morally (Scott, 1969:24). Such conditions become *stigma*, signs or attributes that are deeply discrediting (Goffman, 1963:3). In contrast with those whose deviance is a matter of performance, the deviation of these people is in the meaning of their being.

Primary and Secondary Deviance

Beyond consideration of deviance as an ascribed or achieved status is the need to examine one's entry into a deviant status in sequential terms. In this regard sociologists have suggested two types of deviant: the primary and the secondary (Lemert, 1951:75–76; 1967:40ff). The concept of *primary deviant* refers to those persons whose rule-violating behaviors are ". . . rationalized or otherwise dealt with [by the rule breaker] as functions of a socially acceptable role" (Lemert, 1951:75). One's rule breaking is incidental to the balance of his or her life and the socially approved statuses he or she occupies. Similar to the concept of primary deviant is Becker's *secret deviant* (1973:20), one whose rule-violating conduct is neither publicly recognized nor responded to as such. It is this, the privacy of one's deviation, that the concepts of primary and secret deviant have in common.

But not all rule breakers keep their transgressions secret. And in many cases the signs of one's deviance—drug addiction, being handicapped, blind, obese—may not be effectively hidden. As a consequence, it is felt, such conditions may become a central aspect of the person's life. When that occurs one may be said to be a secondary deviant (Lemert, 1951:75–76; 1967:17–18, Chapter 3). Similar to the notion of secondary deviant is Becker's concept of the *pure deviant* (Becker, 1973:20), one who has broken the rules and is perceived by others to have done so. According to Lemert, secondary deviants are responded to primarily as rule breakers. Ordinary statuses (being someone's child, a spouse, a worker) tend to be obscured as one's audience focuses attention only on the deviant behavior or condition. It is the *attention of others and the actor's response to that attention* that are central to the concept of secondary deviance. Thus, Lemert defines *secondary deviation* as "... a special class of socially defined responses which people [deviants] make to problems created by the social reaction to their deviance" (Lemert, 1967:40). Consistent with the felt need to adjust to other's behavior, the secondary deviant "... is a person whose life and identity are organized around the facts of deviance" (Lemert, 1967:41). In short, the principal distinction between primary and secondary deviation lies in the salience of one's rule-violating behavior.[1]

Master and Auxiliary Status Traits

To say that one's deviance takes on salience means that his or her deviant behavior or condition takes precedence over and supersedes most other status positions. It is as if self and others became blinded to one's social being except for the deviant aspect. As we will later note in greater detail, one's identity may come to be limited to that of deviant. *One comes to represent the thing described.* The priority of this identity over that of a nondeviant has been commented upon by Everett C. Hughes (1945) and Howard Becker (1973).

Hughes makes the distinction between *master and auxiliary status traits.* By master status he refers to those statuses that obscure and take precedence over others. The master status "... tends to overpower, in most crucial situations, any other characteristics which might run counter to it" (Hughes, 1945:357). Associated with a master status is "... a complex of auxiliary characteristics which come to be expected of its incumbents" (Hughes, 1945:353). Thus, *priests* (master status) are expected to be *men* (auxiliary characteristics), *physicians* (master status) are expected to be *male, white,* and *Protestant* (auxiliary characteristics), and *nurses* are expected to be *women.* Other complexes may be thought of.

Linking statuses and traits to deviance, Becker indicates that deviance tends to be a master status. "One receives the status [of deviant] as a result of breaking a rule, and the identification proves to be more important than most others. One will be identified as a deviant first, before other identifications are made" (Becker, 1973:33). Following Hughes, of course, there are many auxiliary

1. Though it is most likely true that this is the most notable distinction between primary and secondary deviance, there is reason to qualify this as a universally applicable distinction. Of major importance in positing the need for qualification is the process of symbolic labeling, with which we will deal at length in Chapter 6.

traits associated with particular deviant master statuses. As noted earlier, homosexuals (master status) tend to be regarded as sexually abnormal, effeminate, insecure, and sensitive (auxiliary traits); marijuana smokers (master status) have been regarded as escapist, weak-minded, and hedonistic (auxiliary traits) (Simmons, 1969:29). By linking these master statuses and their auxiliary traits, the public image of the deviant actor comes to be that of one who is *generally deviant;* that is, deviance is no longer something that is incidental to one's other statuses. Deviance obscures these other matters and becomes the dominant element of one's public self (Becker, 1973:34). One is regarded as essentially deviant.

Let's summarize briefly. As the definition of secondary deviance indicates, one's own and others' reactions to a person's deviant behavior often serve to create problems for the person in question. These are moral problems and have to do with being stigmatized, punished, segregated from society, or otherwise being made the object of social control. Such concerns are felt to be central to the life of some deviants. Their involvement in deviance is therefore often regarded as *qualitatively* different from that of the primary deviant. In the latter case, deviation is hypothesized to be incidental and subordinate to legitimate roles and statuses. The result is that for the primary deviant rule breaking is hypothesized to have relatively few personal and social implications. For the secondary deviant, however, the deviation and ensuing moral problems become central both in terms of self-other relations and one's conception of self. Thus, according to theory, the secondary deviant's life centers upon the fact of his or her rule breaking. We will return to these considerations in Chapter 6.

However salient one's deviance may be, evidence indicates that involvement in deviance is not mutually exclusive of legitimate role playing. Not only is this true in the case of the primary deviant (in which category almost everyone is included at some time or other), but it applies as well to the secondary deviant, for example, people who make their living by means of rule-violating behavior. In their study of black pimps, the Milners discovered that relationships between pimps and their parents and other family members persist, often with only minimal difficulty (Milner and Milner, 1972:144ff). Likewise, Klockars notes that the role of "professional fence" is not incompatible with that of "straight" businessmen (Klockars, 1974:77–78). Finally, Rossman (1976:198) relates cases indicating that pederasty, too, is fully compatible with socially acceptable roles and relationships. These examples demonstrate that, despite popular perceptions, the roles of deviant and nondeviant, even of the secondary type, are far from incompatible. Indeed, as the case of the professional fence suggests, legitimate and deviant roles may sometimes be difficult to separate.

Later we will consider at length the problems experienced by deviants as a consequence of their status. At the same time, consideration will be given to some refinements of the distinctions we have drawn between primary and secondary deviance. At this point it is important to begin consideration of the formal process by which a person takes on the public status of deviant.

Institutionalizing Deviance

Bureaucratization

Once behavior is banned and subject to control by public law, efforts to eradicate it no longer rest in private hands or with private agencies. As noted earlier, banning involves the conversion of private meanings into public laws which, at least in theory, apply to all persons falling under the jurisdiction of the state. As control of behavior passes from private to public hands, the responsibility for processing deviants becomes the task of official agencies—either public or publicly approved. That is, new organizations may be established or existing organizations are assigned the task of enforcing the rules. In some cases a new department may be created within existing organizations. As examples we may note the creation of private groups (that is, nongovernmental) such as Boys Clubs of America, Big Sisters, Big Brothers, and similar organizations. These groups usually receive official endorsement and are thereby given public legitimation as "deviance processing" agencies. (This is not to say that these groups deal exclusively with persons identified as deviant.) Examples of specialized public agencies (governmental) would include police vice and bunco squads, or a special staff within a department of public welfare to investigate cases of welfare fraud, child abuse, and similar matters.

As a step toward institutionalizing deviance, the creation of these groups rests on a prior condition—a relatively clear definition of the nature of the problem and clientele to be dealt with. Logically, this definition precedes assigning such responsibilities since, in the absence of a definition, no rational course of action is likely. For example, assigning responsibility for a given problem to police, medical, social welfare, or some other specialized agency requires a prior definition of that problem. Likewise, whether a particular deviant is remanded to a mental hospital, a jail, a prison, a geriatric or nursing home, or whatever depends on how he or she is officially defined. (As we will see, the assignment of such definitions is quite problematic and may not be taken for granted.) In another case, the admissions staff of a hospital must be provided a definition (that is, an initial diagnosis) of incoming patients in order to know the area or department of the hospital to which the patient should be sent. Cardiac, orthopedic, obstetric, and similar departmental specializations are universal. Beyond this, patients may be classified as critical or seriously ill. In any case, as noted in Chapter 1, how we respond to things is shaped by our definition of them.

Institutionalization of deviance also calls for procedures for enforcing the rules and handling the new category of deviant. These rules and procedures tend to become *organized, systematized,* and *stabilized.* Thus, specific roles (such as a new job classification) may have to be created for the purpose of administering cases. If existing roles are regarded as sufficient for the task, the responsibility may be assigned to them. Thus, particular people do specific things; in accordance with the principles of a division of labor, specific tasks are spread over several functionaries. Stabilization means that by assigning the responsibility of control to an agency, the roles, procedures, and meanings evolved come to have an existence independent of the role incumbents. They become the property of organizations.

Overall, as they appear in a specific organization, these elements of institutionalization reflect bureaucratized methods of handling deviants. Within an agency one finds specific rules, specialization of tasks, a hierarchy of authority, and impersonal interpersonal relations. These conditions are basic characteristics of bureaucratic organizations. Ostensibly they are intended to promote achievement of an agency's goal, most often those of correction, amelioration, containment, and the like. These elements and the meanings that serve as their foundation become part of the social reality of deviance—albeit the reality of specialized groups. These are the realities of deviance found in police departments, social work agencies, agencies for the blind, mental hospitals and clinics, probation departments, prisons, and other organizations created to manage deviants. We may refer to this reality—this general body of information and its associated techniques—as the *theory of office.*[2]

Theory of Office

The concept *theory of office* indicates that the institutionalization of deviance involves more than a simplistic notion of

2. In considering the institutionalization of routines and the theory of office, it is not intended to suggest that these regulatory elements, rules, and so on, become a "straitjacket" denying practitioners the opportunity to display individuality or inhibiting the creation and application of situationally specific meanings. Thus, for example, while every mental health clinic has a theory of office, it is problematic as to which aspect of this *general* body of information will be applied to any *specific* case.

bureaucratized routines. Agencies charged with controlling deviants face a problem in social management—what shall be done with those persons who come to their attention? The theory of office has evolved to provide an answer to this general question. "Office," as used here, refers to a service, to things done to or for others. The theory of office ". . . specifies the number and kind of establishments that will process these deviants . . . [and defines] both the characteristics of its clients and the manner in which they will be admitted and processed. In essence, then, the theory of office concerns itself with registry" (Rubington and Weinberg, 1973:118). As part of the social reality of these processing agencies, the theory of office serves to provide a sense of order and meaningfulness to the task at hand. It seeks to formalize and routinize the *registration* (the defining, classifying, and labeling) and processing of deviants. Finally, the theory of office is evolved and defended for the purpose, not of rendering treatment, per se, but for solving the bureaucratic difficulties faced by these organizations (Newman, 1975).

The relevance of the theory of office goes beyond this. For example, agency functionaries, in their private lives, may not all share the same definitions of the deviants with whom they work. These differences in definition must be reduced if not eliminated; they may not be allowed to interfere with the official task of the agency. As a substitute for the welter of private meanings, official designations (meanings) are evolved and imposed. Thus, many agencies develop typologies of clientele, categories into which otherwise unique persons and problems may be placed for ease of organizational management. Prisons differentiate inmates in terms of the perceived seriousness of their criminal history and their rehabilitative potential. Mental hospitals have their diagnostic categories or "pigeonholes" in terms of which patients are classified and housed. So, too, do *public defenders* (tax-supported defense attorneys for indigent defendants) employ standard categories into which "typical" cases may be placed for routine handling. For example, in order to speed up and reduce the cost of processing criminal cases, public defenders and prosecuting attorneys frequently seek agreement as to how a given case shall be defined (legally classified). To facilitate this process a number of categories called *"normal crimes"* have been established into which public defenders may place cases that lack uniqueness and allow for routine handling. Normal crimes are ". . . those occurrences whose typical features, e.g., the ways they usually occur and the characteristics of the people who commit them . . . are known and attended to by the [public defender]" (Sudnow, 1965:179). Normal crimes frequently dealt with include petty theft, drunk, rape, drug use. A "typical" petty theft is defined as ". . .

about 50-50 Negro-white, unplanned . . . , generally committed on lower class persons and don't get much money, don't often employ weapons, don't make living from thievery, usually younger defendants with long juvenile assaultive records, etc." (Sudnow, 1965:179). A case that substantially satisfies these criteria will likely be dealt with routinely, thereby facilitating the operation of the agency. Similar characterizations of routine cases may be found in probation departments.

The immediate importance of these typologies and categories lies in their contribution to the smooth operation of the agency. It is only in terms of these divisions, typologies, or designations that official agencies are able to deal with their clients within the limits of budget, staff, and other finite resources. As a case in point, prison inmates may have their level of custody changed (from maximum to medium, for example), not to facilitate "rehabilitation" or because of any character change on their part, but to facilitate the harvesting of crops on the prison farm. Legally and ordinarily, maximum security inmates are not allowed outside the walls of maximum security prisons. However, when an insufficient number of inmates are available for harvest (work requiring inmates to go outside prison walls), a change in classification may be conveniently arranged in order to supplement this vitally needed work force (Sykes, 1958:25–31). Conversely, when the definition of the client lacks clarity or does not satisfy the existing organizational apparatus, that is, when the organization is not set up to handle persons whose uniqueness cannot be overlooked, the client may well be expelled. For example, an Associated Press news release from Hackensack, New Jersey, reports that a man in the midst of a sex change operation and who had pleaded guilty to burglary was granted a 90-day suspended sentence—suspended only ". . . because the judge didn't know where the sentence should be served" (*Arizona Republic*, 1977a). A similar case has been reported from Illinois where a man accused of two murders may not be tried for either one. The accused cannot hear, speak, read, or write and is therefore unable to participate in his own defense. For that reason the court has declared him incompetent to stand trial. Until the definitional dilemma is resolved the accused languishes in the Cook County jail (*Newsweek*, 1977:89–90).

To the extent that categories are part of the official apparatus of control agencies, assigning clients to them also serves to legitimize the processing of specific cases. The work of the agency is legitimized. For example, a judgment of "incompetency" by a duly convened board of psychiatrists or others paves the way for the confinement and treatment of one who is designated as mentally ill. Official designation of one as a criminal (conviction) legitimizes imprisonment. A diagnosis legitimizes medical treatment. (Conversely, a successful malpractice suit against a physician necessitates *delegitimizing* the diagnosis; thereby the treatment may be said to have been in error and the physician liable.) It is only in terms of these designations and their meanings that social control agencies may manage the client population. This defining process, along with other aspects of the theory of office, serves to "shape" persons to the needs of the bureaucratic machinery.

The Case of Total Institutions

The nature of this "shaping process" is perhaps obvious to any person who has been inducted into any bureaucratic agency dealing with sizable populations (the military, a university, and the like). To be sure, the extent to which these efforts are engaged in and the consequences for one's conception of self will vary significantly from organization to organization. But they are most apparent and most significant in *total institutions*, organizations that demand total subordination of the client population and that severely restrict association between client and "free" population groups (Goffman, 1961:4–5). Examples of total institutions include, among others, precisely those agencies established to deal with various categories of deviant: homes for the blind, mental hospitals, prisons, and similar places.

Admittance to these agencies is generally accompanied by a variety of rituals serving to eliminate or reduce the individual client's uniqueness or individuality, the uniqueness of self that is inimical to the smooth operation of the agency. As Goffman notes, the vitality and relevance of one's prior conception of self is systematically reduced by a "series of abasements, degradations, humiliations, and profanations of self" (Goffman, 1961:14). For example, as a person enters prison he or she is fingerprinted, photographed (both of which have likely been done numerous times before), subjected to a mortifying rectal (and, if a woman, vaginal) examination, stripped of a name in preference for a number, possibly subjected to a haircut of a standard sort, disinfected and otherwise "cleansed." These and other admissions procedures are called "trimming," "programming," or "being squared away," procedures whereby the new arrival is ". . . shaped and coded into an object that can be fed into the administrative machinery of the establishment, to be worked on smoothly by routine operations" (Goffman, 1961:16).

This shaping is not restricted to the admissions period. Mortifying experiences may be imposed at various points during one's period of incarceration or hospitalization in order to bring obstreperous, boisterous, or otherwise unruly (that is, those who threaten organizational procedures) clients back into line. For example, in *One Flew Over the Cuckoo's Nest*, Nurse Ratched (Big Nurse) ordered a "cautionary cleansing" of the hair and rectum of patients who had participated in a fishing trip contrary to her wishes (Kesey, 1962:227ff). Clearly, defiance is intolerable in total institutions. The consequence may be *contaminative exposure*, the defiling of one's person or things intimately associated with self (Goffman, 1961:25).

Other expressions of "shaping" or bureaucratizing deviant populations to facilitate organizational needs exist in abundance. Upon entering hospitals one is ordinarily divested of personal belongings and issued hospital regulation garb and equipment. Access to personal belongings, ranging from clothing to cigarettes, is restricted in conformity to organizational rules and their rationale. The effect of these restrictions is *personal defacement;* that is, one is ". . . stripped of his usual appearance and of the equipment and services by which he maintains it" (Goffman, 1961:20). Things that are extensions of self are denied.

Mutilation of the body may also be included as part of the "shaping" process. Included are the use of chemotherapy, electroshock therapy, and surgical techniques such as lobotomy (Kesey, 1962:269; Jackson, 1973:42ff; Chambliss, 1971). Even lacking direct imposition of these forms of mutilation, the simple threat they pose may be sufficient to inhibit select behavior patterns and maintain subordination of the client population. Subordination may also be sought by means of *verbal humiliation.* Being required to address institutional personnel as "sir" or by another term of deference (while similar regard is systematically withheld from the client population) is a common example. In some prisons administrative personnel pride themselves on their ability to know and refer to every inmate by number rather than name.

In these and numerous other ways one suffers a mortification or deadening of one's prior self. Behaviors and symbols (including names) expressive of one's uniqueness are obliterated or suppressed, to be replaced by those that are suited to the expectations and needs of the bureaucracy or, in some cases, the society. As one psychiatrist who specialized in "aversive therapy" (a form of mutilation) stated: "These [patients] have no rights: If we can learn something by using them, then that is small compensation for the trouble they have caused society" (Chambliss, 1971:24). It is apparent that rationalizations for such treatment are well developed.

Yet some diminution of the actor's prior self may already have been effected prior to contact with a deviance-processing agency.

Thus, upon discovery of a person's involvement in deviance, others may soon begin to perceive him or her in terms of *stereotypes*, group-shared ideas about the nature of people assigned to specific categories. Let's examine stereotypy as it applies to the institutionalization of deviance.

Stereotypy

For most people, interaction is based to a significant degree on unproven assumptions about the others with whom they deal. The validity of the assumptions is taken for granted. Storekeepers, bus drivers, office workers, teachers, students, and so on, ordinarily are defined in terms at least minimally consistent with their relevant position, the position in terms of which we and they interact. For example, whether a shopkeeper is "kind to animals," "likes kids," or "enjoys rock music," is likely to be irrelevant to his or her evaluation as a shopkeeper because such things have nothing to do with his or her position as shopkeeper. There is, after all, a norm of social interaction that, in the absence of contrary information, encourages people to take one another at face value. Hence, unless contrary evidence is introduced into the situation one is most likely to perceive strangers as at least tolerable, if not nice, persons. Typifications of that sort can best be understood in terms of how they facilitate interaction.

To be sure, these characterizations are not built in total disregard of external matters. As we noted earlier, such things as speech, general demeanor, style of dress, and the like are often used as *symbols*, that is, stimuli that have learned meanings and values attached to them (Rose, 1965:44ff). For example, a smile is generally invested with positive meaning and the clerk, teacher, or fellow student who flashes a smile is likely to be defined differently than one who either frowns or refrains from smiling. It is on the basis of definitions of these symbols, rather than some essential difference in people's character, that much of our social interaction is carried on.

In addition to speech, dress, and other symbols, how we relate to other people is influenced by the meanings assigned to the statuses they occupy rather than to them as individuals. For example, if one has learned to be distrustful of police *as a category*, it is unlikely that the distrust will be dispelled by a particular smiling officer. The distrust directed against police in general is best understood as being based on a stereotype.

Though people are often reluctant to admit they engage in stereotyping, research evidence reveals this to be an extremely widespread practice, so widespread as to suggest that it may well be indispensable for people trying to make sense of and establish order in an impersonal, heterogeneous society (Vander Zanden, 1966:81). And the convenience associated with the use of stereotypes extends to deviants as well as to other categories of persons. Thus, just as people have stereotyped ideas about members of various occupational, racial, religious, and ethnic groups, so, too, do they have stereotyped conceptions of various types of deviants. For example, J. L. Simmons in researching stereotypes of deviants, asked college students to characterize homosexuals, marijuana smokers, and adulterers, among others. In response, ". . . over two-thirds of the students wrote a highly stereotyped portrait of every deviant type, and the responses of those who stereotyped were remarkably similar in content—almost as if they were all echoing the same package of images" (Simmons, 1969:27).

Simmons' findings are perhaps predictable because of the homogenizing effect of mass media and the extremely widespread popularity of certain language forms in America. Indeed, being socialized to stereotypic constructions of deviants is by no means uncommon in our society. They are quite prevalent in everyday speech and the mass media. Thomas Scheff (1966:64ff) notes that ". . . children learn a considerable amount of [stereotyped] imagery concerning deviance very early, and . . . much of the imagery come[s] from their peers rather than adults." Some sense of the prevalence of the stereotypes we have of the mentally ill may be noted in the frequent use of words like "crazy," "nuts," "cracked," "looney," "flipped," "bugs," and others. The content of language is reinforced by media imagery where, in television, for example, the "mentally ill" person

> . . . often enters the scene staring glassy-eyed, with his mouth widely agape, mumbling incoherent phrases or laughing uncontrollably. Even in what would be considered the milder disorders, neurotic phobias and obsessions, the afflicted person is presented as having bizarre facial expressions and actions (Nunnally, 1961:74).

The social reality of criminals is also based to a substantial degree on the stereotyped content of our language and the media (Klapp, 1962:Chapter 2; Quinney, 1963, 1975). These images have become part of the "conventional wisdom" possessed by many Americans bearing on such matters as what criminals and the mentally ill look like, how they behave and, hence, how "normal" people ought to behave toward them.

Consequences of Stereotyping

Engaging in stereotypy has numerous consequences. First, as part of social reality, the content of stereotypes often comes to be regarded as a valid description of the groups to which they refer. For example, as we noted in Chapter 4, though a physician may carry on a demanding daily professional routine despite being addicted to drugs, people persist in believing that "all junkies are nonproductive." Professionally competent addict physicians come to be regarded as "exceptions that prove the rule," that is, that validate the stereotype. On the other hand, the stereotype of physicians (wise, ever alert, and ready to do his or her duty for humanity—personified by Marcus Welby, M.D.) precludes them being perceived as drug addicts (physician and drug addict are, stereotypically, mutually exclusive roles) or even professionally incompetent. By assuming the validity of stereotypes, people think they "know" what a drug addict, a homosexual, a prostitute, and so on is like and feel they are able to recognize one when and if they see one.

Stereotypes also lead people to anticipate objectionable behavior by deviants. For example, antihomosexual forces in California and elsewhere in the 1978 campaign to repeal civil rights ordinances for homosexuals supported their charges not on evidence of what homosexuals *had done* but on what it was feared and expected they *would do*. As a case in point, it is anticipated by homophobic spokespersons that gay teachers *will* seek to seduce or molest their students or *will* seek to entice them into a homosexual life style (*Arizona Gay News*, 1978:4). Such anticipatory fears were writ large in Anita Bryant's homophobic campaign at that same time (*Playboy*, 1978:78). To the extent that stereotypes involve imputing character traits, one may readily make such predictions. To all intents and purposes, then, the actor "becomes" the thing to which the stereotype refers.

Second, largely (if not solely) on the basis of their content, stereotypes serve to bring about the rejection of deviant actors. They serve as a barrier between the deviant and the observer that prevents the latter from relating to a former in any alternative way. The content of the stereotype is taken to be a valid representation of the deviant's *substantial self* (see Chapter 6). That is, the stereotype is often objectified, leading people to assume the deviant "really is that way." Thus, it is not uncommon to find people believing that homosexuals *really are* "limp-wristed faggots" and *can never be* athletic (Garner and Smith, 1976), that blind people *really are* dependent, that fat people *really are* jolly, and so on.

A third and final consequence of stereotyping is that it serves as the basis for the selection of persons to be officially designated as deviant. That is, people are selected to be tagged as deviant not simply because of their involvement in discreditable behavior or, as in the case of the ascribed deviant, because they represent some feared and stigmatized condition. They are singled out because of what stereotypes lead others to think of them. We have already noted at length that differential police reaction to similar behavior among Japanese, black, and white youth was based in part on the stereotyped conceptions police had of these youth. Similarly, it is not uncommon to find schoolteachers stereotyping and judging the younger brother or sister of an "unruly" child they had in their classroom. These everyday examples reveal the ways in which stereotypes influence perception and, in turn, actions toward the persons or groups being stereotyped.

Typification of others influences the conduct of professionals as much as of lay people. A case in point is the way stereotyped perceptions of blind people are used to facilitate the work of some agencies providing services to the blind. Scott (1969) has pointed out that some agencies working with the blind prefer not to deal with all unsighted people, but only with those who conform to the agency's conception of a *rehabilitatable blind person*, the employable blind and the young, categories felt to have the greatest chance for rehabilitation. ". . . One of the major reasons agencies compete for the young and the employable while the rest of the blindness population goes relatively unserved is that they fit the stereotype exploited in fund-raising campaigns relating blindness to youth, work, and hope" (Scott, 1969:100). Scott also notes that agency personnel have mistaken *their concept* of the problems of the blind for *the problems themselves*. Those blind persons whose behavior fails to conform to these conceptions are regarded as "marginal" to the "real work" to be done by such agencies, that is, educational and vocational training. Agencies working with the blind and who employ these stereotypes tend to regard such cases as insoluble and mark them closed. Like the burglar undergoing a sex change operation, mentioned earlier, they tend to be expelled as clients. In short, the agency is predisposed to handle only those cases that conform to its definition of the rehabilitatable blind. Only to the extent that clientele conform to these conceptions can they be fit into the organizational machinery. That is in keeping with the nature of bureaucratized deviance.

Though it is possible to overemphasize the importance of the influence of stereotypes on human behavior, it is nonetheless true that in interaction in general, and in particular with people regarded as deviant (occupying a master status), these conceptions play a critical role. For example, most of us have rather limited contact with persons *known to be* deviant. What we tend to know of such people is therefore derived from accounts carried in the mass media, religious writings, from what friends and neighbors say about them, and from public pronouncements by "the professionals" (police, psychiatrists, and so on). Lacking direct contact and independent verifiable information, we find ourselves in an ambiguous position. How shall we relate to these people? How does one interact with the mentally ill? an alcoholic? a potential suicide? a criminal of some sort? a homosexual? a quadraplegic? In many cases the ambiguity is reduced (not eliminated) by resorting to stereotypes and responding not to the person but to the definition provided by the stereotype. In short, stereotypes assist people to "make sense" of behavior and people they regard as strange, bizarre, or frightening.

The general content of stereotypes, however, is insufficient to provide justification for assigning rule violators to the status of deviant. This is not to suggest that popular stereotypes are sloughed when actors are presented to formal organizations. The need of these agencies for legitimating their activity calls for greater precision and more extensive documentation and evidence about the deviant actor than stereotypes can provide. In particular, while stereotypes refer to *categories* of people in an indiscriminate fashion, the task of control agencies requires information about *specific persons*, information that will provide some sense of consistency between the actor's behavior and character, on the one hand, and the treatment accorded him or her, on the other. As Matza (1969:151) notes, the person who has been *devious* (behavior) must be cast as *deviant* (character). That is, to facilitate the work of the agency, the deviant actor must be made into a case of the thing he or she is alleged to be; behavior (devious) must be linked with character (deviant). To make this link calls for a characterological "transformation" of the actor, a condition effected by the process of *retrospective interpretation* (Lofland, 1969; Schur, 1971). Let's consider this process.

Retrospective Interpretation

We noted in Chapter 1 that moral meanings are expressed in rules, the violation of which may result in the violator being stigmatized and defined as an "outsider." What makes the deviant an outsider is not the deviant act per se. This follows from the fact that while almost everyone breaks rules, often of a serious nature, without being caught or labeled, people persist in thinking only of the *publicly identified* rule breaker as qualitatively different from others. On the basis of this presumed difference, the labeling process is designed to cut known rule breakers off from the rest of society. It is in this "cutting off" and the associated presumption of difference that one finds the essential meaning of the deviant as an "outsider," as a "special kind of person."

Included among deviants who are regarded as "special kinds of persons" are the mentally ill. Charlotte Green Schwartz (1956) has noted that even family members avoid and tend to become alienated from their loved ones who are so diagnosed. As an explanation for this, Schwartz suggests it is because in the perception of others, the mental patient is not just a "different person" but ". . . *he is no longer a person to them. They* sense that something fundamental about the person has been changed. The mental patient is not a person *with* an illness like a man with a broken leg. He is a schizophrenic; in the vernacular, 'he is a mental case'" (Schwartz, 1956:22). The mental patient, then, in contrast to "normals," is a nonperson or in some other way is perceived to be *essentially* different. It is in this sense that the mental patient and other categories of deviant are seen as "special kinds of persons."

One highly public expression of casting a person in this way, of retrospective interpretation, resulting in defining the actor as a "special kind" of person, is regularly noted in newspapers and other media when alleged deviants are subject to biographical scrutiny and (often enough) character reconstruction (Lofland, 1969:149ff). This effort involves trying to link the actor's present deviant behavior with some previously unrecognized character defect. It is assumed that independent evidence of the defect can be discovered in the person's biography. Accordingly, the deviant's biographical history is minutely examined in order to uncover events symbolic of a character consistent with the current deviant episode. Biographical information that is inconsistent with the known deviance may well be discounted or, if it cannot be ignored, may prompt a shift in the way the behavior is explained. For example, if information cannot be discovered that may plausibly be used as an indicator of a defective character (which would explain the deviant conduct), the focus of attention may shift to the psychophysiological realm and the offender may be examined for possible brain damage. In the celebrated case of Patricia Hearst, background information revealed no clues to a fundamental character defect that would provide a plausible explanation for her being a willing participant in the robbery of a Los Angeles sporting goods store and the Hibernia Bank in San Francisco during the time she was alleged to have been a kidnap victim of the Symbionese Liberation Army. In defense of his client, Attorney F. Lee Bailey used the notion of "duress" and "brainwashing." By claiming his client was threatened with being "messed up" unless she participated in the bank robbery, Mr. Bailey was using duress in an effort to make sense of otherwise "unexplainable" be-havior. He also employed the metaphor of brainwashing when he delved into "coercive persuasion" (Moritz, 1976:3; see also Szasz, 1976a and 1976b). These efforts were consistent with the process of retrospective interpretation; new facts are sought and/or old facts are reinterpreted in an effort to establish consistency between the actor's behavior and character (Lofland, 1969:150ff). Finding (or creating) such consistency serves to explain the discreditable conduct and fur-ther legitimizes the label. Evil conduct becomes understandable when engaged in by a "special kind of person," one who, after all, is an "outsider."

Imputational Specialists and Case Records

Contributing to the transformation of one's identity through re-trospective interpretation are a host of functionaries called imputa-tional specialists (Lofland, 1969:136ff) whose task it is to contribute to the unanimity of belief that the actor is characterologically de-viant, that he or she is the type of person he or she is alleged to be. The importance of unanimity derives from the fact that its absence promotes conflict. In the absence of substantial agreement regarding the character of the actor, the legitimacy of regarding and respond-ing to the person as a deviant is jeopardized, and the propriety of the labeling agency is called into question. Lacking the united front that unequivocal agreement provides, the alleged deviant may well claim to have been falsely and unjustly accused and successfully avoid being labeled. Consensus among the labelers, on the other hand, serve to neutralize the accused's effort at resistance. By effect-ing consensus, then, the task of recasting achieves greater legitimacy and is more likely to succeed; that is, the actor will officially be cer-tified as an "outsider" (Emerson, 1969:317; Lemert, 1962:112).

Imputational specialists who contribute to this consensus popu-late the places we have referred to: psychiatric clinics and hospitals, jails and prisons, police stations, welfare agencies, public and pri-vate schools. In each place are people who create and maintain bio-graphical records of those they "serve." These functionaries assemble information about *select* aspects of peoples' life, aspects that will le-gitimate the classification of the person and aid in assigning the actor to the status of deviant. The assembled information gathered from all manner of sources—friends, employers, teachers, fellow workers, neighbors, relatives, ministers—constitutes a case record or case history. Such information is exemplified by the data gathered by probation officers in what are called "presentence investiga-tions."

Undeniably, what goes into a case record is chosen to validate the label, diagnosis, or other attribution. Information that is flattering or contrary to what is alleged of the actor (as of any specific point in time) is often left open to doubt or ignored. Correct answers to questions asked of prospective mental patients may well be ignored, while incorrect answers are dutifully recorded and responded to, that is, taken as evidence of mental illness (Scheff, 1964).

On the other hand, data supportive of the label are expressed unequivocally (Goffman, 1961:155ff). Moreover, given the authority ordinarily vested in the agencies engaged in retrospective interpretation, little of one's biography is beyond scrutiny. From the vast array of materials available are selected the misadventures, examples of poor judgment, regrettable incidents, cases of impetuousness, records of intemperance, and other things (which all people have accumulated in quantity) that may have "symptomatic significance." The events recorded in the case history are, then, just the sort that one would consider "scandalous, defamatory, and discrediting (Goffman, 1961:155–159)." Big Nurse always carried a small pad of paper in her uniform pocket on which to record select events in her patients' daily life. This information was dutifully filed in each patient's record and referred to during "group meeting" (Kesey, 1962:221ff, 252). Goffman suggests that, far from being an exercise in professional neutrality, the collection, accumulation, and collation of such data is a matter of partisanship, serving the interests of organizations that process deviants.

Finally, consistent with bureaucratic methods and the "total" character of many deviance control agencies, the individual person often takes on far less importance than the content of the case record. Institutional procedures are oriented in terms of case content, but almost never are they based on noninstitutional aspects of the deviant population per se. Further, the use of such records may serve to totally depersonalize the individuals to whom they refer. This establishes the distinction between the "body vs. the file." Letkemann notes that while

. . . the body is . . . viewed as a number . . . the file itself is personified. The comments of others are perceived of as a more accurate reflection of the person than the person himself. In fact, the body is perceived of as a false image. "It" may "give you a line," "give you a snow job." In contrast, the file is trustworthy. It contains absolute legal identity, the fingerprints. In addition, it provides us with the body's character—an account of its values and thoughts by way of psychological tests, charts, and reports. The body's ability is also indicated by aptitude and IQ tests. The body's photograph, evidence toward which one is inclined to react in a more personal manner, is tucked away in an envelope at the back of the file (Letkemann, 1973:p. 18).

The Status Degradation Ceremony

The process of retrospective interpretation and the work of the imputational specialist never are more apparent than when their cumulative effect is manifest in the *status degradation ceremony*. Like ceremonies in general, these events consist of rituals serving to bring about and give public acknowledgment to a significant change in a person's social position. Like christenings, circumcisions, puberty rites, confirmations, and marriages, degradation ceremonies signal a change in one's public status. By these rituals ". . . the public identity of the actor is transformed into something looked on as lower in the local scheme of social types" (Garfinkel, 1956:420). Further, at least theoretically, the change in identity effected by these rituals is total. That is the new status reflects not only what a person has done but refers also to their motivational pattern and other aspects of character. Thus, the new identity rests on what a person has done as well as why they are supposed to have done it. Character and behavior are fused in the new identity. The status degradation ceremony, then, contributes significantly to the final conclusion that the deviant actor is the "type of person" who would do what they are alleged to have done.

In the form of court trials, juvenile court hearings, incompetency hearings, psychiatric screening boards, and similar processes, degradation ceremonies are expressive of moral indignation. As such they are not simply amoral transformations of the actor's public identity. They are denunciatory; the actor is stigmatized. In the process of this denunciation the actor's former identity (that of a moral being) is virtually destroyed and a totally new identity established. Thus,

> The work of denunciation effects the recasting of the objective character of the perceived other: The other person becomes in the eyes of his condemners literally a different and new person. It is not that the attributes are added to the old "nucleus." He is not changed, he is reconstituted. The former identity, at best, receives the accent of mere appearance . . . the former identity stands as accidental; the new identity is the "basic reality." What he is now is what, "after all," he was all along (Garfinkel, 1956:421–422).

A significant portion of status degradation ceremonies focuses on the past. That is, it concentrates on what actor *has done* and *has always been*. Degradation ceremonies are also anticipatory; they make reference to the future, to the actor's prospective behavior. That is, transforming the actor motivationally and characterologically results in the implicit (sometimes explicit) prediction that the actor will likely repeat the deviant behavior in question. Such behavior would be consistent with what is now taken to be the person's *essential* nature; it is assumed that in the absence of restraint he or she will engage in similar behavior in the future.[3]

Sometimes the anticipatory nature of these ceremonies becomes explicit. This was noted in a case involving the firing of a self-professed socialist from the faculty of a southwestern state university by that state's Board of Regents. The Regents' action was taken contrary to the recommendations of the university President and two successive faculty committees convened to hear evidence concerning the charges brought against the faculty member. In disregarding these recommendations and announcing their decision, the Board of Regents stated: "In addition, the Board specifically finds that Dr. Starsky . . . would not consider himself *bound in the future* to obey or enforce the rules and regulations of the University and this Board" (Hoult, 1972:237. Italics added.)." In short, despite the evidence having been found wanting by two tribunals, the Board acted in an anticipatory manner, concluding that the interests of the university precluded allowing Starsky to continue to teach. Underlying this decision was the image of Starsky as a socialist. One might guess that the moral and characterological meaning of that label for the Regents prevented them from taking any other position. To them, that was Starsky's "essential" character.

The Court Trial

One example of a degradation ceremony is the court trial. As ordinarily understood and portrayed in the media, the court trial is the arena where issues of fact are dealt with in order to determine guilt and innocence. That is questionable. Viewed as theatre, the trial involves the determination of whether or not the defendant is the type of person capable of doing the particular crime charged. "In other words, is the defendant a social instance of a thief, murderer, rapist, etc.? Can he be made to represent the crime with which he is charged" (Hadden, 1973:270). Two versions of the defendant's character vie with each other, that of the prosecution and

3. The anticipatory element of degradation ceremonies parallels the anticipatory aspect of stereotypes. The similarity is more than accidental. In both instances the actor's character is assumed to be consistent with the "kind of person" who could behave as he or she is alleged to have done. In the case of stereotypy, the characterological properties are assigned informally; in the instance of the degradation ceremony, these traits are attributed in an "official" and formal manner.

that of the defense. Out of these conflicting presentations the jury is required to construct its own version by determining which of the conflicting presentations is the more valid interpretation of the defendant's character. In short, the jury creates social reality.

As the trial proceeds, the attorney for the prosecution and the defense attorney, respectively, seek to establish that the defendant is and is not an instance of the thing charged. The prosecutor tries to create the image of the defendant as one who is different from "normal" people, different for example, from the sort of person who sits on a jury. To counter this effort, the defense attorney may use any of several approaches. He or she may try to create the belief that (1) the act in question was not deviant, (2) that the defendant was not in control of himself or herself (for example, because of insanity or the effect of brainwashing) when the forbidden act was committed, (3) that the defendant did not know the act was prohibited and had no intention of defying the law or producing harmful consequences when he or she did the prohibited thing (ignorance), or (4) that the defendant is a victim of a vendetta by the state and is, in fact, a harmless person (Hadden, 1973:272). Regardless of the image sought, the defense goal is to frustrate creating a discreditable image of the defendant. To the degree that attention is focused on the defendant per se, the trial may well center about retrospective interpretation.

Examples of the use of retrospective interpretation in court trials are abundant in both fiction and fact. A classic fictional expression of the process is found in Camus' *The Stranger* (1954). Shortly after his mother's death, the hero, Monsieur Meursault, chances to meet a petty pimp. In the company of their respective girlfriends, Meursault and the pimp take a weekend outing to the seashore. There they accidentally encounter some Arab enemies of the pimp, an event that ends with Meursault shooting and killing one of the Arabs. During the long pretrial and trial period the judge and prosecutor focus their entire attention on Meursault's character while all but totally ignoring the facts of the alleged crime. Interrogation of the defendant and testimony by witnesses establish that M. Meursault does not believe in God, a condition resulting in his being dubbed "Mr. Antichrist." It is also revealed that Meursault was not distressed by having to send his mother to an institution for the aged; that he displayed "great callousness" by failing to cry or otherwise show appropriate grief at the sad occasion of his mother's funeral; that he did not linger over her fresh grave as a dutiful son is expected to do. Likewise, Meursault is shown to have visited a swimming pool, initiated a sexual liaison with a girl, and attended a comic motion picture on the day after his mother was buried. Such are the elements of "symptomatic significance" for those conducting status degradation ceremonies.

Though having no bearing on the death of the Arab, these revelations regarding M. Meursault's character, in themselves innocent and subject to reasonable interpretation, are presented so as to result in a conviction. During the concluding moments of the trial, the Prosecutor speaks to the jury:

> Not only did the man before you . . . indulge in the most shameful orgies on the day following his mother's death. He killed a man coldbloodedly, in pursuance of some sordid vendetta in the underworld of prostitutes and pimps. That, gentlemen of the jury, is the *type of man the prisoner is* (Camus, 1954:121. Emphasis added.)

To this M. Meursault's attorney replies, "Is my client on trial for having buried his mother, or for killing a man?" (Camus, 1954:121) The prosecutor, stung by the defense attorney's naïvete in failing to note the connection between these two facts, replies: "I accuse the prisoner of behaving at his mother's funeral in a way that showed *he was already a criminal at heart*" (Camus, 1954:122. Emphasis added.).

Sometimes, attorneys' efforts go awry, resulting in prosecution or defense witnesses having other than the desired effect. Thus, in the 1970–71 penalty trial of the members of the Charles Manson "family," the following exchange was recorded between Maxwell Keith, defense attorney for Leslie Van Houten and Dr. Joel Hochman, psychiatric witness for the defense. Regarding this exchange, Prosecutor Bugliosi comments:

> According to Hochman, in talking to him Leslie professed "a kind of primitive Christianity, love for the world, acceptance of all things. And Hochman asked her "Well, professing that, how can it be you would murder someone?" She said, "Well that was something inside of me too."
>
> Maxwell Keith should have stopped right there. Instead, he asked Hochman: "How do you interpret that?"
>
> A. "I think it's rather realistic. I think in reality it *was* something inside of her, despite her chronic denial of the emotional aspects of herself, that a rage was there."
>
> Nor did Keith leave it at that. He now asked: "When you say a rage was there, what do you mean by that?"
>
> A. "In my opinion it would take a rage, an emotional reaction to kill someone. I think it is unquestionable that that feeling was inside of her."
>
> Q. "Bearing in mind that she had never seen or heard of Mrs. LaBianca, in your opinion there was some hate in her when this occurred?"
>
> A. "Well, I think it would make it easier for her not to

know Mrs. LaBianca . . . It is hard to kill someone that you have good feelings towards. I don't think there was anything specific about Mrs. LaBianca.

"Let me make myself clear: Mrs. LaBianca was an object, a blank screen upon which Leslie projected her feelings, much as a patient projects his feelings on an analyst whom he doesn't know . . . feelings towards her mother, her father, toward the establishment . . .

"I think she was a very angry girl for a long time, a very alienated girl for a long time, and the anger and rage was associated with that."

Prosecutor Bugliosi continues:

Hochman was articulating one of the main points of my final summation: namely, that Leslie, Sadie, Katie, and Tex had a hostility and rage within them that pre-existed Charles Manson. They were different from Linda Kasabian, Paul Watkins, Brooks Poston, Juan Flynn, and T. J. When Manson asked them to kill for him, each said no.

Tex Watson, Susan Atkins, Patricia Krenwinkel, and Leslie Van Houten said yes.

So there had to be *something special* about these people that caused them to kill. Some kind of inner flaw. Apart from Charlie (Bugliosi, 1974:441–442. Emphasis added.).

Consistent with that, Prosecutor Bugliosi later addressed the jury as follows: "These defendants are not human, ladies and gentlemen. Human beings have a heart and a soul. No one with a heart and a soul could have done what these defendants did to these seven victims. These defendants are human monsters, human mutations" (Bugliosi, 1974:447–448). Thereby did the Prosecutor give indication of the "something special," the "outsider," to be created at status degradation ceremonies.

Constructing Moral Character: The Juvenile Court

The utility of fictional popularized accounts of degradation ceremonies is limited. That is, they rarely provide insight into the specifics of the processes of categorizing, recasting, and assigning moral character to deviant actors. More useful for that purpose is the systematic work of sociological observers. The comments to follow rest on the work of one such observer, Robert Emerson, and the ceremonial process engaged in by the juvenile court (Emerson, 1969).

Degradation ceremonies are interacts. As applied to the juvenile court, the interaction is largely confined to court officials—probation officers, public defenders and other attorneys, social workers—supplemented by parents and select other witnesses providing information to the court (the juvenile court judge) concerning the defendant and the alleged rule violation. The construction of the offender's moral character is greatly influenced by the types of information provided the court by these witnesses and by the general demeanor of the offender. How and what information is presented to the court will eventually result in the offender being classified as "a normal" or "abnormal" delinquent.

Pitches and Denunciations

Consistent with the general division of delinquents into normals and abnormals are two ways by which information may be presented to the court: the *pitch* and the *denunciation* (Emerson, 1969:104). The pitch refers to a presentation designed to cast the offender in the most favorable moral light and have the delinquent defined as "typical," that is, normal. The pitch is used when probation officers or others wish to keep the accused from being sent to a detention center or being dealt with in some other harsh way. To achieve a lenient disposition or one that will permit some rehabilitative effort calls for emphasizing the youth's socially approved qualities and ignoring, hiding, or normalizing their opposite. The youth must be shown to have redemptive qualities. Pitches, then, are used to normalize the actor and his or her behavior, thereby providing a foundation for the attribution of a socially acceptable moral character.

The second method of presenting information is the *denunciation*. The effort will be to ". . . (a) establish that the present act is of a kind typically committed by a delinquent or criminal-like character and (b) construct a delinquent biography that unequivocally indicates someone of such character" (Emerson, 1969:105). Stated differently, the denunciation is used to stigmatize the delinquent as a prelude to imposing severe and restrictive penalties. Consequently, emphasis is placed on the offender's lack of redeeming qualities, his failings and generally socially unacceptable nature. That is, the offender is seen as abnormal.

Though seeking opposite goals, pitches and denunciations rely on similar techniques and focus attention on the delinquent act and the delinquent's biography. It is these two elements (act and biography) that must be linked in some sensible (meaningful) way to the moral character being presented to the court. We will consider both the act and the biography.

Typing Delinquents

Earlier it was pointed out that deviance-processing agencies bureaucratize their clients and their actions. An expression of that tendency occurs in the juvenile court wherein juvenile offenses are categorized in organizationally convenient ways. Thus, any given delinquent act may be categorized as "typical," "criminal," or "disturbed" (Emerson, 1969:109–110). Associated with each category are distinctive motives (intentions) and distinct kinds of persons (actors). Acts and moral character are perceived to be interdependent. For example, to be perceived as "typical" means that an assault (the illegal act) will be defined as a "fight"—an ordinary event. To be classed as a criminal event, the assault must be seen as a mugging with robbery as the associated motive. The offender's presumed character must be suitably altered to conform to the definition of the act and motive pattern. That is, it is presumed that engaging in criminal assault takes a different "kind of person" than is called for in ordinary fighting. Finally, the "disturbed" category would require the assault to be perceived as "vicious," lacking sensible motivation and occurring for "no reason." Such acts are seen as particularly dangerous, risking possible loss of life, and the work of a "disturbed" person.

The offense of sexual misconduct by a girl may be similarly categorized. If defined as a case of nonrepetitive sexual contact, the situation may be regarded as "typical." Though officially frowned on, it is not likely seen as the behavior of one who has a morally unique character. Should the record reveal that these sexual episodes are regular and persistent, however, the chance exists that they will be defined as "criminal," that is, prostitution. Character would change accordingly. Finally, if these sexual encounters are reported to involve several boys simultaneously and be orgiastic or a "gang bang," the stage is set for assigning the act and actor to the "disturbed" category. Again, then, the act and moral character are intimately associated in the social construction of the delinquent. The link is established in ways that make sense to the court. It is in terms of the meanings of these categories that the court will respond to the case.

But how do court personnel determine the specific category of act and actor to be employed in a particular case? Appreciation of this process is important when one recognizes that not everything about an event or actor is to be found in official records and that the content of the record is subject to highly variable interpretation. The presence or absence of information (for whatever reason) as well as how information is transmitted (for example, with brevity or in full detail) will serve to shape the definition of the act and actor and, in turn, how they are categorized (Emerson, 1969:111). The simple size or bulk of one's file is itself regarded as symbolic of the extent (and seriousness) of one's deviant career. Basically, the "fatter the file" the more extensively and deeply involved in deviance one is assumed to be. Hence, it contributes to the actor being defined as having a more indelibly delinquent moral character. Investigation of seemingly minor issues such as where a runaway spent the night, and linking the answer to the offender's appearance, may also influence the categorization. For example, how likely it is that a physically clean and neatly attired runaway spent the night sleeping in a doorway or a vacant lot? Is the presence of heavy makeup on the "sexually delinquent girl" indicative of a "typical" or a "criminal" (prostitution) case? Does the presence of several highly saleable items in the auto trunk of a suspected juvenile shoplifter suggest a "typical" or a "criminal" case?

In short, categorization of an act and actor is highly problematic, and rests on a combination of several indices which are themselves assigned meanings that allow them to be classed as "typical," "criminal," or "disturbed."

Evaluating Biography

Let's turn to the second area of concern—the actor's biography. In the investigation of the biography, the orientation of court personnel continues to allow for the use of the pitch or the denunciation. The pitch will be used to create the image of a youth whose school record, family situation, known delinquent history, and the like, allows for rehabilitation. On the other hand, a denunciation is likely to be used for the youth whose background shows signs of progressive moral decline and the need for strict restraint and punishment. In either case, consulting the biography aids in the assessment of the actor's moral character as well as helping to "place" the youth in terms of the development of a delinquent career (Emerson, 1969:120–121).

Which presentation is used, pitch or denunciation, depends on the court personnel's definition of where the youth stands vis-à-vis a delinquent career. In turn, the stage of a youth's career is based on (1) his or her general pattern of delinquent behavior (is it characteristically "typical," "criminal," or "disturbed?") and (2) an array of environmental conditions (such as family situation) felt to contribute to serious delinquency (Emerson, 1969:121–132). The first of these concerns generally leads to a standard series of inquiries. Is the present offense one of a series of delinquencies? Has the youth had prior contact with the juvenile court? And, most important, has the youth had previous commitment to a training school—on which basis it may be inferred that a pattern of serious delinquency is well established. Should the presentation be of the denunciatory type, attention will focus on these questions and the details recounted.

Events of a more personal nature will also be investigated. What is the youth's "attitude"; that is, does his or her behavior, especially with respect to the police, the court, and the offense reflect a "hard core" delinquent or a person who is amenable to treatment? How does the offender get along with the staff and other students at school? What attitudinal pattern is reflected in the actor's academic record? Who are the actor's friends and how involved are they in delinquent acts? Information concerning all these matters is likely to be readily available, either in the offender's file or that of others. Each piece of information is subject to collation and interpretation in an effort to "make sense" of the instance of deviance under investigation.

Turning to environmental conditions, investigation of the actor's biography tends to focus on those things presumed to have "causative" importance. Of special importance is family background, particularly parental neglect or other conditions leading to reduced guidance and social control. The amount and kind of parental discipline, general conduct of the home, and whether the parents' behavior conforms to the moral expectations of the court, will effect the court's assessment of the child's moral character and prospects for the future. Basically, the questions posed concern the moral stature of the family. Is the family reputable or disreputable (Emerson, 1969:133; Matza, 1966)? If the latter label is felt to apply to the family, its stigmatizing power may well be transferred to the youth.

Should these inquiries fail to provide information sufficient to allow for categorization of the offender, should the actor's status remain ambiguous, the court may turn to outsiders for assistance (Emerson, 1969:133–136). A person whose reputation is above reproach (such as a priest) and who is familiar with the offender may be called on to provide clarity. Clarity may also be provided by calling on expert witnesses such as a psychiatrist. Whether these or other resource persons are used rests on the apparent need to render character and behavior consistent. It is necessary to determine whether the case in point is typical or atypical. If a case is classed as atypical, the ambiguity of the actor's moral character and, consequently, how the case should be handled, becomes more than usually problematic.

The effort to resolve ambiguities inherent in atypical cases reveals the reciprocal nature of the presumed relation between moral character and behavior (Emerson, 1969:135–136). In typical cases the delinquent act is inconsistent with the actor's "essentially" moral character. In such cases the act is "adjusted" (redefined) to fit the character. If moral character is obscure or uncertain the benefit of the doubt goes to the juvenile. In atypical cases, however, these elements are interactive and consistent; act and biography point to moral character and, in turn, the constructed moral character reflects back on behavior. A consistent relationship between act and biography is thereby established.

Total Denunciation

We conclude with a brief additional comment on denunciations. It has been noted that the "pitch" tends to minimize the socially negative aspects of one's behavior and character. In the denunciation these same qualities are maximized. When carried to the extreme, and to be successful, denunciations preclude defense for the actor's behavior and weaken any support the actor may have for retaining a primarily moral identity. Such cases, referred to as *total denunciations* (Emerson, 1969:137), call for constructing a "hopeless case." That is, the actor must be presented as one who has (1) had several viable opportunities to refrain from rule-violating behavior, but (2) has chosen to ignore or reject them in favor of delinquent conduct. The repetitiveness of the delinquent behavior, its patterned nature, is then used to support the conclusion that the youth is a "hopeless case," beyond reform, suited only for punitive (rather than rehabilitative) disposition. In view of the number of opportunities to "go straight" formerly available and the belief that they were rejected volitionally, the fault is seen to rest solely with the offender. In that sense, there is no defense for the actor's behavior.

Total denunciation disallows a defense in an additional way. First, all parties to the degradation ceremony—officials, witnesses, perhaps family—agree that the actor is a hopeless case. Thus, the actor is fully discredited. Second, disallowing a defense means that there is no meaningful alternative disposition than detention. Such a disposition must be established as a logical and reasonable consequence of the youth having failed to take advantage of the rehabilitative opportunities provided earlier in his or her career. This failure is used to mark the actor's essential character as discreditable. Using "unresponsiveness to rehabilitation" as evidence of character, detention becomes the only viable alternative.

Finally, anyone who would launch a defense of the actor, suggesting he or she is yet a socially redeemable person, anyone who would question the propriety of total denunciation of a thoroughly immoral character, must be discounted and such a position discredited. Alternatively, persons likely to support the youth, such as parents, are often encouraged to join in the denunciation of the actor, at least to the degree of conceding that he or she be sent away for "his or her own good." In brief, parents and others are encouraged to concur in the denunciation. In this regard, total denunciation involves a systematic connection, a *circuit of agents* (Goffman, 1973:100), between court officials, next-of-kin, police, and defense counsel (usually a public defender) who engage in a process of *stripping*, that is, official removal of the symbols of a socially acceptable being.

In sum, then, degradation ceremonies mark a change in one's moral status. However, this moral recasting is not an automatic consequence of one's behavior. Consistent with our comments throughout, it can be seen that court officials do not respond to any objective moral meaning associated with the offender's behavior. The determination of the behavior's moral meaning is problematic; it rests on matters of context, biography, and the presentation of materials to the court. Uppermost in this process is the establishment of a sense of consistency between the actor's behavior and his or her presumed character. In turn, such consistency serves to legitimate the court's disposition of the case. Overall, the decisions reached are consequences of a socially constructed reality.

Impediments to Labeling

The theoretical model employed in this study conceives of people as interactive agents who seek to shape their destiny by interacting with elements in the environment. Consistent with this model, people may not meekly submit to status degradation and moral recasting. As with other aspects of the deviance enterprise, the assignment of moral meanings is problematic, sometimes subject to negotiation. That observation applies as well to the formal induction of people into the status of deviant.

Research evidence clearly supports the idea that the labeling process is influenced by several factors, some posed by the efforts of rule violators to resist labeling and others of a more situational nature. As a consequence, it may not be assumed that formal labeling, once begun, runs its course and automatically results in the actor being compelled into becoming a secondary deviant. Quite the contrary; the sequence of interaction leading to secondary deviance is highly problematic (Lemert, 1951:77). Even though the process may be well advanced, it may be interrupted, its course changed, even reversed. In this section we will consider factors that restrict or permit interruption of the labeling process. In Chapter 7 we will consider ways in which actors respond to labeling *after* it has occurred, how they manage stigma.

Power

One major factor influencing the labeling process is the relative power of the labeler and the labelee. As noted in Chapter 4, the distribution of power in society is rarely, if ever, balanced. It is asymmetrical. But neither is it totally imbalanced such that one party has all, while another has none. This is especially so considering the coalitions, exchange of favors, and other tactics that may be used to enhance one's power position. It should be no surprise, then, that power may be employed in strategic ways by both parties (labeler and labelee) engaged in the labeling process.

One expression of the strategic use of influence to affect labeling is *plea bargaining* (Newman, 1966), whereby defendants in criminal cases plead guilty to reduced charges in return for considerations such as reduced punishment. For his part, the prosecutor is relieved of the necessity of expanding scarce resources to conduct a full-scale prosecution of a relatively minor or routine case. Most pertinent is the fact that these pleas are arranged, arrived at through bargaining by means of which prosecution and defense seek satisfactory consequences. Each has the ability to influence the other and each exercises "skill"—a clear case of intercursive power. The negotiations involve activity that is far from the normative myths constructed concerning the work of the criminal justice system. Certainly, negotiated pleas run counter to ideas such as "the punishment fits the crime," that "rules of evidence" are scrupulously adhered to, and that in the American justice system guilt and innocence are determined in adversary proceedings according to the rules of due process. In fact, between 90 percent and 95 percent of all convictions for crimes in this country are achieved without trial and under conditions substantially at odds with stated ideals (Blumberg, 1967:29; Newman, 1966:3).

Plea bargaining is instructive for students of social reality in that it demonstrates the problematic nature of assessing responsibility. The deviant's responsibility is negotiated and calls for the construction of reality, including the actor's intentions and behavior, as well as the criteria of responsibility. Responsibility, then, is not an absolute (Scheff, 1968: 3-4). Negotiation of such matters is, of course, well known among students, particularly in American colleges and universities. Thus, it is not uncommon for students to "plead their case" before instructors; that is, to seek to avoid having a failing or otherwise unacceptable grade entered in their record. Unacceptable grades have consequences for students' public image, particularly regarding their capacity to learn and/or their apparent failure to "responsibly" play the role of student. The consequence of that image for one's employability is immediately obvious. In short, students, like publicly apprehended deviants, seek to avoid stigma labels by the process of negotiation.

Efforts to negotiate an acceptable self-image may take other forms. One of these is the effort people sometimes make to amass "moral credits" that may be used ("drawn on") at a time when their image as a moral person is jeopardized by public knowledge of wrongdoing. Having these credits available serves to reinforce and validate one's claim to an acceptable social position despite having broken rules. One such case involved an unmarried pregnant high-school girl. Throughout her life this girl took pride in being a "good Catholic girl" who never allowed boys to "take advantage" of her. She then fell in love, submitted to her young man's advances, and became pregnant. Without funds, flight was impossible. For the same reason, and reinforced by very strong religious convictions, abortion was out of the question. Finally, living with her parents in a small town made it readily apparent that in due time her pregnancy would become intolerably public.

The only viable way for this girl to neutralize the anticipated stigma of her pregnancy was to amass moral credits, upon which she could draw when and if she was faced with stigmatization and a spoiled identity. This she did by giving up smoking and what small amount of alcohol she consumed, refraining from parties and other forms of revelry (however mild), doing every extra chore she could to help her parents, working very hard in school to raise her grades—in short, living as ascetic a life as one of her age and circumstance could. In these ways she sought to create a more than usual moral image of self, one that would survive the consequences of revealing her pregnancy.

The effort and ability of some offenders to avoid being labeled may also be noted in the tendency of some actor's to "put on a performance" in the presence of rule enforcers. For example, a woman was stopped by a policeman for speeding. Though she is a highly articulate, intelligent, and liberated person, she immediately went into her "act," speaking and behaving in a helpless, deferential, self-demeaning manner, professing all the time to be ignorant of the rules. She got off with a verbal warning. On leaving the scene she commented "Mark one for me!"

Putting on a performance (Lorber, 1967:303) is by no means unusual when people wish to influence the conduct of others toward oneself (which is almost always). As Goffman notes, one may achieve this control ". . . largely by influencing the definition of the situation which the others come to formulate, and he can influence this definition by expressing himself in such a way as to give the kind of impression that will lead them to act voluntarily in accordance with his own plan" (Goffman, 1959:4).

A demonstration of this was noted by Richard Nagasawa during his investigation of deliqunecy among Japanese-American boys in Seattle, Washington (Chambliss and Nagasawa, 1969). In conversation with these boys, it became clear to Nagasawa that they attempted to influence police definitions of their behavior. For example, playing on the already existing favorable bias police had of them (see page 130), these boys would explain their presence on the streets at unusual hours as a consequence of work or other socially acceptable conditions. During predaylight hours the excuse frequently used was "preparing for newspaper delivery." Late night hours were often explained by proffering they were "detained at a late Boy Scout or other socially acceptable club meeting" (personal communication).

Another factor influencing labeling is the offender's demeanor in the presence of police (Piliavin and Briar, 1964). Youthful offenders who display respect for the police, fear of sanctions, and are penitent (all of which may be feigned) are most prone to be given a formal or informal reprimand and released. Youth who are "fractious, obdurate, and nonchalant," on the other hand, are more likely to be viewed as "tough-guys" or "punks" and arrested (Piliavin and Briar, 1964:210–211).

Finally, resistance to labeling was also noted by Emerson in his work on the juvenile court. This involves a number of protective or defensive strategies. One such strategy is *innocence*, whereby the youth professes technical or factual innocence of the charge. This is particularly effective when evidence is conflicting and the case is inconclusive (Emerson, 1969:144–149). A second strategy is to proffer justifications. These may be of the principled or situational type. *Principled justifications* require "placing" the youth in a situation involving a conflict of principles (not unlike an "appeal to higher loyalties"—see page 67), the resolution of which resulted in the violation. *Situational justifications* are used when one cites the contingencies of his or her actual situation. Thus, the act is acknowledged to be wrong, but the circumstances are said to have been such as to permit an exception. Third and finally, resistances to labeling most frequently take the form of *excuses*, stories designed to reduce the wrongfulness of the act. Well handled, "reasonable excuses allow the court to form and maintain an acceptable evaluation of moral character and in this way further favorable dispositions" (Emerson, 1969:153). Elements used in excuses include duress, accident, ignorance, or that one was innocently led into an act that was planned and initiated by others.

In all these ways individuals may seek to limit the capacity of officials to attach labels. This effort is consistent with the image of man used here. As an expression of man as an interactive agent, people seek to direct and control the actions of others toward themselves. However, as we will see in Chapter 7, efforts to resist and neutralize the *effects of labeling* go well beyond our immediate concerns.

Additional Factors

Social Distance

An additional factor that influences the probability of labeling is *social distance* (the degree of sympathetic understanding between people). As sympathetic understanding increases between labeler and labelee the probability of being labeled decreases. The operation of this rule of typing was noted in research on unwed fathers, men who had impregnated women to whom they were not married. In most of the relationships studied, the couples had been introduced by friends or family members, had attended school together, regarded themselves as regular dating partners, and in a great majority of cases professed to have strong emotional attachment for one another. These characteristics suggest that the couples shared a common group identity—a condition indicative of minimal social distance (maximum sympathetic understanding) and likely to promote minimal typing. This expectation was fulfilled (Pfuhl, 1978). As Rubington and Weinberg have noted (1973:9), the tendency is to grant rule breaking in-group members the benefit of the doubt and withhold the attribution of deviant.

Clarity of Moral Meaning

Another influence on the labeling process is the clarity of moral meaning. "Clarity of moral meaning" refers to the proposition that before actors are labeled their behavior most often is defined as an "uncommon event"—one that might have been otherwise and that violates an important social rule. In the case of unwed fatherhood, referred to above, the important social rule is "don't impregnate unmarried women." Given this rule, these pregnancies were considered "uncommon events" and the responsible men were prime candidates for labeling. Nonetheless, sanctions were never imposed, implying a lack of clear moral meaning. Reconciliation of the apparent inconsistency between rule violation and labeling leads to a consideration of the male role in premarital pregnancy in terms of the distinction between the *morality of intention* and the *morality of consequence*.

"Morality of intention" refers to the tradition in which the criteria of blamefulness includes the actor's purpose, negligence, recklessness, and knowledge (Packer, 1968:105). On the basis of that tradition, the tradition of intention, these unwed fathers are culpable. Each was aware of his purpose (intention), the possible consequences of his behavior (knowledge), and each behaved negligently or recklessly by ignoring (failing to take adequate precautions against) the risk of pregnancy. In that sense the moral meanings seem clear and the men are sanctionable.

Nonetheless, they avoided being labeled, almost in spite of having violated an important social rule. This suggests that in place of the morality of intention a different morality was employed—that of consequence. According to this morality, one's culpability or blamefulness rests *not* on his sexual misbehavior, but on how he behaves following the pregnancy, especially whether he assumes the role of "protector" of the woman. That is, for these men to be officially labeled seems to be unrelated to their sexual conduct or its consequences, the pregnancy. If applied at all, the label is appended in an ex post facto manner, after the men's intentions toward the women become evident. That is, whether or not the man "stood by" the woman was more important than his initial sexual misconduct.

The men in this study and those in a position to label them used a "morality of consequence." Very often men referred to a need to "clean things up," that is, to take steps to reduce or eliminate any problems associated with the pregnancy. Such steps include marrying the woman, helping her to meet medical and living costs, arranging and/or paying all or part of the cost of abortion, and otherwise "standing by" the woman. A morality of consequence was also apparent in the sex codes these men embraced, codes that included the importance of preventing any negative consequences such as pregnancy, venereal disease, and reputational damage as a consequence of sexual behavior. Last, many of the parents of these men and women expressed a morality of consequence by insisting that the man "set things right" or "do the proper thing" with regard to the woman. Fulfillment of the expectations associated with this morality apparently took precedence over the violation of the morality of intention.

The implications of this study may not be generalized to the labeling process as a whole. Nonetheless, it is instructive in that

there appears to be a priority of moralities in terms of which the labeling process is ordered. That is, we have not one rule but two: (1) the rule based on the morality of intention (do not impregnate unmarried women) and (2) the rule based on the morality of consequence (if you get an unmarried woman pregnant, stand by her). What seems clear is that being sanctioned for the former is dependent on violation of the latter, while conformity to the latter may well reduce the probability of invoking the former (Pfuhl, 1978:127–128).

In short, then, whether or not labeling occurs depends to some degree on the clarity of moral meaning, that is, on which moral rule is to be invoked and under what circumstances it shall be invoked.

Odds and Ends

Valuable information concerning the problematics of labeling has come from investigations in the general field of mental health. Studies have shown that several factors, quite apart from the actor's mental state, influence the outcome of investigations to determine legal competency (the legal counterpart of mental illness). These investigations are ordinarily initiated by a complaint filed on the basis of someone's evaluation of the actor's behavior. The outcome of these official investigations (sometimes formal hearings are convened), that is, whether the actor is declared to be legally incompetent, seems to vary with the age of the alleged incompetent, the composition of the investigating committee, and the type of petition filed in the case.

The younger the client the less likely is he or she to be declared incompetent. Perhaps this pattern stems from the positive valuation assigned youth and, conversely, the increased tendency of older people to become economically dependent upon family members. Second, if investigative bodies consist of psychiatrists, the probability increases that a decision of incompetence will result, likely as an expression of the psychiatric construction of reality. Being trained to "find mental illness," psychiatrists do precisely that! Third, as social distance between the petitioner and the alleged incompetent decreases (that is, as petitioner and actor become more intimately associated), so does the likelihood that a judgment of incompetence will result. A petition filed by members of a family against one of its members has less chance of being supported than otherwise. Very likely, reluctance to assign a label of mental illness in such cases reflects community definitions of family interrelations. In any case, it is quite clear that labeling is influenced by factors other than the mental state of the person under examination (Haney and Michielutte, 1968:241).

Additional research on the subject of labeling the mentally ill— this time on lunacy hearings—reveals

. . . that those persons who were able to approach the judge [in a lunacy hearing] in a controlled manner, use proper eye contact, sentence structure, posture, etc., and who presented their stories without excessive emotional response or blandness and with proper demeanor, were able to obtain the decision they wanted, whether it was release or commitment—despite any "psychiatric symptomatology" (Miller and Schwartz, 1966:34).

Finally, it has been shown that the outcome of admission hearings at some state hospitals for the mentally ill are conclusively influenced by whether or not the alleged incompetent is represented at the hearing by an attorney. Thus, in eighty-one admission cases studied, it was found that ". . . 61 (91%) of these without legal counsel (N = 66) were admitted, but only 4 (26%) of those with legal counsel (N = 15) were admitted" (Wegner and Fletcher, 1969:69). It was also found that this relationship between legal representation and admissions decisions held when the patient's behavior was held constant. That is, even when the patient met psychiatric criteria for admission, his or her chances of being admitted were significantly lower with legal representation than without (Wegner and Fletcher, 1969:70–71).

As these data reveal, then, the attribution of a deviant label is far from an automatic or inevitable consequence of rule-breaking behavior. Due to the influence of several factors, many of which are quite tangential to the principal issue of the actor's behavior, labels may be changed (as in the case of plea bargaining) or entirely withheld (as at many incompetency hearings).

However, labeling and the general demeanor of the deviant are not totally independent of one another. Evidence reveals that in some cases the deviant contributes to his own discovery and official stigmatization. One such example was revealed in research comparing homosexuals discharged from military service with honorable discharges and those receiving less than honorable discharges. It was found that the probability of receiving a less than honorable discharge is greater for those homosexuals in the military who are highly active sexually than for those who have infrequent sexual contact. The probability of receiving a LHD is also greater for those who select their homosexual partners from among military personnel. In short, it is not just *doing* homosexuality that influences being labeled and sanctioned. Official labeling is also influenced by the quality and quantity of the actor's behavior (Williams and Weinberg, 1970).

In brief, then, the dynamics of status degradation and labeling are influenced by many factors, the consequence of which suggests that the outcome of these proceedings is far from certain and, like other aspects of the deviance process, may not be taken for granted.

Summary

The focus of concern in this chapter has been the informal and formal procedures by which people come to regard themselves and come to be regarded by others as "being deviant," that is, how one's essential self is recast to conform with what is known of his or her deviant behavior. This has entailed a consideration of deviance as a status, achieved and ascribed, primary and secondary, and the seeming capacity of one's deviant status—a master status—to obscure the balance of one's self.

Extended consideration was also given to the institutionalization of deviance—how responsibility for responding to deviant persons is assigned to bureaucratic organizations, how these organizations operate, and their consequences for the client population. Of major importance is the principal rationale for the conduct of these agencies—the theory of office—and how, taking the form of "total institutions," these agencies socialize the client to a role consistent with one who is seen as essentially deviant. Not the least important element in this process is the influence of stereotypes. Relying on the prior work of "imputational specialists," and by a process of "retrospective interpretation," a biography of the deviant is constructed that validates the label assigned to him or her. In this way the actor's character and behavior may be shown to be consistent. A further consequence is that the conduct of the agency vis-à-vis the client is legitimized. The culmination of much of the labeling process is noted in the degradation ceremony—court trials, and similar procedures.

Overall, "being deviant" is a consequence of a process that may have only marginal relationship to one's prior behavior and the meaning assigned to it. An example of how behavior, actor, and actor's biography are linked together, demonstrative of the problematic outcome of the labeling process, was provided by an extended consideration of the degradation ceremony of the juvenile court.

Part of what renders the outcome of these proceedings problematic—uncertain—is that the decisions reached are negotiable (hence, unpredictable), subject to the influence of several situational factors, and altogether resistable. Consideration was given to several factors influencing the labeling process.

For all of that, some people do get labeled. Their "essential self" does come (at least officially and publicly) to be that of deviant. What are the effects of a "spoiled identity?" We turn now to a consideration of the consequences of labeling and stigma.

Consequences of
Labeling and Stigma

Introduction

Most people who break rules are never publicly identified as such and many who are identified manage to avoid being labeled and stigmatized. In short, the labeling process is problematical. However, it is equally apparent that many people do get labeled, oftentimes indelibly, with the result that their public identity is "spoiled" and they are burdened with the consequences of stigma. The present chapter will deal with the matters of identity spoilage and stigma. Specifically, we will be concerned with the meanings of stigma and what their personal and social consequences may be. The basic issue is how (and if) people become the thing they are named (Manning, 1975:2).

For several years the issue of the social-psychological and social impact of labeling on labelees has been a topic of substantial sociological debate. In order that our present discussion adequately represent this aspect of the labeling process, and to avoid misunderstanding, it will be necessary to deal at length with the theory related to this process. Following that we will examine relevant research findings in terms consistent with the elements of the social definition paradigm. Before turning to these matters, however, let us examine the concepts of *stigma* and *spoiled* identity.

Stigma and Spoiled Identities

The term *stigma* is derived from the Greek, where it refers to a mark or brand (such as imposed on slaves) indicative of the bearer's low *social position* and others' perception of the bearer as an "outsider." Such stigma have also been used to call public attention to people's low *moral position* as, for example, in the case of criminals. This sense of stigma is demonstrated in Nathaniel Hawthorne's famous novel *The Scarlet Letter*, wherein the letter "A" (for adulterer) was required to be worn by the heroine, Hester Prynne. In this case the stigma represents not only one's violation of moral rules, but the despicability and shame bestowed on the person held to be guilty of the offense.

In addition, stigma reflect on the bearer's identity. As noted earlier, the labeling process seeks to establish consistency between behavior and character. In keeping with that effort, one who bears a discrediting stigma is taken to be the same as the thing described by that sign. Thus, the bearer's public or social identity is that of one who is spoiled, morally corrupted, or otherwise tainted (Goffman, 1963:19).

To be sure, not all stigma are alike. Goffman suggests three types

(1963:4–5). First, there are *abominations of the body*, that is, conditions such as physical deformities resulting from birth, illness, or accident that are regarded as repugnant or odious and that may be used to place the individual in a discredited category. These are most often associated with cases of ascriptive deviance. A classic example of one beset with such stigma is Quasimodo, Victor Hugo's hunchback of Notre Dame. Second are *blemishes of character*, qualities inferentially based on one having engaged in things like crime, homosexuality, or political radicalism, having attempted suicide, having been diagnosed as mentally ill, and the like. Again, character and behavior are rendered consistent. As an example, political radicals are often taken to be (characterologically) dangerous, impulsive, and aggressive, while adulterers are often assumed to be (characterologically) immoral, promiscuous, and insecure (Simmons, 1969:29). Finally, there are *tribal stigma*. In Goffman's terms, these are the ". . . stigma of race, nation, and religion, these being stigma that can be transmitted through lineages and [that] equally contaminate all members of a family" (Goffman, 1963:4). Examples include skin color and names that have specific religious and/or national connotations. In most cases, these stigma, like abominations of the body, are matters of ascription rather than achievement.

Regardless of type, all stigma share one sociological feature: they symbolize that one occupies a *master status*. As Goffman notes: ". . . an individual who might have been received easily in ordinary social intercourse possesses a trait that can obtrude itself upon attention and turn those of us whom he meets away from him, breaking the claim that his other attributes have on us" (Goffman, 1963:5). In brief and in theory, stigma denote one's morally spoiled identity, one's social undesirability, and take precedence over other qualities to which one may make claim.

With these few definitions and examples in mind, let us now place the issue of stigma and their consequences in a larger theoretical framework. By examining stigma from the symbolic interactionist perspective we may better appreciate their social and social-psychological consequences.

Consequences of Labeling: Theory

Theoretical Foundations

The origins of the labeling perspective are found in the work of Charles Horton Cooley and George Herbert Mead. These scholars employed a *symbolic interactionist perspective*, a form of social psychology stressing the idea that human behavior and personality rest on man's facility for developing and using language (symbols) to transmit meaning. In this perspective human interaction rests largely on these meanings; hence social interaction becomes symbolic interaction. Most important is the symbolic interactionist contention that one's self-image or self-concept emerges in interaction with others.

Expressive of this contention is Cooley's idea that a person's self-feeling consists of three elements: (1) how we imagine we appear to another person, (2) our imagination of how the other judges our appearance, and (3) a resulting self-feeling (Cooley, 1902:184). As a result of this interactive process people are able to evaluate their behavior, attitudes, and general appearance on the basis of how they think others evaluate these same things. Cooley notes that "we always imagine, and in imagining share, the judgments of the other [person's] mind" (Cooley, 1902:184–85). From such imaginings we derive self-feelings such as shame, pride, mortification, and embarrassment.

The position taken by George Herbert Mead is compatible with that of Cooley. According to Mead, people are able to see themselves as objects as a result of role taking, putting themselves in another's position and identifying with that person (Manis and Meltzer, 1967:9). Taking the role of the other depends on an ability to engage in communication, verbal and/or gestural. It is through the use of symbols that communication is possible and meanings are transmitted. By learning the symbols commonly employed in the groups with which one associates—family, neighborhood, friendship cliques, and so on—a person learns and tends to internalize others' meanings. People are then able to put themselves in others' roles—take the role of the other—and have the perspective of others' become one's own. "The standpoint of others provides a platform for getting outside oneself and thus viewing oneself. The development of the self is concurrent with the development of the ability to take roles" (Manis and Meltzer, 1967:10). This, as well as the development of a self-conception, is the consequence of the socialization process. It is through this general process that identity is acquired. As Peter Berger notes, ". . . identity is socially bestowed, socially sustained and socially transformed" (Berger, 1963:98). It is the transformation associated with stigmatizing labels that concerns us.

Briefly, then, developing a self-concept or self-feelings allows a person to engage in *reflexive activity*, that is, self-interaction, by becoming the object of one's own thoughts. By including others' definitions in these reflexive thoughts, one derives a new perspective toward himself or herself. That is, having self-feelings allows one to act toward (think about) oneself. One has a mental life; people are able to experience their own self.

Finally, as we saw in Chapter 2, people's behavior is often influenced by their self-concept; that is, having self-feelings enables one to control his or her behavior. Having self-feelings and being able to act toward oneself means one is not simply a victim of or responsive to external forces. People are capable of mediating the stimuli to which they are exposed. People are able to check their behavior, redirect it, or permit it to unfold with relatively little inhibition (Manis and Meltzer, 1967:12–13).

Implications: Amplification and Stabilization of Deviance

Let's consider the implication of this theoretical perspective for amplifying and stabilizing people in a deviant status. As we've seen, the labeling process is intended to identify a person as deviant. If the process is successful the labelee comes to occupy the status of deviant and is expected to play the role, that is, display the appropriate behavior. As with any status, deviance is linked to a set of meanings (in this case moral meanings symbolized by the stigma) that are appended to the occupants of the status. Occupying a status and playing the role also results in the incumbent being socialized to the role, including the learning of self-feelings appropriate to that role.

These considerations have led to a major proposition of the labeling perspective, namely that *"rule breakers become entrenched in deviant roles because they are labeled 'deviant' by others and are consequently excluded from resuming normal roles in the community"* (Mankoff, 1971:201. Emphasis in original.). This proposition arose very early in the development of the labeling perspective. Tannenbaum (1938) maintained that to "dramatize" the evil of the wrongful act serves only to perpetuate the conflict between the deviant actor and society, a conflict likely to have negative consequences for the deviant's self-image. Tannenbaum writes:

> From the community's point of view, the individual who used to do bad and mischievous things has now become a bad and unredeemable human being. From the individual's point of view there has taken place a similar change. He has gone slowly from a sense of grievance and injustice, of being unduly mistreated and punished, to a recognition that the definition of him as a human being is different from that of other boys in his neighborhood, his school, street, community. This recognition on his part becomes a process of self-

identification and integration with the group which shares his activities (Tannenbaum, 1938:17).

It was Tannenbaum's view that the community reaction, more than the behavior or character of the individual deviant, was critical in stabilizing people in the position of deviant.

Echoing this position, Kai Erikson maintains that community response to deviants, particularly in the case of those experiencing degradation ceremonies, leaves the deviant in a position from which there may be little or no escape. Underlying community rejection is the negative moral meaning attributed to the deviant and symbolized by the stigma. In turn, ". . . the community's reluctance to accept the deviant back helps reduce whatever chance he might otherwise have for a successful readjustment" (Erikson, 1964:17). Community rejection, then, is alleged to be a fundamental element in people becoming secondary deviants.

Another major contributor to the labeling perspective, Howard Becker, takes a similar position. Becker maintains that "one of the most crucial steps in the process of building a stable pattern of deviant behavior [becoming a secondary deviant] is likely to be the experience of being caught and publicly labeled as a deviant" (Becker, 1973:31). Rule-violating behavior aside, it is claimed, whether or not one's deviant orientation becomes crystallized is at least partly dependent on others' reactions to the alleged deviant. Again, Tannenbaum:

> The first dramatization of the "evil" which separates the child out of his group for specialized treatment plays a greater role in making the criminal than perhaps any other experience. . . . The process of making the criminal . . . is a process of tagging, defining, identifying, segregating, describing, emphasizing, making conscious and self-conscious; it becomes a way of stimulating, suggesting, emphasizing and evoking the very traits that are complained of. . . . The person becomes the thing he is described as being (Tannenbaum, 1938:19–20).

Lemert has also suggested that the individual's conception of self as a deviant and one's involvement in the deviant role rest on ". . . a progressive reciprocal relationship between the deviation of the individual and the societal reaction" (Lemert, 1951:76). The stages of this progressive reciprocal relationship resulting in the stabilization and amplification of one's deviant role are as follows:

1. primary deviation, i.e., one breaks rules;
2. social penalties are imposed; these are

3. followed by more deviation;
4. penalties becoming stronger and are accompanied by rejection of the deviant actor; this is followed by
5. further deviation in association with resentment and hostility directed at those imposing the penalties;
6. deviance is then defined as intolerable resulting in stigmatizing the errant actor;
7. in response to the stigma and penalties actor's deviant conduct is strengthened; this leads to
8. the actor's acceptance of the conception of self as deviant and orients his or her life around the status of deviant (Lemert, 1951:77).

The stabilizing and amplifying consequences of labeling are also alleged to result in the categorization of larger groups of deviants. Employing the term "amplification model," Leslie Wilkins has stressed this aspect of labeling. According to Wilkins,

> The action taken by society and the resulting self-perception of the individuals defined as deviant, lead to the isolation and alienation of the specified individuals.
> This provides the first part of a deviation-amplifying system. The definition of society leads to the development of the self-perception as "deviant" on the part of the "outliers" (outlaws), and it is hardly to be expected that people who are excluded by a system will continue to regard themselves as part of it. The deviant groups will tend to develop their own values which may run counter to the values of the parent system, the system which defined them as "outliers."
> The increased deviance demonstrated by the deviant groups (resulting from the deviation amplifying effect of the self-perception, which in turn may have derived from the defining acts of society) results in more forceful action by the conforming groups against the nonconformists. Thus information about the behavior of nonconformists . . . received by the conforming groups leads to more acts being defined as deviant, or to more stringent action against the 'outliers' " (Wilkins, 1965:92).

Thus, as so-called "conforming groups" and their representatives (police, and so on) receive added information concerning the behavior of "deviant groups," reactions intended to curb that behavior persist, perhaps even increasing in intensity. Wilkins contends that this action-reaction-action cycle is repetitive in nature and may

". . . continue round and round again in an amplifying circuit" (Wilkins, 1965:92).

Applying the amplification model specifically to drug users, Jock Young suggests (1971:33) that the interaction process between deviants and control agents (police) influences both groups. For example,

(i) the police act against the drug-users in terms of their stereotypes;
(ii) the drug-user group finds itself in a new situation, which it must interpret and adapt to in a changed manner;
(iii) the police react in a slightly different fashion to the changed group;
(iv) the drug-users interpret and adapt to this new situation;
(v) the police react to these new changes; and so on.

The deviance amplification cycle may be stated in slightly different terms. First, to be publicly identified as deviant is to be cloaked with the mantle of a master status. In addition to having the capacity to obscure other (perhaps morally acceptable) statuses and the actor's real identity (Payne, 1973:36), an implicit set of expectations is linked to the master status. Not the least of the alleged effects of this status and expectations are the fear and suspicion they arouse in the audience—conditions that may subtly call for the detested behavior. Should the actor conform to the expectations his or her behavior serves only to confirm the original label. The label becomes a self-fulfilling prophecy (see page 130). On the other hand, failure of the deviant actor to conform to the expectations of the deviant status may not be acknowledged (Tannenbaum, 1938:477). On the basis of these circumstances, it is theorized that the moral meaning of one's deviance may become the basis for creating a barrier that prevents the actor from occupying normal statuses or engaging in normal social intercourse. The actor is regarded as a moral pariah and is so treated.

Second, because others may respond to the actor in terms of the master status, and because self-feelings are derived from others' reactions, the actor may come to regard himself and herself in terms consistent with the moral judgments expressed by others and symbolized by the stigmatizing label. These self-attitudes, as well as the limitations placed on one's role-playing opportunities, become central facts of one's life.

Taken together, these conditions lead to the proposition that as a result of responses to the actor's behavior or condition by official control agencies and others in the community, labeling often results in the actor becoming entrenched or "engulfed" in the role of deviant (Lemert, 1967a: Chapter 3; Schur, 1971:67ff; Schur, 1973:115ff; Becker, 1973:31, 179). The actor thus enters the stage of secondary deviance.

In the secondary stage the actor's deviant status is theorized to have social and social psychological consequences. It is also alleged (Tannenbaum, 1938) that being publicly declared deviant serves to perpetuate one's deviant conduct. In short, *community rejection and social control create and maintain deviant careers* (Rose, 1968:43). As an extension of this contention it has been proposed that by following a public policy of *judicious nonintervention* (Lemert 1967b:96–97) or *radical nonintervention* (Schur, 1973:160) many of the long-term negative consequences of labeling may be avoided.

A Cautionary Note

Having introduced several theoretical elements of the labeling perspective and some of their implications for deviant actors, let us briefly identify what these aspects of the perspective *do not* mean.

First, these remarks do not mean that the amplification and stabilization aspects of labeling are simple mechanistic processes wherein the actions of one group (be it deviant or control agent) *compel* or *determine* the actions of others in any specific manner. Quite the reverse is the case. As our model of man indicates, people are interactive agents who *adapt* to and even transcend elements in their environment. As Young indicates, the deviant group is not to be thought of as ". . . a pinball inevitably propelled in a deviant direction, or . . . the police [as] . . . the cushions of the machine that will inevitably reflex into a reaction triggered by the changing course of the deviant group" (Young, 1971:34). Nonetheless, negative responses by the community and its representatives are major environmental conditions with which labeled persons and groups must deal.

Second, to say that labeling (either by self or by members of the community or their representatives) is the foundation for secondary deviance is emphatically *not to locate the origins of rule-violating behavior in people's response to that behavior*. The point is missed if the theoretical proposition outlined here is taken to mean, for example, that mental hospitals drive people insane, that police and prisons force innocent people to engage in crime, or that narcotics treatment facilities make addicts of people. Indeed, as Chapter 2 has made clear, labeling theory has little or nothing to say concerning the etiology—first causes—of rule-violating conduct. Rather, the contention is that prior to being labeled—when one is a primary deviant—one's deviation may be regarded as incidental to a host of nondeviant roles. One is yet officially "innocent." Labeling, however, may significantly alter that condition (Lemert, 1967:17).

Third, these comments are *not to suggest that the responsibility for the rule violator's action is shifted from the actor to the social audience* (Nettler, 1974:209) or that "the moral burden of control is shifted from the victim (the labelee) to the victimizer (the control agents)" (Davis, 1975:172). On the other hand, as indicated in Chapter 5 (see page 166), being labeled is a matter of institutionalizing deviance. In turn, it is theorized that institutionalization may effectively reduce the degree of self-control or self-ordination (see page 58) the actor is able to exercise. Labeling (institutionalization), it is contended, ". . . places the actor in circumstances which make it hard for him to continue the normal routines of everyday life and thus provoke him to 'abnormal' actions" (Becker, 1973:179). In this sense, then, *though it is not a "first cause,"* labeling is believed to intensify, enlarge, and perhaps prolong one's involvement in a deviant role.

Fourth, and finally, these remarks should not be interpreted to mean that labeling *automatically* prevents actors from participating in all forms of normal social interaction (Davis, 1975:174). Whether or not and the degree to which labeling becomes an impediment to such things is problematic, depending on a variety of conditions which we will consider later in this chapter.

With these points in mind, let us now turn to an examination of the data in an effort to determine how validly theory describes the everyday life and experiences of deviant actors.

Consequences of Labeling: Practicalities

That naming things may have profound consequences for the thing named is a truism needing no defense. Its consequences are never greater than when the naming involves the assignment of morally loaded labels. Even children have a sense of this when they bravely utter the rhyme "Sticks and stones may break my bones, but words will never hurt me." What children know from experience is that labels can raise serious doubts and questions about the fundamental worth of the person toward whom they are directed. How smart can one be who is tagged "stupid," how brave one who is labeled a "yellow belly," how strong one who is dubbed "puny," or how manly one who is called "sissy?" In a literal sense, each appellation casts a small moral shadow on the person's essential self.

What children experience is not totally analogous to the experiences of deviants who have been formally labeled in some way or other. However hurtful at the time, these childhood episodes seem characteristically to be short-lived. While that is also the case for many deviants whose behavior or condition is regarded as only nominally or *marginally deviant*, that is, "behavior existing on the border of conventional and deviant worlds" (Briedis, 1975:481) it is a marked departure from the prolonged and agonizing experience of those persons who endure the consequences of stigma for years. As an example, consider the following:

> I was 4 years old when I started school. My mother had told them I was 5; I was somewhat precocious, and she may just have wanted to get me out of the house. But butch haircut or not, some boys in the third grade took one look at me and said, "Hey, look at the sissy," and they started laughing. It seems to me now that I heard that word at least once five days a week for the next 13 years, until I skipped town and went to the university. Sissy and all the other words—pansy, fairy, nance, fruit, fruitcake, and less printable epithets. I did not encounter the word faggot until I got to Manhattan. I'll tell you this, though. It's not true, that saying about sticks and stones; it's words that break your bones (Miller, 1971:48).

In short, it should be acknowledged at the outset that the social psychological and social consequences of stigma and labeling are highly variable, a difference we may appreciate by examining the experience of persons who have been effectively labeled, stigmatized, and whose public identity is therefore changed. We will first examine the consequences of labeling for self-attitudes and follow with a consideration of its social effects.

Social Psychological Effects of Labeling

By means of symbolic interaction one acquires a mental life, is able to experience self, and comes to define himself or herself as others do. These contentions lead to the idea that a change in self-regarding attitudes may well follow one's being publicly labeled deviant (Matza, 1969:143ff; Lemert, 1967:17). That is, when one is formally labeled deviant and undergoes a change in identity, others are most likely to respond to the actor in terms of the deviant status. Theoretically, then, self-regarding attitudes are likely to change. We will consider this change for both secondary and primary categories of deviant.

The Secondary Deviant

The life of the secondary deviant is often organized about the "facts of deviance," referring to the tendency of others to perceive and relate to the labeled deviant in terms of his or her spoiled identity. That is, since the actor is perceived to *be the thing* described by the stigma symbol, his or her identity *is* spoiled. When others respond to the rule breaker in terms of that identity it may be expected to have serious consequences for one's self-attitude.

The way in which self-attitudes and identity may be related is found in the case of the skid row resident. For these men there are three distinguishable yet slightly overlapping identities. The first is the *popular identity*. Commonly labeled "bums," these men are popularly seen as ". . . people who fail abysmally, are dependent on society, lack self-control, drink too much, are unpredictable, and often end up in jail for their criminal behavior" (Spradley, 1970:66). Examination of these labels clearly reveals their dual use, that is, as a means to (1) impute characterological traits to these people and (2) use the traits as evidence of a spoiled identity. For example, "derelict" refers to one who lacks respectability because of *being* neglectful, undependable, and unfaithful. "Transient," in the pejorative sense, refers to one who *is* unsettled, migratory, impermanent, and unstable; on those grounds one cannot be relied on. These personal qualities reinforce the popular belief that the way of life of the skid row wino is "irrational, immoral, and irresponsible" (Spradley, 1970:66).

A second identity these men share is their *medical identity*, the basis of which is the idea that their objective condition (poverty, nomadism, and so on) stems from a disease, specifically, alcoholism. Unlike other illnesses that beset people, alcoholism is perceived to directly influence one's *being*. For example, while people suffer all kinds of disease and illness, it is rare for those conditions to become the basis of a personal noun. One never refers to the victim of a stroke or a heart attack victim as other than a victim. These conditions are not perceived to change the victim's essential self because they do not form the basis for moral judgment. In the case of alcoholism, however, one *becomes* an alcoholic. Similarly, one who suffers paralysis of the lower limbs *is* a paraplegic, one who cannot see *is* blind, and one deprived of hearing *is* deaf. In each instance, at least in American culture, the malady is fused with one's essential character. It matters little that the criteria for some of these conditions, such as alcoholism, lack specificity. Simply, in the nature of stereotypy, one who is perceived to suffer the condition is burdened with the popularly associated traits (Spradley, 1970:66). These traits, however, are pregnant with moral meaning, as the highly stigmatizing aspects of blindness and alcoholism make evident; such people are marked as morally inferior (Scott, 1970:258).

Finally, the skid row resident is concerned with his *legal identity*. Blending with elements of his popular identity, traits associated with the legal identity are morally loaded. Police view these men as vagrants and criminals guilty of at least the moral offense of public drunkenness (Spradley, 1970:67). On the basis of research it is concluded that "in view of the experienced [policeman], life on skid-row is *fundamentally* different from life in other parts of society . . . skid-row is perceived as the natural habitat of people who lack the capacities and commitments to live 'normal' lives on a sustained basis" (Bittner, 1967). Clearly, the quality of life is seen as a consequence of the character of the people living there.

Attitudes held by police are shared by lay people and the press. Howard Bahr reports the negative reaction of a rural person on first encountering skid row people in Chicago:

> We went through "skid row" and saw a "gutter" man which was to be picked up by the paddy wagon when the police see him. There are supposed to be a lot of those men on the street who have passed out from drunkenness. I'm glad we only saw one. I wouldn't dare walk down that street because I was scared just looking at the people (Bahr, 1973:59).

And in the daily press one reads as follows:

> Dirty, disheveled, sometimes dangerous and often traveling in packs, an unprecedented number of panhandlers and bums drift daily around New York City.
> A team of . . . reporters has ranged through New York day and night . . . seeking out the beggars and homeless drifters with neither the will nor the energy to work.
> They found that many of the young alcoholic drifters are potentially violent and will threaten passersby who turn down their touch (Furey, 1973:59-61).

The beliefs that underlie the labels assigned to representatives of deviant categories, for example, that skid row alcoholics are disinclined to be "normal," that the blind are helpless, melancholy, frustrated, and live in a "mental void" (Scott, 1969:4), or that stutterers are constitutionally different from nonstutterers (Lemert, 1951:151) come to be reified, that is, take on "objective" character. This knowledge then constitutes the reality that guides the thoughts and actions of "normals" vis-à-vis the deviant. This reality provides the framework for the evaluation and judgment of the deviant and his or her behavior. It is these beliefs, for example, that lead the sighted person to shun the blind (Scott, 1969:24), that interfere with the establishment of intimate (perhaps sexual) relations between normals and the physically handicapped (Kriegel, 1974:233ff), that encourage police to view the skid row resident with apprehension (Bahr, 1973:231), and that result in skid row residents being

. . . labeled as misfits, degenerates, scum, sub-humans who "swarm" and run in "packs," linked with mass murder, political assassinations, violence, and theft, described as vandals and polluters, eyesores and health hazards, imposing terrors on honest citizens, homeless men are . . . to be kept out, chased away, locked up, segregated in some place with "others of their kind" (Bahr, 1973:63–64).

Alteration of Self-Feelings

Consistent with symbolic interaction theory, evidence reveals substantial support for the idea that self-feelings among some deviants often correspond to the public—medical, personal, or legal—conceptions of the deviant. James Spradley asked men arrested for public drunkenness "What do you feel is the worst thing about appearing in court on a drunk charge?" Fifty-three percent replied it was "the public humiliation" (Spradley, 1970:190–191). Included were one's physical appearance upon entering court and the difficulty of maintaining an acceptable social image. Said one man, "Your appearance, it is degrading to lay in the drunk tank over weekend and appear in court—no shave, no comb to even comb your hair, clothes all wrinkled" (Spradley, 1970:191). People feel defamed. One man commented, "A person is usually sick and dirty from laying on the concrete floor and to have to appear in front of a lot of people in that condition is very humiliating" (Spradley, 1970:191). Others mentioned their fear of confronting and possibly being recognized by court spectators. One man summarized the feelings of many with one word: "degradation."

Degrading experiences for these men are not limited to their appearance in court. From his first encounter with police on the street, the skid row habitué may well be spoken to in highly insulting ways. Some of these insults consist of the terms used by police (among others) to refer to these men: tramp, wino, bum, drunk, dehorn, skid row bastard. Men also report having to endure threats to their person when they have to deal with police. Such threats as "Shut up or we will beat the shit out of you" are designed to inform the person that he is the power subject and that the police are the power holders. Together with the use of defamatory names, these experiences reinforce these men with the idea that theirs is an inferior identity (Spradley, 1970:141).

Also effecting self-conception is the fact that these men are frequently robbed of their possessions by police (reported by 23 percent of Spradley's respondents). This experience effectively informs these men that their claim to respectability and consideration is diminished. In an impersonal society where one's identity is crucially linked to material possessions, especially money, the loss of such symbols and *the apparent lack of means to effect their return*, may well have a critical influence on one's feelings of self (Spradley, 1970:145). Added to this is the ever-present threat of physical assault by police and/or jailers should the man take other than a passive stance regarding his treatment. Thirty-five percent of Spradley's subjects reported that police "rough you up," "hit you," "take shoes to you," "club you," "shake the hell out of you." "work you over," "slam your face on something," "split your head open," "bounce you off his knee," or "drag you someplace" (Spradley, 1970:148–149). One is left only with a profound sense of their vulnerability. As Spradley suggests, the entire experience suffocates any self-assertiveness one may harbor. One is effectively stripped of the opportunity to display any autonomy or self-determination (Sykes, 1958:73–76; Spradley, 1970:161).

These and many other experiences, hidden from public view and denied by officials, comprise the reality and ritualized experience of such men at the hands of the law. These experiences, especially being jailed, are critical in their life.

> . . . [in jail] they find the remaining shreds of respectable identity stripped away as they become participants in an elaborate ritual—that of making the bucket. Identity change takes place for these men as they are labeled "bums," cut off from former roles and identities, treated as objects to be manipulated, and coerced into being acutely aware of the new definitions of social interaction, space, time, and identity which are part of the jail (Spradley, 1970:223–224).

Persisting over an extended time span, such experiences lead the secondary deviant to be engulfed in the deviant role.

Role Engulfment

As used by Edwin Schur (1971:69ff), *role engulfment* refers to the long-term social psychological impact of labeling on the deviant. It is a consequence of others relating to the deviant largely in terms of a spoiled identity. As social interaction is restricted by and limited to aspects of one's deviant identity, that is, as people respond to the actor more and more in terms of the master status of deviant, the master status becomes more salient for the actor as well. Becoming engulfed in one's deviant status, then, is a cumulative process (Schur, 1969:71), the outcome of which is that people may define themselves as others do.

That people may become engulfed in their role as deviants is well demonstrated by the way *some* persons are socialized to the role of the blind. According to Scott, some blind people adopt what he refers to as the "true believer" mode of adjustment. In this case the blind

> . . . adopt as a part of their self-concept the qualities of character, the feelings, and the behavior patterns that others [those who can see] insist they must have. Docility, helplessness, melancholia, dependency, pathos, gratitude, a concern for the spiritual and the aesthetic, all become a genuine part of the blind man's personal identity (Scott, 1969:22).

The expectations that the sighted have of the blind are communicated to the blind in subtle and not-so-subtle ways. Agencies established to "rehabilitate" the blind often expect these people to be more "normal" than sighted people, requiring the blind to meet expectations that sighted people are not expected to meet. For example, in the case of a blind college student, one agency required that he "pass" a Minnesota Multiphasic Personality Inventory test (which, incidentally, has never been standardized for the blind) as a condition of continuing his tuition grant. What sighted student must "pass" (even submit to) such a test in order to obtain scholarship aid, and what, one wonders, constitutes "passing" in this case? Since it is theoretically (and practically) impossible to be more normal than normal, the agency is encouraging its charges to become and remain dependent. Higher education and the opportunities for self-sufficiency it may provide (elements that are consistent with the idea of rehabilitation) are apparently contrary to some of the stereotyped expectations of the blind.

In another sense, however, blind people may be expected to *avoid* displaying attributes of normality. Thus, one student, blind from birth, was unable to write normal script and was restricted to braille. To place a signature on any document, then, called for him to mark an X on the paper. Finding this degrading and onerous, the student was advised to get a signature stamp, a simple device allowing for elimination of the X and a measure of dignity. The suggestion was rejected by the rehabilitation agency working with this student. Instead, the agency insisted that the student learn to write script by hand, a truly formidable task for one who has never seen what hand-writing looks like. In short, the signature stamp may provide the student more freedom than the agency felt he should have and rejected his use of it.

Also contributing to the person's dependency on others and his or her further engulfment is the tendency for some agencies to reject the use of dog guides by the blind and their encouragement of the use of a cane. Canes, according to many blind people, are more restrictive than dogs. Canes are difficult to handle, can be accidently run between the legs of passersby, get caught in revolving doors, become jammed in cracks in sidewalks or sewer grates and are thus easily bent or broken, and are difficult to handle in automobiles and public conveyances unless they are collapsible. Most important, the cane cannot be trained and has no memory. In short, canes are quite limited in their ability to enhance the blind person's mobility, independence, and sense of freedom.

An alternative to the cane is the dog guide, who not only can be trained and who functions on memory, but may also serve as a "bridge" between its blind master or mistress and others. This is particularly the case in that dogs may serve as a substitute for eye contact, conceded to be a vital aspect of initiating and maintaining social interaction. Despite the apparent social and other advantages of a dog, many rehabilitation agencies persist in rejecting their use and opt for reliance on a cane (Scott, 1965:136).

Engulfment is also apparent in the characteristically discouraging approach agencies sometimes take to the employability of the blind person (Scott, 1965:136ff). Agencies often tell their clients that they will be faced with problems when they seek a job, that there are few jobs for the blind, that employers are reluctant to hire the blind, and so forth. What clients are not told is that there are many blind attorneys, physicists, mathematicians, auto mechanics, farmers, and others. That is, the blind are able to occupy a far greater range of occupational roles than stereotypic notions suggest. To restrict the blind person's awareness of such possibilities is to encourage the "true believer" mode of adjustment and promote role engulfment. Again, self-feelings reflect others' definitions.

Engulfment also occurs among others who display abominations of the *body* and are stigmatized on that basis. One such case is that of Mary Benchley, who was born with a markedly deformed lip, a wide, flat, and generally malformed nose, and poorly aligned teeth. Though operated on for a harelip when she was one year old, Mary Benchley's disfigurement persisted. In school Mary's classmates made fun of her, called her names such as "split lip" and "crooked talking," and she was often laughed at by others when called on to recite. As she grew up she was systematically excluded from adolescent groups and was forced to engage in solitary forms of recreation. In seeking employment Mary also found her disfigurement was a handicap. Even minor jobs were denied her, she felt, because the potential employer desired "someone prettier." In seeking surgical correction of her condition at thirty-four: Mary Benchley stated:

> . . . that her whole life had been greatly influenced by her appearance and by her speech defect. While she found it exceedingly embarrassing and difficult to make people fully understand her when she talked (she carried a slip of paper with her name written on it), she felt that her appearance had been the greater handicap in obtaining jobs and making friends. She stated that not only had people ridiculed her and stared at her, but she had been the victim of pity, questions, jokes, and nicknames. *All her life she felt rejected by others because of her deformity, and this caused her to feel depressed, inferior, and anxious* (McGregor et al., 1953:34–35. Emphasis added.).

Engulfment is not restricted to ascriptive deviants. Similar experiences and resultant self-feelings are reported by some law violators. In the following case, that of Ken, a young man from a financially stable background is charged with passing a $20 check without sufficient funds, a result of his failure to keep accurate records of his bank transactions. His sentence was one year on probation. Ken's initial reaction was that the episode was no more than a "minor inconvenience." His friends reacted either with "disbelief or levity." Of his intimate associates, only his family displayed anger or displeasure over Ken having broken the law. To Ken, the most distressing reaction came from the community at large—a small rural town populated largely by single ethnic group. Describing them as "harsh and definite," Ken felt the townsfolk "branded" him a criminal and reacted to him in accord with that definition. He describes the reaction as follows:

> (They reacted like) "you're going to have to watch him now,' 'he's a known criminal now." "he's an outcast," or "you'll have to watch him he could be dangerous," you know. Completely (banned)!
> At first, I just looked at it like, they had to be putting me on. I mean their reaction was so (unbelievably) violent. . . . Uh, my God! what is this? You know, (I just couldn't believe it was happening).
> Then—I thought maybe (the) next thing they would tell

me is I'm a hardened felon, you know, I go out and knock people in the head for money.—I couldn't believe it—but *that's the type of community we had. "If you was good—you was good. If you was bad—you was horrid!"* Uh, it's just one of those type deals (Frazier, 1976:135. Emphasis in original.).

To add to these difficulties, the parents of Ken's girlfriend refused to admit him to their house, would not permit the girl to come to the door, and told Ken never to come to their house again (Frazier, 1976:136).

On the basis of repeated experiences of this sort, Ken reports that his attitude toward self commenced to change.

> . . . when I got this from people it started making me very bitter . . . you know, like, "what the hell—*if I'm going to be named a criminal I might as well be one I guess." I never went out and done anything, I mean . . . but that was my outlook.* And getting more and more so. I mean, "if they're going to condemn me for that, what was their reaction gonna be if I actually did do something serious." Uh, actually I got a little more defensive from then on . . . (Frazier, 1976:136. Emphasis in original.).

Clearly, we note in Ken's case the tendency of the master status to take precedence, influencing the way others related to Ken. Apparently, to the townsfolk, the only salient identity Ken had was his spoiled identity.

The Primary Deviant

In contrast with secondary deviance, it is maintained that primary deviance ". . . does not lead to symbolic reorganization at the level of self-regarding attitudes and social roles "(Lemert, 1967a:17). That is, it is hypothesized that as a result of their essentially "private" nature, the acts of primary deviants have less impact on and fewer consequences for the person's conception of self and relations with others. This hypothesis rests on two major conditions.

First, it is contended that as a primary deviant one's rule-violating behavior is incidental to a large array of socially approved roles. In this case "incidental" means that regardless of the frequency with which the acts are engaged in, they have less priority and salience than one's rule-abiding behavior. Second, that one's transgressions are unknown to public agencies means these people are defined as more or less "innocent"—at least in a public and official sense. Certainly, the individual is aware of his or her rule violations. However, because of their essentially "private" nature (that is, they do not become the subject of a public forum), the rule breaking does not intrude on self-other relations. Because the bulk of the actor's roles (to which others respond) are socially approved, people tend to interact with the primary deviant as a moral person. One attends school, works, goes to church, has a drink with a friend, rings doorbells for a political candidate, and so on. The others with whom these things are done provide support for a conception of self as law abiding. One's public and *substantial self* (the totality of one's self-evaluations) remains moral. If one's rule-breaking behavior has any impact on self-evaluation, the impact is limited to the person's *situated self* (that portion of self restricted to rule-breaking episodes). As a consequence, no essentially deviant image is reflected back to the actor. Theoretically, then, it is possible for the primary deviant to maintain a moral conception of self. However logical, and though it may apply to the overwhelming bulk of rule breakers, the foregoing proposition does not apply to all. To appreciate the exceptions calls for the examination of symbolic labeling.

Symbolic Labeling

The social psychological consequences of rule breaking for some unlabeled persons may be understood by examination of *symbolic labeling*, the application of stigma without benefit of public ceremony (Warren and Johnson, 1972). However important they may be for those experiencing them, degradation ceremonies are experienced by very few rule breakers. Formal labeling is atypical. Goode (1975:580) notes that "most of the people who would be considered 'deviants' were their behavior to become known to the general public do not conform to this [public labeling pattern]." According to Gagnon and Simon (1968:353), the bulk of the male homosexuals they studied were subjected to no formal stigmatizing process. The atypicality of formal labeling has also been noted by Warren and Johnson (1972), who, like Gagnon and Simon, contend that most homosexuals never have their personal sexual activities become a public issue. Despite that, many members of the gay community studied by Warren "defined themselves as essentially *being homosexual*, and tend to organize their lives around the fact of possessing this *symbolic* (as opposed to publicly applied) *stigma* "(Warren and Johnson, 1972:77. Italics in original.).

What seems true of homosexuals seems equally plausible for a wide array of other categories of deviants. Many other persons

> . . . appear to be largely symbolically labeled as deviants in American society; thus, their "escalation" to the status of secondary deviance (with its implications of a [de-

viant] "substantial-self") results *not* from (official) *acts of labeling,* typically at least, but through more informal and amorphous processes of *being-labeled,* or having an identity infused with the cognizance of its public opprobrium (Warren and Johnson, 1972:77. Italics in original.).

Lest it be overlooked, the fundamental distinction here is between the formal, *official process of labeling,* on the one hand, and the more frequent, albeit less determinate process of *being labeled,* that is, labeling one's self as a consequence of an awareness of the public meaning of one's actions.

Symbolic labeling is wholly consistent with symbolic interactionist theory. As we have noted, people have a mental life. They are able to engage in self-scrutiny, interact with themselves (behave reflexively), evaluate their acts and condition in terms of public rules and meanings and, consequently, develop self-regarding attitudes. Symbolic labeling rests on precisely these elements. Given (1) cognizance of social rules and the moral opprobrium they symbolize, (2) acknowledgment to self that one is engaged in disapproved behavior, and (3) a sense of the low esteem in which "such persons" are held, the rule violator may then proceed to label himself or herself in ways consistent with public meanings. The outcome may well include a revision of one's substantial self.

To appreciate this process it is only necessary to recall that symbolic labeling occurs in a context replete with expressions of the public meanings of deviant acts and actors. For example, even in the absence of formal conversation on the topic, sexually active teenagers may be well aware of their parents' negative judgment of premarital sexual conduct. Isolated derogatory comments about venereal disease, premarital pregnancy, or remarks about "parents not being able to trust young people" are often sufficient for the teenagers to infer these meanings (Briedis, 1975:482–483). On a more public level, jokes about fat people, minority people, the mentally retarded (moron jokes), the physically handicapped, "queers," drunks, persons with speech impediments, and so on, each provide the sort of knowledge that leads to humiliation and self-denigration—not unlike the consequences of formal degradation ceremonies. One author describes the humiliation resulting from exposure to these materials:

> Sometimes I find myself drawn as if into a net by the abuses and sneers of the hostile world. I hear the vile joke or the calumnious remark, and must sit in silence, or even force a smile as it were in approval. A passenger enters an elevator and remarks, "When I come out of a barber shop, I have a feeling I smell like a fag. I better watch out or some god-

damn queer'll pick me up on the way home." The operator laughs, and I find myself forcing a smile, joining in the humiliating remark that is, unknowingly, directed against myself (Cory, 1951:10).

Everyday language also reveals the low esteem in which some people are held. This is exemplified in the case of people who are short. Our vocabulary is filled to capacity with taken-for-granted idiomatic expressions demeaning shortness: "putting people down," "belittling people," "being shortsighted," "getting the 'short end' of the stick," and "being shortchanged" are but a few examples (Feldman, 1971). And, of course, who can forget popular songs about short people?

In many instances people suffer the consequences of their condition in silence and secrecy, revealing their torment only anonymously. This is demonstrated in the following letter, written to the author of a biographical piece on being homosexual:

I have been working on this letter and trying to send it for more than three months now. . . . I have been married for over 20 years, have a daughter who is 20 and in college, and another who is 18 and will start college in the fall. We have a beautiful home and, I feel, a good life together. My wife is my best friend, but she has a very Victorian view of sex; it is performed more as a duty than anything else. . . . For me the thrills, excitements and beauties of sex have always come from men. I don't like the lying, the hiding, the excuses that go on because of my situation. I would like to open the door and have gay friends to my house and have the knowledge accepted. Has this ever been done successfully? If so, how? How can you change a person's mind when "homosexual" is a very dirty word, although they have lived over 20 years with one, lovingly? Any ideas, please? (Miller, 1971:69)

Similar experiences and expressions are shared by many other categories of primary deviants. They serve to socialize the deviant, provide evidence of the disdain in which he or she is held, and inform the rule breaker of the presumed difference between so-called "normals" and the substantial self of "people like them." On the basis of this socialization the primary deviant may well experience social psychological difficulties.

Guilt, Shame, Transparency, and Bedevilment

Among the difficulties faced by the primary deviant are guilt and shame. Manifest by feelings of self-disgust and other negative attitudes, and often accompanied by a verbal expression of a desire to withdraw from public view ("I could have crawled in a hole and pulled it in after me!"), guilt and shame derive ". . . from a horror of being disapproved of by others, particularly by meaningful or significant others, and from the fact that the values of these others have often been accepted by the rule breaker" (Sagarin, 1975:315). Guilt and shame may be expected, then, among those persons who anticipate others will judge their behavior negatively. The self-abnegation that is so much a part of guilt feelings is a derivative of symbolic interaction; one judges himself or herself as one *expects* others will judge him or her.

Knowing their behavior is banned and punishable means, too, that rule violators must face the prospect of losing social acceptability among some persons if information about their behavior becomes widely known. As a result, they face the task of managing their secret. They are concerned with *transparency*, that is, with whether or not they will be able to keep their secret and from whom it ought to be kept (Matza, 1969:150). For example, a liberated young woman who had sexual affairs with several men reported having guilt feelings on the basis of her awareness of her parents' attitude toward premarital sex. She commented as follows:

Dr. D: Earlier you said you feel guilty.

JM: Because of my parents. My parents don't know about my personal life. I imagine they have had their suspicions at times, but my mother is adamant about sexual experience before marriage. It would destroy her if she knew about me, I think (Denes, 1977:35).

Similarly, research on unwed fathers revealed that men experience considerable *bedevilment* (Matza, 1969:146ff) as a consequence of their involvement in these extramarital pregnancies. That is, they anticipate losing social acceptability among some persons if information about their behavior becomes public. Upon learning of these pregnancies men characteristically were concerned that public knowledge of their involvement would bring down the law on them, that their families would reject them, that it would be grounds for expulsion from school or other groups, and that friends and neighbors would reject them. As a result, they had to confront the problem of transparency and the task of managing their secret (Pfuhl, 1978; Breidis, 1975:484–485).

The horrors of discovery may be noted in other contexts, as well. For example, to reduce the potential threat of discovery, to protect their anonymity and avoid unwarranted intrusion, men who frequent *tearooms* (a public place, often a restroom, where impersonal homosexual encounters occur) take great precautions

(Humphreys, 1970:26, 131; Corzine and Kirby, 1977). These precautions, principally information control, serve to ". . . exclude the potentially threatening and uninitiated intruder, . . . [and] protect participants from biographical disclosure; and locales are chosen for an ease of access that keeps wives, employers, and others from discovering the deviant activity" (Humphreys, 1970:131). The lack of such controls increases the threat that one will be discovered and exposed; the consequence is ". . . a double nightmare of flight from fear and pursuit of satisfaction" (Humphreys, 1970:133).

Worry over discovery is also characteristic of many persons who drink a great deal but wish not to acknowledge they are alcoholics. Sometimes the drinker seeks to avoid disclosure by attempting to be humorous about his or her behavior. At other times the drinker engages in outright deceit and lying (Hough, 1974:17).

Finally, it is important to note that concern over these matters is not necessarily a result of the frequency or the public declaration of one's involvement in rule violations. This is evident in Rossman's recent (1973 and 1976) works on *pederasts*, males over eighteen years of age who engage in sexual acts with adolescent boys. Many of the men studied by Rossman had engaged in a sexual act with a boy only once or twice in their entire life and, at the time of the research, had not had sexual contact with boys for several years. Nonetheless, these men lived in constant fear that their past would be revealed. Caution, fear, and secrecy—from officials, psychiatrists, and one another—characterize these mens' lives. Any publicity, research, or public attention is greatly feared, so much so that some pederasts threatened Rossman's life should he persist in investigating this topic (Rossman, 1973:30).

The foregoing examples point out the very real difficulty of distinguishing between so-called secondary and primary deviants on the basis of their respective social psychological experiences. It must be recognized that the major social psychological distinction between these categories of deviants (that secondary deviation entails substantially altered psychic structure and self-regarding attitudes, while primary deviation has only limited implications for these matters) involves differences of degree rather than kind. The matter of salience seems not to differentiate the primary and secondary deviant. Nor may these categories be consistently separated by the presence and absence of problems associated with stigma, attempts to avoid its anticipated consequences, or the organization of life around the facts of deviance (Lemert, 1967a:40–41). As regards the social psychological consequences of one being labeled and stigmatized, then, it may well be that much of the assumed difference between primary and secondary deviation ignores the practical aspects of everyday life.

Social Consequences of Stigma

It has been pointed out that the labeling process may result in the erection of barriers against the deviant's participation in the normal social life of the community. As one assumes the master status of deviant, along with appropriate character traits, one's identity becomes that of the "outsider," one who cannot be trusted (Becker, 1973:1). Despite the irrelevance of one's deviance to any particular social role, the deviant may be denied access to a variety of nondeviant positions. For example, though a person's sexual preference may have nothing to do with his or her ability to play a given occupational role, certains jobs may be closed to persons known or suspected to be homosexual. This situation has been reported on by David Kopay, former collegiate and professional football player who recently publicly acknowledged his homosexuality. In Kopay's experience, despite his being qualified to fill the role of football coach, the public rejection of homosexuals prevented his being employed in that capacity (Kopay and Young, 1977:61–63, 182). Similarly, the International Association of Chiefs of Police have adopted a resolution opposing homosexuals being hired for police work. The rationale behind this resolution is that the role of policeman is totally inconsistent with one being an "open, obvious, ostentatious" homosexual (*Arizona Republic*, 1977b). The U.S. Air Force took a similar position in the case of Tech. Sergeant Leonard Matlovich following a public acknowledgment of his homosexual preferences. In seeking to oust Matlovich from the Air Force the argument was made that "the presence of homosexuals in the service . . . could impair recruitment; other young men might feel anxious about living in close quarters with them. . . . [H]omosexuals cannot command respect as officers and non-coms and are prey to blackmailers" (*Time*, 1975a). A similar case, though lacking details, has been reported for homosexual WACS (*Time*, 1975b).

These cases reflect people's tendency to perceive deviants as inimical to the smooth integration of roles characteristic of "normal" social existence. As Becker notes, ". . . societies are integrated in the sense that social arrangements in one sphere of activity mesh with other activities in other spheres in particular ways and depend on the existence of these other arrangements" (Becker, 1973:35). Work, family, educational and religious roles, for example, when carried out in "normal" ways are regarded as being supportive of (or at least neutral toward) one another. When carried out in "deviant" ways (that is, when occupied by deviants), however, these roles become antithetical to one another. According to the dominant reality, people who are deviant possess traits rendering them incapable of satisfying normal role expectations. Thus, many people are loath to allow homosexuals to play the role of teacher, fearing their children will be corrupted (*Playboy*, 1978:78). People are taken to be the same as the thing symbolized by the label; they have a moral defect. The alleged moral defect "fixes" them in the position of "outsider" and helps shape others' responses. As our examples show, a basic response is to avoid contact in order to prevent contamination.

Contamination

To contaminate something is to pollute, corrupt it, or otherwise render it impure. To a great extent, the restrictive social conditions faced by many rule breakers reflect the efforts of people to avoid the contamination of territories by deviants (Lyman and Scott, 1967). As used here, territories are multiple: public, home, interactional, and body. *Public territories* are those areas to which one has freedom of access by reason of citizenship. Nations, schools, cities, and similar public areas are examples. Closely related and not always distinguishable from public territories are *home territories*, places where people ". . . have a relative freedom of behavior and a sense of intimacy and control over the area" (Lyman and Scott, 1967:238). Clubhouses, country clubs, gay bars, and hobo jungles are cases in point. Third are *interactional territories*, any place where people may engage in social interaction. That is, every interact occurs in some physical place (someone's apartment, a street corner, a tavern) which, for the duration of the interact, is enclosed by an "invisible boundary." These interactional territories may be noted by people's resistance to their being penetrated by persons other than the interactants. Finally, there is *body territory*, ". . . the space encompassed by the human body and the anatomical space of the body" (Lyman and Scott, 1967:241). That body territories exist may be noted in the way people selectively grant and withhold the right of others to view and touch their body. Their territory has been described as the most sacred of all, as evidenced by the numerous restrictions societies establish concerning the time, place, and relationship between persons who may legitimately view and/or touch the naked body of another, engage in sexual intercourse, and so on. Marriage, of course, ordinarily converts body territory into home territory by granting rights that would not otherwise be extended (Lyman and Scott, 1967:241).

Each of these territories may be (and is) encroached upon and misused by those who *violate* them (by making unwarranted use of a territory), *invade* them (cross their boundaries without entitlement), or *contaminate* them (render them impure by use or definition). In the first instance, children may play hide and seek in a cemetery, while a man may make use of a public restroom designated for women only. In the second case, "adult" bookstores or theaters or taverns may be established in close proximity to schools and churches, or in residential areas from which they had previously been absent. By reason of this type of invasion the third form of encroachment, contamination, may occur. That is, in the perspective of some persons and groups, a territory may be rendered impure by such usage.

Viewed in terms of these forms of territories and the ways they may be violated, many of the restrictions imposed on deviants may be rendered meaningful. Given a sense of the deviant as a pariah, someone afflicated with a grave moral defect, the "normal" person or group may well feel the deviant's presence constitutes an encroachment of one sort or another. The rapist is one who *violates* bodily territory. If the victim is a married woman, the rapist is violating the spouse's home territory. The attempt to convert public restrooms into meeting places (tearooms) by homosexuals and the wildcatting of beaches by nude bathers may be seen as *invasions* of public territory. Should such efforts succeed, the encroachment may be regarded as an instance of contamination.

If a nondeviant segment of the community regards the presence of the deviant as an intolerable encroachment, any of several reactions may be expected. One possible reaction is *turf defense,* a popular expression of which is the case of the delinquent gang that seeks to physically resist the invasion of its territory by a rival gang. More consistent with the standard conception of deviance, however, is the recent case in Chicago wherein residents of the Edgewater district banded together (with support from the Chicago Police Department's Gang Crime Unit) to resist thefts, muggings, harassment, and other crimes being committed against the residents by a local gang (Law Enforcement Assistance Administration, 1977:3, 7).

A second reaction in defense of territory is *insulation,* ". . . placement of some sort of barrier between the occupants of a territory and potential invaders" (Lyman and Scott, 1967:246). Several examples of this are regularly observed. The use of their native language by foreign students on university campuses or by residents of an ethnic enclave (such as a Chinatown) keeps "outsiders" at bay. More common is the careful use of facial expression to communicate to others that an interactional territory ought not be invaded.

Finally, there is the tactic of *linguistic collusion,* used to protect interactional and home territories. Most often this defense takes the form of an elaborate linguistic form that outsiders may not readily penetrate and that automatically renders them ineligible for participation. The special argot developed by some occupational groups (such as musicians), ethnic groups (such as blacks), and other groups are cases in point.

As applied to the case of deviants, many of the restrictions imposed on them reflect a tendency toward defense or protection of one or another territory. For example, in taverns (often regarded as home territories) efforts are often made to regulate, if not suppress, open displays of homosexual affection in order to protect the license of the establishment (Cavan, 1966:71–72). To protect interactional territory, youngsters who are obese or who have a physical handicap are often quite bluntly excluded by peers from participation in regular activities.

Other Restrictions

Other social limitations associated with various stigma go beyond territorial protection. For example, those with felony convictions may experience restrictions on employment. Evidence of this is contained in Schwartz and Skolnick's (1964) study of the effects of a criminal court conviction on employability. Schwartz and Skolnick conclude that a convicted felon is substantially more likely to encounter employment difficulties than a person having no convictions; indeed, the person without a record is nine times more likely to receive a positive response from a potential employer than an equally qualified person with a criminal record. What is even more revealing about Schwartz and Skolnick's data, however, is that those who were accused but later acquitted (officially declared innocent) was very likely to experience employment problems. This, it should be noted, is likely to occur despite the idea that one who is acquitted of a crime is innocent (legally) and, according to our system of justice, should not be subject to sanction (Schwartz and Skolnick, 1964:108–109). These data suggest, then, that labeling, including cases later found to be in error and undeserved, may serve as a barrier to full social participation.

Severe limitations on employment are also reported among the disabled (Safilios-Rothschild, 1970:262ff). To be sure, employment opportunities available to the disabled vary with the subject's age, sex, race, educational level, work history, degree and type of disability, and so on. Nonetheless, overall, only a fraction of the employable disabled are employed. Those that are employed tend, on the average, to have less severe afflictions and be better educated (Safilios-Rothschild, 1970:263). The disabled who are employed tend to receive fewer promotions and are often restricted to less prestigious jobs than ones they held prior to being disabled. Added to this is the tendency for some employers to subject disabled employees to constant observation and evaluation—more constant than that imposed on able-bodied workers. These experiences, social in nature, have sometimes profound influence on the self-feelings of the disabled. To be limited to work roles beneath one's level of ability and training is humiliating, evidence of one's devalued position. Acceptance by others, then, is partial. For some it is likely that a forthright rejection would be preferable to halfhearted acceptance (Safilios-Rothschild, 1970:263–264).

Exclusion is also well demonstrated in the case of the mentally ill. In studying hospitalized mental patients, Charlotte Green Schwartz (1956) discovered that such patients receive very few visits from relatives or friends. Visits that did occur were anxiety provoking and visitors (with the exception of the patient's mother) tended not to return. Half the patients studied had no visits from persons other than family and, of those having visits, 41 percent were single or occasional visits. In seeking to account for this pattern of avoidance and isolation of patients Schwartz's informants indicated (as we have noted, page 176) that mental patients are nonpersons. "They are afraid of what a "nonperson" might do because he no longer is guided by the controls "people" have" (Schwartz, 1956:22). Such comments are clearly consistent with theory: alleged characteristics of deviants are perceived as inimical to "normal" social interaction.

Further support for theory is found in the research by Phillips (1963) and by Loman and Larkin (1976). Phillips' study investigated factors related to the rejection of the mentally ill, focusing specifically on the "... extent to which people's attitudes toward an individual exhibiting disturbed behavior are related to their knowledge of the particular help-source that the individual is using or has used" (Phillips, 1963:963). In this study "help-source" refers to clergy, psychiatrists, marriage counselors, mental health clinics or hospitals, and the like, where people may go to seek help when they feel they have an emotional or mental health problem. It was hypothesized that "individuals exhibiting identical behavior will be increasingly rejected as they are described as not seeking help, as utilizing a clergyman, a physician, a psychiatrist or a mental hospital" (Phillips, 1963:965). Interviews concerning five case abstractions representing a variety of mental health conditions were conducted with a sample of 300 married white females. Data supported Phillips' hypothesis, that is, "an individual exhibiting a given type of behavior is increasingly rejected as he is described as seeking no help, as seeing a clergyman, as seeing a physician, as seeing a psychiatrist, or as having been in a mental hospital" (Phillips, 1963:968). To be sure, Phillips did discover some moderate variation in patterns of rejection. However, even controlling for the influence of age, religion, and social class failed to diminish the principal relationship, namely, that regardless of the variation of behavioral form, persons described as needing assistance with emotional problems are rejected. Apparently, the more clearly the help-source signifies (labels) the help-seeker as a person with mental health problems, the greater the tendency toward rejection.

A study of the rejection of the mentally ill by Loman and Larkin (1976) reached similar conclusions. In this study an effort was made to determine the relative influence of three independent variables (actor's behavior, actor's account of that behavior, and labels) on two dependent variables: (1) audience rejection and (2) assessment of the social competence of persons declared to be mentally ill. The "audience" in this study consisted of students enrolled in a general sociology course who were exposed to two different videotaped counseling sessions reflecting ". . . fairly reasonable and common explanations of [a student's] poor academic progress" (Loman and Larkin, 1976:557). In one version of the counseling session the lack of academic progress was accounted for by the impersonality of the school atmosphere and the attitudes of the teachers. In the second version the "distressed student" accounted for academic difficulties in ways that could readily be interpreted as paranoid. Data revealed that the actor's behavior and the account of that behavior (two of the independent variables) had little relationship to audience rejection of assessment of competence (dependent variables). However, the "label" was significantly associated with both dependent variables. That is, rejection and a low assessment of the subject's social competence were associated with labeling. Loman and Larkin contend that this association reflects people's agreement with the stereotypic characterizations implied by the label (Loman and Larkin, 1976:560). Again, then, it appears that the meaning conveyed by labels, *irrespective of manifest behavior*, is significantly associated with how people respond to deviant actors.

The socially restrictive consequences of stigma may also be found among ascriptive deviants, such as persons who are obese or who are short. Employers often establish physical fitness criteria for employees regardless of whether the criteria are pertinent to job performance (Barker, 1948:31). Failure to satisfy these criteria may result in unemployability, however "fit" one may be in other respects. Such things as obesity, deafness, or disability due to the loss of a limb or paralysis, may result in intense social ostracism if only because these conditions are felt to interfere with many aspects of life, public and private. Regarding obesity, evidence suggests that being excessively overweight has an influence on college acceptance, particularly among females (Cahnman, 1968:290). According to the New England School Study,

> Twice as many obese persons were found in the high school female population than in the female college population (23.3 percent vs. 11.2 percent), with a less large but still considerable difference for boys (18.0 percent vs. 13.7 percent). Correspondingly, two-thirds more of the non-obese girls went on to college than the obese (51.9 percent vs. 31.6 percent) and only three-fifths as many non-obese females than obese began to work directly after high school without further training of any kind (17.4 percent vs. 28.9 percent); the difference between non-obese and obese males was insignificant. There was no significant difference for females as well as for males regarding motivation to attend high-ranking colleges, academic performance, and social class (SES or origin), whether they were obese or not (Cahnman, 1968:290).

The consequences of stigma also extend into the most private spheres of life. The exclusion of the "fat boy" from a game of ball and the avoidance of the heavy girl as a dating partner are common examples. For those with defective hearing, limited ability to communicate effectively with friends and family may have serious consequences. The hard of hearing man

> . . . has trouble understanding what his wife is saying, especially if he is reading the paper, and his wife is talking while she is making noise in the kitchen. This kind of situation frequently leads at first to a mild dispute and later to serious family tension.
>
> The wife accuses the husband of inattention, which he denies, while he complains in rebuttal that she mumbles. Actually, he eventually does become inattentive when he realizes how frustrating and fatiguing it is to strain to hear. When the same individual tries to attend meetings, to visit with friends, or go to church services and finds he cannot hear what is going on or is laughed at for giving an answer that is unrelated to the subject under discussion, he soon, but reluctantly, realizes that something is wrong with him. He stops going to places where he feels pilloried by his handicap. He stops going to the movies, the theater or concerts, for the voices and the music are not only far away but frequently distorted. Little by little his whole family life may

be undermined, and a cloud overhangs his future and that of his dependents (Sataloff, 1966:342–343).

Persons having a physical disability may experience isolation and other social consequences. Fink, Skipper, and Hallenbeck (1968) report that as the mobility of physically disabled wives decreases, so, too, does the husband's satisfaction with the companionate aspect of the marital relation. Husbands of severely disabled wives often attempt to spend more time at home with their wives, but often find this less than satisfactory, especially because this frequently calls for a suspension of activities in which both persons once engaged and from which they derived considerable pleasure. Included here are mundane but important things like visiting friends, attending movies, and going on automobile trips. As one husband commented

Well, it hurts if you can't get out with the family and do things that other families do. Such as, for instance, through the paper you see a show you'd like to see. Other families say, "Well, let's go." They put on a clean shirt and they do, and that's had its effect on me. . . . You can't just pick up and do something on the spur of the moment. It just can't be done. To go somewhere it takes planning, to be sure there's electrical outlets where you're going for the respirator. If we go to the show, I always go there first, talk to the manager, find out where we are going to be, see there's AC current there for her equipment. So it's not an easy thing just to go visiting (Fink, Skipper, and Hallenbeck, 1968:68).

These restrictions bring us to a consideration of "courtesy stigma."

Courtesy Stigma

Several of the examples cited in the preceding paragraphs reveal that the consequences of stigma are not restricted to those to whom it is directly applied. The term *courtesy stigma* points to the fact that stigma often ". . . spreads from the stigmatized individual to his close connections . . ." (Goffman, 1963:30). Examples include the spouse and offspring of the mental patient (Yarrow, Schwartz, Murphy, and Deasy, 1955), the families of mentally retarded children (Birenbaum, 1970), families of convicted felons, parents of gays (Miller, 1971), and many others who, by reason of social constructions, come to share some of the discredit assigned to the stigmatized individual. For such persons and groups an intimate affiliation with a stigmatized person may become a social psychological as well as a social impediment.

Social psychologically, courtesy stigma often result in painful self-examination and, on the basis of recipe knowledge, self-condemnation and guilt. These conditions are well represented among parents of homosexuals, many of whom believe they have "failed" their homosexual child (Simpson, 1977:15). Such feelings are sometimes built on the psychoanalytic idea that homosexuality arises out of maladaptive parent-child relations (Bieber, 1962:Chapters III and IV). Expressive of this guilt and self-blame is the following letter, written by a parent to a homosexual author:

> I blame myself for the fact that my son is homosexual. I know that it is a nearly incurable disease. I confessed my son's predicament—he is 16—to our family doctor, and he said that in rare cases the disease can be cured, but he said that the cure is a long and costly one and would be far beyond our means . . . He said that while the boy may not be an actual menace to society, there is always the possibility of arrest and disgrace. . . . Do you think we should send him away someplace? Are there hospitals where for a minimal charge he might . . . ? I would hope that he would be well treated. . . . We have never discussed the fact that he is— queer. His father refuses to allow the subject to be mentioned in our home (Miller, 1971:73).

Paralleling the self-blame and torment in the preceding case, is the fear of stigma that often accompanies one's spouse being declared mentally ill. As one wife said, "I live in a horror—a perfect horror—that some people will make a crack about it to Jim (the child) and suppose after George [the husband] gets out that everything is going well and somebody throws it up in his face. That would ruin everything. I live in terror of that . . ." (Schwartz, 1956:20).

Associated with these concerns is the fear that people will be disrespectful, suspicious, or fearful of the husband upon his release from the mental hospital. "The wives feared that their husbands would suffer from social discrimination—their husbands would not be able to get jobs; they would be avoided by old friends; their children would be excluded from play groups; and, in general, their family would be looked down upon" (Schwartz, 1956:21).

These fears are not limited to the subjective level. For many people they become the basis of action designed, it is hoped, to prevent their realization. For example, the wives of men who are mentally ill often avoid telling others of the husband's condition or reveal no more than is absolutely necessary. This tactic, however, may give rise to new difficulties while solving old ones.

Many wives had to invent devious excuses [for their husband's absence] backed up with still more excuses and explanations. They had to be careful about who knew and who did not. Some tended to cut off old associations by avoiding them or moving away, leaving no forwarding address. With neighbors and friends they acted strained and remote. There was always the fearful possibility that the "truth" might be discovered. Life for such a wife became complicated and uneasy. Her fears led her to limit her relationships with others precisely when she needed them more than ever. Her own behavior cut her off from many little services friends might perform for her. It also reduced the possibility that she could talk about her problems and difficulties to a sympathetic listener. . . . This behavior—which, by the way—is often undertaken at the husband's request—is an attempt to "protect" him from unfriendly attitudes, but it does so at the expense of *isolating both the wife and the husband* (Schwartz, 1956:21. Emphasis in original).

Some of these same tendencies are found among parents of children who have been declared mentally retarded. For such people, interfamily visiting is often curtailed, fewer invitations are extended, vacations may be highly limited, and entire families may change their place of residence (Schonell and Watts, 1956:217).

Not all persons and groups closely associated with the stigmatized seek to minimize public awareness of the affiliation and/or the stigma. Some become deeply involved in the world of the stigmatized and abandon all efforts to maintain an image of normality (Birenbaum, 1970:196). Yet it is apparent that for many persons, being identified as an affiliate of one who is stigmatized can be a painful social psychological and social condition.

Deviance Amplification

Our earlier theoretical discussion noted that negative community responses to the deviant, especially (but not only) responses of social control agencies, are alleged to promote the amplification and perpetuation of deviance. It was Tannenbaum's (1938) contention that *dramatization of evil* led both to the actor having a negative definition of self (identity) and perpetuation of rule violations (behavior). Sharing in this view are Becker (1973), Erikson (1964), Wilkins (1965), and Lemert (1967a). Each contends that community rejection of the actor may encourage *career deviance*, that is, movement of an individual from the status of primary deviant, through a sequence of movements and positions, to that of secondary deviant wherein identity and behavior are principally deviant (Becker, 1973:24–39). In short, labeling stabilizes deviance; ". . . deviation begets deviation" (Lemert, 1967a:25). However logical this proposition may appear, its validity is best determined on the basis of the evidence.

Examining the Evidence: Pro

A considerable number of studies provide data supportive of the amplification hypothesis. Many of these studies focus on juvenile delinquents. In New Hampshire, Davis (1973) concluded that a positive relation exists between a person's involvement with a juvenile justice system and his or her subsequent involvement in delinquency. Using a sample of Washington high-school students, Baker (1973) found that youth who had been labeled delinquent became more involved in delinquency even though they had little or no commitment to delinquency. Evidence supporting amplification has also been reported by Klein (1974). Comparing police departments having high and low rates of juvenile *diversion* (channeling youth away from the criminal justice system), Klein shows that recidivisim rates among youth are higher among departments engaging in less diversion (where offenders are treated formally and channeled into the justice system) than among departments that have high diversion rates (Klein, 1972:297).

Still further support comes from Gold and Williams (1969) semi-experimental study of thirty-five pairs of matched apprehended and unapprehended juvenile offenders. "In 20 of the 35 comparisons, the apprehended member of the pair subsequently committed more offenses than his unapprehended control. In 10 of the 35, the unapprehended control committed more offenses. Five pairs committed an equal number" (Gold and Williams, 1969:8). In an earlier study conducted in Flint, Michigan, Gold (1970) reached similar conclusions. Again using matched apprehended and unapprehended delinquents, Gold found that ". . . in 11 of the 20 pairs, the apprehended youngsters *went on to commit* more offenses than the unapprehended youngsters, in four they committed less, and five the same number" (Gold, 1970:107. Emphasis added). In short, Gold concludes that not only does apprehension fail to deter, it appears to be a stimulant to further violations.

More recent research (Farrington, 1977) using a population of 383 British youth as subjects revealed similar results. Farrington compared the self-reported delinquency scores of 285 unlabeled youth with those of 98 publicly labeled youth. "In agreement with the deviance amplification hypothesis, the 98 publicly labeled youths had very significantly higher self-reported delinquency scores at age 18 than the . . . 285 non-labeled youth" (Farrington, 1977:114). Subsequent examination of his data, to test the plausibility of alternative explanations of his findings, led Farrington to persist in his support of the amplification hypothesis as it applies to delinquents.

But does the amplification hypothesis apply to categories of deviants other than delinquents? In one instance, as we have noted earlier, agencies established to rehabilitate the blind frequently encourage (if not require) their subjects to ". . . play the kind of deviant role traditionally reserved for the blind" (Scott, 1965:138). To the extent the client meets agency expectations, stereotypic beliefs are actualized; the client becomes the "true believer" and is entrenched in his or her deviance in terms of both identity and behavior.

A similar condition is noted by Fred Davis's (1961) study of polio victims. In a number of ways the polio victim's handicap becomes the issue of principal concern in relations with able-bodied persons. First, the handicap becomes the center of attention, a condition to which others respond first and foremost in both speech and action. Second, the handicap, as perceived by the able-bodied, may overwhelm all other attributes the handicapped person may have (reminiscent of the notion of "master status"), with the result that interaction is shaped by these perceptions (definitions). Third, attributes the handicapped person may display that contradict the disability tend to be subordinated, while those consistent with the handicap tend to be emphasized. This is characterized by the experience of one of Davis's subjects, a particularly pretty woman, who often hears new acquaintances say "How strange that someone so pretty should be in a wheel chair" (Davis, 1961:124). Finally, the handicap becomes a source of interactional ambiguity for both the able-bodied and the handicapped person. For example, to what activities is it appropriate to invite the handicapped? And under what circumstances should the handicapped person accept or decline the invitation? Regardless of the answer, each question may be seen to focus on the handicap. To the extent the handicap becomes the central issue *around which other aspects of life are organized*, we may say the handicapped person is entrenched in the position of a career deviant.

Additional support for the amplification hypothesis stems from research on mental illness. In his analysis of mental illness as a social status, Thomas Scheff (1966:84ff) proposes that amplifying one's position in the role of the mentally ill is encouraged by two processes leading the patient to accept that role. The first process involves rewarding the patient for playing the deviant role, that is, concurring in the diagnosis and behaving accordingly. This process is promoted by the doctor's "apostolic function" (Balint, 1957) and partly by the unequal distribution of power between patient and physician. *Apostolic mission* or *function* means that doctors usually have well-developed and firmly held ideas about how people with particular illnesses should act. In the diagnosis process the physician subtly (or otherwise) encourages the patient to accept the diagnosis he or she thinks is appropriate. Acceptance is greatly enhanced by the physician's power over the patient. This is a consequence of the physician being ". . . well trained, secure, and self confident in his role in the transaction, whereas the client is untutored, anxious, and uncertain about his role. Stated simply, the subject, because of these conditions, is likely to be susceptible to the influence of the [physician]" (Scheff, 1968:6). The physician's efforts are reinforced by the action of other staff and hospital patients. For example, Caudill et al. (1952) have pointed out that conversation and interaction between patients on psychiatric wards often revolves about how valuable it is for patients to accept that they are in a mental hospital and that if a patient wants to "get well" and be released they had best work with (accept the social reality of) the physician, a lesson McMurphy never seemed to learn during his stay in the "Cuckoo's Nest" (Kesey, 1962). How patients encourage one another to accept a deviant identity is noted in the following exchange between patients (Scheff, 1966:86):

New Patient: "I don't belong here. I don't like all these crazy people. When can I talk to the doctor? I've been here four days and I haven't seen the doctor. I'm not crazy."
Another Patient: "She says she's not crazy." (Laughter from patients.)
Another Patient: "Honey, what I'd like to know is, if you're not crazy, how did you get your ass in this hospital?"
New Patient: "It's complicated, but I can explain. My husband and I. . . ."
First Patient: "That's what they all say." (General laughter.)

The second process leading to amplification is that deviants are sometimes punished if they seek to abandon the deviant role and return to a normal role (Scheff, 1968:87). As an example, we have already observed the employment and other restrictions imposed on ex-convicts and the disabled, and the general exclusion of the mentally ill (see pages 227–231). Such discrimination, extending into social and marital areas as well as the occupational, serves to block the deviant's efforts to reassume a normal role. Thus, not only is one rewarded for accepting the deviant role, but he is punished if he tries to abandon that position.

Finally, let's look at the heavy drinker and the role of alcoholic. Pittman and Gillespie (1967:106ff) propose that public policies designed to reduce alcoholism serve only to stabilize people in that position and to perpetuate the problem. As a consequence of a "Deviancy Reinforcement Cycle," depicted in Figure 6-1, what commences as drinking (or even heavy drinking) on the level of primary deviance is transformed into the status of public drunk on the level of secondary deviance. Thus,

> beginning with position A, symbolizing the various factors that . . . [precede the] behavior, the actor proceeds to position B. This position . . . represents the prodromal or pre-

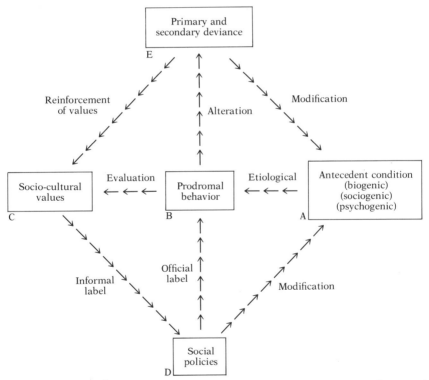

Figure 6-1 Model of deviance reinforcement cycle. Letters a-e indicate theoretical sequence of events; arrows indicate theoretical direction of influence. Source: David J. Pittman and Duff G. Gillespie, "Social Policy as Deviancy Reinforcement: The Case of the Public Intoxication Offender." Pp. 106–124 in David J. Pittman, ed., *Alcoholism.* New York: Harper and Row, Publishers, 1967.

liminary stage of the actor's involvement in deviance. Such behavior . . . is subject to evaluation in terms of currently existing sociocultural values (position C). It is at point C . . . that the definition *deviant* is attached to the behavior, at least informally. Should the behavior . . . violate the values and interests of a sufficiently large segment of the population in a sufficiently intense way, the labeling process may occur in formal rather than informal terms. Such formal labeling, a matter of invoking social policy, is represented by position D. Thus, for example, at position C we might have a person who is frowned on by his associates because he occasionally drinks to excess. Should this behavior persist and should the drinker be arrested for being drunk and disorderly or driving while intoxicated, the previously informal label may well be augmented by the formal label (position D). The informal label *heavy drinker* is replaced by the label *public drunk* (Hardert et al., 1974:280–281).

This abstract argument is presented in practical terms by Jacqueline P. Wiseman in her (1970) study of skid row men. Those men who seek employment as part of a rehabilitation effort have a particularly difficult time.

In part, this is because . . . his union membership has lapsed during drinking bouts, or he cannot get a job in his trade as an electrician, metal worker, or one of the other crafts because so much of this work is tied in with contacts demanding security clearance for all workers.

To be unbondable means that the Skid Row man cannot work on many jobs connected with the handling of money or expensive equipment. His status as an alcoholic (or ex-alcoholic) means he cannot work around heavy machinery because of high-risk insurance provisions. Add to this his age, his loss of current experience in his field, and the suspiciously long gaps in his job record (which are hard to explain in any case), and the picture of a virtually unemployable man emerges (Wiseman, 1970:229).

In summary, evidence and commentary based on examination of juvenile delinquents, the blind, polio victims, the mentally ill, ex-convicts, the disabled, and the alcoholic support the view that labeling, by a complex interactive process, may encourage the entrenchment of people in the role of secondary deviant and stabilize them in that position. But, one may ask, is there no contrary evidence? Indeed, there is.

Examining the Evidence: Con

One argument in opposition to the amplification hypothesis is that labeling has no permanent consequence on the deviant. For example, as a result of his study of physician drug addicts, Charles Winick (1964) notes that few doctors are prosecuted for this form of rule breaking and, in contrast to the "street" addict, most physicians who had been treated for addiction at the U.S. Public Health Service Hospital remained off drugs, were not stigmatized, and maintained a successful professional life.

A study of physicians charged with medical malpractice reveals similar conditions. Schwartz and Skolnick (1964) report that of fifty-eight physicians interviewed about the occupational consequences of these malpractice lawsuits, ". . . fifty-two reported no negative effects of the suit on their practice, and five of the remaining six, all specialists, reported that their practice *improved* after the suit" (Schwartz and Skolnick, 1964:11. Emphasis in original.).

These studies suggest that the very protective stance taken by members of the medical profession toward its members may serve to guard physicians, even those who err, from the burden of stigma experienced by lower-class deviants and those who lack the power base (Hessler, 1974:151; Schwartz and Skolnick, 1964:115). Another factor likely protecting the physician from long-term negative effects of stigma is high occupational status. Given the popular definition of that status, including physicians' alleged devotion to service and competence, and the associated tendency of lay people to defer to doctors just because they are doctors, it is unlikely that these members of the upper world would be subject to prolonged disprivilege. In this regard one cannot help recalling the relative lack of deviance amplification in the case of former Vice-President Spiro T. Agnew as a result of his having engaged in political corruption and tax evasion (*Newsweek*, 1973) or in the cases of Charles Colson, John Dean, and other highly placed persons involved in the Watergate affair.

A second argument contradicting the amplification hypothesis is that in some cases labeling, rather than perpetuate deviance, actually reduces it. This argument is consistent with the more traditional view that punishment deters (Sutherland and Cressey, 1974:326–328). In her study of shoplifters, Mary Owen Cameron (1964:151) reports there was "very little or no recidivism" among adult pilferers who were apprehended by store detectives but not turned over to police or formally charged. Cameron suggests that the adult pilferer does not think of himself or herself as a thief prior to apprehension (which, she says, is an illusion); arrest and interrogation breaks down such illusions. Coupled with fear, shame, and remorse, together with a lack of support from friends and family, the destruction of these illusions as "front work" forces pilferers to regard themselves as others do, that is, as rule breakers. The horror of that perception for some people is enough to deter further violations (Cameron, 1964:161–166).

A second example of how labeling may deter further rule breaking is found in the case of alcoholics who are members of Alcoholics Anonymous. In his study of the therapeutic dynamics of AA, Milton Maxwell (1967) suggests that two factors associated with self and/or formal labeling combine to aid the alcoholic to achieve sobriety. First, the drinker must accept the fact that he or she has a drinking problem he or she cannot control alone and that anything less than total abstention is impossible. This amounts to acknowledging and accepting the label and identity of the alcoholic. Second, and combined with the alcoholic identity, are the feelings of disillusionment and despair, followed by the discovery of hope. As many alcoholics say, they feel "licked," "down and out," "beaten," that they have their "backs to the wall," or are at "the end of their rope." Such despair, however, is frequently combined with (dissipated by?) hope in the form of a recovered alcoholic, someone who has shared their despair and escaped it. Maxwell comments,

> A meaningful [to the actor] coming together of disillusionment and hope seems to be a very individual matter. It may occur early as in the case of what A.A.'s call "high bottoms." It may not occur until after many years of suffering ("low bottoms"), and it may not occur at all, but there is nothing fateful about it. . . . Whether disillusionment and hope intersect early or late, it appears that both are prerequisites for readiness to seek or accept help (Maxwell, 1964:214).

Resolving the Pros and Cons

It is readily apparent that the arguments and evidence bearing on the amplification hypothesis are in substantial conflict. But all is not hopeless confusion. One may resolve this conflict and make sense of the competing claims by noting that while labeling may and often is associated with people becoming more firmly entrenched in the deviant role, such entrenchment and amplification (becoming a "career deviant") is not inevitable; many other factors intervene between *being* labeled (formally or informally), on the one hand, and *career deviance*, on the other. Let's examine some of these intervening factors.

Ascriptive vs. Achieved Rule Breaking

Appreciation of the consequences of labeling for career deviance calls for distinguishing between ascriptive and achieved deviance (see pages 162–163). In the case of the highly visible ascribed deviant, such as the obese, the dwarfed, the blind, or the ugly, social reaction may be a sufficient base for one to become entrenched in the deviant role. Such persons ". . . are not handicapped because their physical and/or visible traits prevent them from playing any particular roles but rather because of the invidious labeling process and the absence of factors which might tend to mitigate its effects" (Mankoff, 1971:207). Given its involuntary character, the deviance and status assigned these groups is dependent upon social reaction and has nothing to do with the acts or intentions of the actor. Therefore, in the case of the ascribed deviant, labeling may be considered a necessary basis for career deviance to occur.

In the case of achieved deviants, however, the relationship between labeling and amplification or career deviance is less clear. On the basis of evidence derived from examination of embezzlement, marijuana use, and homosexuality, Mankoff suggests that people frequently become involved in deviant careers *in the absence of public labeling* and stigma. Thus, he contends, social reaction is not a *necessary condition* of (one that always precedes) career deviance. Neither, Mankoff suggests, is social reaction a *sufficient* condition (one that is always followed by its effect) of career deviance among achieved deviants. Many people who are labeled are, for a variety of reasons, able to adapt to this condition in ways unavailable to the ascribed deviant (Mankoff, 1971:209–211). In short, career deviance is less likely to be associated with labeling in the case of the achieved than in that of the ascribed deviant.

Power and Socioeconomic Status

The opportunity of the labeled deviant to avoid becoming involved in career deviance may be greatly enhanced by his or her *power*, that is, the control he or she may exert over others' behavior by whatever means available, including the use of economic wealth. For example, if the long-term consequences of labeling involve discrimination or occupational restrictions, these may be compensated for or substantially lessened depending on the power of the offender. Indeed, it would appear that in some cases the actual wielding of power is unnecessary; *merely having access to power* may be sufficient to forestall the negative potential of labeling. As a case in point, let's examine the outcome for both corporations and individuals of what has been termed the "Incredible Electrical Conspiracy," ". . . the biggest criminal case in the history of the Sherman [Antitrust] Act" (Smith, 1961:132). This case involved charges of price fixing, rigging of bids, and the dividing of markets on the manufacture and sale of electrical equipment with an annual value of $1.75 billion. The conspiracy extended over a period of eight years and included the largest manufacturers and distributors of electrical equipment in the United States (General Electric, Westinghouse, Allis-Chalmers, McGraw-Edison, Carrier, and twenty-four other companies of varying size).

For their part in this conspiracy the offending corporations were fined a total of $1,787,000, with the largest fines being levied against G.E. ($437,500) and Westinghouse ($372,500). To corporate giants, such fines are piddling, ". . . no more unsettling than a $3 parking fine would be to a man with an income of $175,000 a year" (Gies, 1977:120). More substantial were the damage claims against these corporations by municipalities and other purchasers of their equipment. Despite their size (alleged to total about $160 million dollars in 1964) a company like General Electric could charge these costs off against taxes (Gies, 1977:120).

In addition to "paying" fines of a relatively inconsequential sort, evidence suggests these corporations suffered no appreciable (if any) damage to their public image (identity). A survey of national newspaper coverage in the days immediately after the defendants admitted their guilt revealed that the case received very little media coverage. Only 16 percent of the papers surveyed (of a sample of 15 percent of all newspapers sold in the United States) gave front-page coverage to the story. Those that did give it front-page coverage gave it no more than one column. Fifty-four percent gave one column or less on an inside page, and 30 percent never mentioned the story (*Notes and Comment*, 1971). A second newspapers survey (of thirty newspapers accounting for 20 percent of all newspaper sold in the United States), taken after the sentences were handed down, revealed that

> . . . *forty-five percent of the newspapers in the survey kept the story of the sentencing off the front page.* Fewer than a handful of the surveyed papers mentioned the names of any of the sentenced corporations other than General Electric and Westinghouse, and most of the newspapers devoted substantially all their headline space and coverage to the executives who

received prison sentences. None of the newspapers emphasized that the *corporations* were actually guilty of committing *crimes* (*Yale Law Journal*, 1971:288–289. Emphasis in original).

In this case, then, moral stigma appears to have been withheld from the corporations who were fined. Words like "crime," "guilt," and "corporation" were never linked together. Thus, the image of the corporation was protected, no blacklisting of the offending companies occurred, and business as usual was the order of the day.

But what of the executives? Prior to their indictment these men had played roles leading to the idea that they were "pillars of the community," including church deacons or vestrymen, president of the chamber of commerce, hospital board member, Community Chest fund raiser, bank director, Little League organizer, and the like. As one might expect, several of these men were dismayed over the prospect of being relegated to the status of "jailbirds" (Smith, 1961). As things turned out, they had little to worry about. Of forty-five corporation executives who were involved, seven received jail sentences of thirty days and twenty-four were given suspended jail sentences. The maximum fine imposed on these men was $12,500 and in one case that entailed two conspiracies (Smith, 1970:530). The seven who went to jail were later described by officials as model prisoners, got a five-day reduction in sentence for good behavior, and were released. One ". . . executive resigned from his original job, indignant that his salary had not been paid while he was in jail, and shortly thereafter he was appointed president of another corporation at an estimated annual salary of $65,000" (Geis, 1970:311). About a month after paying his penalty, a second executive assumed the presidency of another company at an annual salary of $74,000 (Geis, 1977:129).

The general outcome of this case is remarkably consistent with Sutherland's (1945) classic analysis of the differential implementation of law in white-collar crime cases. It was Sutherland's contention that a combination of fear of and admiration for businessmen prompted courts to be more lenient when judging their violations than those of more stereotypic offenders. This leniency and the image that "the man of business is a man of virtue" is also facilitated by the cultural homogeneity between the media and industry as interest groups (Sutherland, 1945:72). Given the combination of these factors, the modest penalties in this case and the absence of protracted stigma are not surprising. These results are consistent with the cases of addict physicians and physicians charged with malpractice cited earlier. We may propose, then, that the career consequences of labeling will vary inversely with the power and socio-economic status of the labelee. Status and power are insulators against the long-term effects of deviance amplification.

Motives

Whether or not labeling promotes career deviance may also hinge on the *motives* (see page 73ff) for the behavior. The motives that underlie the actor's decision to engage in rule breaking do not cease to operate after the initial violations occur. On the basis of such motives, for example, deviance based on protest (as we have noted in the case of blacks and women) and civil disobedience and in some forms of systematic theft, the actor may pursue a deviant career despite the absence of formal labeling and regardless of an opportunity to refrain from rule breaking and reassume a non-deviant status. In short, it is quite plausible that people persist in deviance (become career deviants) because they like what they are doing or are otherwise committed to the behavior (Mankoff, 1971:211–212).

Other Factors

On the basis of their own and other's research, Thorsell and Klemke (1972:397–402) suggest that a variety of other conditions may influence deviance amplification. First, they propose that when labels are assigned confidentially (as by private organizations rather than public agencies) to people who have limited commitment to deviant behavior (many shoplifters, for example), the probability of deviance amplification is reduced. Second, they suggest that when the labelee identifies with the labeler, and shares the labeler's general moral sense, labeling is most likely to retard further deviance. This proposition is consistent with the work of Maxwell, cited earlier, and that of Carol A. B. Warren (1974b). Contrary to the amplification hypothesis, Warren reports, first, that negative labeling by former members of the stigmatized category (such as ex-cons, ex-drug users, and ex-alcoholics) promotes identification between labeler and labelee and stimulates a change in the deviant's life style and behavior. Second, Warren reports that labeling occurring within the confines of a voluntary membership group (such as a weight loss group) is more likely to promote a positive change in the labelee's behavior and identity than when labeling occurs in total institutions such as jails or prisons (Warren, 1974:307–308).

Third, Thorsell and Klemke suggest that the nature of community response to the labeled deviant is critical as an insulator against one's becoming entrenched in the deviant status. Especially important are positive, supportive relations with significant others such as family and friends. Such relations serve to maintain social integration between the labelee and the larger community; the disintegrative potential of labeling is thereby frustrated.

Finally, these writers propose that when labels can be relatively easily removed, as in the case of "closing" records of juvenile delinquents or "sealing" other public documents, the actor has less chance of becoming involved in career deviance. Simply stated, the record and the label are no longer visible and, hence, do not work to shape relationships between offenders and others. Offenders are given a "second chance."

Summary

Our aim in this chapter has been to examine the social-psychological and social consequences of stigma and identity spoilage. Employing an interactionist approach, theory suggests that the attribution of stigmatizing labels to actors, and behaving toward actors in terms of the moral meaning of those labels, may well result in a substantial transformation in their public identity and self-concept. By and large, the evidence we have examined, taken from a wide variety of ethnographic and other researches, supports the contention that many persons who are publicly labeled do, indeed, suffer social psychological consequences, specifically a decline in self-feelings. For the most part we may say that such feelings reflect (1) the social relations between deviant actors and their condemners, (2) the actor's internalization of the moral meaning linked to his or her deviant status, and (3) the fact that deviant actors are often responded to by others rather exclusively in terms of their deviant, that is, spoiled, identity.

Suffering these consequences is not restricted to those who are publicly labeled. Through the process of symbolic labeling undetected rule breakers—primary deviants—may label themselves and experience the burden of guilt and shame and the fear of public disclosure. These social psychological consequences, identified as role engulfment, are most properly seen as the outcome of a cumulative process.

In addition to the social psychological consequences, stigma may also carry grave social results, extending not merely to the deviant actor, but, by way of courtesy stigma, to those with whom they may be intimately associated. Most important, we have attempted to show that these consequences stem not from any indelible characterological or other defect possessed by the actor, but from the audience definition of the deviant as unacceptable, morally defective, and, hence, difficult to relate to in normal ways. These definitions are sustained by negative stereotypy. Consistent with these meanings, we have seen that normals often erect barriers to avoid contact with and contamination by those they regard as defective. These barriers obstruct normal social interaction and, in turn, may encourage some stigmatized persons and groups to become more deeply involved in the deviant role, that is, to have their deviance amplified.

Evidence bearing on the validity of the deviance amplification hypothesis is conflicting. Much of this conflict reflects the state of the sociological art, methodological matters, and other issues beyond the scope of this volume (Meade, 1974). Nonetheless, by refining our perspective it is possible to make sense of the broad and conflicting claims. Consistent with that we have examined several factors that research and logic suggest influence the amplification process.

First, we distinguished between ascribed and achieved deviance, suggesting that the influence of labeling on one's behavior and identity is more problematic (less certain) in the case of the achieved than the ascribed deviant. This, it is contended, is a consequence of the greater role of voluntarism in the case of achieved than ascribed deviance.

Second, we focused on the labelee's ability to wield power and his or her location in the social structure. Simply, representatives of some groups are better able to insulate themselves from the effects of labeling on behavior and identity.

Third, we noted that the motives underlying one's involvement in rule-violating behavior may well encourage career deviance independent of labeling. Motives, then, may render labeling quite incidental to some cases of career deviance.

Finally, a host of other influential elements have been discussed, including (1) the circumstances under which labeling occurs, (2) the labelee's commitment to rule-breaking behavior, (3) the identification between labeler and labelee, (4) the nature of others' responses to the labelee, especially within primary groups, and (5) whether or not the label may be easily expunged.

Taken together, these refined considerations suggest it is inappropriate to make unqualified claims that *in and of itself* labeling has either positive or negative effects on target populations. In the final analysis, the effect of labeling and stigma is mediated by a variety of interrelated elements. Not the least of these is the actor's ability to manage stigma. It is to that issue that we now turn.

Managing
Stigma

Introduction

An earlier chapter stressed a model of man emphasizing people's active role in shaping their destiny. Accordingly, people interact with, adapt to, and sometimes overcome elements in their world. Rarely do they submit passively or allow themselves to be buffeted about, willy-nilly, by whatever forces come their way. As an example, we noted people's efforts to negotiate with labelers (see Chapter 5) in an attempt to resist or modify the tags placed upon them. A second example of people's effort to shape their destiny involves *stigma management*, that is, any of a variety of methods employed, individually or collectively, either to control information about their spoiled identity or otherwise alter the meanings attributed to them and thereby reduce the social significance of their deviance. In this chapter we will examine the many ways in which deviant persons and groups seek to manage their stigma.

In considering efforts to manage stigma, no suggestion is made or implied that such efforts are universal or that these attempts are successful to any specific degree. For one thing, as Goffman has noted, the idea of stigma is simply inapplicable to some people. That is, it is entirely plausible ". . . for an individual to fail to live up to what we effectively demand of him, and yet be relatively untouched by his failure; insulated by his alienation, protected by identity beliefs of his own, he feels that he is a full-fledged human being, and that we are the ones who are not quite human" (Goffman, 1963:6). Second, some deviants concur with public attributions and accept their stigma and shame, as we may note among minority group members who express self-hatred (Vander Zanden, 1966:430–439). In neither of these instances do people confront and deal with the stigma directly, preferring, in the first case to ignore it and in the second to capitulate and accept it as valid.

Differing from these instances is the tendency of many stigmatized people to deal more directly with their stigma. Some acknowledge the stigma and seek to correct or otherwise overcome it. For example, people who are paralyzed struggle to walk, run, or engage in other physical activity characteristic of "normals," while the *transsexual*, one who, through surgery and socialization seeks a gender and/or sex identity other than that to which he was born, undergoes psychotherapy, hormone injections, and radical surgery to replace a penis with an artificial vagina (Humphreys, 1972:137; Kando, 1973). Still other deviants may use their stigmatized condition to achieve secondary gains, for example, to explain or justify other shortcomings or deficiencies. The stigma becomes an excuse for ill-success to which it has no relevance (Goffman, 1963:10).

The aspects of stigma management with which we will deal differ from these in that we are concerned with those modes of adjustment pertinent to situations in which normals and the stigmatized are in contact. What is most important to bear in mind is that *to be deviant* (as distinguished from *doing deviance*) necessarily calls for another to recognize the actor as having engaged in some untoward behavior or as displaying some condition leading to ascriptive deviance. Management of one's stigma, therefore, becomes a *social matter*; that is, an effort must be made to control information bearing on one's condition. For some this may take the form of trying to avoid the disclosure of damaging information; for others it may involve trying to make one's stigma less obtrusive. For still others it may entail trying to bring about a change in the meaning (definition) customarily assigned to the stigma one possesses. Whatever form management takes, however, to be successful calls for an effort to influence the construction of reality. The stigma must be dealt with if the actor wishes to minimize his or her differentness. These comments require some qualification.

Analysis of stigma may profit by noting the variation in the public nature of stigma. In some cases people possess stigma that are not readily or immediately noticed by or known to others. Examples would include sterility in a male, a person's ethnic origin, the fact that one is a former mental patient or prison inmate. In general, this would also include those who have been symbolically labeled and have managed to keep their deviance secret. Such cases of stigma fall into the category of the *discreditable*. In contrast are those persons whose stigma is self-evident (blindness, obesity, a physical handicap, skin color) or is or may be assumed to be known by others. These cases represent the *discredited*. Our consideration of stigma management will follow this distinction as it pertains to individualized efforts to manage stigma.

Individualized Stigma Management

The Discreditable

Secrecy and Information Control

Erving Goffman suggests that persons who are discreditable often confront the problem of whether "to display or not to display; to tell or not to tell; to let on or not to let on; to lie or not to lie; and in each case, to whom, how, when and where" (Goffman, 1963:42). People who carry an undisclosed stigma may have to reckon with the possibility that those who accept them may do so unwittingly, that is, without knowing, and that were their stigma known to others their acceptance (which is based on ignorance and unintentional) would be replaced by rejection. In an effort to avoid rejection those who possess an undisclosed stigma have a pervasive need for secrecy.

This concern for secrecy has been noted by Humphreys (1970) and by Corzine and Kirby (1977) in their studies of impersonal sexual encounters among men. Concern for secrecy during these sexual encounters, often entered into in public restrooms ("tearooms") and other public settings such as roadside rest areas, is marked by the emergence of the role of *watchqueen*, a watchman or lookout, usually in a public restroom, who remains alert to the possible intrusion by police or other strangers who may pose a threat to those engaged in sex (Humphreys, 1970:26–27). Even where no such role exists, concern for secrecy remains paramount. To the extent that these encounters involve persons who are married, or engaged in professions, or who otherwise maintain an acceptable public identity, it is rare that participants exchange personal information. Telephone numbers, addresses, and surnames are seldom given out. Other information is purposely left vague or ambiguous in order to prevent being identified and having one's involvement disclosed (Corzine and Kirby, 1977:173). In other cases, those who are discreditable may attempt to *pass*, that is, by controlling information about themselves seek to occupy a status by fraudulent means. In either case, secrecy is of utmost importance. Deviants must give careful attention to the management or control of information about themselves that would disclose their discreditable condition.

Information control involves a variety of techniques. First, it may entail avoidance of contact with *stigma symbols*, signs that would call attention to or reveal one's debased or deviant condition (Goffman, 1963:43). For example, it has been suggested that, historically, for a black person to pass and establish a totally white identity called for "sociological death and rebirth." That is, passing required a black person to sacrifice his or her educational credentials if they were acquired at a black school, to abandon all contact with family and friends so as to avoid the risk of being identified, and to suffer the loss of work and other references who might reveal one's racial identity (Drake and Cayton, 1962:163). Among feminized transsexuals, passing may require name changes, a move to a new community, as well as new friends, jobs, and so on. (Kando, 1963:98; Bogdan, 1974). Similarly, unwed fathers occasionally abandon the pregnant woman or encourage her to take up residence in some distant place. By avoiding all contact with the pregnant woman (who symbolizes his failing) the man seeks to control information concerning his moral rule violation (Pfuhl, 1978).

A second technique of information control involves the use of *disidentifiers*, symbols used to prevent one being conceived of as deviant (Goffman, 1963:44). Again referring to premarital pregnancies, a number of couples marry prior to the birth of the baby. Regardless of other reasons for marrying, one acknowledged result is the legitimation of an otherwise illicit union and ensuing birth. In that way the principals are provided a positive image, one that would at least protect them against the full impact of having their deviance revealed (Christensen, 1953; Pfuhl, 1978).

A pervasive concern over disclosure leading to the use of disidentifiers is also found among Mexican male homosexuals. Much of this concern stems from the tight grasp the Mexican family maintains over unmarried male members. Given this grasp, these men greatly fear being seen in the company of effeminate males or being seen entering or leaving places where known homosexuals gather—both of which are prima facie evidence of one's own homosexuality. To avoid disclosure of homosexuality, these men frequently maintain social contacts with women, periodically engage in heterosexual intercourse with prostitutes, and publicly whistle or make suggestive remarks at passing girls (Carrier, 1976).

The use of disidentifiers may become an inextricable part of the discreditable deviant's life. This is particularly true among many homosexuals who wish not to reveal their sexual preference. How thoroughly secrecy may be woven into the fabric of life is revealed in Barbara Ponse's research among lesbians. For example, maintaining secrecy may necessitate adjustment of speech patterns. One of Ponse's respondents reported that as a result of having cultivated a self-protective sensitivity, she became so accustomed to anticipating her utterances that she lost a great deal of spontaneity in her speech and at times found herself being quite inarticulate (Ponse, 1976:318). In other instances lesbians cultivate speech patterns intended to misinform their audience about their sexual preference. For example, in order to establish and maintain a heterosexual image, many women will speak publicly about their boyfriends or unrequited love affairs. Others may establish a standing relationship with a man so as to have a male companion on select occasions (Ponse, 1976:318). Another disidentifying device used by some lesbians is to habitually dress in ways suggestive of their being "super feminine" or straight (Ponse, 1976:319). In all these ways people seek to avoid projecting cues that may reveal their homosexual preference.

Managing undisclosed stigma may call for a third tactic: leading a *double life*. Leading a double life requires imposing severe restrictions on one's choice of associates and friends. For example, other than highly impersonal and instrumental contacts, some homosexuals refuse to have any association with heterosexuals. Having a drink after work with a co-worker or dropping by a neighbor's residence to talk, are things to be scrupulously avoided lest one's identity be revealed. When intermingling between homosexuals and heterosexuals does occur, there remains the question of whether or not to tell, to lie, and to whom. Leading a double life is often an attempt to resolve the tensions and anxieties that arise from this intermingling. Thus, many people who are gay strictly separate their homosexual and heterosexual friends. The success of this tactic is debatable, as the following informant notes:

> Oh boy, I've lived a double life like you wouldn't believe all my life and sometimes the pressure was so enormous I thought I was going to explode. We'd sit around and have coffee, the girls in the office, and they'd say . . . this woman looks like a man . . . Omygod that's a queer and I'd sit there and listen to this kind of stuff and . . . until I'd just get violent sometimes. And there's been a few times when it's been all I could do just to keep from jumping up and saying, "Look you guys have lunch with me, we've socialized together for fifteen years. I'm queer!" I've wanted to do it so bad that you know, I uh, almost explode! Because you know . . . Why? I mean, what would I have accomplished anyway—I would have lost more than I had gained (Ponse, 1976:327–328).

The foregoing suggests that the preservation of secrecy calls for the development of ". . . a more heightened awareness and a sharper perspective on ordinary affairs and everyday encounters than those for whom concealment is not an issue" (Lyman and Scott, 1970:78). Conditions of ordinary social interaction that "normals" take for granted often must be given considerable attention by those seeking to conceal their stigma. As we have noted, spouses of mental patients go to great lengths to conceal the family stigma. Stutterers frequently develop tricks to disguise their speech problem such as anticipating the inclination to use "difficult" words and then selecting a less troublesome substitute. The colostomy patient finds it necessary to select a theater seat so located as to provide quick and easy access to a lavatory. And the covert homosexual must watch every word and gesture for fear of revealing his or her true self. In each case the paramount concern is to never relinquish control over information about self.

The development of this sensitivity is not without unintended consequences. For example, at the same time and precisely because it helps them to maintain a heterosexual identity, the reliance on a male companion may frustrate some lesbians' desire to become more involved in the gay community. The price of a heterosexual image, then, is at least partial isolation from intimate association with one's reference group. As Ponse remarks, "the veils of anonymity are often as effective with one's own as with those from whom one wishes to hide" (Ponse, 1976:319).

Another price the discreditable must sometimes pay is the strain and tension secrecy imposes on what would otherwise be quite ordinary and relaxed situations. For example, casual conversation with co-workers or others about friendships, about how one spent a weekend, or the types of leisure activity one engages in may become the basis for heightened tension lest one "slip" and reveal his or her true self. Secrecy, to have the desired effect, may call for one to lead a double life, replete with fear, alienation (from one's true self as well as others), and dissonance. At the very least, for many who are discreditable, leading such a double life calls for uninterrupted vigilance for fear that damaging information will fall into the "wrong" hands.

The Role of Others

The management of discreditability is aimed at influencing others' perceptions and, hence, affecting self-other relations. The outcome of these efforts, however, does not rest solely with the deviant actor. In many cases successful management is achieved only with the active assistance of one's audience. Quite often this "assistance" takes the form of a mutual pretense between the deviant and others, a false or *counterfeit secrecy* (Ponse, 1976:323). In such instances, despite mutual awareness, both the deviant and the nondeviant audience tacitly agree to preserve the fiction that there is nothing different or unusual about the deviant or his or her actions. For example, Ponse cites a case of counterfeit secrecy between a lesbian and her mother. In this instance, despite incontrovertible evidence to the contrary, a facade of heterosexuality (normality) was maintained, with both parties refusing to discuss the situation. Conversation between mother and daughter excluded such topics as boyfriends, marriage, childbearing, and other things that would call for recognition of the unrecognizable (Ponse, 1976:325–326). This same strategy has been noted among some Mexican male homosexuals, many of whom continue to live in the parental home long after the age when young men in the United States may be expected to have established their own residence. Between such men and their families, and even when their homosexuality is known to several members of the family, there may exist a "conspiracy of silence" or "counterfeit secrecy."

"The homosexually involved individuals thus continue to act in such a way that they do not expose themselves to unknowing relatives, neighbors, or friends. They may continue to maintain the fiction, for example, that some day they will marry and have children; and social occasions at the house may be organized as though their interests were heterosexual" (Carrier, 1976:367).

As in the case of leading a "double life," counterfeit secrecy demands a price. The obscuring and denial of one's true self in this way not only serves to reinforce the idea of one's unacceptability and some degree of self-alienation, but serves also as the basis for erecting barriers between self and others from whom one might conceivably obtain emotional support. Topics of conversation and areas of interaction become highly attenuated and social relationships become strained. The tension one seeks to avoid may be intensified by the very means employed to reduce it.

The Discredited

Not all efforts to control information succeed. As a consequence, one's stigma may become known; the actor "moves" from the position of the discreditable to that of the discredited, joining those whose failing is self-evident or otherwise known to others. These are the people who wear their stigma on their sleeve. In contrast to the problem of the discredited, which is to control information, the discredited face the problem of seeking to reduce the relevance of the stigmatized condition, attempting to maintain a positive, if not normal, self-image and public identity. Like the discreditable, the discredited employ a variety of tactics in an effort to achieve this goal.

Deviance Disavowal

One tactic used by the discredited is to engage in *deviance disavowal*, that is, to repudiate or deny that their behavior or condition is abnormal (Davis, 1961). This process is particularly to be noted among the physically handicapped and other ascriptive deviants. Seen as an effort to *normalize*, deviance disavowal seeks to render normal and morally acceptable that which has heretofore been regarded as immoral and unacceptable (Davis, 1961:126). As such, the process of disavowal, if successfully carried out, serves to normalize relations between the deviant and normals.

As a technique of managing stigma, deviance disavowal has been observed among those convicted of sexual offenses against children (McCaghy, 1968). According to McCaghy, convicted child molesters frequently allude to the influence of alcohol as an explanation of their behavior. As a way of normalizing the situation, alluding to alcohol allows the offender to admit the deviance without accepting the associated moral responsibility. As an example, men state (McCaghy, 1968:48):

"If you been drinking a lot your passions get aroused."
"I was intoxicated and couldn't account for myself."
"I was drunk. I didn't realize their age and I was half blind. I've always been a drinker."
"Drinking is the reason. I could always get women. I can't figure it out. A man's mind doesn't function right when he's got liquor on it."

At the same time, these men contend that the offense would never have occurred had it not been for their intoxicated condition. In one motion these men attempt to account for their behavior, absolve themselves of responsibility for their wrongdoing, and present the self-image of a normal, socially acceptable (moral) person. Thus, they make a bid to be seen as persons who have many of the same positive social attributes possessed by others. Their problem is perceived to be simple: they sometimes drink to excess and then do "stupid things." However, the "stupid thing" is not symbolic of the molester's essential or substantial self. Thus, the effort is made to "normalize" his identity despite having to acknowledge his deviance.

The Disavowal Process

To the extent it occurs, the disavowal process follows three discernible stages. The first stage is marked by *fictional acceptance of the deviant as normal and equal to others*. Interaction between normals and the deviant is characterized by politeness, curiosity, and privacy. Ordinarily one may expect the normal to exhibit some curiosity about aspects of the deviant that symbolizes his or her differentness, be it obesity, a physical handicap, a record of wrongful behavior, and the like. Despite this curiosity, the norms supporting the value of privacy require that people ". . . . refrain from remarking or otherwise reacting too obviously to those aspects of [deviant] persons which in the privacy of our thoughts betoken important differences between ourselves" (Davis, 1961:126). Thus, despite curiosity, people generally tend to honor the norms of privacy and conduct themselves according to the standards of politeness. Feigning avoidance of the thing that is very much on people's mind amounts to *civil inattention.*

That such fictions are engaged in is noticeable by the horror that sometimes arises when they are violated, especially by innocent children. As an example, note the instance of a very overweight babysitter, who was greeted by her three-year-old charge with the loud exclamation "You're fat!" Davis tells of another occurrence provided him by a young woman informant with a physical handicap.

> I was visiting my girl friend's house and I was sitting in the lobby waiting for her when this woman comes out of her apartment and starts asking me questions. She just walked right up. I didn't know her from Adam, I never saw her before in my life. "Gee, what do you have? How long have you been that way? Oh gee, that's terrible." And so I answered her questions, but I got very annoyed and wanted to say, "Lady, mind your own business" (Davis, 1961:127).

Feigning normalcy and equality permits the existence of the fiction of "no difference" between the deviant and others. Most important, this permits prolongation of the interaction to the point that normals may relate to the deviant in terms other than those linked to his or her deviance. At this point the second stage of deviance disavowal commences—*the facilitating of normal role taking by the deviant.* This stage is reached when the normal person is able to interact with the deviant in terms of one or more statuses other than that of the deviant status. Interaction is no longer bounded by the characterological imputations linked to the master status of deviant. Terms like blind, crippled, and so on, can be used without embarrassment when talking with a blind or handicapped person. Often this stage is actively promoted by the effort of the deviant to project images, attitudes, and concepts of self other than those of a deviant.

Development of this stage of deviance disavowal necessarily calls for reciprocity between the deviant and the normal. That is, as the deviant disavows his or her "abnormality" and makes a bid for redefinition of self, the nondeviant must respond in a manner consistent with the cues proffered by the deviant. The nondeviant's support of the effort at disavowal serves to confirm the deviant's bid for self-redefinition; equally important, it helps promote a "normalization" of traits possessed by the deviant that may originally have been taken as evidence of his or her deviance. When interaction between the deviant and normals reaches a level such that the deviant condition is no longer regarded as a handicap, it may be said that one has "broken through" the interactional limitations imposed by the master status (Davis, 1961:128). Interaction becomes spontaneous rather than forced, natural rather than artificial.

Having "broken through," the person engaged in deviance disavowal faces the third and last stage of the process—*institutionalizing* (that is, sustaining) *normalized relationships.* Institutionalization does not mean that the special condition of the deviant (for example, that he or she cannot see, or is confined to a wheelchair, or has a prison record) is ignored. Rather, it means that these conditions are ultimately acknowledged and worked into the "normalcy" that prevails between deviant and others. Davis suggests this normalization is reached in either of two ways.

First, there is "overnormalization," in which a person ". . . . normalizes his perceptions to such an extent as to suppress his effective awareness of many of the areas in which the handicapped person's behavior unavoidably deviates from the normal standard" (Davis, 1961:130). This pattern exists when the normal person, *unthinkingly*, schedules events, appointments, activities, and so on, that are inconvenient, embarrassing, or uncomfortable for the deviant. A case in point is making reservations for dinner at a popular (hence, crowded) restaurant without telling the management that one of the diners will be confined to a wheelchair. In short, the deviant is being encouraged to "give up" his or her abnormality.

The second method is the reverse of the first. In this case the normal individual, in repudiation of stereotypic definitions of the deviant, joins the deviant in their marginal status and seeks to affirm his or her belief in the deviant's capabilities. In effect, the normal joins the deviant in defiance of the stereotypic definitions of the larger community (Gowman, 1956:71). An expression of this repudiation is found in those cases where the normal person mildly and jokingly chides the paraplegic for being "so damned helpless." For persons who embrace the stereotypic conception of the physically handicapped, such a remark is horrifying in that it violates the standards of "good taste" and civil inattention. However, for those involved in normalized relations, the perception of such remarks as horrifying is taken as evidence of the definer's lack of enlightment. Essentially, such remarks serve to announce that the handicap is defined as a "small part" of the individual (Levitin, 1975:552).

Deviance Avowal

In contrast to disavowal, some people attempt to manage their stigma and avoid or limit devaluation by *acknowledging their condition* while simultaneously working to effect a positive social identity and achieve positive social statuses (Levitin, 1975:550–551). By

openly declaring that they are handicapped or otherwise stigmatized, these people may be said to engage in *deviance avowal* (Turner, 1972). For example, people who are temporarily handicapped
sometimes use the technique of avowal by proclaiming that "this
deviance will *not always* be me" (Levitin, 1975:551). In taking this
path, the deviant individual is not simply resisting the label *permanently handicapped*, but seeks to discourage the idea that *any* such
label is appropriate. That is, he or she resists the application of any
label that symbolizes the removal of the attribution of normality.

Avowing one's deviance while making a bid for normality may
demand considerable time, effort, and imagination of the stigmatized person. For example, avowal may call for an effort to relate the
details of the particular condition to any normal who will listen. In
telling the story, emphasis will be placed on the prognosis of early
recovery (even when this is not medically justifiable), thereby emphasizing the temporary nature of the condition. The basic message
is that ". . . . this handicap will *not always* be who I am" (Levitin,
1975:554). Examples of this effort include the temporarily disabled
person who announced the temporary need of a wheelchair and its
anticipated "disappearance" by painting "Houdini" on the chair
(Levitin, 1975:552). Another device used by temporarily handicapped persons is to inquire of normals about their own past illnesses or handicaps, thereby reminding them that they, too, were
once afflicted and limiting the normal's opportunity to draw "lines"
between himself or herself and the handicapped person.

This same effort may be engaged in by the permanently handicapped person but with one major change. For these people the
basic message to be transmitted is that their ". . . . handicap is *not
all* of who I am" (Levitin, 1975:554). This message is supplemented
by the effort to present information about the "untainted" aspects of
self.

For both the temporarily and the permanently handicapped,
broadcasting these details and providing cues that would permit
normals to relate to them in terms of a nondeviant role, facilitates
their own normal role taking (as in the second stage of the disavowal process). Should this effort be successful and the preferred
definition be accepted by normals, the final stage of normalizing
relations between deviants and others is reached.

Moreover, avowal seeks to separate the *deviant condition* from
the *deviant role*. As Turner (1972:311) has pointed out, "overaggres-
siveness" (deviant condition) may be linked to a deviant role in the
case of the *nouveau riche* or the Jewish businessman but may be separated from the role in the case of the Junior Chamber of Commerce
young man of the year; in the latter instance, one cannot, by defini-

tion, be *overly* aggressive. In this case the "deviance" is overlooked, forgotten, or redefined. It is this that those who use deviance avowal seek to achieve.

Stigma Management and Socialization

Use of the techniques of disavowal and avowal to successfully manage encounters with nondeviants or normals does not come easily or automatically. The techniques must be learned as part of the ongoing biography of the deviant. The deviant must be socialized to his or her role. Promoting that socialization are other deviants with whom one may interact directly and indirectly (as through the media) and from whom cues may be acquired on how to minimize role problems.

Examples of this socialization may be found in journals and other printed material serving select deviant populations. One such journal is *Paraplegia News,* which contains articles written by "insiders" to help handicapped persons adjust to their condition, find fulfillment, and handle the distressing behavior of nonhandicapped persons. Such an article is Sue Odgers' (1978) "Sex on Wheels," outlining for the disabled female what "kinds of men" may be encountered and how they may be dealt with.

Humor may also serve to sensitize and assist people to manage their stigma. Many of the journals carry cartoons designed to promote deviance disavowel or avowel, normalize the handicap, and assist the actor to anticipate and respond to recurring events. Thereby, it is hoped, problems may be reduced and stigma managed more gracefully.

The audience toward whom these devices are aimed also includes the "normal" population. Successful stigma management often calls for changing the normal's perception of and behavior toward the nondeviant. Ideally, the stereotyped conceptions of deviants and their presumed characterological defects must be addressed and altered, thereby promoting greater empathy for the deviant on the part of the nondeviant.

Exemplifying this effort is the Lily Tomlin characterization of Crystal, the Terrible Tumbleweed (*Paraplegia News,* 1978:24–25). In this characterization, admittedly a burlesque, Crystal is a young quadraplegic woman confined to a CB equipped "blow-job" wheelchair dubbed the Iron Duchess. Conforming to anything but the stereotype of a quadraplegic, Crystal is traveling coast to coast in her chair; thus far she has traveled 1,900 miles in one year and seven months. When she arrives in California, says Crystal, she will go hang gliding at Big Sur, perhaps the first (and maybe the last) quadraplegic to do so. Liberally sprinkled with gallows humor (in the middle of one hang-gliding experience Crystal got her catheter caught in a crosswire and crashed), Tomlin's characterization is designed to bring to the attention of normals things the rules of good taste and civil inattention require be avoided. By the use of satire, Tomlin implicitly questions the appropriateness of such restrictions and of stereotypes, subjecting the latter to ridicule. In their place (hopefully) is empathy and a greater sensitivity to the needs and capabilities of the handicapped.

The success of this effort is admittedly problematic and unknown. Among Tomlin's mail are letters from normals indicating that such frankness is more than some people can manage. Others perceive the characterization to be in bad taste. But among handicapped persons, Crystal is well accepted as a means of telling their story ". . . . with warmth, honesty, total humanity and humor (*Paraplegia News*, 1978:24).

Accounts: Excuses and Justifications

In addition to the foregoing techniques of stigma management, people whose deviance is known frequently seek to manage their moral burden by using any of a variety of *accounts*, statements designed ". . . . to explain unanticipated or untoward behavior" (Scott and Lyman, 1968:46). Two kinds of accounts are *excuses* and *justifications*.

Excuses consist of a variety of fairly standard, socially approved phrases or ideas used by people to bring about a softening of the moral breach they are involved in and to relieve themselves of responsibility for the deviant condition (Scott and Lyman, 1968:47). One type of excuse is the *appeal to accidents*. This is employed when people claim their conduct and its consequences are the result of things (for example, an environmental irregularity such as a hazard or a momentary bodily weakness) over which they have no control. A second type of excuse consists of *appeals to defeasibility*. As an example, one may seek to absolve himself or herself of responsibility by claiming to have acted on the basis of ". . . . misinformation arising from intentional or innocent misrepresentation of the facts by others" (Scott and Lyman, 1968:48; Sykes and Matza, 1957:667). Had valid information been available, they contend, they would have acted differently; its absence serves as a mitigating force. A third category of excuse includes those that rest on *biological drives*. For example, popular phrases such as "boys will be boys" and "that's what you'd expect from a woman" refer to the idea that some behaviors are governed by sex-linked traits. As a result, behavior is fatalistically attributed to conditions over which people are believed to have no influence. Again, then, people are granted some measure of relief from responsibility. A fourth and final type of excuse is *scapegoating*, excusing their behavior on the basis of traits (negative) possessed by others. For example, a Mexican girl excuses her behavior by claiming that "I was always getting into fights because some girls are vipers; they get jealous, tell lies about each other, and start trouble" (Lewis, 1961:143). Given the unacceptable traits of others, the actor's behavior becomes explainable and the actor is less blameworthy.

In addition to excuses are *justifications*, ideas that ". . . neutralize an act or its consequences when either is called into question" (Scott and Lyman, 1968:51). The unique feature of justifications is that they call for an acknowledgment of the wrongfulness of the *type* or *category* of act in question while seeking to have the *specific instance* in question defined as an exception. For example, taking the life of another person is generally wrong. Yet, as we have noted, it is justified under conditions of war, self-defense, and other exceptions.

When the act and its consequences are called into question, when the seeming contradiction between the general rule and the specific case is raised, people may resort to any of a variety of justifying ideas to account for their behavior while keeping the general rule intact. Called "techniques of neutralization," many of these devices were considered in Chapter 2.

To these techniques of neutralization must be added two other forms of justification: the *sad tale* and *self-fulfillment*. "The sad tale is a selected (often distorted) arrangement of facts that highlight an extremely dismal past, and thus 'explain' the individual's present state" (Scott and Lyman, 1968:52; see also Goffman, 1961:150–151). As an example, Harold Greenwald (1958:32–36) relates the "sad tale" of a call girl whose biography included the experience of the depression of the 1930's, a period of residence in an orphan asylum, being sent to a series of foster homes (in one of which the foster father allegedly forced her to perform fellatio on him and in another she was regularly punished for things she had not done), loneliness, and so on, finally culminating in her engaging in sex in return for material reward. This array of conditions is regarded as an explanation and justification for the woman's prostitution.

In employing *self-fulfillment* one justifies his or her rule violation on the ground that it is an aid to a higher and more complete realization of praiseworthy goals. For example, the ingestion of some drugs (such as peyote, marijuana, LSD) is justified by some people on the ground that these chemicals "expand consciousness" and enhance one's sensibility to people and things in the environment. Syllogistically, sensitivity is good (self-fulfilling), the chemicals enhance one's sensitivity, therefore the ingestion of these chemicals is justifiable.

Covering

A final technique used by individuals to manage a discredited condition is *covering*, referring to an array of tactics whereby one seeks to present one's stigma in the least offensive way, that is, to minimize the stigma so as to ease any associated tension (Goffman, 1963:102–104). One method of covering seeks to divert attention from one form of stigma to a second, hopefully lesser, stigma. As an example, Goffman cites the blind person who wears dark glasses symbolizing his or her blindness, in an effort to cover defacement or disfigurement that may exist in the region of the eyes (Goffman, 1963:102–103). A second form of covering is that in which the discredited person avoids behaviors that would call attention to his or her stigma and increase the chance of interfering with social interaction. As an example, Goffman refers to the near-blind person who refrains from reading in public since to do so would require bringing the page to within a few inches of his or her face. Such a display would call attention to the handicap and perhaps contribute to problems of acceptance by others and interaction with them (Goffman, 1963:103).

As a final example of covering we may note the effort by some homosexuals to make themselves more acceptable to heterosexuals by imitating the normative pattern of stable heterosexual marriage. By establishing stable relationships, including in some cases having their relationships solemnized with religious ceremony, displaying fidelity, and avoiding signs of promiscuity, homosexuals hope to ". . . ease the burdens of oppression by stressing acceptable modes of behavior and diverting attention from those traits that straight society finds intolerable" (Humphreys, 1972:139–140).

Collective Management of Stigma

The several stigma management techniques thus far considered are essentially individual modes of adaptation; their successful use seldom calls for the assistance of more than a few others. We turn now to a final mode of adaptation, one calling for group or collective effort.

In an office building corridor hangs a poster displaying the silhoutte of a person in a wheelchair. The caption reads: "You gave us your dimes. Now we want our rights." In San Francisco and other cities many prostitutes have organized and are hustling for their rights as well as dollars. They have joined COYOTE, "a loose woman's organization" (the acronym stands for "Call Off Your Old Tired Ethics"), aiming to ". . . reform the way American society hassles, punishes and stigmatizes its prostitutes" (*The Missoulian,* 1973). In the fall of 1976, Free Spirit, the gay student organization at a major western state university, sponsored a "gay awareness" week designed to change what gay people regard as misconceptions concerning homosexuality, and to educate the public and promote understanding by straights of gay life. And, again in San Francisco, Bob Goldman's National Stuttering Project is attempting to "off the pig," that is, have the cartoon character Porky Pig declared a menace, and promote the self-enhancement of the nation's 2.6 million stutterers (*Time,* 1977).

Each of these examples reflects the militance of an apparently growing and increasingly varied number of *voluntary associations* (groups seeking to promote the common interest of the membership, affiliation being noncoercive) established by those who are deviant and stigmatized. Included are associations of those who are deviant by ascription as well as by achievement. They are the people— dwarfs, alcoholics, gamblers, the overweight, drug addicts, homosexuals, the aged, and mental patients, among others—who have, largely since the 1960's, sought to establish an organizational apparatus with which to solve some of the dilemmas of deviance. In the following section our concern will be focused on these associations, their origins, the forms they take, and the role they play in the larger phenomenon of deviance.

Origins of Voluntary Associations

Among some sociologists there exists the belief that the presence of voluntary associations among deviants represents a relatively new phenomenon in history; at least the impression is given that the prevalence of such groups has increased markedly in the past few decades (Sagarin, 1969; Becker, 1970). While perhaps true in general, the applicability of this notion likely varies with the specific group under consideration, the virulence of social opposition directed toward it, its size and power relative to nondeviant groups, and several other factors. Adding to the confusion in this general realm is the fact that, until recently, the history of the activity of some groups, especially their involvement in resistance, has lacked investigation (Katz, 1976:335). The idea that the recent appearance of voluntary associations among deviants represents a new phenomenon (as against the increased visibility and expansion of a long-standing tendency) also fails to reckon with the fact that "the tree presupposes a root." In point of fact, secret societies, with which some present-day voluntary associations have continuity, were quite common among preliterate peoples and have a history dating from the most ancient times (Heckethorn, 1965).

Secret Societies

What is meant by the term *secret societies?* These may be defined as associations placing a premium on secrecy and that engage in ritual designed to maintain that secrecy. In sharp contrast with groups that admit anyone to membership and keep nothing from outsiders, secret societies are "organized around the principles of exclusiveness and secrecy" (MacKenzie, 1967:14). Recruitment is selective and activities are protected from public scrutiny. Beyond this similarity of organizational style, secret societies have historically exhibited considerable variations in focal concerns: religious, political, scientific, military, as well as criminal and antisocial. Among the better-known groups of the latter sort were Chinese secret societies, many of which ". . . enrolled criminals, miscreants, delinquents, and outcasts as members and mercenary thugs" (Lyman, 1974:23). Beyond that, Chinese secret societies provided an organizational base from which to launch both individual and collective protests against oppression. "By joining a secret society, an individual acquired a sworn fraternity of comrades, a protective group, and the force to counter the strength of the traditional societies" (Lyman, 1974:41). A purely native American secret society is the Invisible Empire Knights of the Ku Klux Klan.

Secret societies are often formed by persons engaged in behavior defined as deviant by the dominant standards of society. To that extent, such societies may be said to emerge out of and provide an index of social conflict in a society. This is particularly the case for those whose activities are perceived to be heretical, revolutionary, or in some other sense threatening to vested interests in the society. The secrecy of such groups is understandable as a "cover" (MacKenzie, 1967:300).

In addition to providing a "cover," secret societies have other attractive features. One of these is secrecy itself. As Georg Simmel notes, the element of secrecy greatly colors the integration of those who share the secret vis-à-vis those who do not. For those involved, sharing fosters a sense of mutual confidence and trust; without these conditions the protective advantage of secrecy is lost. In the absence of secrecy, the discreditable becomes the discredited (Simmel, 1950:346).

Another feature of secret societies is their aristocratizing effect on the membership. That is, "by joining one another, those who want to distinguish themselves give rise to the development of an aristocracy, i.e., a sense of themselves as a superior and privileged class, which strengthens and . . . enlarges their position and self consciousness . . . "(Simmel, 1950:364–365). By separating and forming a group, people may acquire a sense of their specialness, their identity; belonging to such groups becomes honorific. This element is readily recognized among members of Greek letter societies on American college and university campuses. As a counter to degradation, the importance of this aristocratizing effect for those who have been publicly discredited or who experience symbolic labeling is obvious.

Finally, belonging to secret societies provides members with a sense of freedom denied them by legitimate society. Of particular importance to those engaged in banned behavior is the fact that within the confines of the secret organization exist opportunities to behave in ways that public social regimentation and the threat of punishment seek to extinguish. Indeed, Simmel proposes that the ". . . widespread diffusion of secret societies is usually proof of public un-freedom, or a tendency toward . . . political oppression" (Simmel 1950:361). Belonging to a secret society provides the opportunity (freedom) to express one's uniqueness (for example, one's deviance) while minimizing the costs and danger of being open. Such societies provide for association with sympathetic others and the opportunity to express oneself without fear of censure. Within the limits of its safety, the secret society permits one to abandon the *fronts* (the managed images of self) so necessary for those engaged in deviance (Goffman, 1959:22ff).

The Deviant Community

The development and maintenance of these secret worlds has continuity with the creation of communities of deviants. *Community* here refers not to a physical thing, a geographical area having a political identity and name. Rather, in the sense used here, community is a psychic and social thing, a state of mind and a set of relationships. It is the "sense of oneness, of brotherhood and sisterhood" (Warren, 1974a:13) shared by people who are set apart by their ethnicity, sexuality, disability, or behavior. It is a social thing in that it consists of people whose life style reflects their oneness with others.

To say communities are psychic and social things does not mean they cannot be found in physical places. Among professional thieves of the 1920's and 1930's these "places" included the speakeasies, restaurants, saloons, cigar stores, and other places where professional gangsters congregated (Sutherland, 1937:158–159). For the homeless men and women, vagabonds of the road of that same era, social centers existed in the form of "jungles" or ". . . places where the hobos congregated to pass their leisure time outside the urban centers" (Anderson, 1923:16). In such places matters of interest to hobos were discussed, songs sung, stories told, meager foodstuffs shared, and solidarity established among people who had turned their backs on the world and who were at ease with one another (Reitman, 1975). Among homosexuals such places are the baths, bars, gymnasia, motels, clubs, resorts, and other locations catering to that population. Among striptease dancers it is the gay bars and hotels where these women may gather under at least minimally hospitable circumstances (McCaghy and Skipper, 1969).

Communities such as these do not arise in a simple, deterministic, or mechanistic fashion. Nor are they automatic consequences of societal condemnation of the people who populate them. Rather, these communities develop out of the choices people make to affiliate with persons like themselves. In some cases, for example, segregated ethnic and highly visible racial minorities, one may have few viable options from which to choose. For most of those who are discredited and discreditable, however, affiliation allows for the expression of what is best not revealed in the presence of nondeviants. For homosexuals involvement in the "gay world" permits one to experience the delights of one's sexuality, to hold hands with a lover, to engage in honest communication, to feel one is indistinguishable from others. For striptease dancers, community means an opportunity to interact with others without being perceived and treated as a sex object (McCaghy and Skipper, 1969). For dwarfs it means an opportunity to escape the prying stares of normals and to experience a semblance of an ordinary social life (Sagarin, 1969:203).

In seeking after such experiences, deviants are not noticeably different from nondeviants. What does appear to be unique is that heretofore secret societies (by definition) and deviant communities have spawned few *public* associations. However, as noted, the past few decades have seen an unprecedented upsurge in their number. Let's consider the bases for that change.

Organizing for Change

How may we account for the recent increase in the number and visibility of voluntary associations among deviants? The answer is neither altogether clear nor very precise. Very likely, the increasing number and variety of such associations, and especially their public nature (as compared with secret societies), are linked to a variety of social changes occurring over the past century or more. Of major importance is urbanism and all it represents (Sagarin, 1969:29). As urbanism increased, so, too, did the opportunity to effect anonymity. People were permitted to remain faceless and nameless in increasingly large cities. Under these circumstances people had greater opportunity than ever before to meet with like-minded others and indulge their appetites despite the opposition of public morality.

If anonymity was not immediately available, increasing geographic mobility made possible the short- (or long-) term change in geographic location. By means of quick trips to nearby urban places, a "man could organize and join an association, go to its meetings, and then return to the quiet surroundings of his home and neighbors with few people knowing about his membership. Thus the anonymous society—as opposed to the secret one—was born" (Sagarin, 1969:29).

Another possible contributor to the growth of voluntary associations among deviants was the increasing tendency, during the 1920's and 1930's, of Americans to look upon many deviations as a reflection of an underlying emotional disorder, one calling for sympathy rather than punitive condemnation. Helped along by the increasing popularity of the ideas of Sigmund Freud and psychoanalysis, it is suggested, the shame and stigma associated with some deviations began to decline (Sagarin, 1969:30). Thus, "the rise of dime-store psychoanalysis—the easy explanation of deviant or odd behavior as the product of childhood traumas that might have happened to anyone—has helped the public to absolve deviants of responsibility for what they do" (Becker, 1970:343). Taken together, these views may be said to have encouraged an increasing tolerance (that is, a change in the definition) of some forms of deviance by promoting an image of the rule breaker as something other than a ". . . sinner whose consignment to hell is a foregone conclusion" (Becker, 1970:343). This changing reality of deviance tends to promote increased organizational (especially political) activity among segments of the deviant population.

Closely linked to this changing definition of deviance is the increasing public tolerance of some behaviors previously regarded only as revolting. Rather than condemnation, over the course of several generations ordinary people have become more inclined to attribute deviance to extenuating circumstances, to accept the idea that deviants can be reformed, and less inclined to take harsh punitive action against them (Becker, 1970:343). Most recently these tendencies have paralleled court decisions intended to restrict the use of extralegal methods by law-enforcement agencies controlling deviants. For example, public officials have been prohibited by courts from interfering with the right of protest organizations to demonstrate peacefully, such actions being protected by the 1st and 14th

Amendments to the constitution guaranteeing the right to assemble peacefully and seek redress of grievances (Boggan et al., 1975:14).

Supplementing the tendency to withhold harsh punishment is the seeming reluctance in some areas to deny constitutional protection to deviant minorities. In some cases this reluctance is apparently based on the fear that to deny such rights to one group, however despised, may bode ill for other groups in the future. One example is the defeat at the polls in California of the so-called Briggs Amendment, which would have required the dismissal and prevented the hiring of known homosexuals as teachers in that state's public schools (Gregory-Lewis, 1978:7ff). A second example involves the 1978 Seattle, Washington, initiative to repeal that city's gay rights law. The Seattle City Council unanimously condemned the initiative as "misguided, confused, dangerous, deceitful, frightening and un-American" (Anderson, 1978). That sentiment was echoed by the Community Relations Committee of the Jewish Federation of Seattle. In a resolution that Committee condemned the repeal of civil rights for gays, claiming it ". . . is a denial of human and civil rights which, if allowed to pass, could become part of an epidemic, which will spread to other individuals who are minorities by virtue of their race, religion, sex, political beliefs or natural origin" (Anderson, 1978). The initiative was defeated at the polls by an approximate 3:2 margin (*Mayerson*). What is most important for our purposes is that victories of this sort serve to stimulate and encourage similar efforts among other groups who perceive themselves to be oppressed.

Finally, and perhaps more important then the other factors mentioned, is the influence of the social protests of the 1960's and 1970's. Of special significance has been the development of the counterculture during that time and the agonizing political upheavals concerning black liberation and America's role in Vietnam (Altman, 1971). Prior to that time, control of the public morality of this nation was, by and large, in the hands of the WASP (Schrag, 1970). At least on the public level no viable challenge to that hegemony existed prior to the development of black protest in the 1960's and, simultaneous with that, the challenge of youth. Each in their way, blacks and youth demanded the right to their own culture and insisted on its legitimacy. Each collectivity called for a new social reality and new identities. In doing so, they provided a model to be followed by other groups who felt oppressed.

Promoted by these several conditions, recent years have seen a rapid increase in the number and variety of voluntary associations among deviants of almost every stripe. Within this vast array of collectivities, however, there exist rather marked differences. Let's consider these differences.

Types of Associations

Not all organizations of deviants are alike. Indeed, such organizations may be classified on two different dimensions: (1) the *dominant method* by which they seek to achieve their objective and (2) the *attitude* of the association with respect to the major or legitimate values of society. Let's explore these two dimensions.

Expressive and Instrumental Groups

Regarding the dimension of dominant method, two major types of association may be identified, the *expressive* and the *instrumental*. Expressive groups are those that ". . . exist primarily to furnish activities for members" (Gordon and Babchuk, 1959:25). Serving members' needs is an end in itself. Thus, the principal concern of expressive groups is to provide for the social, recreational, and other needs of the membership. Often there is an interest in providing information (legal, medical, and the like) or services (food, transportation, education) for the followers. For the most part, expressive groups do not concern themselves (that is, confront and seek to deal) with issues of the larger society. By and large, these groups tend to be apolitical, choosing to foster any of various methods of *evading stigma*, that is, helping the individual to correct his or her "fault" or "defect," aiding people to adopt a socially acceptable life style, or providing the support and succorance of other stigmatized persons (Humphreys, 1972:141). Essentially, the posture of expressive groups promotes adaptation to (rather than removal of) stigma.

The second type of organization included under this dimension is the instrumental. These are groups that ". . . serve as social influence organizations designed to maintain or create some normative conditions or change" (Gordon and Babchuk, 1959:25). They are designed primarily to resist or promote change. This is not to suggest that these organizations are unconcerned with the welfare of members; indeed, just the opposite is the case. Rather, these associations are ". . . designed to benefit members by organizing them to change, in some small way, what to them [is] a significant aspect of the social system" (Sagarin, 1969:84). Unlike expressive groups, instrumental types seek to *counter* or *remove* the stigma attributed to their differentness (Humphreys, 1972:141). As we will see, it is these associations that are involved in the politicization of deviance (Horowitz and Leibowitz, 1968).

Conformative and Alienative Groups

The second dimension by which we may differentiate voluntary associations concerns the group's orientation toward legitimate social values. Again, two major orientations are discernible. First is the *conformative* type, referring to those groups that embrace and are in close accord with major social values (Lyman, 1970:37). Despite their sometime interest in social change, these groups do not address themselves to *basic* social values and institutional arrangements. Rather, attention is focused on a realignment of social priorities, the altering of specific social policies, or changes in select laws. In other cases conformative groups may work to alter the moral meaning of their particular brand of deviance. However, in seeking these changes, conformative groups pose no challenge to the existing political, religious, economic, or other institutions of society.

The second type of group to be noted under this dimension is the *alienative*, referring to those groups hostile to the major legitimate values and institutions of society (Lyman, 1970:37). Though less prevalent, this type of group tends toward a radical or revolutionary posture. *As perceived by their membership*, the problems such groups face are endemic to the society, a consequence of the way the society is structured and operates. As such, the alienative group is hostile to and "attacks"—for the most part, verbally—dominant social values and institutions.

Combining the dimensions of organizational method with that of value orientation, we may establish a fourfold classification or typology of voluntary associations. This schema is shown in Table 7-1. Representing *ideal types*, that is, a hypothetical conception of a phenomenon against which actual situations (in this case, groups) may be compared, it must be recognized that the location of actual groups in this framework reflects a somewhat imperfect placement. It is imperfect, first, because the groups identified do not reflect in practice the unqualified commitment to or display of the ideal traits linked to each type. Second, in the course of time the complexion of groups changes in substantial ways. As a case in point, one need only contrast the Ku Klux Klan of the 1880's with the rechartered Ku Klux Klan of today, or compare the Black Panther Party at present with the Black Panther Party in its heyday in the late 1960's (Marine, 1969). Despite these imperfections, this typology permits the establishment of a working classification of voluntary associations. Let's examine the major types.

The first type of association is the *instrumental-conformative*, examples of which include several of the groups mentioned in the preceding paragraphs. Prominant among these is COYOTE, the principal goal of which is to decriminalize (if not to legitimize) prostitution. The goals and activities of COYOTE are disseminated through an official newspaper called *Coyote Howls*. We may also include under this heading the National Stuttering Project, which

TABLE 7-1

A Typology of Voluntary Deviant Associations*

Dominant Method	Attitude Toward Dominant Social Values	
	Conformative	Alienative
Instrumental	COYOTE	Redstockings
	National Stuttering Project	The Feminists
	Gay Activist Alliance	Women's International Terrorist Conspiracy from Hell
Expressive	Weight Watchers	
	Recovery	Old Order Amish
	Little People of America	Black Muslims

*Adapted from: Stanford Lyman, The Asian in the West, Reno/Las Vegas, Nevada: Western Studies Center, Desert Research Center, 1970: 37.

includes in its program such instrumental concerns as ending job discrimination against stutterers. Finally, there is the Gay Activist Alliance, an organization of homosexual men and women seeking freedom of expression of their "value and dignity as human beings." Calling for the elimination of specific political, economic, and other conditions they feel inhibit them (a selective focus of attention), this organization sponsors pickets and demonstrations, circulates informational pamphlets and a bimonthly publication, and maintains a speakers bureau. Each in its way, these organizations seek social change, but not to the detriment of the basic fabric of society.

Equally prevalent are groups of the *expressive-conformative* type. One popular group of this sort is Weight Watchers, a commercial organization composed of overweight persons. The official purpose of this association is to provide dietetic advice and information to members and, in weekly meetings, provide support and encouragement for those who are dieting. Another organization of this type is Recovery, a self-help group established to provide social and rehabilitative assistance to former psychiatric patients. Nationwide, this organization has a reported 7,000 members and approximately 1,000 local chapters. Finally, there is Little People of America. This organization limits membership to persons who are 4' 11" in height or less and to either proportionate or disproportionate dwarfs. LPA provides an information exchange for members, assists dwarf couples wishing to adopt children of that type, assists "normal" parents who have dwarf children, and in other ways seeks to assist members to solve problems unique to little people.

The third type of association is the *instrumental-alienative*. Representative of this category are a wide variety of women's liberation groups reflecting varying degrees of political activism and radicalism. Generically, these organizations are referred to as the Women's Liberation Movement. Many of the specific organizations affiliated with this movement are unstructured and unconnected, and reflect widely differing ideologies. Specific groups representative of the alienative wing of the movement are Redstockings, Women's International Terrorist Conspiracy from Hell (WITCH), and The Feminists. According to the Redstockings Manifesto, the enemy is men; women are oppressed by men who, as a class, use the dominant institutions as tools of oppression. Men control the cultural, political, and economic institutions, as well as having the force to retain their position as oppressors. All men are rewarded by the existing system. That system must go. The Feminists, a splinter group from the New York National Organization for Women (NOW), call for the elimination of marriage and family as we now know them because they perpetuate traditional male-female role playing. Likewise, "political institutions such as religion [must be eliminated] because they are based on philosophies of hierarchical order and reinforce male oppression of females" (Papachristou, 1976:235). Similar sentiments are echoed by WITCH.

Finally, there are organizations we may refer to as *expressive-alienative*. Characteristic of this type is the Old Order Amish, a religious group once confined to Lancaster County, Pennsylvania, but now found in twenty states as well as Central and South America and Canada. A splinter group of the Mennonite Church, the Old Order Amish are believers in a literal translation of the Bible and regard themselves as a "chosen people," a "royal priesthood." As such, they have rejected almost all aspects of modern industrial civilization. This includes their homes and clothing which are stark (but highly functional) by modern standards, the rejection of bodily adornments of *all* kinds, the rejection of automotive vehicles and bicycles, the tendency to shun elections except to vote against school board candidates who are unsympathetic to their views, and the rejection of insurance and federal social security, preferring to rely on mutual aid for individual assistance (Kephart, 1976). In these many ways the Old Order Amish reflect their expressive tendencies as well as their steadfast rejection of (alienation from) modern American life and values.

A second group fitting the expressive-alienative category is the

Black Muslims, a religious body having the characteristics of both a *sect* (a small, ascetic religious group, sometimes having a charismatic leader, rejectful of integrating with the dominant social order, and tending to develop its own subculture), especially of the aggressive type (Yinger, 1957:153), and a *cult* (a small, unstable religious body built around a leader—of charismatic—and ". . . concerned almost wholly with problems of the individual, with little regard for questions of the social order). Both sects and cults tend to deviate from the established social order and the dominant churches of the society. The Black Muslims fit such specifications. They demonstrate their alienative tendencies by their repudiation of established religious bodies in this country and their effort to become aligned with Islam (Lincoln, 1961:218), as well as their call for black separation, that is, a repudiation of political integration with white society (Lincoln, 1961:87–93). Their expressive tendencies are revealed in their emphasis on group solidarity, mutual aid, self-discipline, and general conformity of the membership to a stringent code of personal and social morality (Lincoln, 1961:80).

Thus, in brief, it may be seen that voluntary associations cover a broad spectrum and display divergent styles and goals.

The Deviant as Moral Entrepreneur

Having considered the historical and contemporary basis for voluntary associations of deviants, as well as their variety, let us now turn to a consideration of the role played by those organizations in the broad context of the deviance process. Viewed as expressions of a *general social movement*, that is, an uncoordinated and general shift in the values of people (Blumer, 1955:200), the social changes we have noted (particularly the youth movement and black liberation) signaled the emergence of new orientations and sensitivities among large segments of our population. People were exhibiting a new sense of self, a general dissatisfaction with their position in the social structure, and a desire for an extension of rights and privileges heretofore unrealized. To be sure, the directions toward which people were striving, the new images of self and the values being sought, and so on, may be said to have been vague during the early period of this movement. Yet out of such periods of indefiniteness come specific social movements (women's liberation, gay liberation, fat liberation) and the myriad voluntary associations that identify themselves with the more general humanitarian movement (Mauss, 1975: 45). Let's give thought to these associations viewed as moral entrepreneurial groups, small parts of a larger social momement.

Forming Entreprenurial Groups

Commencing as loose-knit, unstructured entities, the small but dynamic units that comprised the general humanitarian movement slowly solidified and proliferated. Specific recognizable organizations appeared. What was amorphous and scarcely noticed was suddenly transformed. Almost before people were aware ". . . the social movement [passed] like a wave across the social surface . . . microscopic indicators [of unrest] coagulated into recognizable groups" (Humphreys, 1972:56).

Vague statements of purpose became clarified. Uncoordinated general shifts in people's values began to take direction, indeed, several directions, depending on the specific values and interests of the groups involved. Small concretions emerged out of the friendship networks that comprised the communities of deviants.[1] The question is how this happened.

A Sense of Dissatisfaction

Earlier it was proposed that the work of the moral entrepreneur begins with a sense of dissatisfaction with some facet of the status quo (see page 123). That observation is as applicable to deviant groups as to any other. In the case of deviants the dissatisfaction arises out of their individual and collective experience (biography), particularly the experience of social oppression and the burdens linked with stigma. Given their shame and despicable public condition, many who are discredited are "driven out" of legitimate society and often enough have little chance of returning. Others are subjected to a variety of forms of social oppression, be it legal-physical, occupational-financial, or ego-destructive (Humphreys, 1972:Chapter 2). For some people it is discrimination, for others it is prejudice, and for some it is the ignominy of being approached with the tolerance granted an "inferior" by a "superior." For those who remain in the "closet, there is the ever-present need to engage in "front work," to maintain a facade of normality, to be on one's guard, to never let on or reveal that aspect of self. In short, each type of deviant, by definition, comprises a class of social rejects, such rejection being a manifestation of social policy.

These experiences may be softened and their consequences modified slightly by one's involvement in the deviant community. It is in

1. How each group emerges will, of course, reflect elements unique to the organization's purpose, time, place, and the persons forming the organization. For an example of the process and problems involved in the formation of such a group, see Laud Humphreys, *Out of the Closets: The Sociology of Homosexual Liberation* (Englewood Cliffs, N.J.: Prentice-Hall, 1972), pp. 79–84, an account of the establishment of the Mandrake Society, a homophile organization.

the context of that community that one must view this experience. As elements of these communities we may include beliefs and interests. *Beliefs* refer to the convictions and the sense of reality shared by those who have experienced stigmatization and who participate in and share the deviant subculture. Beliefs come to be shared as a result of people congregating and interacting with one another. As in the case of rule creators in general, these interpersonal relations lead to an awareness of and a heightened sensitivity to the experience of oppression and the need for change. Through association the deviant becomes aware that he or she is not alone, that other like-minded and sympathetic persons exist. Others, particularly in the aggregate, come to be perceived as a source of refuge in a malevolent environment.

However, the "easing" of problems provided by participation in the deviant community is not to be confused with their "final solution." The deviant community does not comprise the totality of experience. To some extent deviants of every stripe must continue to be involved in the life of the larger society. As such, they continue to be the *experiencing persons*, those who suffer the impact of the dominant reality and for whom that reality is a problem (Toch, 1965:7). It is from the ranks of those who perceive conditions as problems that participants in expressive and instrumental groups are drawn. It is as an element of their biography that people experience the hardships of stigmatization and are thereby disposed to join associations established to alleviate those hardships.

The Quest for Change

Beyond experiencing problems and defining them as intolerable, people must regard change and the resolution of problems as an attainable goal. Change must be conceivable. To embrace the idea that change is possible and become involved in associations working to promote it rests, finally, on the individual's conscious desire to engage in that enterprise (Toch, 1965:12). Together with like-minded others, such persons may be said to be in search of meaning and change.

Persons in search of meaning may be regarded as people who are "sensitive" and alert to ideas and proposals that have relevance to their problem, especially those ideas that promote a solution. Such persons may be said to be *susceptible* (Toch, 1965:12). That is, susceptible persons are suggestible and likely to engage in selective perception. Being oriented toward change, they are more than ordinarily prone to perceive others' proposals as promising vehicles of change. Susceptibility, of course, is a matter of degree, just as its manifestation may take an active or passive form (Toch, 1965:13).

Affiliation with such movements is often decided on the basis of the appeals proffered by members of the movements. Like other moral entrepreneurs, spokespersons for social movements seek to "hawk" their product, to render it appealing to those who are susceptible. Indeed, the appeals made by such persons are often explicitly addressed to the elements of susceptibility. Given this tendency, appeals are likely to be found meaningful by audience members. It is when susceptible people encounter beliefs they define as appealing that they come to affiliate with the movement. As examples of appeals made to elements of susceptibility, we may point to the Little People of America. Appeals made to dwarfs and midgets to join this organization speak to increasing their medical knowledge about their physical condition,[2] to helping people with occupational problems and other inconveniences, and, most important, to providing members with an opportunity to expand their social life by meeting other little people (Weinberg, 1968:67). The appeal of "trim down" or weight watching organizations often speaks to people's wish to be relieved of the "disease" or "sin" of being overweight (Allon, 1973). As with other organizations, these examples demonstrate that appeals are couched in terms consistent with the interests and goals of potential members. Often the appeals offer satisfaction of a variety of needs.

An equally important element of appeals is the *ideology* put forth by various movements. As used here, ideology is the beliefs a group of people hold in common and what it is they expect to achieve as a collectivity (Toch, 1965:21). Ideological statements help define the organization in terms of specific beliefs and goals. For example, the National Organization for the Reform of Marijuana Laws (NORML) identifies its goals as seeking an end to all criminal penalties for possession and use of marijuana. The National Association to Aid Fat Americans seeks to change the social reality of obesity; it is dedicated to the proposition that "fat can be beautiful." The American Sunbathing Association, a nudist organization, identifies its goal as the cultivation of healthy minds and healthy bodies. Sometimes, of course, the meaning of ideological statements is not so apparent as these examples suggest. In some instances the meanings are more latent than literal. An example is found in the case of the KKK, the

2. The accumulation and dissemination of medical information concerning dwarfism reflects an abiding concern among dwarfs and midgets for the physical basis of their condition and its correction and prevention. As an example, biologists engaged in research in the field of recombinant DNA anticipate that isolation of the gene governing human growth will ultimately provide a cure for dwarfism. See Howard, Ted, and Jerry Rifkin, *Who Should Play God?* (New York: Dell Publishing Company, 1977:31.

purpose of which is obscurely phrased as follows: the ". . . protection and maintenance of distinctive institutions, rights, privileges, principles and ideals of pure Americanism and to the defense and preservation of the Constitution as originally written and intended" (*Encyclopedia of Associations*, 1978:887). Obscure or not, such statements serve not only to differentiate between groups but also to link organizational goals with members' interests.

In summary, the formation of entrepreneurial groups of deviants (which together comprise a *specific* social movement) may be said to arise out of the same general conditions and processes that give rise to moral entrepreneurial groups in general. These conditions are dissatisfaction with the status quo—a shared perception that existing conditions are intolerable and that change is desirable and conceivable (Humphreys, 1972:48).

Tactics of Change

As we indicated earlier, all voluntary associations are not alike. In the remarks to follow, reference will be to instrumental groups, those concerned with some aspect of the normative condition of society.

Troubles and Issues

In pursuing change, instrumental groups of deviants use tactics similar to those used by other moral crusaders. One tactical similarity is the effort to demonstrate that, despite popular beliefs to the contrary, the existing public policy regarding a specific type of deviance is contrary to the public interest, broadly conceived. For example, efforts will be made to demonstrate that the existing policy toward the deviant minority (discrimination, oppression, and so on) could readily be visited on other groups now considered to be legitimate. Or it may be suggested that the cost to society of maintaining and perpetuating a condition of deviance (as with criminalizing and imposing harsh penalties for marijuana use and possession and other victimless crimes) is excessive and counterproductive. Thus, prior to its becoming a relatively popular perspective, NORML was making the point that zealous enforcement of marijuana laws diverts significant numbers of law-enforcement personnel and other resources from policing more important and socially damaging matters, for example, violent crime (NORML, n.d.:1). In this way the problem faced by the deviant minority is enlarged to encompass others; the cost of the "cure" to society at large is so construed as to suggest it is greater than the disease. As with other moral entrepreneurial tactics, then, "troubles" are converted into "public issues."

Gaining Legitimacy

A second tactical similarity between deviant and nondeviant moral entrepreneurs lies in the effort to enlist the support of prestigeful and respectable others in order to legitimate one's claims. As a case in point, an issue of *Coyote Howls*, the official newspaper of COYOTE, points out the supportive relationship and mutuality of goals between Margo St. James (founder and leader of COYOTE) and Father dePaul Genska, a Franciscan monk who administers a group serving the needs of street women in New York City. If COYOTE and a segment of the Roman Catholic Church share goals, apparently COYOTE cannot be all bad (*Coyote Howls*, 1978b:9). To further promote the legitimacy of COYOTE's purposes, the same issue of *Coyote Howls* reprints portions of a letter written by Mrs. Dorothy Wachter (mother of Margo St. James) to First Lady Rosalynn Carter on the occasion of Mother's Day, 1978. The letter, first, seeks to draw parallels between their respective children; second, points out how blessed mothers are who have children such as theirs; and, third, makes reference to the "dedicated" and "crusading" work engaged in by Margo St. James (*Coyote Howls*, 197a:4). One may easily regard this effort as a calculated attempt to elicit some legitimating support from the First Lady. Finally, we may note COYOTE's legitimating efforts by its attempt to link itself with the largest women's movement of the 1970's. Thus the following squib: "Is it true the 2nd Coyote Banner, lost at the [International Women's Year] Convention, is currently hanging in the Smithsonian to forever memorialize the efforts of hookers to be part of the women's movement of the 70's?" (*Coyote Howls*, 1978b:9)

As a second instance of seeking legitimacy through testimonials, NORML lists as members of its Advisory Board several prominent physicians, attorneys, educators, and religious personalities.

Use of the Media

A third tactical similarity between deviant and nondeviant moral crusaders is their resort to the media to achieve visibility, attract adherents, and solidify the ranks of followers, efforts that are seemingly indispensable. We have already noted the wide variety of devices—many of which involved the media in one form or another—used in the campaign in China to "liberate" the bound foot of Chinese women. A similar historical example of resort to the media is found in the case of the Scientific Humanitarian Committee, a German organization formed in 1897 and regarded as the first gay liberation group. In 1903 that group published a pamphlet entitled *What People Should Know About the Third Sex* in order to provide a ". . . generally understandable and convincing piece of propaganda that will make it possible to reach the broadest layers of the public with a refutation of the false conceptions that still often hold sway about the nature of Uranianism [homosexuality]" (Lauritsen and Thorstad, 1974:14). The pamphlet went through nineteen editions within four years.

In a similar way, many contemporary groups create and maintain their own official publications such as we noted in the case of COYOTE. Other examples include the KKK's monthly publication entitled *The Klansman*, the monthly newsletter of the LPA, and the Gray Panthers' (a group serving the interests of the aged) quarterly newsletter and book. Circulated among members, these publications heighten their awareness of events of interest to the group, promote interaction, and encourage members to engage in letter writing and other activity intended to bring about desired change. Of course, such materials are circulated to government administrators and others close to the seats of power whose support is indispensable for the success of the movement. Supplementing these efforts are the established (profit-making) newspapers and magazines serving a select segment of the deviant population. Examples include *The Advocate* (a newspaper) and *Alternate* (a magazine) serving gays, and *Paraplegia News, Mainstream,* and *Accent on Living,* all of which serve the disabled.

As we saw in the case of the nude bathers (Chapter 4), a problem for deviant spokespersons is having their activity and perspective defined as newsworthy by newsworkers and, hence, deserving of recognition. In playing the role of "newsmaker" and seeking access to media channels, spokespersons for deviant interests often find it necessary to establish at least a "counterfeit" legitimacy in order to have their perspective broadcast. One method used to overcome obstacles to news coverage is to effect an image of legitimacy by establishing an organizational identity (one that is more apparent than real, more hoped for than realized) specifically for the purpose of presenting self to media newsworkers (Altheide, 1978). Thus, though it met with success with the media and was largely effective in its efforts to "save the nude beaches," The Committee to Save Eden Beach never consisted of more than a handful of people (Douglas, Rasmussen, and Flanagan, 1977:218). A second method of securing media coverage calls for *staging* events that have a high probability of being defined by newsworkers as worthy of coverage. Thus, it is not uncommon for deviant associations to purposely generate events likely to receive media coverage. For example, groups opposed to nuclear electrical generating plants have staged acts of civil disobediance in order to promote confrontation with police, have themselves arrested, force a court trial, and then use the media and the court as vehicles to bring their message to the attention of a larger audience (Shuey, 1978:3, 25).

Reconstructing Reality

A final parallel between the tactics of deviant and other moral crusaders is their construction of realities. As we saw in Chapter 4, a major task of the moral entrepreneur is to create "new moralities," to alter the meaning of conditions, behavior, and so on. In the case of the deviant moral entrepreneur this effort most often takes the form of "reconstructing reality," that is, seeking to alter the etiologic and other beliefs established and disseminated by "legitimate" moral entrepreneurs. A prime example of seeking to alter such beliefs and meanings is the effort of the Scientific Humanitarian Committee to which we referred earlier. A second example is found in the efforts of a California organization called the Fat Underground to counter popular beliefs concerning the advantages and consequences of dieting. The Fat Underground maintains that dieting is not an aid to better health, serves no lasting purpose, and may actually "wreck" people's health by contributing to increased stress and high blood pressure. Further, they state that "reducing is a $10 billion industry annually [in the U.S.]. Someone is making a lot of money off the public's fear of fat. Your (temporary) loss is their gain and they want to keep it that way" (*Before You Go On a Diet*, n.d.).

Similarly, gay liberationists have long worked to promote a change in the popular beliefs concerning the causes and character of homosexuality. For nearly a hundred years the American Psychiatric Association maintained that homosexuality was a mental disorder. Then, in 1973, the APA reclassified homosexuality as a "sexual orientation disturbance." Unlike the earlier classification of homosexuality, the sexual orientation disturbance is restricted to those who are troubled by their sexual orientation. In and of itself, said the APA, homosexuality is neither abnormal or normal (*New York Times*, 1976, Sec. 1:6). Whether this reclassification was accomplished independent of direct pressure from gay liberation groups is problematic. What is relevant is that the change is consistent with the effort of the homophile movement to create a new reality of homosexuality, altering it from a disease or mental disorder to a "way of life" equal to heterosexuality.

Another example of the reconstruction of reality is found in the case of alcoholism. Though references to alcoholism as a disease appeared as early as the eighteenth century (Catanzaro, 1968:5), a systematic movement to institutionalize that view was not evident prior to the 1930's, when a physician, W. D. Silkwood, with the support of Alcoholics Anonymous, proposed that alcoholism is an allergy. Somewhat later, E. M. Jellinek consolidated the view of alcoholism as a disease with the publication of his book *The Disease Concept of Alcoholism* (1960). Though not accepted by everyone, and despite the difficulty of isolating uniform, consistent, and progressive symptoms, the idea of alcoholism as disease has paved the way for a general redefinition: alcoholism is now popularly regarded as "problem drinking" (McCaghy, 1976:271–272). This redefinition is more than "mere semantics." By this change people who are perceived to be alcoholic are relieved of the moral burden once carried by those labeled as "drunks." With alcoholism being considered an illness, the social response to the inebriate leads to treatment and rehabilitation rather than punishment; excess consumption of alcohol is converted from a legal to a medical problem.

A final example of an effort to alter existing moral meanings by crusaders dubbed deviant is the case of legalized abortion. Over the span of the past fifteen years, largely through the efforts of the National Association for the Repeal of Abortion Laws, representatives of the women's liberation movement, and other crusaders, the meaning of abortion has been altered for a substantial segment of the population. With abortion long described as a barbarous ritual, cloaked in secrecy and available only at exorbitant rates paid to quacks and criminals operating in dingy "kitchen table" surroundings, restrictive abortion laws were generally seen as necessary to protect women from the unscrupulous and to safeguard the family. Accordingly, restrictions in law were staunchly supported by and were incorporated into the basic tenets of fundamentalist faiths and the Roman Catholic Church. In sharp contrast, groups favoring repeal of restrictive abortion laws saw these regulations as "totally evil," inhumane, and unjust. They perceived abortion as a medical issue to be decided privately between women and their physicians. To have the choice of abortion, ". . . was simply the right of personal decision, the right of a woman to control the creative powers of her body, to bring into the world only a child she truly wanted and loved" (Lader, 1973:xiii).

Though it may not be attributed solely to the efforts of prorepeal forces, it is no less worth noting that in recent years there has been a substantial change in public attitudes toward abortion. Thus, based on independent nationwide samples of college and noncollege youth, a report by Daniel Yankelovitch shows that between 1969 and 1973, during which years the abortion revolution was in full flower, the proportion of noncollege youth regarding abortion as morally wrong declined from 63 percent to 48 percent. The general moral code of college youth is reported to be even less strict in that only 32 percent of the people interviewed in 1973 regarded having an abortion as morally wrong (Yankelovich, 1974:87, 91, 93). Clearly, moral meanings are changeable and do change. One can hardly dismiss the influence of moral enterpreneurs in effecting these changes.

Altering Public Policy

As indicated in Chapter 4, the creation of "new moralities" is intended to have either instrumental or symbolic consequences. To be sure, no direct link may be established between changes in moral meanings and individual actions. Nonetheless, we may observe alterations in public policy that are consistent with the emerging moral meanings sought after by crusading deviant minorities. With that as a "measure of success," at this time let's inquire briefly into the outcome of the moral entrepreneurship of deviant groups. At the outset it is well to recognize that, in an area so fraught with currents and cross currents of moral meaning, where each success is almost immediately tempered by a setback, few if any sweeping generalizations may be proffered. More prudent, it appears, is to note that winning battles must not be equated with winning "wars." It is perhaps also true that the experience (whether of success or failure) of one segment of the deviant population has no necessary relationship to the experiences of other segments. Here, then, we will focus on specifics, withholding more general impressions for later.

One area that has undergone substantial change is alcoholism. As we noted, the view that alcoholism is a disease, though not without its critics, has become well established. Consistent with this change in definition has been the establishment over the nation of alcohol detoxification centers and diversionary treatment programs (Siegal) 1973). As alternatives to incarceration, this change in public policy is a marked departure from tradition, according to which behaviors associated with drinking (such as public drunkenness) were defined as crime, the responsibility of the police and court system. Problem drinkers, ranging from the intoxicated driver to the inebriated felon, are increasingly defined as needing rehabilitation rather than punishment. Among the expected consequences of the institutionalization of this perspective is a reduction in the burdens borne by police and courts. Thus, the city of Boston reported 12,627 arrests for public drunkenness in 1973. In 1974, one year after decriminalization, there were 8,755 reported cases of protective custody for public intoxication, a reduction of 39 percent (Rubington, 1975:413). In the span of six years, 1969 through 1974, police-inebriate contacts were reduced more than 10,000. As a result of less frequent contact between police and inebriates may also come changes in the definitions these groups have of each other and in the definition inebriates have of self (Rubington, 1975).

A second area that has undergone extensive redefinition over the past several years is marijuana use. Groups working to decriminalize marijuana possession (such as NORML and Amorphia—now combined with NORML) have been instrumental in broadcasting information indicating the nonrational nature of antimarijuana legislation and law enforcement. With the aid of representatives of the medical profession, it is now increasingly recognized that marijuana ranks among drugs causing only infrequent and relatively superficial harm (Goode, 1972:183). Forming into lobbies and pressure groups, these organizations present testimony before state legislative bodies in an effort to bring about a reduction in criminal penalties for marijuana possession. En toto, these groups appear to have experienced success in many jurisdictions. In 1973 Oregon reduced the penalty for marijuana violations to a fine. In 1975 Alaska, California, Colorado, and Maine followed suit, as did New York, in 1977. Reform proposals have been considered in several other states. In 1978 New Mexico legalized the therapeutic use of marijuana for glaucoma victims. Similarly, in September, 1978, California Attorney General Evelle Younger, then campaigning for the office of Governor of California, predicted the legalization of pot in that state in 1979 (*L.A. Herald-Examiner*, 1978). Of course, not all the impetus to reform marijuana laws results from the effort of moral entrepreneurial groups; legal change is also linked to the issue of tax revenues. Thus, in Florida, through which hundreds of tons of pot are smuggled each year, one law-enforcement officer stated: "If we legalized marijuana and sold it through state stores . . . the state would make out like a bandit . . . Just think about taxes . . . We wouldn't need any property taxes, sales taxes or a lot of other taxes" (Boyle, 1978). In the final analysis, the "color" of decriminalization may be green.

The changing reality and public policy regarding drugs is not restricted to marijuana. Dr. Peter Borne, Deputy National Chairman of Jimmy Carter's presidential campaign in 1976 said the time was right for a reexamination of the nation's heroin policy, suggesting consideration needs to be given its decriminalization and the establishment of clinics where addicts may be treated and heroin dispensed. Further, Dr. Robert DuPont, head of the National Institute of Drug Abuse under the Ford administration, had suggested that penalties for possession of all drugs should ultimately be eliminated. These sentiments are echoed by other groups. The National League of Cities has considered the feasibility of establishing heroin maintenance clinics. In September, 1976, a San Diego, California, grand jury suggested legal changes be made in drug laws permitting the creation of such clinics. The Massachusetts Council of Churches, representing sixteen Protestant denominations, has urged the same thing (Arnold, 1976).[3]

To be sure, these proposals are not without opposition from numerous interest groups. Nonetheless, it is instructive to compare the fact of these tolerant utterances by respected groups in the 1970's with the silence or utterly repressive posture taken by almost all jurisdictions only a decade or so earlier.

A third category of deviance subject to widespread public attention over the past several years is homosexuality. In 1971 a gay candidate was elected president of the student body of the University of Minnesota. In that same year, East Lansing, Michigan, and San Francisco became the first cities to enact civil rights protections for gay people; in Hawaii sodomy statutes were repealed. As we have seen, in 1973 the American Psychiatric Association removed homosexuality from its list of mental disorders. In 1974, then U.S. Representative Bella Abzug (N.Y.) introduced a bill in Congress to ban discrimination against gay people, and Elain Noble, an avowed lesbian, was elected to the Massachusetts House of Representatives. In 1975 Pennsylvania Governor Milton Shapp ordered an end to discrimination in hiring gays for state jobs; in California a bill was signed into law decriminalizing consensual sex between adults; the U.S. Civil Service Commission announced an end to its policy prohibiting employment of homosexuals; six additional states repealed sodomy statutes and ten more cities passed gay rights ordinances. In 1977, Dade County (Miami), Florida, passed and then repealed an ordinance banning discrimination against gay people in housing and employment. In that same year several other cities repealed similar ordinances, largely because of the mobilization of opposing sentiment by Anita Bryant and sympathetic others. In 1978, however, such repeal efforts were resoundingly defeated in California and Seattle, Washington. It is perhaps true that the decade of the 1970's has likely witnessed more change in public policy concerning gay rights than any other.

The activism and sometime militance of liberation activists is not confined to groups concerned only with voluntaristic deviance. Equally active are the handicapped. Thus, the handicapped have been identified as a "new minority," an "awakening minority" that

3. These proposals, coming as they do from persons and groups regarded as eminently respectable, serve not simply as an index of the degree to which social reality has changed, but also to further heighten the legitimacy of deviant groups crusading for more substantial change in laws and social policy. Such statements are doubly welcome for the crusader, of course, since, coming from respectables, they are almost automatically perceived by newsworkers as worthy of publication and dissemination.

is ". . . finally making themselves heard by lobbying for bills that will aid their cause, by attending city council meetings, and by addressing service clubs" (Watson, 1978:20). Following the model established by other instrumental groups, the handicapped have learned that "action brings reaction."

Of major concern to the handicapped are such things as the inaccessibility of public transportation facilities, restricted educational and occupational opportunities, the widespread existence of architectural barriers that severely restrict the handicapped's access to public and private buildings, and the weak enforcement of federal laws concerning discrimination against the handicapped among recipients of federal funds. To seek solutions to these and other conditions, handicapped citizens have launched an organizational effort—including the formation of the American Coalition of Citizens with Disabilities (comprised of fifty-five different organizations) for the purpose of lobbying and demonstrating to achieve their goals. Exemplifying their effort to promote change, the California Association of the Physically Handicapped (with the aid of other groups) has petitioned to have the Federal Communications Commission consider the inclusion of the disabled in equal employment opportunity regulations. Directing their petition to the FCC may result in all the nation's radio and TV facilities being made physically accessible to the disabled and preclude their being refused employment on the basis of their handicap (Marx, 1978:18). Other successes achieved by the handicapped include the decision by San Francisco authorities to make the Market Street trolleys in that city accessible to wheelchair citizens. All trolley stops will have raised platforms on a level with the trolley entrance. And, to promote the hiring of the handicapped, the Tax Reform Act of 1976 was revised to provide a tax relief incentive to employers who hire the disabled (*Paraplegia News*, 1977:28, 35).

Examples of the influence of these groups to bring about change in public policy could be expanded indefinitely. More important is the implication of these many cases, namely, that over the span of slightly more than a decade deviance has become *thoroughly politicized* in this nation (Horowitz and Liebowitz, 1968). We will conclude with a consideration of that issue.

The Politicization of Deviance

The alterations in social reality and public policy with which we have dealt have implications of the utmost significance for the understanding and analysis of the phenomenon of deviance. Surely and obviously, deviance has been brought into the realm of politics, into the realm of making and administering public policy. Deviance has been politicized. Equally obvious is the fact that this is where deviance commences—with the transformation of interests into public rules and the banning of behavior. What is significant about recent developments, however, is that the traditional conflict between power holders and power subjects, between defenders of the public morals and deviants, has been substantially altered. Traditionally that conflict has been seen in moral terms by participants as well as observers. Progressively, the conflict is being perceived in political terms.

As an adjunct to the politicization of deviance is the fact that it is increasingly unlikely that issues of deviance will be defined as absolute and unarguable. To the consternation of many segments of our society, traditional moral meanings, especially concerning sexual matters, are increasingly likely to be defined as problematic and negotiable. The moral credibility of those who rank high in the local scheme of things is no longer taken for granted. The authority of persons and groups is no longer something to which people—especially those who have long been defined as politically marginal—automatically defer and assign moral superiority. Even presidents admit to looking on women "with lust" and to having "committed adultery" in their heart (*Playboy*, 1967:87). Authority, it appears, is a "target to shoot at" (figuratively, of course), to challenge, or, perhaps, to try to coopt for the purpose of achieving one's goals. Gone are the days when people actually believed that "you can't fight City Hall." Indeed, the implication of the politicization of deviance is that the entire political arrangement (including the existing structure of public rules and their enforcement, the idea that politics is the art of compromise, and established authority) is being called into question along with the moral judgments used to bolster its legitimacy (Horowitz and Leibowitz, 1968:296).

The developments we have examined also indicate that deviant groups, in increasing number and diversity, have abandoned the traditionally subordinate political role assigned them by representatives of legitimate society. Thus, as Becker has noted, despite the fact that power subjects frequently complained of the treatment accorded them by power holders, rarely, if ever, did the power subjects seek to alter their position vis-à-vis the power holders (1967:241). Rarely, too, did deviant groups seek to have their position legitimized by the public at large; rarely were the stigmatized seen openly campaigning for votes either for a candidate of their choice or to bring about approval or rejection of an initiative or a referendum on the ballot. The increasing popularity of these and similar tactics signals the fact that ". . . deviants have become more self-conscious, more organized, more willing to fight with conventional society than ever before. They are more open in their deviance, prouder of what they are and less likely to be treated as others want to treat them without having some voice in the matter" (Becker, 1970:344).

Increasingly abandoned, too, is the idea that the stigmatized and the oppressed shall be satisfied with being "ministered to" in therapeutic terms. Indeed, the activities we have recounted indicate progressive rejection of the very basis of such an idea, namely, that "being different" is in some way pathological, a condition necessarily calling for "correction" by psychiatry, surgery, social work, counseling, or some combination of these. This amounts to an utter rejection of the "correctional" orientation that has so long dominated in the field of deviance. Such rejection, of course, is the other side of the coin of self-acceptance among those heretofore rejected by legitimate society.

Finally, recent developments indicate that ". . . the line between the social deviant and the political marginal is fading. It is rapidly becoming an obsolete distinction" (Horowitz and Leibowitz, 1968:285). Indeed, it may already have become obsolete. If so, and though we must allow for the possibility of change, its obsolescence may spell the end of an elitist conception of the political process wherein only majorities were held to rule (with the possible exception of a few powerful minorities). Politically active deviant associations are a marked departure from the traditional model and give testimony to the flourishing of "minoritarian" politics (Horowitz and Leibowitz, 1968:288).

These changes are wholly consistent with the model of man and society used throughout this volume. Politicization of deviance is reflective of persons who deal actively with their environment, who *interact with* rather than simply *respond to* external pressures. The collective effort of these groups to confront, manage, and overcome their stigma is reflective, too, of deviance as a conflict process between sometime subordinates and sometime superordinates. Consistent with our earlier analysis of power and lawmaking, the work of these voluntary associations reveals that law is indeed an instrument for the realization of the values and interests of groups having power.

Summary

In this chapter we have examined the diverse means by which people seek to deal with stigma. To facilitate analysis of stigma management by individuals, a distinction was made between the *dis-*

creditable and the *discredited*. Among the discreditable, stigma management appears to involve a rather universal set of properties, including the manipulation of *stigma symbols*, a reliance on *disidentifiers*, and the sometime need to lead a "double life." Such techniques are acknowledged to have varying degrees of success, depending on the circumstances under which they are used and one's facility in employing them. Even with the active complicity of others, as in the case of counterfeit secrecy, however, the use of these devices may sometimes exact a substantial price, including self-alienation and the substitution of one set of tensions for another.

Turning to the discredited, those whose stigma is publicly known, we noted the use of deviance *disavowal*, a process having three analytically discernible stages, each of which is intended to facilitate normalization of relations between deviants and others. Essentially, we noted, disavowal is a process wherein the deviant makes a claim to normality and the nondeviant honors that claim; the key to successful disavowal is reciprocity. A second technique of management among the discredited is deviance *avowal*, whereby one's deviance is acknowledged while simultaneously indicating it is only one part of self. Essentially, avowal is an effort to avoid being engulfed by the *master status*.

Stigma management may also be promoted by socialization to the deviant role. A major element in that socialization is to recognize and overcome the stereotyped typifications of the deviant role. Other "tools" used to manage one's moral burden include *excuses*, which seek to reduce the moral breach in which one has been engaged, or *justifications*, which are intended to deny the negative moral implications associated with one's actions. Justifications may take the form of any of several *techniques of neutralization, sad tales*, or *self-fulfillment*. The use of these techniques is a commonplace occurrence wherein people employ a variety of verbal devices (one is tempted to say "tricks") in order to absolve themselves of moral responsibility and to promote a redefinition of their actions. In a microscopic sense, people are engaged in an effort to create a reality that will permit modification of others' definition of the actor and, in turn, a modification of the actor's status as a discredited person.

Turning from individual to collective methods of stigma management, extensive consideration was given to various forms of *voluntary associations*. To better understand these associations their origins were examined, noting their continuity with *secret societies*, and linking their recent increase in number and visibility with a variety of changes in American society over the course of the past century. Of most immediate importance in explaining their present status are the political upheavals experienced by the U.S. during the

1960's and 1970's, and the broader humanitarian social movement of this period.

Viewing these associations as moral entrepreneurial groups, we also examined their activities and the existential conditions to which they are related: the experience and definition of conditions as intolerable and the resulting desire to pursue change. In examining the tactics used by instrumental groups, several similarities were noted between them and other moral crusaders. That such similarity exists reflects the widespread institutionalization of the means to alter public policy and create "new moralities" by collective effort. Most important, it is suggested, these activities reflect a fundamental change in the nature of deviance in this society—a shift requiring deviance to be viewed as a political rather than a moral and therapeutic issue.

Epilogue

For those who have followed our analysis to this point, let us now summarize, draw a few conclusions, and engage in a bit of projection.

Early in the book we said we had no "final truths" to impart. Given our perspective, it should now be evident that "final truths" concerning moral matters are anything but final, being more a reflection of the value orientation of their author than of the world they are supposed to describe. What we have tried to provide is more modest, a mode of analysis enabling people to understand and, hence, cope with deviance as an aspect of humanly created social order.

Our analysis of deviance as a social construction has taken us full circle, from the effort of moral entrepreneurs to assign negative moral meaning to conditions that distress them (pessimize them), to the processes by which these meanings become institutionalized, and back to the effort of "outsiders" to normalize their condition. Hopefully, this endeavor has resulted in establishing a firm distinction between rule breaking and deviance; between the *actions* and *conditions* of people, on the one hand, and the *social reaction* to them, on the other. Equally important, it is hoped, is that this exercise has explicated the process by which these distinctions are established, maintained, and changed, revealing that deviance is a social creation resulting from the attribution of moral meanings to people and things. By noting the recurrent and cyclical nature of this process we may readily conclude that deviance is unending. It is part and parcel of the ongoing business of people seeking to create and maintain order in a heterogeneous and conflictful environment. However, to suggest that this order is a social construction and dependent on defining is *not to say* it is *merely* a matter of semantics, that is, a matter of words. To be sure, deviance entails the attribution of meanings (as the word "semantics" suggests), but it entails far, far more. It is by naming things that people make sense of the sociocultural world and organize their responses to it. To suggest, then, that the social construction of deviance reduces to mere semantics (as if that were nothing) is to ignore man's ability to objectify his creations, mock those whose lives are burdened by the consequences of these objectified meanings, and, in general, to trivialize the entire process.

In concluding our study we might ask where this analysis leaves us. For example, is one to conclude from this study that the solution to deviance is simply to cease making rules? That is, if deviance results from rule making, is the "cure" for deviance to end rule making? Theoretically and logically that may be so. But practically it is a vacuous suggestion since it neither alters peoples' interests, allays their fears, nor reduces the bodily and/or psychological harm from which they seek protection. Or, again, does the foregoing analysis lead to the idea that the "cure" for deviance is to adopt an ethic of "anything goes?" That is, does the solution lie in withholding moral meanings from the activity and conditions of others? Were that suggestion to be taken seriously and made the basis of social policy, one suspects that policy would soon be labeled "suicidal." Reasoning thusly leads to the idea that "across-the-board-normalization" is the ultimate answer. Viewed practically, however, such a notion is equally foolish in that it ignores the idea that reality is multiple, that interests and values, however parochial, are often assigned cosmic importance and defended to the death. In short, such proposals fail to reckon with the fundamental aspects of the definitional model and are not based on a valid representation of everyday life.

To say that it is a persisting aspect of collective life does not preclude the idea that deviance, as it has in the past, will continue to change. First, we may confidently expect continued change in those conditions and activities defined as deviant. One example is pornography; what today is regarded as salacious and hard-core will tomorrow be defined as "avant garde." Today's "antagonists of profanity" will be tomorrow's "patrons of perversity" (Palmer, 1977:96). As another example, consider the recent changes in life style in our society. A few decades ago departures from the traditional monogamous marriage and family pattern (such as group marriage, bisexual and homosexual liaisons, communal living, open cohabitation) were regarded as fundamental threats to the values on which such marriages were felt to be based. Presently these patterns are more likely to be defined amorally as "alternative life styles," discussed on TV talk shows, subject to examination in textbooks and courses on marriage and family, and engaged in and espoused by people of widely differing persuasions.

As this book goes to press two well-publicized cases give evidence of these changes in moral meaning. In Oregon is the case of Greta and John Rideout, the latter perhaps the first American husband to be charged with raping his wife (*Times*, 1979a). Regardless of his having been acquitted of the charge, the fact that husbands (even though in only one state) may be tried on such charges indicates the introduction into law of very fundamental changes in the official definition of marital roles and responsibilities. Perhaps more radical is the California case of *Marvin* v. *Marvin* in which actor Lee Marvin is being sued by his former "live-in girlfriend" Michelle Triola Marvin to recover half of the $3.6 million he allegedly earned during the six years they resided together. Twenty years ago it would have been unthinkable to all but a few persons that a woman, at best a paramour, at worst a concubine, would sue for recovery of property from a man with whom she had lived without benefit of matrimony. The changed meaning of such relationships is expressed in the decision of the California Supreme Court ruling that Michelle Marvin did have the right to sue. After noting the change in social customs concerning cohabitation in our society, the court decided it should not ". . . impose a standard based on alleged moral considerations that have apparently been so widely abandoned by so many" (*Time*, 1979b:46). At the very least, these cases indicate that it is no longer reasonable to posit the idea that monogamy, with its emotional and sexual exclusivity, is the only socially acceptable means of expressing and satisfying the need for human intimacy. Nor is it morally tolerable to increasing numbers of people that wives be defined and treated as property. As alternatives to these patterns become more prevalent so, too, does their "normality."

A final example of the dynamics of moral meaning may be seen in the recent changes in the public and official definitions of "crimes without victims," a term, incidentally, that had little or no currency prior to the mid-1960's and the publication of Edwin Schur's small volume entitled *Crimes Without Victims* (1965). During the intervening years there has been a veritable flood of information gathered on these phenomena, much of it linked to efforts to bring about decriminalization and legalization. To appreciate the change, one need only consider recent policy innovations regarding abortion, drug use, homosexuality (especially among consenting adults), prostitution, and gambling. Increasingly, it seems, the pressure grows to have such behaviors declared to be not the law's business (Geis, 1972). Such pressure attests to the ongoing process of normalization.

We should note, as well, that banning is an equally vital part of the deviance process; here, too, we may expect change. That is, just as we may be moving in the direction of normalizing yesterday's sins and "bad taste," we simultaneously are pessimizing things that up to now have been taken-for-granted aspects of life or that are products of recent technological innovations. Included in the first category is the increasing public concern over behavior engaged in by public officials and government agencies (such as the FBI and CIA), corporate crime, destruction of the environment, and similar issues. As an example of the latter sort it seems reasonable to expect the application of negative moral meaning to the increasing biological exploration of and experimentation with "genetic engineering." For many people, including those who are professionally involved, research and experimentation in recombinant DNA is neither a moral nor an ethical issue; rather, it is seen as a matter of "public health" (Howard and Rifkin, 1977:33). However, as the practical implications of such procedures become more apparent and widely known—implications that include the spread of experimental cancer, mass death and genetic destruction, and the creation of threatening life forms which, once created, can neither be controlled nor their effects reversed—may we not anticipate a growing sensitivity to this issue and the formation of interest groups, if not to prevent surely to seek control over the current direction of the eugenics movement in our society?

This is not the place, nor is it our intention, to explore these matters in detail. Our purpose is merely to suggest that our analysis leads to the proposition that normalizing and banning are part of the same general deviance process; they are distinguishable only by the interests and perspectives of the groups that are instrumental in promoting one view or the other.

Our analysis suggests a second area of change. Recent public policy changes in our society indicate we are at the leading edge of what may come to be seen as a time of *increasing public fairness*. Placing the developments of the past decade or more in historical perspective and appraising them in terms of an intercursive power model suggests we may have reached the point when to declare conditions immoral, deviant, or criminal will become progressively more difficult. Indeed, this increased difficulty seems to be a consequence of the increased politicization of deviance. That is, given their newly achieved sense of power and the willingness of previously oppressed groups to employ countervailing tactics to secure and/or protect their interests, as well as the institutionalization of the means to "fight City Hall," we may have passed the point in our society's development when rule makers easily and willingly comply with requests to criminalize or otherwise stigmatize people and behavior. This is well demonstrated in the abortion issue. Regardless of one's definition of abortion, the conflict that has ensued these many years reveals that we can no longer expect the entire nation to "jump" to the "moral rope" of heretofore dominant and powerful interest groups, not even the Roman Catholic Church. This is to be expected as the moral pluralism (multiple realities) of our society becomes increasingly manifest in the political arena.

As a corollary, we may look for the process of banning to require progressively more evidence of the "objective harm," that is, overtly demonstrable damage, associated with conditions and behavior to be declared deviant. As a result we may anticipate a narrowing of the parameters of official deviance. Existing rules declaring behaviors deviant will continue to fall into disuse ("administrative decriminalization"), others will be formally repealed or otherwise modified, and new rules rather more difficult to enact.

However, as used here, "fairness" does not mean we have seen the end of "backlash" and other expressions of resistance. We will continue to have moral crusaders abroad in the land and, for many segments of the population, three steps "forward" will likely be balanced against one "backward." Nor does public fairness mean there will be an end to resentment among those who feel offended or threatened by one or another group. For that reason we will continue to experience intergroup struggles for moral superiority, a struggle to which there seems no end. The achievement of superiority by one group necessarily means rendering another group inferior. At root, however, persistence of these conditions and increased public fairness are not mutually exclusive.

Contrary to the position taken by persons of the "antipermissiveness" school, we see no evidence in these changes that our society (from a moral perspective) is "going to hell in a handbasket," or that we are headed for a state of utter moral degradation. "Moral degradation" is the term applied by the disaffected to situations that distress them greatly, over which they have little or no control, and to which they have not yet reconciled themselves. Viewed more dispassionately, all we may note with assurance is that public moral codes are changing, that the boundaries between public and private morality may be shifting. This is to be expected as the representatives of progressively more and varied forms of behavior seek legitimation for their ways and effective resistance to change declines. (It should be noted that a decline in opposition to normalizing deviant conditions *does not* equate with an increase in support for these conditions. Akin to our earlier discussion—see Chapter 4—of the declaratory argument, the absence of resistance is not to be taken as an endorsement.) Once again, if moral meanings are human constructions rather than natural law expressions, it may be a bit ambitious to expect them to stand for all time, absolutely. What we may expect, absolutely, is that deviance, like the poor, will always be with us.

Glossary

abominations of the body conditions of one's person resulting from birth, illness, or accident that are commonly regarded as repugnant and perceived as *stigma*.

achieved status a social position occupied by reason of the official or public definition of a person's behavior; contrasts with *ascribed status*.

advocacy journalism the tendency of some journalists to play the role of special pleader without, simultaneously, playing the counter role of critical questioner.

affinity a general condition leaving one more or less attracted to engaging in a specific pattern of behavior.

alienative group one that is hostile to or rejects major legitimate values and institutions of the society.

anomie a condition in which norms are lacking for the governance of individual and group behavior; in the absence of such norms the social system (or portions thereof) are rendered meaningless and people resort to adaptive behaviors held to be deviant.

appeal to higher loyalties a technique of neutralization wherein one justifies his or her rule breaking as a result of being faced with equally binding but mutually exclusive obligations; whichever obligation is satisfied automatically results in violation of the other.

ascribed status a social position occupied on the basis of the official

or public definition of a quality a person is assumed to possess; contrasts with *achieved status*.

auxiliary status traits a set of subsidiary or secondary conditions usually associated with persons occupying a *master status*.

avowal, deviance a technique of stigma management whereby an actor acknowledges his or her abnormal condition while simultaneously seeking a positive social identity and social status.

awareness the point when rule creating commences; when would-be rule makers perceive objective conditions as a threat to their interests.

banning assigning or infusing an activity or condition with negative moral meaning; to proscribe the activity as bad, evil, immoral, wrong.

bedevilment a concern of some rule breakers that if information about their deviation becomes public they will suffer a loss of social acceptability.

blemishes of character personal qualities attributed to persons known or thought to have engaged in immoral conduct and that are, themselves, stigmatizing.

bureaucratization the process of developing formal organizations and roles, a division of labor, and systematic procedures to deal with specific phenomena. See *institutionalization*.

canons of the scientific method a series of postulates forming the foundation of the scientific method.

career deviance a sequence of movements and stages through which one passes, resulting in being identified publicly as deviant, excluded from nondeviant activities, and defining self as deviant.

circuit of agents a network of role players who concur in the official *denunciation* and *stripping* of an actor of his or her social acceptability.

coalition formal or informal, covert or overt cooperative relations between groups, usually for the pursuit of limited goals.

commitment a felt obligation to persist in a line of action because of the anticipated negative consequences of discontinuing that line of action.

condemnation of condemners a technique of neutralization in which one focuses attention on his or her condemners and their alleged immorality; intended to render the accused relatively less reprehensible in appearance.

conflict perspective the idea that society is the arena of disagreement and conflict between various segments of society regarding values, interests, and morality. See *consensus perspective.*

conformative group one that tends to embrace dominant social values.

consensus perspective the idea that the members of society are in essential agreement as to the core values and moral meanings extant in the society; has several implications in sharp contrast with those of the *conflict perspective.*

contaminative exposure defiling or dishonoring of one's person or things associated with one's self.

contracultural referring to values held to be inconsistent and in conflict with the values held to prevail in the larger society.

counterfeit secrecy a mutual pretense between a deviant and others wherein, despite their shared knowledge of the actor's deviation, neither makes reference to it in speech or action.

courtesy stigma the stigma experienced by those (parents, friends, and so on) intimately associated with persons directly stigmatized.

covering (cover) the use of a variety of devices or tactics designed to help one present his or her stigma in the least offensive way or to minimize its impact.

criminal anthropology a later-nineteenth and early-twentieth-century school of criminology stressing the idea that criminals are unique from a hereditary and evolutionary perspective; initially led by Cesare Lombroso.

culture area a physical area defined in terms of the cultural homogeneity of the people populating it.

declaratory argument in law, the belief that the absence of a law against a thing is equal to official endorsement of that thing.

denial of injury a technique of neutralization in which the wrongfulness of one's actions is reduced by redefining the wrongful action; theft becomes "borrowing," assault becomes a "fist fight," and vandalism becomes a "prank," and so on.

denial of responsibility a technique of neutralization in which deviant actors attribute their behavior to the pressure of external forces over which they have no control.

denial of the victim. a technique of neutralization in which the victim is "transformed" into a deserving target of the offender's wrath; the victim becomes an "evildoer," while the rule breaker becomes a "moral avenger."

denunciation at a status degradation ceremony, a method presenting information so as to stigmatize the actor and promote the imposition of severe and restrictive penalties; contrast with *pitch.*

determinism (deterministic) any philosophy stressing the causal influence of conditions and events felt to be necessary to the occurrence of subsequent conditions or events.

differential association a highly popular social psychological theory of behavior indicating that people learn criminal and deviant behavior by the same social psychological process involved in learning noncriminal and nondeviant behavior.

disavowal, deviance the tendency of some deviant actors to repudiate or deny that their condition or behavior is abnormal; the effort to normalize that which heretofore has been defined as abnormal.

discreditable referring to that segment of the deviant population whose deviation is not publicly known, who have been symbolically labeled, and who manage to keep their deviance secret.

discredited referring to those persons whose stigma is self-evident or may be assumed to be known by others.

disidentifier any symbol used to prevent one being identified as deviant.

diversion a technique used in some places to divert youthful offenders from the criminal justice system; involves "treating" rule breakers informally rather than processing them through the institutionalized justice system.

dualistic fallacy an idea (now regarded as false) suggesting the existence of essentially different qualities between deviants or criminals and normals or noncriminals; deviants and nondeviants are therefore held to be mutually exclusive segments of the population.

empiricism a series of operations or methods used in doing science; emphasizes the importance of sensory experience as the basis of knowledge.

epidemiology a term derived from medicine, referring to the study of the distribution of deviant conduct in society and the expression of this distribution in statistical terms.

etiology the study of the cause or origins of a thing; in deviance, of the actions regarded as immoral.

excuse one form of an account or explanation for behavior that allows the actor to avoid acceptance of full responsibility for the act.

expressive group one that exists principally for the purpose of serving the immediate personal and/or social needs of the membership. See *instrumental group.*

externalization one aspect of the process rendering subjective meanings objective; refers to the overt manifestation of initially subjective meanings, preferences, techniques, and the like.

holy crusade the efforts of moral entrepreneurs that are defended and supported by scriptural and other worldly references.

human ecology the study of the spatial and temporal distribution of people and institutions.

ideal type a hypothetical conception of a phenomenon against which actual expressions of the thing may be compared.

institutionalization the processes associated with bureaucratized methods: development of organized and systematized rules and roles and the stabilization of these as the "property" of formal organizations. See *bureaucratization*.

instrumental goals in law, referring to the use of law to directly influence the actions of others.

instrumental group one that exists principally for the purpose of serving as a "social influence organization," seeking to resist or promote change; in contrast to expressive groups, instrumental groups tend to be political. See *expressive group*.

integral power usually applied to a situation wherein the distribution of power is so unbalanced as to appear unilateral. See *intercursive power*.

intercursive power usually applied to a situation in which power is distributed in a bilateral or multilateral fashion, albeit unequal (asymmetrical) in its distribution. See *integral power.*

interest groups groups organized on the basis of shared and distinctive interests of the members, generally functioning to perpetuate and serve the interests of the membership.

internalization the process (in socialization) whereby seemingly objective knowledge is acquired by people resulting in the fusing of self and others.

justification an explanation for one's behavior wherein one accepts responsibility for the action but denies any immoral or negative aspect to the action.

justification, principled a justification that entails a conflict of principles, the resolution of which is alleged to be the basis of one's rule-violating action.

justification, situational a justification resting on actual or alleged situational conditions and that permit the wrongful act being defined as an exception.

legitimacy a legal, authorized, and public status.

master status a status that tends to supersede and obscure other statuses one may simultaneously occupy.

moral absolutes universal moral standards and meanings held to apply at all times and places; moral absolutism; contrasts with *moral relativism*.

moral entrepreneurs groups (seldom individual actors) who take the initiative and engage in the "business" of (1) defending existing moral rules, (2) seeking to change existing moral rules, or (3) seeking to create moral rules where none exist.

moral relativism the belief that moral meanings are situationally rooted, changeable, and dependent upon man's construction of them; contrasts with *moral absolutism.*

morality of consequence a moral code in which one's blamefulness rests on the results of his or her initially wrongful actions, including whether or not these consequences are dealt with by the actor. See *morality of intention.*

morality of intention a moral code in which one's blamefulness is based on his or her purpose, knowledge, negligence, and recklessness. See *morality of consequence.*

motives the complex of meanings individuals regard as sufficient reason for their behavior.

multiple factor approach now largely discredited, used by early students of social phenomena, characterized by emphasis on statistical relationships as an indicator of causality, the notion that "evil causes evil," and a general lack of theoretical sophistication.

mutilation of the body any of a variety of techniques resulting in one being maimed or his or her person altered significantly; chemotherapy, shock therapy, and surgical techniques may be included.

myth(s) socially constructed tales serving to explain events; in the case of deviance, myths often seek to cast rule breaking in counterinstitutional terms.

neutralize to treat or accommodate to a negatively defined condition, thereby bringing about an altered definition of it.

nominalism a philosophical position stressing the idea that there are no universal essences.

normal crimes a range of offenses commonly dealt with by public defenders and which, therefore, may be handled in routine ways.

normalize to perceive the unusual or the atypical as ordinary and normal.

objectivation an aspect of the process of rendering subjective meanings objective; entails the naming of things, the name (independent of the referent) taking on a reified character. Applies to knowledge in general.

objective referring to the idea that events and qualities of events and conditions are external to human consciousness, that is, existing independent of mind; the reverse of *subjective.*

office, theory of an aspect of the institutionalization process; a rationale for the methods employed by formal organizations to fulfill their task; renders the task meaningful and provides a sense of order.

ontology the study of being and reality, and the essence and relations of things.

optimize to treat something in optimistic ways despite a general negative definition of the thing.

pederast (pederasty, pedophilia) one who has an erotic craving for children, sexual attraction to children, deriving sexual gratification from them.

personal defacement the marring or spoiling of one's ordinary appearance by removal of the materials and services by which that appearance is maintained.

pessimize a neologism identifying the tendency to perceive things negatively and, on that basis, regard them as intolerable.

phrenology the study of the shape of the skull to determine one's mental faculties.

physiognomy the art of seeking to determine one's temperament and character on the basis of the configuration of the face.

pitch at a status degradation ceremony, a method of presenting information so as to cast the offender in the most favorable moral light; contrasts with *denunciation.*

plea bargaining a process whereby defendants in criminal cases and prosecutors negotiate a plea, usually of guilt; the defendant may receive a reduction in the charge and/or penalty, while the prosecutor is freed of the necessity of expending scarce resources in acquiring a conviction.

positivism the idea that the proper way to study reality and man is to employ the methods of science. See *empiricism.*

power following Wrong, ". . . the production of intended effects by some men on other men." In general terms, a variety of means used to control the behavior of others.

pressure groups interest groups that work to protect their interests by recourse to public law.

primary deviant a person whose rule breaking is incidental to his or her principal involvement in socially acceptable behaviors; akin to *secret deviant.* The initial stage in a deviant career is called *primary deviance.*

primary sexual identity one's fundamental sexual inclination, either heterosexual, homosexual, or bisexual; not to be confused with sex roles, sex norms, or other cultural prescriptions or proscriptions, or one's actual behavior.

probabilism as a substitute for rigid *determinism,* the idea that certain conditions and events are more or less likely (rather than certain) to produce some subsequent condition or event.

psychopathy a condition of emotional abnormality held to underlie a variety of morally objectionable behaviors.

psychosis severe personality disturbance.

pure deviant similar to *secondary deviant;* one whose rule breaking is known and responded to by others.

rate a ratio relating the size of one number to that of another.

recipe knowledge general normative information concerning what is and is not considered correct and on which people base routine daily activities.

reflexive activity self-interaction; one becomes the object of his or her own thoughts or action.

retrospective interpretation a complex cognitive process in which the character of a known deviant actor is rendered consistent with his or her behavior; involves characterological transformation.

role engulfment long-term social psychological consequences of labeling; a cumulative process akin to *deviant career* wherein one's deviant identity becomes increasingly central in his or her relations with others.

scapegoating attributing one's problems to the alleged deficiencies or weaknesses of others.

secondary deviance an advanced stage in a *deviant career* characterized by the centrality or salience of others' reactions to one's rule breaking; one's life becomes organized about the facts of his or her deviance.

secret deviant one whose rule breaking is neither publicly recognized nor responded to as such. Similar to *primary deviant*.

secret society an association organized around the principles of exclusiveness and secrecy of membership; activity of the group may be highly variable (religious, political, and so on) and either deviant or nondeviant.

self-concept a complex of meanings or definitions people have of themselves, acquired in interaction with others.

self-fulfilling prophecy an initially false definition of things that is reacted to in such a way as to promote its validation.

situated moral meanings the application of general or abstract moral meanings to specific situations and their consequent departure from the abstract meaning.

situated self self-regarding feelings associated with specific roles and statuses.

situated transactions a series of interactions between two or more persons limited to the time and place they are in one another's physical presence.

social disorganization a sociological perspective viewing problem behavior as a consequence of variable rates of change among the social and cultural parts of the social system.

social distance the degree of sympathetic understanding between people or groups of people.

social reality the meanings (definitions, conceptions, and typifications) people assign to things in their environment and in terms of which they seek to introduce order to their world.

status degradation ceremony any of a variety of public rituals intended to bring about and give public legitimacy to a reduction in one's public status.

stereotypes group-shared ideas about the nature of a category of people.

stigma a sign or symbol indicating the bearer's low social and/or moral position.

stigma management any of a variety of methods used individually or collectively to promote control of information about one's deviation and spoiled identity; efforts to alter moral meaning attributed to persons having a spoiled identity so as to reduce the significance of their deviance.

stigma symbols signs that call attention to one's deviation or spoiled identity.

stripping official removal of the symbols by which one identifies himself or herself as a socially acceptable person.

structural functionalism an analytical perspective stressing the interrelationship between the parts of the social system and their respective consequences one to another.

subjective referring to those things having their origin in the mind, perception, or consciousness of the actor; contrasts with *objective*.

substantial self the totality of one's self-evaluations.

symbolic goals in law, the use of law to legitimate the goals and purposes of some groups without directly influencing others' actions.

symbolic interactionism a form of social psychology stressing the idea that human behavior and personality rest on people's ability to create and use symbols to transmit meaning.

symbolic labeling self-labeling; the application of stigma without benefit of public ceremony.

symbolic universe an integrated set of ideas/meanings providing a sense of orderliness and legitimacy to the elements comprising the institutional order.

symbols stimuli that have learned meanings and values attached to them.

tearoom a public place, such as a restroom, where impersonal homosexual encounters occur.

techniques of neutralization any of a variety of methods or "devices" used to reduce (neutralize) the binding force of moral norms on the actor and assist him or her to maintain a socially acceptable image of self despite having violated rules. See *appeal to higher loyalties, condemnation of condemners, denial of injury, denial of responsibility*, and *denial of the victim*.

territories, home places where one has freedom of behavior and a sense of intimacy, as well as control over the area.

territories, interactional places where people engage in social interaction; the space in which a specific interact occurs.

territories, public places to which one has access by reason of citizenship.

territory, body the space encompassed by one's body.

test case in law, a court case promoted by interest groups in the belief that the decision is likely to influence future cases resting on similar points of law and in which the interest group has an abiding concern.

total institutions organizations that demand total subordination of the client population and that severely restrict interaction between clients and nonclients.

transfer of authority the investing of ideas, proposals, and the like with legitimacy on the basis of the prestige of those with whom they are identified, such as heroes, esteemed public figures, and others.

transparency a concern on the part of rule breakers that others may "see through" them and perceive them as deviant.

transsexual one who, through surgery and socialization, seeks a change in gender and/or sex identity.

tribal stigma conditions such as nationality, skin color, and so on that are transmitted through lineages or families and regarded by others as stigmatizing.

turned on used in two senses: (1) aware of and knowledgeable about a thing as a result of experience; (2) converted to a behavior as a result of experiences defined as pleasureable and satisfying.

variable any phenomenon that can change, be measured, or be quantified.

voluntary association a group seeking to promote the common interest of the membership, affilation being noncoercive.

willing a condition in which one is open or free to engage in a given pattern of behavior at a specific time and place.

Bibliography

Adler, Patricia and Peter
1976   Tiny-Dopers: Deviant Socialization in a Period of Flux. Unpublished.

Advocate, The
1975   "L.A. Police Department's Position on Gay People." February 26:8.

Akers, Ronald L.
1964   "Socio-Economic Status and Delinquent Behavior: A Retest." *Journal of Research in Crime and Delinquency* 1 (January):38–46.
1973   *Deviant Behavior, A Social Learning Approach.* Belmont, Calif.: Wadsworth Publishing Company.

Alinsky, Saul D.
1972   *Rules for Radicals, A Practical Primer for Realistic Radicals.* New York: Random House (Vintage).

Allon, Natalie
1973   "Group Dieting Rituals." *Society* 10 (January/February):36–42.

Altheide, David Lynn
1974   The News Scene. Unpublished Ph.D. dissertation. San Diego: University of California.
1976   *Creating Reality, How TV News Distorts Events.* Beverly Hills, Calif: Sage Publications.

Altman, Dennis
1971   *Homosexual Oppression and Liberation.* New York: Avon Books, The Hearst Corporation.

American Druggist
1968   "The Pharmacist as a Drug Addict." December 2, 1968. Cited in Paul R. Elmore and Larry Cohen, "Addiction Among Pharmacists and Physicians," Pacific Sociological Association, Anaheim, Calif., April, 1970.

American Psychiatric Association
1974   "Homosexuality Dropped as Mental Disorder." *Monitor* 5 (February):1ff.

Anderson, Nels
1923   *The Hobo, The Sociology of the Homeless Man.* Chicago: University of Chicago Press.

Anderson, Robert T.
1968   "From Mafia to Cosa Nostra." Pp. 269–279 in Marcello Truzzi, ed., *Sociology and Everyday Life.* Englewood Cliffs, N.J.: Prentice-Hall.

Anderson, Scott P.
1978   "Dispatch." *The Advocate.* October 4:8ff.

Anonymous
1974 "Shooting Up: Autobiography of a Heroin Addict." Pp. 59–68 in Jerry Jacobs, ed., *Deviance: Field Studies and Self Disclosures.* Palo Alto, Calif.: National Press Books.

Aptheker, Herbert
1943 *American Negro Slave Revolts.* New York: International Publishers.

Arizona Republic (Phoenix)
1975 "Priests Ordered to Refuse Communion to Women in Groups." April 9:A-14.
1977a "Jail Avoided by Defendant in Sex Change." March 9:B-11.
1977b "Chiefs of Police Oppose Homosexuals as Officers." October 7:A-8.
1978 "Anita Bryant Wants Sex, Violence Off TV." January 23:A-4.

Arnold, Mark R.
1976 "Should Heroin be Legal?" *National Observer* (October 23).

Ashman, Charles R.
1973 *The Finest Judges Money Can Buy and Other Forms of Judicial Pollution.* Los Angeles: Nash Publishing Co.

Bahr, Howard M.
1973 *Skid Row, An Introduction to Disaffiliation.* New York: Oxford University Press.

Baker, Richard P.
1973 A Concomitant Look at Commitment and Labeling Theory: Divergent but Compatible Accounts of Delinquency Causation. Unpublished Ph.D. dissertation, Washington State University.

Balint, Michael
1957 *The Doctor, His Patient, and the Illness.* New York: International Universities Press.

Barber, Bernard
1973 "Resistance by Scientists to Scientific Discovery." Cited in William J. Chambliss, ed., *Sociological Readings in the Conflict Perspective.* Reading, Mass.: Addison-Wesley Publishing Co.

Barker, Roger G.
1948 "The Social Psychology of Physical Disability." *Journal of Social Issues* 4 (Fall):28–38.

Barnes, Harry Elmer, and Negley K. Teeters
1951 *New Horizons in Criminology,* 2nd ed., Englewood Cliffs, N.J.: Prentice-Hall.

Bay, Christian
1967 "Civil Disobedience: Prerequisite for Democracy in a Mass Society." Pp. 163–183 in David Stolz, ed., *Political Theory and Social Change.* New York: Atherton Press.

Becker, Howard S.
1960 "Notes on the Concept of Commitment." *American Journal of Sociology* 66 (July):32–40.
1963 *Outsiders, Studies in the Sociology of Deviance.* New York: Free Press.

1966   *Social Problems, A Modern Approach,* editor. New York: John Wiley and Sons.
1970   *Sociological Work, Method and Substance.* Chicago: Aldine Publishing Company.
1973   *Outsiders, Studies in the Sociology of Deviance,* rev. ed. New York: Free Press.

Before You Go On A Diet
n.d.   Fat Underground, P. O. Box 597, Venice, California 90291.

Bell, Daniel
1962   *The End of Ideology,* rev. ed. New York: Free Press.

Bell, Robert R.
1971   *Social Deviance, A Substantive Analysis.* Homewood, Ill.: The Dorsey Press.

Bennett, Lerone, Jr.
1965   *Confrontation: Black and White.* Baltimore: Penguin Books.

Berelson, Bernard, and Patricia J. Salter
1946   "Majority and Minority Americans: An Analysis of Magazine Fiction." *Public Opinion Quarterly* 10 (Summer):168–190.

Berger, Peter L.
1963   *Invitation to Sociology, A Humanistic Perspective.* New York: Doubleday Anchor.

Berger, Peter, and Thomas Luckmann
1967   *The Social Construction of Reality.* New York: Doubleday and Co.

Berkowitz, Leonard, and Nigel Walker
1967   "Laws and Moral Judgements." *Sociometry* 30 (December):410–422.

Berrigan, Philip
1971   *Prison Journals of a Priest Revolutionary.* New York: Ballantine Books.

Bieber, Irving, et al.
1962   *Homosexuality, A Psychoanalytic Study of Male Homosexuals.* New York: Vintage Books.

Birenbaum, Arnold
1970   "On Managing a Courtesy Stigma." *Journal of Health and Social Behavior* 11 (September):196–206.

Bittner, Egon
1967   "The Police on Skid-Row: A Study of Peace Keeping." *American Sociological Review* 32 (October):699–715.

Blaustein, Albert P., and Clarence C. Ferguson
1957   *Desegregation and the Law: The Meaning and Effect of the School Desegregation Cases.* New Brunswick, N.J.: Rutgers University Press.

Bloch, Herbert A., and Gilbert Geis
1970   *Man, Crime, and Society,* 2nd ed. New York: Random House.

Blumberg, Abraham S.
1967   *Criminal Justice.* Chicago: Quadrangle Books.

Blumer, Herbert
1955   "Collective Behavior." Pp. 165–222 in Alfred McClung Lee, ed., *Principles of Sociology.* New York: Barnes and Noble.
1956   "Sociological Analysis and the Variable." *American Sociological Review* 21 (December):683–690.

Bogdan, Robert
1974   *Being Different: The Autobiography of Jane Fry.* New York: John Wiley and Sons.

Boggan, E. Carrington, et al.
1975   *The Rights of Gay People, The Basic ACLU Guide to a Gay Person's Rights.* New York: Avon Books, The Hearst Corporation.

Boyle, Bob
1978   "Legalizing Pot Could Net State Big Tax Money." *Florida Times-Union* (Jacksonville), August 13.

Bredemeier, Harry C., and Jackson Toby
1972   *Social Problems in America,* 2nd ed. New York: John Wiley and Sons.

Briar, Scott, and Irving Piliavin
1965   "Delinquency, Situational Inducements and Commitment to Conformity." *Social Problems* 13 (Summer):35–45.

Briedis, Catherine
1975   "Marginal Deviants: Teenage Girls Experience Community Response to Premarital Sex and Pregnancy." *Social Problems* 22 (April):480–493.

Brodie, Fawn
1945   *No Man Knows My History.* New York: Alfred A. Knopf.

Brown, Claude
1966   *Manchild in the Promised Land.* New York: Signet Books.

Brown, Richard H.
1977   "The Emergence of Existential Thought: Philosophical Perspectives on Positivist and Humanist Forms of Social Theory." Pp. 77–100 in Jack D. Douglas and John M. Johnson, *Existential Sociology.* New York: Cambridge University Press.

Bryan, James H.
1967   "Apprenticeships in Prostitution." Pp. 146–164 in John H. Gagnon and William Simon, eds. *Sexual Deviance.* New York: Harper and Row.

Bugliosi, Vincent (with Curt Gentry)
1974   *Helter Skelter, The True Story of the Manson Murders.* New York: W. W. Norton and Company.

Bullough, Vern L.
1974   "Is Homosexuality an Illness?" *The Humanist* 34 (November/December): 27–30.

Burns, W. Haywood
1963   *The Voices of Negro Protest in America.* New York: Oxford University Press.

Burt, Cyril
1925. *The Young Delinquent.* New York: Appleton-Century-Crofts.

Bustamente, Jorge A.
1972 "The 'Wetback' as Deviant: An Application of Labeling Theory." *American Journal of Sociology* 77 (January):706–718.

Cahnman, Werner J.
1968 "The Stigma of Obesity." *The Sociological Quarterly* 9 (Summer): 283–299.

Cameron, Mary Owen
1964 *The Booster and the Snitch, Department Store Shoplifting.* New York: The Free Press of Glencoe, Macmillan Company.

Camus, Albert
1954 *The Stranger.* New York: Vintage Books/Random House.

Carmichael, Stokely, and Charles V. Hamilton
1967 *Black Power.* New York: Random House (Vintage).

Carrier, J. M.
1976 "Family Attitudes and Mexican Male Homosexuality." *Urban Life* 50 (October):359–375.

Catanzaro, Ronald J.
1967 "Psychiatric Aspects of Alcoholism." Pp. 31–45 in David J. Pittman, ed., *Alcoholism.* New York: Harper and Row.
1968 *Alcoholism, The Total Treatment Approach.* Springfield, Ill.: Charles C. Thomas, Publisher.

Caudill, W., et al.
1952 "Social Structure and Interaction Processes on a Psychiatric Ward." *American Journal of Orthopsychiatry* 22 (April):314–334.

Cavan, Ruth S.
1928 *Suicide.* Chicago: University of Chicago Press.
1969 *Juvenile Delinquency: Development, Treatment, and Control.* 2nd ed. Philadelphia: J. B. Lippincott Company.

Cavan, Sherri
1966 *Liquor License.* Chicago: Aldine Publishing Company.

Chambliss, William J.
1969 *Crime and the Legal Process.* New York: McGraw-Hill Book Company.
1971 "A Visit to San Miguel." *The Humanist* 31 (July/August):24–25.
1973 "The Saints and the Roughnecks." *Society* 11 (November/December):24–31.
1975 *Criminal Law in Action.* Santa Barbara, Calif.: Hamilton Publishing Company.

Chambliss, William, and Richard H. Nagasawa
1969 "On the Validity of Official Statistics: A Comparative Study of White, Black, and Japanese High-School Boys." *Journal of Research in Crime and Delinquency* 6 (January):71–77.

Chambliss, William J., and Robert B. Seidman
1971 *Law, Order, and Power.* Reading, Mass.: Addison-Wesley Publishing Company.

Christensen, Harold T.
1953 "Studies in Child Spacing: I—Premarital Pregnancy as Measured by the Spacing of the First Birth from Marriage." *American Sociological Review* 18 (February):53–59.

Clark, John P., and Eugene Wenninger
1962 "Socio-Economic Class and Area as Correlates of Illegal Behavior Among Juveniles." *American Sociological Review* 27 (December):826–834.

Clausen, John A.
1976 "Mental Disorders." Pp. 103–139 in Robert K. Merton and Robert Nisbet, eds., *Contemporary Social Problems*, 4th ed. New York: Harcourt Brace Jovanovich.

Clinard, Marshall B.
1964 *Anomie and Deviant Behavior, A Discussion and Critique.* New York: The Free Press.

Cloward, Richard A., and Lloyd E. Ohlin
1960 *Delinquency and Opportunity, A Theory of Delinquent Gangs.* Glencoe, Ill.: The Free Press.

Cohen, Albert K.
1955 *Delinquent Boys: The Culture of the Gang.* Glencoe, Ill.: The Free Press.
1966 *Deviance and Control.* Englewood Cliffs, N.J.: Prentice-Hall.
1970 "Multiple Factor Approaches." Pp. 123–126 in M. E. Wolfgang, L. Savitz, and N. Johnston, eds., *The Sociology of Crime and Delinquency.* 2nd ed. New York: John Wiley and Sons.

Cohen, Lillian
1954 *Statistical Methods for Social Scientists: An Introduction.* New York: Prentice-Hall.

Connell, Noreen, and Cassandra Wilson
1974 *Rape: The First Sourcebook for Women.* New York: New American Library

Conrad, Peter
1975 "The Discovery of Hyperkinesis: Notes on the Medicalization of Deviant Behavior." *Social Problems* 23 (October):12–21.

Cooley, Charles Horton
1902 *Human Nature and the Social Order.* New York: Charles Scribner's Sons.

Cory, Donald Webster
1951 *The Homosexual in America: A Subjective Approach* New York: Greenberg.

Coyote Howls
1978a "Letters to the Madam." n.d. Volume 5 (Ball Edition):4.
1978b "Hooker Convention Movie: 'Hardwork'—Wine, Women and Gospel." n.d. Volume 5 (Ball Edition):9.

Corzine, Jay, and Richard Kirby
1977   "Cruising the Truckers: Sexual Encounters in a Highway Rest Area." *Urban Life* 6 (July):171–192.

Dahrendorf, R.
1959   *Class and Class Conflict in Industrial Society.* Stanford, Calif.: Stanford University Press.

Davis, Fred
1961   "Deviance Disavowal: The Management of Strained Interaction by the Visibly Handicapped." *Social Problems* 9 (Fall):120–132.

Davis, Kingsley
1966   "Sexual Behavior." Pp. 322–372 in Robert K. Merton and Robert A. Nisbet, eds., *Contemporary Social Problems,* 2nd ed. New York: Harcourt, Brace and World.
1971   "Sexual Behavior." Pp. 313–360 in Robert K. Merton and Robert Nisbet, eds., *Contemporary Social Problems,* 3rd ed. New York: Harcourt Brace Jovanovich.

Davis, Nanette J.
1975   *Sociological Constructions of Deviance, Perspectives and Issues in the Field.* Dubuque, Iowa: W. C. Brown Company Publishers.

Davis, Richard L.
1973   The Labeling Perspective and Juvenile Delinquency. Unpublished Ph.D. dissertation, University of New Hampshire.

Dawley, David
1973   *A Nation of Lords.* New York: Doubleday.

Denes, Magda
1977   *In Necessity and Sorrow, Life and Death in an Abortion Hospital.* Baltimore: Penguin Books.

Dentler, Robert A., and Lawrence J. Monroe
1961   "Early Adolescent Theft." *American Sociological Review* 26 (October):733–743.

Dickson, Donald T.
1968   "Bureaucracy and Morality: An Organizational Perspective on a Moral Crusade." *Social Problems* 16 (Fall):143–156.

Dictionary of American Biography
1930   "Anthony Comstock." Volume IV. New York: Scribner's Sons.

Ditton, Jason
1977a   "Perks, Pilferage, and the Fiddle: The Historical Struggle of Invisible Wages." *Theory and Society* 4 (Spring):39–71.
1977b   *Part-Time Crime, An Ethnography of Fiddling and Pilferage.* London: The Macmillan Press.

Dohrenwend, Bruce P.
1975   "Sociocultural and Social-Psychological Factors in the Genesis of Mental Disorders." *Journal of Health and Social Behavior* 16 (December):365–392.

Douglas, Jack D.
1967   *The Social Meanings of Suicide*. Princeton, N.J.: Princeton University Press.
1970   *Deviance and Respectability*, editor. New York: Basic Books.
1971a   *American Social Order, Social Rules in a Pluralistic Society*. New York: Free Press-Macmillan.
1971b   "The Rhetoric of Science and the Origins of Statistical Social Thought: The Case of Durkheim's Suicide." Pp. 44–57 in Edward A. Tiryakian, ed., *The Phenomenon of Sociology*. New York: Appleton-Century-Crofts.

Douglas, Jack D., and Paul K. Rasmussen, with Carol Ann Flanagan
1977   *The Nude Beach*. Beverly Hills: Sage Publications.

Drake, St. Clair, and Horace R. Cayton
1962   *Black Metropolis, A Study of Negro Life in a Northern City*. New York: Harper and Row.

Dunford, Franklin W., and Philip R. Kunz
1973   "The Neutralization of Religious Dissonance." *Review of Religious Research 15* (Fall):2–9.

Durham v. United States, 214 F.2d 862, 874–75 (D.C. Cir.) 1954.

Durkheim, Emile
1951   *Suicide, A Study of Sociology*. (Translated by John A. Spaulding and George Simpson). New York: Free Press-Macmillan.

Elliott, Mabel A., and Francis E. Merrill
1961   *Social Disorganization*. 4th ed. New York: Harper and Row.

Emerson, Robert M.
1969   *Judging Delinquents, Context and Process in Juvenile Court*. Chicago: Aldine Publishing Company.

Encyclopaedia Britannica
1974   "John Brown." *Micropaedia*, Vol. II:308; "Carry Nation." *Micropaedia*, Vol. VII:207. Chicago: Helen Hemingway Benton.

Encyclopedia of Associations
1978   Invisible Empire Knights of the Ku Klux Klan." Volume 1, National Organizations of the U.S. Section 9, Public Affairs Organizations. Chicago: Gale Research Co.

Ennis, Philip H.
1967   *Criminal Victimization in the United States, A Report of a National Survey*. Washington, D.C.: U.S. Government Printing Office.

Epstein, Edward Jay
1977   "Peddling a Drug Scare." *Columbia Journalism Review* (November/December):51–56.

Erikson, Kai T.
1964   "Notes on the Sociology of Deviance." Pp. 9–21 in Howard S. Becker, ed., *The Other Side, Perspectives on Deviance*. New York: Free Press.

Etzioni, Amitai
1964   *Modern Organizations.* Englewood Cliffs, N.J.: Prentice-Hall.

Fairfield, L.
1959   "Notes on Prostitution." *British Journal of Delinquency* 9 (January):164–173.

Faris, R. E. L., and H. Warren Dunham
1939   *Mental Disorders in Urban Areas: An Ecological Study of Schizophrenia and Other Psychoses.* Chicago: University of Chicago Press.

Farrington, David P.
1977   "The Effects of Public Labeling." *British Journal of Criminology* 17 (April):112–125.

Federal Bureau of Investigation
1976   *Uniform Crime Reports.* Washington, D.C.: U.S. Government Printing Office.

Feldman, Saul D.
1975   "The Presentation of Shortness in Everyday Life—Height and Heightism in American Sociology: Toward a Sociology of Stature." Paper presented before The American Sociological Association, Denver, Colorado.

Fink, Arthur E.
1938   *Causes of Crime: Biological Theories in the United States, 1800–1915.* Philadelphia: University of Pennsylvania Press.

Fink, Stephen L., James K. Skipper, Jr., and Phyllis N. Hallenbeck
1968   "Physical Disability and Problems in Marriage." *Journal of Marriage and the Family* 30 (February):64–73.

Fontana, Vincent J.
1973   *Somewhere a Child Is Crying, Maltreatment—Causes and Prevention.* New York: New American Library, Mentor Books.

Fox, Richard G.
1971   "The XYY Offender: A Modern Myth?" *Journal of Criminal Law, Criminology and Police Science* 62 (March):59–73.

Franklin, John Hope
1956   *From Slavery to Freedom: A History of American Negroes,* 2nd rev. ed. New York: Alfred A. Knopf.

Frazier, Charles E.
1976   *Theoretical Approaches to Deviance: An Evaluation.* Columbus, Ohio: Charles E. Merrill Publishing Co.

Freeman, Howard E., and Ozzie G. Simmons
1961   "Feelings of Stigma Among Relatives of Former Mental Patients." *Social Problems* 8 (Spring):312–321.

Frutig, Judith
1975   "Griffen Seeks Probe on Hoffa Mystery." *The Christian Science Monitor,* December 4:50.

Furey, Thomas
1961   "Wave of Bums Sweeps Over Parks, Streets." *New York World Telegram.* November 1: 1 and 3, in Howard M. Bahr, *Skid Row, An Introduction to Disaffiliation.* New York: Oxford University Press.

Gable, Richard W.
1958   "Political Interest Groups as Policy Shapers." *Annals* 319 (September):84–93.

Gagnon, John H., and William Simon
1968   "Homosexuality: The Formulation of a Sociological Perspective." Pp. 349–361 in Mark Lefton, James K. Skipper, and Charles H. McCaghy, eds., *Approaches to Deviance: Theories, Concepts, and Research Findings.* New York: Appleton-Century-Crofts.

Galliher, John F., and Allyn Walker
1977   "The Puzzle of the Social Origins of the Marihuana Tax Act of 1937." *Social Problems* 24 (February):367–376.

Garfinkel, Harold
1956   "Conditions of Successful Degradation Ceremonies." *American Journal of Sociology* 61 (March): 420–424.

Garner, Brian, and Richard W. Smith
1976   "Are There Any Gay Male Athletes? An Empirical Survey." Unpublished paper presented before Society for the Scientific Study of Sex, San Diego, California.

Garrett, Henry E.
n.d.   *How Classroom Desegregation Will Work.* Richmond, Va.: Patrick Henry Press.

Geis, Gilbert
1972   *Not the Law's Business? An Examination of Homosexuality, Abortion, Prostitution, Narcotics and Gambling in the United States.* National Institute of Mental Health. Washington, D.C.: U.S. Government Printing Office.
1977   "The Heavy Electrical Equipment Antitrust Cases of 1961." Pp. 117–132 in Gilbert Geis and Robert F. Meier, eds., *White Collar Crime, Offenses in Business, Politics, and the Professions.* New York: The Free Press.

Geller, Allen, and Maxwell Boas
1969   *The Drug Beat.* New York: McGraw-Hill Book Company.

Gibbs, Jack P., and Walter T. Martin
1964   *Status Integration and Suicide.* Eugene, Ore.: University of Oregon Press.

Glaser, Daniel
1956   "Criminality Theories and Behavioral Images." *American Journal of Sociology* 61 (March):433–444.
1958   "The Sociological Approach to Crime and Correction." *Law and Contemporary Problems* 23 (Autumn):683–702.
1962   "The Differential Association Theory of Crime." Pp. 425–442 in Ar-

nold M. Rose, ed., *Human Behavior and Social Processes*. Boston:
Houghton Mifflin Co.
1971 *Social Deviance*. Chicago: Markham Publishing Company.
Goddard, H. H.
1912 *The Kallikak Family*. New York: Macmillan Company.
1922 *Human Efficiency and Levels of Intelligence*. Princeton: Princeton
University Press.
Goffman, Erving
1959 *The Presentation of Self in Everyday Life*. New York: Doubleday
Anchor Books.
1961 *Asylums, Essays on the Situation of Mental Patients and Other Inmates*. New York: Doubleday Anchor Books.
1963 *Stigma, Notes on the Management of Spoiled Identity*. Englewood
Cliffs, N.J.: Prentice-Hall.
1973 "The Moral Career of the Mental Patient." Pp. 95–105 in Earl
Rubington and Martin S. Weinberg, eds., *Deviance, The Interac-
tionist Perspective*. New York: The Macmillan Company.
Gold, Martin
1966 "Undetected Delinquent Behavior." *The Journal of Research in
Crime and Delinquency* 3 (January):27–46.
1970 *Delinquent Behavior in an American City*. Belmont, Calif.: Brooks,
Cole Publishing Co.
Gold, Martin, and Jay R. Williams
1969 "National Study of the Aftermath of Apprehension," *Prospectus, A
Journal of Law Reform* 3 (December):3–38.
Goode, Erich
1972 *Drugs in American Society*. New York: Alfred A. Knopf.
1975 "On Behalf of Labeling Theory." *Social Problems* 22 (June):
570–583.
Goode, William J., and Paul K. Hatt
1952 *Methods in Social Research*. New York: McGraw-Hill Book Com-
pany.
Gordon, C. Wayne, and Nicholas Babchuk
1959 "A Typology of Voluntary Associations." *American Sociological Review* 24 (February):22–29.
Gouldner, Alvin W.
1970 *The Coming Crisis of Western Sociology*. New York: Equinox, Avon
Books.
Gowman, Alan G.
1956 "Blindness and the Role of the Companion." *Social Problems* 4
(July):68–75.
Gray, Diana
1973 "Turning Out: A Study of Teenage Prostitution." *Urban Life and
Culture* 1 (January):401–425.

Greenwald, Harold
1958   *The Call Girl, A Social and Psychoanalytic Study.* New York: Ballantine Books.

Gregory-Lewis, Sasha
1978   "Politics, Californians Face Proposition 6 and Will It Be Written, Mene, Mene, Tekel Upharsin?" *The Advocate,* November 15:7ff.

Gusfield, Joseph R.
1955   "Social Structure and Moral Reform: A Study of the Women's Christian Temperance Union." *American Journal of Sociology* 61 (November):221–232.
1967   "Moral Passage: The Symbolic Process in Public Designations of Deviance." *Social Problems* 15 (Fall):175–188.

Hacker, David W.
1977   "She's Against Gay Rights." *National Observer,* March 12:1, 16.

Hadden, Stuart C.
1973   "Social Dimensions of Jury Decision Making." *International Journal of Criminology and Penology* 1 (August):269–277.

Hall, Jerome
1952   *Theft, Law, and Society.* 2nd ed. Indianapolis: Bobbs-Merrill.

Halverson, Guy
1975   "The Politics of the Gun Trade." *The Christian Science Monitor,* November 14:19.

Haney, C. Allen and Robert Michielutte
1968   "Selective Factors Operating in the Adjudication of Incompetency." *Journal of Health and Social Behavior* 9 (September):233–242.

Haney, Robert W.
1960   *Comstockery in America.* Boston: Beacon Press.

Hanson, Norwood Russell
1965   *Patterns of Discovery.* Cited in Richard Quinney, *The Social Reality of Crime.* Boston: Little, Brown and Company, 1970.

Hardert, Ronald A., et al.
1974   *Sociology and Social Issues.* San Francisco: Rinehart Press.
1977   *Sociology and Social Issues,* 2nd ed. Hinsdale, Ill.: The Dryden Press.

Harris, Richard N.
1973   *The Police Academy: An Inside View.* New York: John Wiley and Sons.

Hartung, Frank E.
1965   *Crime, Law, and Society.* Detroit: Wayne State University Press.

Haselden, Kyle
1968   *Morality and the Mass Media.* Nashville, Tenn.: Broadman Press.

Hazlett, Bill
1976   "30,000 Children Sexually Abused, LAPD Reports." *Los Angeles Times,* November 19:I, 3, 25.

Heckethorn, Charles William
1965   *The Secret Societies of All Ages and Countries.* New Hyde Park, N.Y.: University Books.

Henslin, James M.
1971   "Criminal Abortion: Making the Decision and Neutralizing the Act." Pp. 113–135 in James M. Henslin, ed., *Studies in the Sociology of Sex.* New York: Appleton-Century-Crofts, Meredith Corporation.

Hern, Warren M.
1972   "The Politics of Abortion." *The Progressive* 36 (November):26–29.

Hertz, Robert
1960   *Death and the Right Hand.* Glencoe, Ill.: Free Press.

Hessler, Richard M.
1974   "Junkies in White: Drug Addition Among Physicians." Pp. 146–153 in Clifton D. Bryant, ed., *Deviant Behavior, Occupational and Organizational Bases.* Chicago: Rand McNally Publishing Company.

Hills, Stuart L.
1971   *Crime, Power, and Morality: The Criminal-Law Process in the United States.* Scranton, Pa.: Chandler Publishing Company.

Hinkle, Roscoe C., Jr., and Gisela J. Hinkle
1954   *The Development of Modern Sociology, Its Nature and Growth in the United States.* New York: Doubleday and Company.

Hirschi, Travis, and Hanan C. Selvin
1967   *Delinquency Research, An Appraisal of Analytic Methods.* New York: Free Press.

Holzner, Burkart
1972   *Reality Construction in Society*, rev. ed. Cambridge, Mass.: Schenkman Publishing Company.

Hood, Roger, and Richard Sparks
1970   *Key Issues in Criminology.* New York: World University Library, McGraw-Hill Book Company.

Hooker, Evelyn
1958   "Male Homosexuality in the Rorschach." *Journal of Projective Techniques* 22 (March):33–55.

Hooton, E. A.
1939   *Crime and the Man.* Cambridge: Harvard University Press.

Horowitz, Irving Louis, and Martin Leibowitz
1968   "Social Deviance and Political Marginality: Toward a Redefinition of the Relation Between Sociology and Politics." *Social Problems* 15 (Winter):280–296.

Horton, Paul B., and Gerald R. Leslie
1965   *The Sociology of Social Problems*, 3rd ed. New York: Appleton-Century-Crofts.

Hough, Henry Beetle
1974   "Becoming an Alcoholic." Pp. 15–32 in Charles H. McCaghy, James K. Skipper, Jr., and Mark Lefton, eds., *In Their Own Behaif: Voices from the Margin*, 2nd ed. New York: Appleton-Century-Crofts.

Hoult, Thomas Ford
1969   *Dictionary of Modern Sociology*. Totowa, N.J.: Littlefield, Adams and Co.
1972   *March to the Right*. Cambridge, Mass.: Schenkman Publishing Co.
1974   *Sociology for a New Day*. New York: Random House.

Howard, Ted, and Jeremy Rifkin
1977   *Who Should Play God? The Artificial Creation of Life and What It Means for the Future of the Human Race*. New York: Dell Publishing Company.

Hughes, Everett Cherrington
1945   "Dilemmas and Contradictions of Status." *American Journal of Sociology* 50 (March):353–359.

Humphreys, Laud
1970   *Tearoom Trade, Impersonal Sex in Public Places*. Chicago: Aldine Publishing Company.
1972   *Out of the Closets, The Sociology of Homosexual Liberation*. Englewood Cliffs, N.J.: Prentice-Hall.

Jackson, Don
1973   "Dachau for Queers." Pp. 42–49 in Len Richmond and Gary Noguera, eds., *The Gay Liberation Book*. San Francisco: Ramparts Press.

Jellinek, E. M.
1960   *The Disease Concept of Alcoholism*. New Haven, Conn.: College and University Press.

Johnson, Michael P.
1973   "Commitment: A Conceptual Structure and Empirical Application." *The Sociological Quarterly* 14 (Summer):395–406.

Kando, Thomas
1973   *Sex Change, The Achievement of Gender Identity Among Feminized Transsexuals*. Springfield, Ill.: Charles C. Thomas, Publisher.

Kaplan, Abraham
1964   *The Conduct of Inquiry*. San Francisco: Chandler Publishing Co.

Katz, Jonathan
1976   *Gay American History, Lesbians and Gay Men in the U.S.A.* New York: Thomas Y. Crowell Company.

Kephart, William M.
1976   *Extraordinary Groups, The Sociology of Unconventional Life-Styles*. New York: St. Martin's Press.

Kesey, Ken
1962   *One Flew Over the Cuckoo's Nest*. New York: Signet, New American Library.

Kirkpatrick, Clifford
1955   *The Family, As Process and Institution.* New York: The Ronald Press.

Kitsuse, John I.
1962   "Societal Reaction to Deviant Behavior: Problems of Theory and Method." *Social Problems* 9 (Winter):247–256.

Kittrie, Nicholas N.
1971   *The Right to be Different, Deviance and Enforced Therapy.* Baltimore: The Johns Hopkins Press.

Klapp, Orrin E.
1962   *Heroes, Villains, and Fools: The Changing American Character.* Englewood Cliffs, N.J.: Prentice-Hall.

Klein, Malcolm W.
1974   "Labeling, Deterrence, and Recidivism: A Study of Police Dispositions of Juvenile Offenders." *Social Problems* 22 (December):292–303.

Klockars, Carl B.
1974   *The Professional Fence.* New York: The Free Press.

Kopay, David, and Perry Deane Young
1977   *The David Kopay Story, An Extraordinary Self-Revelation.* New York: Bantam Books.

Kotarba, Joseph A.
1975   "America Acupuncturists: The New Entrepreneurs of Hope." *Urban Life* 4 (July):149–177.

Kriegel, Leonard
1974   "On Being Crippled." Pp. 233–246 in Charles H. McCaghy, James K. Skipper, Jr., and Mark Lefton, eds., *In Their Own Behalf: Voices from the Margin,* 2nd ed. New York: Appleton-Century-Crofts.

Krisberg, Barry
1975   *Crime and Privilege, Toward a New Criminology.* Englewood Cliffs, N.J.: Prentice-Hall.

Kuhn, Thomas S.
1970   *The Structure of Scientific Revolutions,* 2nd ed. Chicago: University of Chicago Press.

Lader, Lawrence
1973   *Abortion II: Making the Revolution.* Boston: Beacon Press.

Lastrucci, Carlo L.
1967   *The Scientific Approach, Basic Principles of the Scientific Method.* Cambridge, Mass.: Schenkman Publishing Company.

Latham, Aaron
1976   "The Pike Papers: An Introduction." *The Village Voice* (supplement), February 16:70.

Lauritsen, John, and David Thorstad
1974   *The Early Homosexual Rights Movement (1864–1935).* New York: Times Change Press.

Law Enforcement Assistance Administration Newsletter
1977   "Mother of 10 Leads Fight Against Gang." December 6:3ff.

LeGrand, Camille E.
1973   "Rape and Rape Laws: Sexism in Society and Law." *California Law Review* 61 (May):919–941.

Lejins, Peter
1951   "Pragmatic Etiology of Delinquent Behavior." *Social Forces* 29 (March):317–321.

Lemert, Edwin M.
1951   *Social Pathology, A Systematic Approach to the Theory of Sociopathic Behavior.* New York: McGraw-Hill Book Company.
1962   "Paranoia and the Dynamics of Exclusion." Pp. 106–115 in Earl Rubington and Martin S. Weinberg, eds., *Deviance, The Interactionist Perspective*, 2nd ed. New York: The Macmillan Company.
1967a *Human Deviance, Social Problems, and Social Control.* Englewood Cliffs, N.J.: Prentice-Hall.
1967b "The Juvenile Court—Quest and Realities." Pp. 91–106 in *Task Force Report: Juvenile Delinquency and Youth Crime.* President's Commission on Law Enforcement and Administration of Justice. Washington, D.C.: U.S. Government Printing Office.

Lemkau, Paul V., and Guido M. Crocetti
1967   "Epidemiology." Pp. 225–232 in Alfred M. Freedman and Harold I. Kaplan, eds., *Comprehensive Textbook of Psychiatry.* Baltimore: The Williams and Wilkins Company.

Letkemann, Peter
1973   *Crime as Work.* Englewood Cliffs, N.J.: Prentice-Hall.

Levitin, Teresa E.
1975   "Deviants as Active Participants in the Labeling Process: The Visibly Handicapped." *Social Problems* 22 (April):548–557.

Levy, Howard S.
1966   *Chinese Footbinding, The History of a Curious Erotic Custom.* New York: Walton Rawls, Publisher.

Lewis, Oscar
1961   *Children of Sanchez.* New York: Random House.

Lincoln, C. Eric
1961   *The Black Muslims in America.* Boston: Beacon Press.

Lindesmith, Alfred
1940   " 'Dope Fiend' Mythology." *Journal of Criminal Law and Criminology* 31 (May/June):199–208.

Lisansky, Edith S.
1968   "Drinking and Alcoholism: Psychological Aspects." Pp. 264–268, Vol. 4, *International Encyclopedia of the Social Sciences.* New York: The Macmillan Company.

Lofland, John
1969   *Deviance and Identity.* Englewood Cliffs, N.J.: Prentice-Hall.

Loman, L. Anthony and William E. Larkin
1976   "Rejection of the Mentally Ill: An Experiment in Labeling." *The Sociological Quarterly* 17 (Autumn):555–560.

Los Angeles Herald-Examiner
1978   "Legalization of 'Pot' Predicted by State Attorney General." September 13.

Lorber, Judith
1967   "Deviance as Performance: The Case of Illness." *Social Problems* 14 (Winter):302–310.

Lowrey, Lawson G.
1944   "Delinquent and Criminal Personalities." Pp. 794–821 in J. McV. Hunt, ed., *Personality and Behavioral Disorders.* Vol. II. New York: Ronald Press.

Lowry, Ritchie P., and Robert P. Rankin
1969   *Sociology, The Science of Society.* New York: Charles Scribner's Sons.

Luckenbill, David F.
1977   "Criminal Homicide as a Situated Transaction." *Social Problems* 25 (December):176–186.

Lyman, Stanford M.
1970   *The Asian in the West.* Reno/Las Vegas, Nev.: Western Studies Center, Desert Research Institute.
1974   *Chinese Americans.* New York: Random House.

Lyman, Stanford M., and Marvin B. Scott
1967   "Territoriality; A Neglected Sociological Dimension." *Social Problems* 15 (Fall):236–249.
1970   *A Sociology of the Absurd.* New York: Appleton-Century-Crofts, Meredith Corporation.

Macgregor, Frances Cooke, et al.
1953   *Facial Deformities and Plastic Surgery, A Psychosocial Study.* Springfield, Ill.: Charles C. Thomas, Publisher.

MacKenzie, Norman
1967   *Secret Societies.* New York: Holt, Rinehart and Winston.

Manis, Jerome C., and Bernard N. Meltzer, eds.
1967   *Symbolic Interaction, A Reader in Social Psychology.* Boston: Allyn and Bacon.

Mankoff, Milton
1971   "Societal Reaction and Career Deviance: A Critical Analysis." *The Sociological Quarterly* 12 (Spring):204–218.

Manning, Peter K.
1971a   "Fixing What You Feared: Notes on the Campus Abortion Search." Pp. 137–166 in James H. Henslin, ed., *Studies in the Sociology of Sex.* New York: Appleton-Century-Crofts, Meredith Corporation.

1971b   "The Police: Mandate, Strategies, and Appearance." Pp. 149–193
    in Jack D. Douglas, ed., *Crime and Justice in American Society*. In-
    dianapolis: Bobbs-Merrill Company.
1975   "Deviance and Dogma." *The British Journal of Criminology* 15
    (January):1–20.
Marine, Gene
1969   *The Black Panthers*. New York: Signet/New American Library.
Maris, Ronald W.
1969   *Social Forces in Urban Suicide*. Homewood, Ill.: Dorsey Press.
Marx, Paul
1978   "Legislation Corner." *Mainstream, Magazine of the Able-disabled* 3
    (September):18.
Matza, David
1964   *Delinquncy and Drift*. New York: John Wiley and Sons.
1969   *Becoming Deviant*. Englewood Cliffs, N.J.: Prentice-Hall.
Mauss, Armand L., and Associates
1975   *Social Problems as Social Movements*. Philadelphia: J. B. Lippin-
    cott Company.
Maxwell, Milton A.
1967   "Alcoholics Anonymous: An Interpretation." Pp. 211–222 in David
    A. Pittman, ed., *Alcoholism*. New York: Harper and Row.
Mayerson, Robert
1978   "Saving the Queen City's Honor." *Seattle Sun*, November 15:1ff.
McCaghy, Charles H.
1968   "Drinking and Deviance Disavowal: The Case of Child Molesters."
    Social Problems 16 (Summer):43–49.
1976   *Deviant Behavior: Crime, Conflict and Interests Groups*. New York:
    The Macmillan Company.
McCaghy, Charles H., and James K. Skipper, Jr.
1969   "Lesbian Behavior as an Adaptation to the Occupation of Strip-
    ping." *Social Problems* 17 (Fall):262–270.
Meade, Anthony C.
1974   "The Labeling Approach to Delinquency: State of the Theory as a
    Function of Method." *Social Forces* 53 (September):83–91.
Merton, Robert K.
1957   *Social Theory and Social Structure*, rev. ed. Glencoe, Ill.: Free
    Press.
Merton, Robert K., and Robert Nisbet
1971   *Contemporary Social Problems*, 3rd ed. New York: Harcourt Brace
    Jovanovich.
Michael, Jerome, and Mortimer J. Adler
1933   *Crime, Law and Social Science*. New York: Harcourt Brace and
    Company.
Miller, Dorothy, and Michael Schwartz
1966   "County Lunacy Commission Hearings: Some Observations of
    Commitments to a State Mental Hospital." *Social Problems* 14
    (Summer):26–35.

Miller, Merle
1971   "What It Means to be a Homosexual." *New York Times Magazine*, January 17, 1971:9ff; October 10, 1971:67ff.

Miller, Walter B.
1958   "Lower Class Culture as a Generating Milieu of Gang Delinquency." *Journal of Social Issues* 14 (No. 3):5–19.

Mills, C. Wright
1943   "The Professional Ideology of Social Pathologists." *American Journal of Sociology* 49 (September):165–180.
1959   *The Sociological Imagination*. New York: Oxford University Press.

Milner, Christina and Richard
1972   *Black Players, The Secret World of Black Pimps*. Boston: Little, Brown and Company.

Missoulian
1973   "Hookers' Guild Formed in 'Frisco." June 26:12.

Molotch, Harvey, and Marilyn Lester
1974   "News as Purposive Behavior: On the Strategic Use of Routine Events." *American Sociological Review* 39 (February):101–112.

Montagu, Ashley
1968   "Chromosomes and Crime." *Psychology Today* 2 (October):43–49.

Moritz, Frederic A.
1976   "Hearst: What Evidence to Bar?" *The Christian Science Monitor*, February 6:3.

Movahedi, Siamak
1975   "Loading the Dice in Favor of Madness." *Journal of Health and Social Behavior* 16 (June):192–197.

Murphy, Fred F., Mary M. Shirley, and Helen L. Witmer
1946   "The Incidence of Hidden Delinquency." *American Journal of Orthopsychiatry* 16 (October):686–696.

National Commission on Marihuana and Drug Abuse
1972   *Marihuana: A Signal of Misunderstanding*. Washington, D.C.: U.S. Government Printing Office.

National Commission on the Causes and Prevention of Violence
1970   *Law and Order Reconsidered*. New York: Bantam Books.

National Observer
1977   "Views from Readers: On Anita Bryant and 'Gays.'" April 16:12.

National Organization for the Reform of Marijuana Laws
n.d.   *Statement in Support of the Need to Reform Marijuana Laws*. Washington, D.C.

Nettler, Gwynn
1974   *Explaining Crime*. New York: McGraw-Hill Book Company.

Newcomb, Theodore M.
1950   *Social Psychology*. New York: The Dryden Press.

Newman, Donald J.
1966   *Conviction: The Determination of Guilt or Innocence Without Trial*. Boston: Little, Brown and Company.

Newman, Graeme R.
1975   "A Theory of Deviance Removal." *British Journal of Sociology* 26 (June):203–217.

Newsweek
1973   "This is Your Veep." October 22:25–36.
1975   "The Story of Patty." September 29:20–40.
1977   "The Silent One." November 7:89–90.

New Times Weekly
1977   "From Drive-in Banking to Call-in Robbery." October 26–November 11:4.

New York Times
1970   June 5; 1:4; 38:2.
1973   *New York Times Index, A Book of Record.* Vol. I. New York: New York Times Company.

Norton, Nancy Lee, and Geoffrey Stokes
1977   "Right-to-Life: Documents Reveal Improper Financing." *Village Voice,* November 28:12.

Notes and Comment
1971   "Corporate Crime." *Yale Law Journal* 71 (December):280–306.

Nunnally, Jum C.
1961   *Popular Conceptions of Mental Health; Their Development and Change.* New York: Holt, Rinehart and Winston.

Nye, F. Ivan
1958   *Family Relationships and Delinquent Behavior.* New York: John Wiley and Sons.

Odgers, Sue
1978   "Sex on Wheels." *Paraplegia News* 31 (April):38–39.

Packer, Herbert L.
1968   *The Limits of the Criminal Sanction.* Stanford: Stanford University Press.

Papachristou, Judith
1976   *Women Together.* New York: Alfred A. Knopf.

Paraplegia News
1977a   "Trolleys to be Partly Accessible." January:28.
1977b   "Barrier Busters Get Tax Break." January:35.
1978   "Crystal the Terrible Tumbleweed." April:24–25.

Partridge, Eric
1970   *A Dictionary of Slang and Unconventional English,* 7th ed. New York: The Macmillan Company.

Payne, William D.
1973   "Negative Labels: Passageways and Prisons." *Crime and Delinquency* 19 (January):33–40.

Perry, Joseph B., Jr., and Erdwin H. Pfuhl, Jr.
1963   "Adjustment of Children in 'Solo' and 'Remarriage' Homes." *Marriage and Family Living* 25 (May):221–223.

Pfohl, Stephen J.
1977   "The 'Discovery' of Child Abuse." *Social Problems* 24 (February): 310–323.

Pfuhl, Erdwin H., Jr.
1978   "The Unwed Father: A 'Non-Deviant' Rule Breaker." *The Sociological Quarterly* 19 (Winter):113–128.

Phillips, David P.
1974   "The Influence of Suggestion on Suicide: Substantive and Theoretical Implications of the Werther Effect." *American Sociological Review* 39 (June):340–354.
1977   "Motor Vehicle Fatalities Increase Just After Publicized Suicide Stories." *Science* 196 (June):1464–1465.

Phillips, Derek
1963   "Rejection: A Possible Consequence of Seeking Help for Mental Disorders." *American Sociological Review* 28 (December):963–973.

Piliavin, Irving, and Scott Briar
1964   "Police Encounters with Juveniles." *American Journal of Sociology* 70 (September):206–214.

Pittman, David J., and Duff Gillespie
1967   "Social Policy as Deviancy Reinforcement: The Case of the Public Intoxication Offender." Pp. 106–124 in David J. Pittman, ed., *Alcoholism*. New York: Harper and Row.

Platt, Anthony
1969   *The Child Savers, The Invention of Delinquency*. Chicago: University of Chicago Press.

Playboy
1976   "Playboy Interview: Jimmy Carter." November: 63–86.
1978   "Playboy Interview: Anita Bryant." May: 73ff.

Polsky, Ned
1967   *Hustlers, Beats, and Others*. Chicago: Aldine Publishing Company.

Ponse, Barbara
1976   "Secrecy in the Lesbian World." *Urban Life* 5 (October):313–338.

Powell, Elwin H.
1958   "Occupation, Status, and Suicide: Toward a Redefinition of Anomie." *American Sociological Review* 23 (April):131–139.

Powell, Lyman P.
1940   *Mary Baker Eddy, A Life Size Portrait*. New York: L. P. Powell.

President's Commission on Law Enforcement and Administration of Justice
1967   *The Challenge of Crime in a Free Society*. Washington, D.C.: U.S. Government Printing Office.

Quinney, Richard
1965   "A Conception of Man and Society for Criminology." *The Sociological Quarterly* 6 (Spring): 119–127.
1969   *Crime and Justice in Society*, editor. Boston: Little, Brown and Company.

1970   *The Social Reality of Crime.* Boston: Little, Brown and Company.
1973   "There's a Lot of Folks Grateful to the Lone Ranger: With Some Notes on the Rise and Fall of American Criminology." *The Insurgent Sociologist* 4 (Fall):56–64.
1975   *Criminology, Analysis and Critique of Crime in America.* Boston: Little, Brown and Company. ·

Radzinowicz, Leon
1966   *Ideology and Crime.* New York: Columbia University Press.

Reasons, Charles E.
1970   "A Developmental Model for the Analysis of Social Problems: Prostitution and Moral Reform in Twentieth Century America." Pacific Sociological Association, Anaheim, Calif., April, 1970.
1974   "The 'Dope' on the Bureau of Narcotics in Maintaining the Criminal Approach to the Drug Problem." Pp. 144–155 in Charles E. Reasons, ed., *The Criminologist: Crime and the Criminal.* Pacific Palisades, Calif.: Goodyear Publishing Company.

Reckless, Walter C.
1950   *The Crime Problem.* New York: Appleton-Century-Crofts.

Reid, Sue Titus
1976   *Crime and Criminology.* Hinsdale, Ill.: The Dryden Press.

Reiss, Albert J., Jr.
1961   "The Social Integration of Queers and Peers." *Social Problems* 9 (Fall):102–120.

Reiss, Albert J., Jr., and David J. Bordua
1967   "Environment and Organization: A Perspective on the Police." Pp. 25–55 in David J. Bordua, ed., *The Police: Six Sociological Essays.* New York: John Wiley and Sons.

Reitman, Ben L.
1937   *Sister of the Road, The Autobiography of Box-Car Bertha.* New York: Harper and Row.

Ritzer, George
1975   *Sociology, A Multiple Paradigm Science.* Boston: Allyn and Bacon.

Robin, Gerald D.
1969   "Employees as Offenders." *Journal of Research in Crime and Delinquency* 6 (January):17–33.
1970   "The Corporate and Judicial Disposition of Employee Thieves." Pp. 119–142 in Erwin O. Smigel and H. Laurence Ross, ed., *Crimes Against Bureaucracy.* New York: Van Nostrand Reinhold Co.

Rodriquez, Octavio
1974   "Getting Straight: Reflections of a Former Addict." Pp. 83–89 in Jerry Jacobs, ed., *Deviance: Field Studies and Self-Disclosures.* Palo Alto, Calif.: National Press Books.

Rose, Arnold M.
1965   *Sociology, The Study of Human Relations,* 2nd ed. New York: Alfred A. Knopf.

1968   "Law and the Causation of Social Problems." *Social Problems* 16 (Summer): 18–40.

Rosett, Arthur, and Donald R. Cressey
1976   *Justice by Consent: Plea Bargains in the American Courthouse.* Philadelphia: J. B. Lippincott Company

Ross, Robert, and Graham L. Staines
1972   "The Politics of Analyzing Social Problems." *Social Problems* 20 (Summer):18–40.

Rossman, Parker
1973   "The Pederasts." *Society* 10 (March/April):29–35.
1976   *Sexual Experience Between Men and Boys: Exploring the Pederast Underground.* New York: Association Press.

Rotenberg, Mordechai
1974   "Self-Labeling: A Missing Link in the 'Societal Reaction' Theory of Deviance." *The Sociological Review* 22 (August):335–354.

Rubington, Earl
1975   "Top and Bottom: How Police Administrators and Public Inebriates View Decriminalization." *Journal of Drug Issues* 5 (Fall):412–425.

Rubington, Earl, and Martin S. Weinberg
1973   *Deviance, The Interactionist Perspective,* 2nd ed. New York: The Macmillan Company.
1977   *The Study of Social Problems,* 2nd ed. New York: Oxford University Press.
1978   *Deviance, The Interactionist Perspective,* 3rd ed. New York: The Macmillan Company.

Safilios-Rothschild, Constantina
1970   *The Sociology and Social Psychology of Disability and Rehabilitation.* New York: Random House.

Sagarin, Edward
1969   *Odd Man In, Societies of Deviants in America.* Chicago: Quadrangle Books.
1975   *Deviants and Deviance, An Introduction to the Study of Disvalued People and Behavior.* New York: Praeger Publishers.

Sataloff, Joseph
1966   *Hearing Loss.* Philadelphia: J. B. Lippincott Company.

Scheff, Thomas J.
1964   "The Societal Reaction to Deviance: Ascriptive Elements in the Psychiatric Screening of Mental Patients in a Midwestern State." *Social Problems* 11 (Spring):401–413.
1966   *Being Mentally Ill: A Sociological Theory.* Chicago: Aldine Publishing Company.
1968   "Negotiating Reality: Notes on Power in the Assessment of Responsibility." *Social Problems* 16 (Summer):3–17.

Schmid, Calvin F.
1928   *Suicides in Seattle, 1914 to 1925.* Seattle: University of Washington Publications in the Social Sciences.

Schonell, F. J., and B. H. Watts
1956   "A First Survey of the Effects of a Subnormal Child on the Family Unit." *American Journal of Mental Deficiency* 61 (July):210–219.

Schrag, Peter
1970   "America's Other Radicals." *Harper's Magazine,* August:35–46.

Schuessler, Karl F., and Donald R. Cressey
1950   "Personality Characteristics of Criminals." *American Journal of Sociology* 55 (March):476–484.

Schur, Edwin M.
1965   *Crimes Without Victims, Deviant Behavior and Public Policy.* Englewood Cliffs, N.J.: Prentice-Hall.
1971   *Labeling Deviant Behavior, Its Sociological Implications.* New York: Harper and Row.
1973   *Radical Nonintervention, Rethinking the Delinquency Problem.* Englewood Cliffs, N.J.: Prentice-Hall.

Schwab, John J., and Ruby B. Schwab
1973   "The Epidemiology of Mental Illness." Pp. 58–83 in Gene Usdin, ed., *Psychiatry: Education and Image.* New York: Bruner/Mazel Publishers.

Schwartz, Charlotte Green
1956   "The Stigma of Mental Illness." *Journal of Rehabilitation* 22 (July/August):7–29.

Schwartz, John L.
1976   "Officer Calls on Legislators to Examine Smut for a Day." *Phoenix* (Arizona) *Republic,* April 26:A-1, 12.

Schwartz, Richard D., and Jerome H. Skolnick
1964   "Two Studies of Legal Stigma." Pp. 103–117 in Howard Becker, ed., *The Other Side, Perspectives on Deviance.* New York: The Free Press of Glencoe.

Scott, Marvin B., and Stanford M. Lyman
1968   "Accounts." *American Sociological Review* 33 (February):46–62.

Scott, Robert A.
1965   "Comments About Interpersonal Processes of Rehabilitation." Pp. 132–138 in Marvin B. Sussman, ed., *Sociology and Rehabilitation.* Washington, D.C.: American Sociological Association.
1969   *The Making of Blind Men.* New York: Russell Sage Foundation.
1970   "The Construction of Conceptions of Stigma by Professional Experts." Pp. 255–290 in Jack D. Douglas, ed., *Deviance and Respectability, The Social Construction of Moral Meanings.* New York: Basic Books.
1972   "A Proposed Framework for Analyzing Deviance as a Property of Social Order." Pp. 9–35 in Robert A. Scott and Jack D. Douglas, eds., *Theoretical Perspectives on Deviance.* New York: Basic Books.

Secord, Paul F., and Carl W. Backman
1964   *Social Psychology.* New York: McGraw-Hill Book Company.

Shaskolsky, Leon
1973   "The Legal Institution: The Legitimizing Appendage." Pp. 294–337 in Larry T. Reynolds and James M. Henslin, eds., *American Society, A Critical Analysis.* New York: David McKay Company.

Shaw, Clifford R., and Henry D. McKay
1942   *Juvenile Delinquency and Urban Areas.* Chicago: University of Chicago Press.

Shaw, Colin
1969   "Television and Popular Morality: The Predicament of the Broadcasters." Pp. 117–127 in Paul Halmos, ed., *The Sociology of Mass Media Communicators.* Sociology Review Monograph No. 13. University of Keele.

Sheldon, William H.
1949   *Varieties of Delinquent Youth, An Introduction to Constitutional Psychology.* New York: Harper and Brothers.

Sherif, Muzafer
1961   "Conformity-Deviation, Norms, and Group Relations." Pp. 159–198 in Irwin A. Berg and Bernard M. Mass, eds., *Conformity and Deviation.* New York: Harper and Brothers.

Short, James F., Jr.
1958   "Differential Association with Delinquent Friends and Delinquent Behavior." *Pacific Sociological Review* 1 (Spring):20–25.
1960   "Differential Association as a Hypothesis: Problems of Empirical Testing." *Social Problems* 8 (Summer):14–25.

Short, James F., Jr., and F. Ivan Nye
1958   "Extent of Unrecorded Juvenile Delinquency, Tentative Conclusions." *Journal of Criminal Law, Criminology, and Police Science* 49 (November/December):296–302.

Shuey, Chris
1978   "The Nuke Fight Escalates." *New Times Weekly* 10 (December 6–13):3, 25.

Siegel, Harvey H.
1973   *Alcohol Detoxification Programs: Treatment Instead of Jail.* Springfield, Ill.: Charles C. Thomas, Publisher.

Simmel, Georg
1950   *The Sociology of Georg Simmel.* Kurt H. Wolff, editor and translator. New York: The Free Press.

Simmons, J. L.
1969   *Deviants.* Berkeley, Calif.: Glendessary Press.

Simpson, Ruth
1977.   *From the Closet to the Courts, The Lesbian Transition.* New York: Penguin Books.

Sirjamaki, John
1953   *The American Family in the Twentieth Century*. Cambridge: Harvard University Press.

Skolnick, Jerome H.
1966   *Justice Without Trial: Law Enforcement in a Democratic Society*. New York: John Wiley and Sons.

Skolnick, Jerome H., and Richard Woodworth
1967   "Bureaucracy, Information, and Social Control: A Study of a Morals Detail." Pp. 99–136 in David J. Bordua, ed., *The Police: Six Sociological Essays*. New York: John Wiley and Sons.

Smith, Philip M.
1955   "Broken Homes and Juvenile Delinquency." *Sociology and Social Research 39* (May/June):307–311.

Smith, Richard Austin
1970   "The Incredible Electrical Conspiracy." Pp. 529–548 in Marvin E. Wolfgang, Leonard Savitz, and Norman Johnston, eds., *The Sociology of Crime and Delinquency*, 2nd ed. New York: John Wiley and Sons.

Spradley, James P.
1970   *You Owe Yourself a Drunk*. Boston: Little, Brown and Company.

Sprout, Harold and Margaret
1965   *The Ecological Perspective on Human Affairs; with Special Reference to International Politics*. Princeton, N.J.: Princeton University Press.

Steinhoff, Patricia G., Roy G. Smith, and Milton Diamond
1971   The Characteristics and Motivations of Women Receiving Abortions. Unpublished.

Storr, Anthony
1964   *Sexual Deviation*. Baltimore: Penguin Books.

Sudnow, David
1965   "Normal Crimes." Pp. 174–185 in Earl Rubington and Martin S. Weinberg, eds., *Deviance, The Interactionist Perspective*, 2nd ed. New York: The Macmillan Company.

Sutherland, Edwin H.
1937   *The Professional Thief, By a Professional Thief*. Chicago: University of Chicago Press.
1947   *Principles of Criminology*. 4th ed. Philadelphia: J. B. Lippincott Company.
1950a "The Diffusion of Sexual Psychopath Laws." *American Journal of Sociology* 56 (September): 142–148.
1950b "The Sexual Psychopath Laws." *Journal of Criminal Law and Criminology* 40 (January/February):543–554.
1956a "Crime of Corporations." Pp. 78–96 in Albert Cohen, Alfred Lindesmith, and Karl Schuessler, eds., *The Sutherland Papers*. Bloomington: Indiana University Press.

1956b "Critique of the Theory." Pp. 30–41 in Albert Cohen, Alfred Lindesmith, and Karl Schuessler, eds., *The Sutherland Papers*. Bloomington: Indiana University Press.
1956c "Is 'White Collar Crime' Crime?" Pp. 62–77 in Albert Cohen, Alfred Lindesmith, and Karl Schuessler, eds., *The Sutherland Papers*. Bloomington: Indiana University Press.

Sutherland, Edwin, and Donald R. Cressey
1974 *Criminology*, 9th ed. Philadelphia: J. B. Lippincott Company.

Sykes, Gresham M.
1958 The Society of Captives, A Study of a Maximum Security Prison. Princeton: Princeton University Press.
1972 "The Future of Criminality." *American Behavioral Scientist* 15(3):403–419.

Sykes, Gresham M., and David Matza
1957 "Techniques of Neutralization: A Theory of Delinquency." *American Sociological Review* 22 (December):664–670.

Szasz, Thomas S.
1966 *The Myth of Mental Illness*. New York: Dell Publishing Company.
1976a "Some Call It Brainwashing." *The New Republic* 174 (March 6):10–12.
1976b "Mercenary Psychiatry." *The New Republic* 174 (March 13):10–12.

Taber, Merlin, Herbert C. Quay, Harold Mark, and Vicki Nealey
1969 "Disease Ideology and Mental Health Research." *Social Problems* 16 (Winter):349–357.

Tannenbaum, Frank
1938 *Crime and the Community*. Boston: Ginn and Company.

Taylor, Ian, Paul Walton, and Jock Young
1973 *The New Criminology, For a Social Theory of Deviance*. New York: Harper Torchbooks.

Taylor, Robert Lewis
1966 *Vessel of Wrath, The Life and Times of Carry Nation*. New York: New American Library.

Terry, W. Clinton, III, and David F. Luckenbill
1976 "Investigating Criminal Homicides: Police Work in Reporting and Solving Murders." Pp. 79–95 in William B. Sanders and Howard C. Daudistel, eds., *The Criminal Justice Process, A Reader*. New York: Praeger Publishers.

Thomlinson, Ralph
1965 *Sociological Concepts and Research, Acquisition, Analysis, and Interpretation of Social Information*. New York: Random House.

Thorsell, Bernard A., and Lloyd W. Klemke
1972 "The Labeling Process: Reinforcement and Deterrent." *Law and Society Review* 6 (February):393–403.

Thrasher, Frederic M.
1927 *The Gang*. Chicago: University of Chicago Press.
1963 *The Gang*. abridged ed. Chicago: University of Chicago Press.

Time
1975a "Armed Forces: Homosexual Sergeant." June 9:18–19.
1975b "Male and Female." June 16:73.
1976 "What Price Honor?" June 7:18–29.
1977 "Let's Hear It for Stutterers' Lib!" October 31:98–101.
1978 "Nightmare in Jonestown." December 4:16–30.
1979a "Rape? No." January 8:61.
1979b "The Paladin of Paramours." January 15:46–47.

Toby, Jackson
1957 "The Differential Impact of Family Disorganization." *American Sociological Review* 22 (October):505–512.

Toch, Hans
1965 *The Social Psychology of Social Movements*. Indianapolis: The Bobbs-Merrill Company.

Toffler, Alvin
1970 *Future Shock*. New York: Bantam Books.

Turk, Austin T.
1976 "Law as a Weapon in Social Conflict." *Social Problems* 23 (February):276–291.

Turner, Henry A.
1958 "How Pressure Groups Operate." *Annals* 319 (September):63–72.

Turner, Ralph H.
1972 "Deviance Avowal as Neutralization of Commitment." *Social Problems* 19 (Winter):308–321.

U.S. Bureau of the Census
1972 *Census of Housing: 1970*, Hc(1)-B1. Washington, D.C.: U.S. Government Printing Office.

U.S. Department of Health, Education, and Welfare
1970 *Report of the XYY Chromosomal Abormality*. National Institute of Mental Health, Public Health Service Publication No. 2103. Washington, D.C.: U.S. Government Printing Office.

U.S. Department of Justice (Law Enforcement Assistance Administration)
1975 *Criminal Victimization Surveys in 13 American Cities*. Washington, D.C.: U.S. Government Printing Office.

Unitarian Universalist World
1976 "Coalition Opposes Anti-Abortion Plan." February 15:1–2.

Vander Zanden, James W.
1966 *American Minority Relations, The Sociology of Race and Ethnic Groups*, 2nd ed. New York: Ronald Press.

Varni, Charles A.
1972 "An Exploratory Study of Spouse-Swapping." *Pacific Sociological Review* 15 (October):507–522.

Vold, George B.
1958 *Theoretical Criminology*. New York: Oxford University Press.

Vose, Clement E.
1958   "Litigation as a Form of Pressure Group Activity." *Annals* 319 (September):20–31.

Waldo, Gordon P., and Simon Dinitz
1967   "Personality Attributes of the Criminal: An Analysis of Research Studies, 1950–65." *Journal of Research in Crime and Delinquency* 4 (July):185–201.

Walker, Nigel, and M. Argyle
1964   "Does the Law Affect Moral Judgments." *British Journal of Criminology* 4 (October):570–581.

Wallace, Samuel E.
1965   *Skid Row as a Way of Life.* Totowa, N.J.: Bedminster Press.

Wallerstein, James S., and Clement J. Wyle
1947   "Our Law-Abiding Law-Breakers." *Probation* 25 (March/April):107–112.

Warren, Carol A. B.
1974a   *Identity and Community in the Gay World.* New York: John Wiley and Sons.
1974b   "The Use of Stigmatizing Social Labels in Conventionalizing Deviant Behavior." *Sociology and Social Research* 58 (April):303–311.

Warren, Carol A. B., and John M. Johnson
1972   "A Critique of Labeling Theory from the Phenomenological Perspective." Pp. 69–92 in Robert A. Scott and Jack D. Douglas, eds., *Theoretical Perspectives on Deviance.* New York: Basic Books.

Watson, Lyndon
1978   "Awakening of the New Minority." *Paraplegia News* 31 (May):20.

Weber, Max
1946   "Science as a Vocation." Pp. 129–156 in Hans H. Gerth and C. Wright Mills, eds., *From Max Weber: Essays in Sociology.* New York: Oxford University Press.
1962   *Basic Concepts in Sociology.* New York: Philosophical Library.

Wegner, Dennis L., and C. Richard Fletcher
1969   "The Effect of Legal Counsel on Admissions to a State Mental Hospital: A Confrontation of Professions." *Journal of Health and Social Behavior* 10 (March):66–72.

Weinberg, Martin
1957   "Sexual Modesty, Social Meanings, and the Nudist Camp." *Social Problems* 11 (Winter):311–318.
1968   "The Problems of Midgets and Dwarfs and Organizational Remedies: A Study of the Little People of America." *Journal of Health and Social Behavior* 9 (March):65–71.
1973   "Becoming a Nudist." Pp. 277–290 in Earl Rubington and Martin S. Weinberg, eds., *Deviance, The Interactionist Perspective,* 2nd ed. New York: The Macmillan Company.

Weis, Kurt, and Michael E. Milakovich
1974   "Political Misuses of Crime Rates." *Society* 11 (July/August):27–33.

West, D. J.
1967   *Homosexuality.* Chicago: Aldine Publishing Company.

Westley, William A.
1970   *Violence and the Police: A Sociological Study of Law, Custom, and Morality.* Cambridge, Mass.: The MIT Press.

Whitam, Frederick L.
1975   "Homosexuality as Emergent Behavior." Paper presented at the 46th annual meeting of the Pacific Sociological Association, Victoria, British Columbia, April 17–19.
1977a   "The Homosexual Role: A Reconsideration." *The Journal of Sex Research* 13 (February):1–11.
1977b   "Childhood Indicators of Male Homosexuality." *Archives of Sexual Behavior* 6 (No. 2):89–96.

White, Ralph K., Beatrice A. Wright, and Tamara Dembo
1948   "Studies in Adjustment to Visible Injuries: Evaluation of Curiosity by the Injured." *Journal of Abnormal and Social Psychology* 43 (January):13–28.

Wicker, Tom
1971   "The Harrisburg Story." *New York Times,* August 8. Cited in Robert Ross and Graham L. Staines, "The Politics of Analyzing Social Problems." *Social Problems* 20 (Summer 1972):24.

Wilde, William A.
1969   Official News: Decision Making in a Metropolitan Newspaper. Unpublished Ph.D dissertation, Northwestern University.

Wilkins, Leslie T.
1965   *Social Deviance: Social Policy, Action, and Research.* Englewood Cliffs, N.J.: Prentice-Hall.

Wilkinson, Karen
1974   "The Broken Family and Juvenile Delinquency." *Social Problems* 21 (June):726–739.

Williams, Colin J., and Martin S. Weinberg
1970   "Being Discovered: A Study of Homosexuals in the Military." *Social Problems* 18 (Fall):217–227.

Williams, Jay R., and Martin Gold
1972   "From Delinquent Behavior to Official Delinquency." *Social Problems* 20 (Fall):209–229.

Williams, Nancy
1974   *"Sex for Money."* Tempe, Arizona: The State Press (November 14).

Williams, Robin
1960   *American Society, A Sociological Interpretation,* 2nd ed. rev. New York: Alfred A. Knopf.

Winick, Charles
1964   "Physician Narcotic Addicts." Pp. 261–279 in Howard S. Becker, ed., *The Other Side, Perspectives on Deviance.* New York: The Free Press.

Winslow, Robert W.
1973   *Crime in a Free Society,* 2nd ed. Belmont, Calif.: Dickenson Publishing Company.

Wiseman, Jacqueline P.
1970   *Stations of the Lost, The Treatment of Skid Row Alcoholics.* Englewood Cliffs, N.J.: Prentice-Hall.

World Almanac and Book of Facts
1977   New York: Newspaper Enterprise Association.

Wrong, Dennis H.
1961   "The Oversocialized Conception of Man in Modern Sociology." *American Sociological Review* 26 (April):183–193.
1968   "Some Problems in Defining Social Power." *American Journal of Sociology* 73 (May):673–681.

Yankelovich, Daniel
1974   *The New Morality, A Profile of American Youth in the 70's.* New York: McGraw-Hill Book Company.

Yarrow, Marian Radke, et al.
1955   "The Psychological Meaning of Mental Illness in the Family." *Journal of Social Issues* 11 (No. 4):12–24.

Yinger, J. Milton
1957.   *Religion, Society and the Individual, An Introduction to the Sociology of Religion.* New York: The Macmillan Company.

Yochelson, Samuel, and Stanton E. Samenow
1976   *The Criminal Personality.* Vol. I: A Profile for Change. New York: Jason Aronson.

Young, Jock
1971   "The Role of Police as Amplifiers of Deviancy, Negotiators of Reality and Translators of Fantasy." Pp. 27–61 in Stanley Cohen, ed., *Images of Deviance.* Baltimore: Penguin Books.

Author Index

Subject Index